Meaning and Modernity

Meaning and Modernity

Religion, Polity, and Self

EDITED BY

Richard Madsen, William M. Sullivan,
Ann Swidler, and Steven M. Tipton

EPILOGUE BY

Robert N. Bellah

UNIVERSITY OF CALIFORNIA PRESS

Berkeley   Los Angeles   London

Stanley Hauerwas's "On Being a Christian and an American" was previously published in Hauerwas, *A Better Hope: Resources for Confronting Capitalism, Democracy, and Postmodernity,* pp. 23–34 (Grand Rapids: Brazos Press, 2000). Revised by permission.

University of California Press
Berkeley and Los Angeles, California

University of California Press, Ltd.
London, England

Library of Congress Cataloging-in-Publication Data

Meaning and modernity : religion, polity, and self / edited by Richard Madsen . . . [et al.]; epilogue by Robert N. Bellah.
   p.   cm.
Includes bibliographical references and index.
ISBN 0-520-22656-9 (alk. paper) — ISBN 0-520-22657-7 (pbk. : alk. paper)
   1. Religion and sociology—United States.   2. United States—Religion.
3. Postmodernism—Religious aspects.   4. Symbolism.   I. Madsen, Richard, 1941–
BL60 .M37   2002
306.6—dc21   2001027616

10 09 08 07 06 05 04 03 02 01
10 9 8 7 6 5 4 3 2 1

CONTENTS

ACKNOWLEDGMENTS

Thanks to Jim Clark, director of the University of California Press, for encouraging our efforts to create this book—and for all of his work over the years to help us publish and update *Habits of the Heart*. And special thanks to Reed Malcolm, our editor at the Press, for guiding this book through to publication.

We are grateful to Judy Haier of the University of California, Berkeley, Sociology Department for her help in organizing correspondence to our far-flung authors and to Dale Bretches of the University of California, San Diego, Anthropology Department for his help in organizing the final draft of the manuscript. Thanks also to Paula Friedman for her superb copy editing and to Jean McAneny for overseeing the book's production.

Our deepest debt of gratitude is to Robert Bellah, whose vision inspires this work. The essays in this book were written to honor him. But he has honored us with his wise, profound, and eloquent epilogue.

INTRODUCTION

Richard Madsen, William M. Sullivan, Ann Swidler,
and Steven M. Tipton

POSITIVISM, POST-MODERNISM, AND SYMBOLIC REALISM

There is a painful contradiction between what modernity promises and what it delivers. It promises—indeed demands—intellectual, moral, and political emancipation. Yet it delivers an iron cage. Modern persons aspire to express themselves as autonomous individuals, even as their choices are firmly channeled into paths laid down by the modern market economy and bureaucratic state. The social sciences embody these contradictions.

On the one hand, positivist social science seeks to explain the rules of economic, political, or social behavior in terms of the strategic choices made by individuals who wish to maximize their self-interests. Not only rational choice theory, but even more mainstream or politically radical strands of the social sciences presume a deeply utilitarian understanding of social life, in which preferences and calculations of advantage are treated as givens (or as objects to be controlled) and therefore severed from connections to any concrete sense of identity, purpose, or meaning. Morality, religion, and the whole normative dimension of social life get either pushed out of sight or explained away as resultants of more important, or more real, factors. What goes typically unnoticed and unremarked is how this apparently straightforward approach locks its adherents into a closed universe of diminished meaning and possibility.

In contemporary intellectual life, the main alternative to this positivist vision is the movement commonly called post-modernism. Its leading figures, such as Michel Foucault, Jacques Derrida, and Pierre Bourdieu, attempt to carry the modern demand for intellectual, moral, and political emancipation to its radical conclusions.

One of the defining moments of modern consciousness was the recognition that the social and religious order is a human construction for which human beings ultimately have to take responsibility. Foucault's great progenitor, Nietzsche, saw this truth in all its painful implications. He drew from it the radical conclusion that all existing values had to be overturned in a radical revaluation of all values. Post-modernism is in some sense simply a continuation of Nietzsche's project, expanding the task of dismantling values beyond Christianity, Nietzsche's main target, to the values that define modernity itself: reason, freedom, and the autonomous self. Foucault adopted Nietzsche's technique of "genealogy" to trace out the layers of practice and meaning that constitute the modern subject—both its interior subjectivity and its supposed "rights." He attempted to unmask the claims of the scientific disciplines to omniscient neutrality by showing their deep links to practices of power; to reveal the irrational, almost haphazard, agglomeration of practices constituting what claimed to be rational methods of dealing with poverty, madness, or crime; and to show how the modernizing drive toward freedom and autonomy was itself an effect of the extension and deepening of practices of power.[1]

Pierre Bourdieu, while less a self-conscious post-modernist than Foucault, employs a similar logic. He tries to show that the things sacred to modern elites—their judgment, their taste, their hierarchy of academic values—are social constructions that reproduce inequalities. He aspires to reveal how fields of power and their associated values become established, and, by so doing, he aims to subvert the "misrecognition" upon which power depends: where the logic of claims to truth, beauty, or brilliance is made transparent, inequality and power can no longer hide. Thus Bourdieu takes apart, and tries to render impotent, the hidden means by which power and wealth would assert superiority—of taste and cultivation, of knowledge and originality, of generosity.[2]

For its proponents, this post-modern unmasking of the social fictions that hide the bars of the iron cage holds the promise of inducing human beings to rebel against such constraints. There is good reason, however, to doubt that legitimating symbols can be rendered powerless by being made transparent. Indeed, the evidence of social history is that human beings rebel against oppression not when illusions are replaced by transparent truths, but when meaningful traditions define right and wrong, justice and injustice, good and evil.[3] And religious traditions, above all, have been able to speak truth to power, to invoke meanings that transcend and thus make demands on human beings, even the most powerful among them.

Whatever their personal political or religious sympathies, however, most contemporary social analysts take for granted that modernity, and now postmodernity, have won the battle against religion, and now against the Enlightenment ideals of rationality and freedom. These analysts presume that, if religion, moral obligation, reason, and freedom are only human creations, then these ideals, however desirable, have no authoritative status in human social life. But post-modernist nihilism is not the only realistic response to the dilemmas of modernity.

In this book we present exemplars of a third way, an intellectual vision that offers an alternative to positivism and post-modernism, a vision that attempts realistically to confront the dilemmas of modernity but offers hope of transcending them. Central to this vision is the notion of "symbolic realism," a term coined by Robert N. Bellah, one of the preeminent sociologists of religion, modernity, and democracy in this century. Bellah argued that religious symbols, created by human beings as ways of grasping the ultimate conditions of existence, could nonetheless have transcendent meanings that made powerful claims on individuals and communities for moral self-understanding and judgment.[4] It is this vision of the centrality of symbols and of the nature of traditions as living realities that animates this volume.

This view holds that, because of the ways symbols operate—defining the world, constituting social groups, and bridging conscious and unconscious meanings—symbolically constituted realities transcend particular individuals and groups. Thus they anchor human life in a transcendent reality. Though this vision can be traced back to Emile Durkheim and was carried to American sociology through the work of Talcott Parsons, it has been largely ignored by much recent social science. Bellah gave it renewed life and new theoretical depth. Unlike earlier approaches to religion and morality, symbolic realism accepts that religious truths are mutable rather than immutable, and it looks with favor, even hope, to the possibility that human beings can reappropriate and transform the meanings they inherit. Through such reappropriations, and sometimes through painful struggle with the core meanings that define self, social order, and the divine, human beings can alter the course of personal and social history. Thus, the humanly constructed nature of wider realities—truth and justice, as well as moral obligation and divine grace—is not a reason to abandon them; it does, however, remind us that we share responsibility for them.

These essays have been written to honor Robert N. Bellah. By no means, however, do the authors simply reproduce or even extend Bellah's ideas. They write in their own voices about their own substantive concerns, but within a broad tradition of symbolic realist thought. They represent a variety of disciplinary perspectives—sociology, history, philosophy, and theology—while having in common a concern with the way religious traditions have shaped modern civilizations and with the moral meanings that frame contemporary social and political choices. We hope by these essays to illustrate the range and the depth of the work that can be done within the symbolic realist tradition, and we hope that these essays will help new generations of scholars to carry that tradition forward.

THE INTERPRETIVE APPROACH

By their style of argument as well as their substantive claims, these essays offer a critique of modernity that moves beyond a naively relativist, antinomian ethics and an agnostic epistemology. They embrace a morally engaged, interpretative approach to social reality. Let us highlight some of the distinctive features of such an approach.

First, it bases itself on what the Aristotelians would have called "practical reason"—reason aimed at true wisdom in the practical tasks of enabling human societies to flourish. Pursuit of such wisdom requires not only mental sharpness but moral virtue, not simply knowledge of facts about social life, but critical engagement with the values that define a society and set its priorities.

Pursuit of such wisdom is a never-finished task. An interpretive social science seeks a deepened, clarified understanding of the cultural subject matter it shares with those it studies, who are in search of meaning too. Such sharing is not simply a matter of arriving at intersubjective consensus among the similarly socialized. It embraces critical, public dialogue about the meaning of primary texts and symbols shared by a community, about the canons of reasoned discourse used to arrive at such meanings, and about the analogies commonly used to imagine the unfamiliar in terms of the familiar. The essay "Mythic Gestures" by Jeffrey Alexander and Steven Sherwood in this volume analyzes the rhetorical style that Robert N. Bellah developed to carry out such a dialogue.

Because the webs of significance that humans share are not seamless, and no culture is a unitary, timeless whole, every interpretation makes sense of the world from a particular point of view, situated in social space and historical time, and unfolds within a certain tradition of interpretation. Modern societies not only feature divisions of class and caste-like groups defined by distinctive interests, ideologies, and styles of life. They also encompass contrasting traditions and "moral languages." So, every interpretation of a culture takes part in a "conflict of interpretations," in Paul Ricoeur's phrase, and this conflict characterizes, indeed constitutes, culture as a multi-vocal conversation and argument.[5] It is a conversation about how we ought to live in accord with reality as it is, and how we ought to think about how to live.

Such interpretive social science seeks practical wisdom in a synoptic view—at once philosophical, historical, and sociological—of the interrelation between the mores and moral character of persons in groups and the order of the institutions they inhabit—family, religion, politics, and economy. Without renouncing specialized expertise, a morally engaged interpretive social science recognizes the public calling of its continuing citizenship in the society at large, with the implication of public social responsibility. As the essays in this volume, particularly Bellah's powerful epilogue, illustrate, deep engagement with fundamental moral questions can be the stimulus to ideas of great intellectual range and force.

With an eye to democratic decision making in a self-governing society, social science as public philosophy seeks to animate and enlighten public dialogue about the diverse social goods, practices, and ways of life persons share in a good society. These ultimate meanings and values, in all their variety and contrariety, are embodied in social institutions. Indeed, institutions are the settings for moral dramas, in which we act out our understandings of who we are and how we ought to live. Thus, for example, free markets in American society dramatize the interplay of individual interests and opportunities in mutual exchange, and religious congregations dramatize biblical ideals of neighbor-love and forgiveness in mutual reconciliation. Steven M. Tipton's essay, "Social Differentiation and Moral Pluralism," analyzes the ways in which the moral diversity of modern society is embodied and dramatized in its institutional diversity.

In this view, institutions are essentially and dialectically moral, and therefore open to serious moral debate and questioning. Institutional pluralism permits us to look critically at the logic of one institution from the standpoint of another. For, if "institutions think," as Mary Douglas puts it, what they think about is one another in terms of their own moral logics and metaphors.[6] This enables us to judge and compare institutions in terms of moral logics of social and personal virtues as well as of rights, responsibilities, and duties. It enables us to test institutions in terms of moral metaphors like the model of the family as a school of justice and love, or the political economy as a public household. Do our institutions actually serve and live up to the moral purposes claimed for them? Do their underlying moral values and axiomatic assumptions actually accord, or do they hold us captive to moral contradictions within or across particular social spheres? Ann Swidler's essay, "Saving the Self: Endowment and Depletion in American Institutions," is an example of how such questions can be posed to an American public.

A morally engaged interpretive social science invites its fellow citizens to join it in public discussion, and through this to contest and remake its arguments, not merely to follow them as readers or students. For without such a public, social science as public philosophy will neither fulfill its own moral ends nor sustain its own moral inquiry.

SUBSTANTIVE CONCERNS

Because of its commitment to thinking about the relationship between major institutions, this interpretive approach to social science enables scholars to articulate, and to grapple with, some of the most fundamental concerns of humans at the beginning of the new millennium. This book illustrates the range of these concerns, all touched upon by Robert N. Bellah at some point in his career.

Modernity

A primary concern involves the very meaning of modernity itself. Some scholars would define modernity basically in economic terms, in terms of the complexity of the industrial division of labor or of the pervasiveness of the market economy or, today, of the extensiveness of new information technologies. Others would define modernity in political terms, such as the replacement of personal forms of rule with impersonal bureaucracies. Still others would define it in sociological terms like the liberation of individuals from primary ties to family and local community into a "lonely crowd" of consumers. Finally, others would define modernity in terms of secularization, the substitution of religious faith by systematically organized skepticism.

The morally engaged social science exemplified in these essays, however, insists on taking a synoptic view. Modernity is a dynamic relationship between economy, polity, society, and culture. Although each of these various institutional realms is influenced by the other, each also follows a relatively autonomous path of development. What we think of as modern societies are complex configurations of more or less modern institutions, and each society has a somewhat different configuration. In the U.S. version of modernity, for example, there is extreme emphasis on the centrality of an open market economy and tremendous pressure on the state, family, and even church to accommodate themselves to the logic of the market. Japan, on the other hand, is a modern society, but (to the frustration of American diplomats trying to negotiate trade agreements) the Japanese market economy is not so open as that of the United States; the Japanese government takes a more directive role in guiding the economy, and family relationships are more cohesive (some would say rigid). Many Continental European societies follow yet other patterns. Thus there are different versions of modernity and different paths to modernity.

At the beginning of his career, Robert N. Bellah wrote a seminal book on Japan, *Tokugawa Religion*, which confronted such differences between Japanese and American modernization.[7] This book was published at a time when most social scientists assumed that there was really only one version of modernity, the one fully exemplified by the United States. Insisting on the multiplex nature of modernity, Bellah argued that the key reason for Japan's difference from the United States derived from the difference between Japanese and Western religious systems. In the present volume, the essay by S. N. Eisenstadt revisits some of the issues raised by Bellah over four decades ago. Eisenstadt argues that differences in Japanese and American religious traditions led to contrasting—yet, in a way, mirror-image—modes of constructing collective identity and social order.

Philip Gorski's essay, on the other hand, highlights the complexity of modernization even within the West. Max Weber argued that it was the evolution of Calvinist Christianity that created the "spirit of capitalism" in Northern Europe. The political theorist Michael Walzer extended this thesis to argue that Calvinism provided a template for the revolutions that created the modern Western political order. Gorski argues, however, that Calvinism did not necessarily lead to such revolutions. It did so only within certain configurations of political, social, and economic institutions. Thus, even in the West, even in countries with a strong Calvinist influence, there were different paths to early modernity. Richard Madsen's essay, moreover, shows that there are many different forms of modernity existing today, in the West as well as around the globe; Madsen attempts to create a theoretical framework for comparing these forms, especially for showing how changes in religion may differentially affect their future development.

All of these essays, then, insist that religion and morality cannot be reduced to economics and politics, and yet they show that religion and morality are constantly being refashioned through dialogue between the legacies of the past and the challenges of the present. These contemporary challenges are defined by complicated configurations of institutions. Grounded in different traditions and faced with different challenges, different societies move along different paths toward modernity and represent different kinds of modernity.

This vision is not only intellectually satisfying in its ability to take into account new forms of complexity, it is morally and politically hopeful. If there is no iron law that guides the process of modernization, there is not necessarily any iron cage at the end of the process. One can conceive of forms of modernity that are more or less conducive to human flourishing; one can recognize that one can have a lot to learn from other societies, not just those that dominate the present but also those that flourished in the past. And one can take responsibility for helping to create better societies within the modern world.

The Conditions of Democracy

A practical corollary to this vision is that the social sciences are openly recognized as moral sciences, with links to the classical philosophical and normative concerns of the humanities. Scholars who follow this approach do not define their task simply in terms of solving theoretical puzzles or fashioning new tools for more efficient scientific investigation. They see their task as one of responding to the major moral challenges of their time. This certainly does not preclude investigations of the past or of other cultures; it is, indeed, only through such investigations that present challenges can become clear. Yet, like Bellah, who began his career with comparative studies of Japan and ended up writing acclaimed books on America, even the most cosmopolitan scholars, such as those whose essays are collected here, have always written with a special eye to the moral dilemmas of their own societies. It is therefore fitting that a substantial number of the essays written for this book focus explicitly on the United States. There is a strong concern with the capacity of American religion to criticize the injustices and heal the fragmentation of the version of capitalist modernity found in the United States today.

Some of these authors, like Harvey Cox and John Coleman, worry that the American market economy and consumer culture have become so strong that American religion may not be able to have much impact on the society. Others, like Albert Raboteau and Robert Wuthnow, are more hopeful, demonstrating the power of prophetic voices in the past and the capacity of American religion to reassemble in new ways to meet the needs of the present.

Chief among these needs is a way to maintain the vitality of democracy in an interdependent world ever more dominated by global markets, powerful corporations, and massive governments. All of the problems about democracy that were classically analyzed by Tocqueville are still with us: the tension between freedom and equality, between individualism and social solidarity. The history of the United States and of other democratic republics has been one of attempts to create social institutions that realized, to some acceptable degree, high democratic ideals that could never be fully realized, and to constantly reform these institutions under changing conditions.

But at the beginning of the twenty-first century, these tensions have grown sharper, and older means for resolving them no longer work. In their essays, Charles Taylor, Nina Eliasoph, and Stanley Hauerwas force us to scrutinize the tensions within the democratic ideal. For Taylor, a major source of tension today is the democratic vocation to inclusiveness—the vocation to bring everyone, no matter what gender, religion, ethnicity, into equal participation in a self-governing polity—and the opposing pressure to exclude those who by their differences threaten the common sense of identity necessary for self-governance. This tension will become greater as modern communication and commerce bring increasing migration into democratic countries, while making everyone more aware of every sort of social difference. Taylor argues that classical liberalism, the dominant political philosophy of Anglo-American democracies, fails to provide any basis for resolving this tension. It is based simply on tolerance, a kind of benign neglect of privatized differences. Taylor thinks that a more robust sense of common purpose is needed if modern democracies are to meet the challenges of self-governance. This sense can only come from an approach that does not simply tolerate social difference but welcomes it and embraces dialogue with it because it provides an indispensable way to expand understanding of what it means to be fully human.

Nina Eliasoph offers a probing investigation into some impediments to, but also some potential stimuli for, deepened civic conversation in America. Particularly intriguing are her suggestions about the important role that human service bureaucrats and educators can play in furthering such conversation—if they take seriously their responsibilities to be good citizens and not simply technocrats.

Such dialogue among the diverse members of a democratic polity is a matter less of exchanging theories than of sharing stories. This is not necessarily a pleasant exercise. It can be extremely painful, because, as Stanley Hauerwas points out, serious stories—about our most profound religious convictions, for example—cannot easily be reconciled with the bland liberalism that sets the conventions for public speech in America today. In his essay, Hauerwas says that Christians should engage in a deep, intense argument with American culture, an argument driven by a profound sense of tragedy and a keen sense of the need for repentance.

Finally, William Sullivan offers a basis for hope by showing how in England—and to a considerably lesser degree in the United States—there emerged a "clerisy" of public intellectuals who helped create a more humane capitalism and who built the institutions of the modern welfare state. Intellectuals like Keynes and Beverage were far from mere technicians. They encased their economics and organization-building in visions drawn from a broad humanistic perspective, grounded in a knowledge of history, philosophy, and, not least, theology. For the most part, the learned professions, at least as institutionalized in the United States, no longer nurture such public intellectuals—yet such intellectuals are not completely absent. Throughout his long career, Robert N. Bellah has been such an intellectual. The authors of these essays aspire to such a vocation as well, and their work has contributed, at least indirectly, to the refashioning of our academic institutions necessary to sustain responsible public intellectuals.

In the end, this book is animated by an anti-reductionist vision, which insists on drawing into an inclusive conversation the manifold material and spiritual dimensions of society. In the concluding essay of his *Beyond Belief,* Bellah quotes William Blake, "Twofold always / May God us keep / From single vision / And Newton's sleep." The authors in this book struggle to maintain such a twofold vision and hope to inspire others to do the same.

ONE

"Mythic Gestures"

Robert N. Bellah and Cultural Sociology

Jeffrey C. Alexander and Steven J. Sherwood

One's life and work are an effort to find a form which will reconcile inner needs and outer pressures. The form itself is unique and personal even though both the inner needs and the outer pressures are transpersonal. In my life there has been a long preoccupation with fragmentation and wholeness and it is this which has made religion such an abiding concern.
ROBERT N. BELLAH, *Beyond Belief: Essays on Religion in a Post-Traditional World*

One of the curious but invariably neglected aspects of any social theory is the fact that it has a form as well as a content.
ALVIN GOULDNER, *The Coming Crisis of Western Sociology*

There are many ways to consider the career of Robert N. Bellah. He is: sociologist of religion, Japanologist, Americanist, historian of sociology, public intellectual, teacher, and mentor. Our interest here is to consider Bellah's fundamental contribution to the development of a field called the sociology of culture—or, as we would prefer to identify it, cultural sociology. Such a consideration requires discussing Bellah in relationship to the Parsonian tradition, within which he worked for a good part of his life, the tradition that, like every good son, he had to transcend to make his own profound contribution—even while, paradoxically, he extended the scope and vision of Talcott Parsons's.

A fundamental premise of this essay—one that resonates with Bellah's own aesthetic—is that form and content are as intimately and inextricably related in sociology as in the arts or, for that matter, in any other intellectual endeavor. Sociologists, no less than artists, confront the problem of style, of the form in which the content of their work is conveyed. And style, like theory, is seldom the product of individual idiosyncrasy or of sui generis creation; typically, it is a matter of internalization. The profound challenge facing the sociologist who would aspire to intellectual maturity is to assimilate the tradition in order to externalize it anew, to use tradition to achieve the substantive and stylistic skills necessary to creativity, to internalize a master's orientation in order to find a way to transcend it—or, at least, innovate within it. Traditions are not killed by innovation and innovators, but by stylistic stagnation and intellectual conformity. It is only through the contributions of those who break with traditions that traditions survive. Let us begin to understand this productive tension between the master, Parsons, and his master-student, Bellah, by starting with the marked difference in sensibility. The central vision of Bellah's work and career lies in his belief that to understand ourselves as social subjects we must also understand ourselves as religious subjects; it is this religious sense that makes fragmentation and wholeness such significant and recurring concerns in Bellah's *oeuvre*. Here Bellah stands in clear contrast to Parsons, for whom wholeness and fragmentation at the level of the subject seldom constituted interests worthy of attention. Such matters were never fundamental, but pathological, merely "strains" in an otherwise homeostatic system. Parsons always felt that totalistic concern, and the experience of fragmentation that it paradoxically produced, were mediated by values and institutions. If society had a fundamental purpose for Parsons, it was precisely to provide such remedial mediation. Society was enabling, not constricting.

This substantive difference between master and master-student is represented in form, in contrasts of style. Parsons's ideas about society were always anchored in an abstract model, an anchor that seemed to warrant the formal style within which it was conveyed. The dearth of autobiographical references in the vast Parsonian corpus reflects the fact that Parsons saw his theoretical structures as his medium of communication. His theory *was* his style. By contrast, Bellah and his close friend and collaborator Clifford Geertz—they were Parsons's two most important cultural students—would both be far more biographical and personal, drawing not only on fieldwork and theory but from the zeitgeist and their personal experience. It was for this reason that Bellah and Geertz could so easily negotiate the linguistic turn.[1]

It is in terms of Bellah's negotiation of this linguistic turn that we wish to understand and periodize some critical aspects of his middle-period work. We wish to examine the shifts in this work in terms of what we can understand, in retrospect, to have been the emerging field of cultural sociology. In this process, we display our hermeneutical orientation: cultural sociology is, unlike "ideology," not just something that applies to others, to other people, cultures, or social structures; it just as powerfully shapes the consciousness and self-consciousness of the interpreter of social reality. We shall try to understand this experiential relationship between Bellah and his sociology through two moments in the development of cultural sociology. The first was the late 1960s and early 1970s, when Bellah turned from the dominant, static Parsonian paradigm to "Civil Religion in America." We shall characterize this first development as simultaneously a much more sophisticated and dynamic elaboration of Parsonian theory and a transcendence of it. The second moment, in the mid-1970s, came with Bellah's decisive "break" with Parsons, exemplified in *The Broken Covenant*. In the conclusion to this essay, we will sketch an argument that space restrictions prevent us from developing more fully, namely, the importance of Bellah's "religious" reading of Durkheim and the role this played in the development of the third, contemporary phase of cultural sociology.

The career of Robert N. Bellah will be presented here, in other words, against the profound growth of the theoretical and methodological self-consciousness of cultural sociology.

CULTURAL SOCIOLOGY I:
THE ORIGINS IN "CIVIL RELIGION IN AMERICA"

Like other forms of representation, sociology has always confronted the stylistic conflict between formal classicism and informal naturalism. While the theoretical model and the methodology of controlled experiment have connected sociology to the formal transparency of scientific language, the fact is that, in discursive terms, models and experiments are always conveyed in more naturalistic ways as well, through narrative, trope, and metaphor. The linguistic understanding of social science simply has made this discursive aspect much more apparent, allowing a post-positivist literature to develop that explores the boundaries between science and the humanities.

In his 1959 debunking of Parsons as a substantively irrelevant "grand theorist," C. Wright Mills condemned particularly his elliptical, obtuse prose, which suggested that, in his empty formalism, words were parading as insights. Ironically, it is precisely such a "convoluted" prose style that has come to be associated with the sociological discipline at large, "sociologese" being the standard pejorative for anyone who speaks in its jargon. If Parsons was in any way exceptional, in fact, it was only because he was particularly good at it. This was recognized in a backhanded fashion by Alvin Gouldner, who exclaimed over "the paradoxical aspect for those who merely complain about Parsons's literary style" and suggested that it was "through the sheer force of his conceptualizing rhetoric" that "more than any other modern social theorist [Parsons] has persuasively communicated a sense of the reality of a social system, of the boundaried oneness and coherent wholeness of patterns of social interaction."[2]

If to establish form is also to establish content, then substantive changes will be accompanied by changes in form. The middle-period writings of Robert N. Bellah, along with those of Geertz, served as a critical bridge between what we would call formal and informal Parsonianism; in so doing, they also bridged mid- and late-twentieth-century sociology, the difference between which can be seen in the very emergence of cultural sociology as a robust rather than apologetic form. One of Parsons's signal contributions to sociological theory was to lay the groundwork for the exploration of culture. We wish to suggest, however, that it was only through the writings of Bellah and of Geertz that this framework has been passed on to sociology at large. This transmission made cultural sociology possible.

That Bellah's *Beyond Belief* and *The Broken Covenant*—and, for that matter, Geertz's *The Interpretation of Cultures*—were not only seminal texts in the 1970s but continue to exhibit vitality today is due as much to their aesthetic form as to their intellectual content. In content, they exploit a key tenet of Parsons's theory, the critical nexus between religion and culture and the ramifications of this connection for social action, particularly politics. Prior to Parsons, these categories had largely been segregated, even in the work of Max Weber. The analytic and synthetic scope of Parsons's theory allowed him, by contrast, to assert the interdependence not only of these crucial categories but also of every previously segregated sphere of society. Yet, although Parsons could assert this interdependence hypothetically, it required the empirical interventions of Bellah and of Geertz to liberate this profound insight from the complex and largely unapproachable theoretical edifice encasing it. An important part of this liberation was stylistic, the appropriation of Parsonian systematics into a more accessible, humane, hermeneutically oriented style. Bellah and Geertz both became successful as former specialists of "primitive," or non-Western, religion who employed these hermeneutic perspectives to reveal the cultural aspects of modernized Western societies. Yet, the *way* that these writers presented culture had as much to do with the revolutionary impact of their work as *what* they said. Bellah and Geertz were able to create a substantive argument for the structural integrity of culture without engaging an aesthetic form that contradicted it—which had been Parsons's mistake when he conceptualized culture as some monumental and monolithic abstraction. In this regard, one need only compare Parsons's multitudinous, highly schematic definitions of culture with the supple and rich definitions in the famous cultural essays of his two prodigal sons.

In *Beyond Belief*, we find an exemplary illustration of how form and function came together in Bellah's initial turn toward culture and away from Parsons. To this collection of essays, which famously included the only just published "Civil Religion in America," Bellah appended another piece, "The Systematic Study of Religion." Dating from over ten years earlier, 1955, and never previously published, this essay lays out his conception of the relation of religion to society, in a fully complex and abstract Parsonian way. Looking not at all different from something Parsons himself might have written, "Systematic" is replete with arrows and boxes, and lays out the interconnections between the various spheres of the "action system" (A-G-I-L) and their ramifications for religion, religious symbol systems, and religious institutions. While Bellah characterizes this piece as having been created when he was "still caught in the unfolding of the Parsonian theoretical scheme," he rather gamely asserts that "much of it is easily accessible and, I think, still of some interest."[3] If so, the interest is only to demonstrate how cramping AGIL formalism was to Bellah's ability to explore the relationships between religious and other aspects of social reality. We get to see what the sociology of Robert N. Bellah would have been like had he never weaned himself from the fourfold paradigm. It is not a pretty sight.

Fortunately, weaning took place, and we have "Civil Religion in America" as a result. However, if by 1968 Bellah had evolved beyond Parsonian style, he remained deeply ambivalent about leaving Parsons's substantive paradigm behind. On the one hand, from the perspective of a cultural sociology, there is a revolutionary dimension to "Civil Religion," for it applies to a secular and modern society such "religious" and "primitive" concepts as mythical narrative and sacred time. On the other hand, the 1968 essay upholds the very kind of modernization perspective that, then and now, stops cultural sociology dead in its tracks.

"Civil Religion" is a largely affirmational work. Appearing on the tail end of the modernization approach of the 1950s and 1960s, it fits, for the most part, within Parsons's evolutionary ambit. Indeed, a key to understanding "Civil Religion" is Bellah's earlier essay on "Religious Evolution," which emerged from the 1962–63 seminar on social evolution he taught at Harvard with Parsons and S. N. Eisenstadt. In this still deeply impressive theoretical effort, Bellah had offered the compelling claim that "neither religious man nor the structure of man's ultimate religious situation evolves . . . but rather religion as a symbol system."[4] On the cusp of cultural sociology, Bellah implies here that religiosity and religious symbolism penetrate the secular arenas of modernity in a more primitive, less differentiated manner than is suggested by Parsons's formal, linear, and much more cleancut model. This opening is foreclosed, however, by Bellah's insistence that, in the scheme of human history, the evolution of religious symbol systems ensures that "at each stage the freedom of personality and society has increased relative to the environing conditions," with the result that "religious evolution has implied at almost every point a general theory of social evolution."[5] This is the roadblock that modernization theory throws up, a barrier that militates against the new possibility of a cultural sociology. Bellah follows here Parsons's singular appropriation of Weber's religious sociology, a reading that acknowledges modernity as the sacralization of the secular but conceptualizes this sacralization primarily in ethical and developmental, rather than symbolic and imagistic, ways. There has been the greater penetration of religious standards into the social world, but they have taken on a generalized, universalized, and abstract form. Bellah's optimistic conception of the social actor during this period clearly echoes that of his teacher:

> The fundamental symbolization of modern man and his situation is that of a dynamic multidimensional self capable, within limits, of continual self-transformation and capable, again within limits, of remaking the world, including the very symbolic forms with which he deals with it, even the forms that state the unalterable conditions of his own existence.[6]

So it is that when Bellah looks at what Rousseau called "civil religion" in relation to American society, what he sees is largely a positive and adaptive ethical regulation. He defines civil religion as "certain common elements of religious orientation that the great majority of Americans share," as a set of beliefs that "reaffirms the religious legitimation of the highest political authority."[7] Characterizing the famous inaugural address of John F. Kennedy, Bellah suggests, "The whole address can be understood as only the most recent statement of a theme that lies very deep in the American tradition, namely the obligation, both collective and individual, to carry out God's will on earth."[8]

While allowing for the continued intrusion of religious elements into the political sphere, this element of Bellah's discussion affirms the comfortable synthesis of secular and religious culture.

> The American civil religion was never anticlerical or militantly secular. On the contrary, it borrowed selectively from the religious tradition in such a way that the average American saw no conflict between the two. In this way the civil religion was able to build up without any bitter struggle with the church powerful symbols of national solidarity and to mobilize deep levels of personal motivation for the attainment of national goals.[9]

Thus, civil religion is neither specifically sectarian[10] nor a substitute for Christianity.[11] Rather, civil religion describes the continuing moral interpenetration between religion and secular cultures in the political sphere, such that, as Bellah states in his essay on religious evolution, "it will be increasingly realized that answers to religious questions can validly be sought in various spheres of 'secular' art and thought."[12] There are clouds on the horizon, to be sure. Bellah asserts that the American Revolution and the Civil War represented America's first two "times of trial" and that the then-current era of the mid-Sixties is America's "third time of trial," mentioning specifically the problem of "responsible action in a revolutionary world," and, more obliquely, Vietnam. Yet, overall, the tone is one of cautious hope and optimism, for the telos of civil religion is "concerned that America be a society as perfectly in accord with the will of God as men can make it, and a light to all the nations."[13]

Yet if "Civil Religion" remains within Parsons's theoretical orbit in significant and ultimately restrictive ways, there are other, equally important ways in which it decidedly does not. Stylistically, Bellah has already transcended this orbit. He achieves his own "voice," leaving theoretical classicism far behind. Further, in achieving his own profoundly personal and prophetic voice, he has also produced a new content, what Hayden White[14] would later call "the substance of form." Drawing on the inaugural addresses of John F. Kennedy and Abraham Lincoln, as well as on the latter's Gettysburg Address, Bellah deftly deploys hermeneutic, phenomenological, and myth analysis—the rudiments of the late-Durkheimian, "anti-Weberian" repertoire that would later become so central to cultural sociology. Adopting a thickly narrative form that Parsons had abjured, Bellah introduces heroes (Lincoln and Kennedy) and weaves a redemptive plot centered on America's "mission," anchored in the nation's renewal and rebirth during the Civil War. He explicitly refers to the typological sources of America's civil religion narrative: "Behind the civil religion at every point lie biblical archetypes: Exodus, Chosen People, Promised Land, New Jerusalem, and Sacrificial Death and Rebirth."[15] While such references now seem rather commonplace, for a sociologist in the 1960s, even more so one so closely associated with the "abstract upgrading" of Parsons's system, these were revolutions in both substance and form. Rather than refer to cultural objects and patterns in the abstract, as Parsons had, Bellah actually set them in motion, drawing on them to evoke the architecture of meaning in a secular faith. Rather than see the continuity of cultural control only in morally regulative terms, and conceive of its repercussions primarily in terms of institutional effects, Bellah was beginning to explore the *internal*, meaning-making aspects of cultural patterns in their own right. He had transformed Parsons's structure of style into his own style of Parsons's structure.

CULTURAL SOCIOLOGY II:
THE "BROKEN COVENANT" AND CRITICAL SOCIOLOGY

"Civil Religion in America" might be considered the first significant document of contemporary American cultural sociology. Although Clifford Geertz significantly deepened and extended cultural analysis in two much more theoretically self-conscious essays, "Ideology as a Cultural System" and "Religion as a Cultural System," written earlier in the decade, it would take some time for these to establish their disciplinary (and cross-disciplinary) influence. Bellah, on the other hand, is dealing with something specific and immediately compelling in a moral sense, something that neither Parsons nor Geertz ever fully confront—the idea of America. Parsons taught a course on American society throughout his career at Harvard and left a substantial but incomplete manuscript volume (which unfortunately remains unpublished) titled *The American Societal Community*. Geertz contended with specific aspects of American culture, such as the metaphorical aspects of the

Taft-Hartley Act. Still, neither fully engaged, as did Bellah, in explicit cultural commentary on America—and it is at least partly for this reason that neither became public intellectuals in the same way. Cultural commentary on "America" is generally restricted either to lay social commentators or to professional intellectuals whose central interest is in debunking the *idea* of America, for example, David Riesman with *The Lonely Crowd* or C. Wright Mills in *The Power Elite*. While Parsons had engaged in debates with these critics, these discussions had never attained wider visibility. One reason is that affirmation, especially within intellectual and academic circles, is never as compelling as criticism. The other is that Parsons's abstract and complex formalism made his ideas inaccessible to a more public audience. Bellah's increasingly cultural sociology, employing a hermeneutic that rested in shared sensibility, was.

While the critics of Parsons were no less strident in the early 1970s, they had moved from his model's formal aspects to its political implications. The reasons for this shift were anchored not only in the prevailing social movements of the time but also in the adaptation, by Parsons's bitterest enemies, of the very degree of abstraction and sophistication ("grand theory") that Parsons himself employed. This was especially true in the cultural realm pioneered by Parsons and his students. The "linguistic turn" was beginning to take hold, and cultural sociology to burgeon in Europe. Aided by the turbulent social climate and stagnant economies of the time, and informed by the growing appreciation of Gramsci, Habermas, Lévi-Strauss, Barthes, and such contemporary British cultural Marxists as Raymond Williams and E. P. Thompson during the 1970s, Stuart Hall and his colleagues and students at the University of Birmingham established the first self-conscious school of what is still known as "cultural studies." It was as passionately anti-American in its content as it was proto-American in its increasing level of Parsonian abstraction. (Perhaps this realization was what moved Gouldner late in his life to find an increasing appreciation for Parsons.) Cultural sociology, like theoretical sociology, could define itself only in relation to Parsons and his school, even if obliquely.

In "Civil Religion in America," Bellah had been developing cultural sociology in a much less ideological fashion. Yet cultural sociology, like theory, is never an autonomous enterprise. Sociology is as much shaped by its environment as it is a factor in shaping it. The turbulent years of the late 1960s and early 1970s were the milieu in which Bellah was working. He had purposefully moved in 1967 from Harvard to the University of California, Berkeley—or, as he described it, from "magisterial order" to the "wide-open chaos of the post-Protestant, post-modern era."[16] As this master-student had already developed substantial independence, theoretically and stylistically, from Parsons, his geographic move could only reflect a further deviation. As Bellah himself put it, "[t]he move from Harvard to Berkeley . . . was an outward expression of an inward change."[17]

By the time *Beyond Belief* was published in 1970, Bellah, now in Berkeley, projected a strong ambivalence, protesting that he still considered his own work "more a development than a repudiation of Parsonian theory."[18] By the time of the publication of his next major work, *The Broken Covenant*, in 1975, however, Parsons was neither referred to nor footnoted at all. *The Broken Covenant* would be Bellah's first crystallized and fully autonomous response to his new environment, the America of the 1970s.

The Broken Covenant is a profound and provocative work. Based on a series of Weil Lectures first given at Hebrew Union College/Jewish Institute of Religion in Cincinnati in 1971, it represents a clear break not only with the more optimistic presuppositions of Bellah's earlier work but also with Parsons. In comparison to the New Testament feel of "Civil Religion," the new work is very much Old Testament—much more prophetic, hortatory, and apocalyptic. In responding to the culmination of Vietnam, the Watergate crisis, and the gamut of social-movement issues in American culture, Bellah asserts that America can no longer be a "light to the world," that instead it must concern itself first with internal reform and "conversion." Loosely described by one reviewer as a "jeremiad with footnotes," *The Broken Covenant* indeed represents the opening of a new era both in cultural sociology and in the career of Bellah, who has chosen to work not so much in the critical tradition of the Frankfurt school as in the critical tradition of such earlier American figures as Winthrop, Mather, and Garrison, all of whom he cites. In finding his own, more critical voice, Bellah embarks on a long and fruitful journey as a reader of America's soul, delinking the close relationship he had earlier posited between religion and culture and arguing that the latter has drifted too far from the former. Indeed, this is the very definition of the "jeremiad," which remonstrates the community for forgetting its sacred obligations in carrying out God's plans and purposes and attempts to shame it back into submission to God's will.[19] This is the distinctive voice that will mark Bellah's career henceforth, up to and including his more famous collaborations in the 1980s and 1990s, *Habits of the Heart* and *The Good Society*. It is a voice that argues that America's "punishment" for deviating from her spiritual commitments is, ironically, her very material "success." Bellah writes, "we have plunged into the thickets of this world so vigorously that we have lost the vision of the good."[20] Americans, he asserts, suffer not from a lack of means and goods but instead from a failure of "our central vision."[21]

Let us briefly outline the work that went into Bellah's conversion to a more critical stance regarding American society and its values. The gist of his argument is that American values are founded simultaneously upon two

competing tradition-complexes. The first is an amalgam of values embodying "virtue," represented by the Puritans who first founded the colonies
in concert with principles of republicanism and civic responsibility. The
second refers to an instrumental ethic of self-interest, which is said to have
emerged especially from the end of the Civil War and from the ascendance
of what Bellah for the first time calls "corporate capitalism." The first set
of values is reflected in America's mythic heritage and embodied in such
keystones as the Declaration of Independence and, especially, Lincoln's
Gettysburg Address and Second Inaugural Address. The second is already
reflected in such works as Benjamin Franklin's *Autobiography* but seems to
emanate largely, in its most corrosive aspect, from the industrial advances
of the last century. Bellah's argument is that the second set of values has,
in modern America, increasingly come to displace the more originary elements of "virtue"—hence the loss of vision.

To make such an argument, Bellah clearly must revise the theoretical
foundations he drew from Parsons. The most fundamental change is to
abandon the evolutionary, developmental impetus he had shared with Parsons until the early 1970s. The implication of this abandonment is not only
a move toward ideological pessimism; it also has analytic, purely theoretical
implications. It allows Bellah to pose a confrontation between normativity
and amoral, instrumental self-interest, a confrontation that Parsons thought
he had permanently displaced when he had proposed his synthetic model
of the "unit act" in *The Structure of Social Action* almost forty years before.
When, in the decade after, Parsons introduced the pattern variables, he had
proposed not only that self-interest is itself normatively regulated, but that
modern societies cannot function if primary emphasis is given to normative
self-interest. Bellah's argument in *The Broken Covenant* that virtue has been
increasingly replaced by self-interest draws precisely the opposite conclusion. Drawing from his studies of the professions, Parsons had argued that
the pattern variables provide the specific values that enable professions
to be seen as "callings" embodying virtues rather than as instrumental, self-
interested occupations. Bellah's critique is premised upon the assertion that
this is no longer the case. Why? Because the development of corporate capitalism has perverted this relationship. In Parsonian terms, Bellah is arguing that the social actor no longer operates voluntaristically but is constrained—by cultural and institutional tensions—toward self-interested
and instrumental behavior. This is the utilitarian actor that, in *The Structure
of Social Action,* Parsons had argued against. From the perspective of that
work, indeed, Bellah has walked right into the "utilitarian dilemma," the
theoretical trap that Parsons blamed for Western social theory's insensitiv-
ity to moral and cultural concerns. Bellah asserts that what for Parsons was
theoretical bad faith is, in contemporary America, an empirically "bad" reality: "The major tendency in the society at large seems to be erosion rather

than reaction or reconstruction,"[22] there is a "declining sense of moral obligation," "freedom [has come] to mean freedom to pursue self-interest,"[23] the "self-interest of the isolated individual" is preeminent.[24]

In "Civil Religion in America," secular morality represented an inclusive and integrative fusion of critical and salvationary elements. By contrast, near the end of *The Broken Covenant*, Bellah writes that "today . . . civil religion is an empty and broken shell."[25] Where, in "Civil Religion in America," secular and religious cultures had been seen as converging, here they are starkly opposed. In the earlier essay, American society itself had been a legitimating principle; civil religion, Bellah had written, was "genuinely American and genuinely new." In *The Broken Covenant*, "America" is neither new nor particularly genuine. Where earlier there had been an optimistic, if cautious and self-critical, hope for evolution, here there is only Bellah's grim intonation that America must recognize her "broken covenant," realize that the reality falls far short of the ideal. If redemption comes, it is no longer through our own efforts but as an act of grace. Bellah continues to assert that American society is facing its third time of trial, but now he says, "[i]t is a test of whether we can control the very economic and technical forces, which are our greatest achievement, before they destroy us."[26] Bellah has moved away from the convergence between culture and religion, toward a more specifically religious, radical Protestant, rejection of the world. Secular and religious dimensions of American society are much more strongly differentiated, as the form of the jeremiad requires. The condemnation of secular society requires the invocation of the higher standard that religious discourse represents, that is, the distinction between material and spiritual bases of satisfaction, between "virtue" and "self-interest."

The irony is that, even while impugning the health and robustness of American culture, in *The Broken Covenant* Bellah provides cultural sociology with its most robust model yet. For he broaches explicitly something no contemporary other than Roland Barthes had seriously considered, the power of myth. "It is the role of symbols and myths at the level of personal life both to stimulate and mobilize psychic energy and to provide form and control for it," Bellah writes.[27]

> Myth does not attempt to describe reality; that is the job of science. Myth seeks rather to transfigure reality so that it provides moral and spiritual meaning to individuals or societies. Myths, like scientific theories, may be true or false, but the test of truth or falsehood is different.[28]

By recognizing myth as a variable in its own right, and by exploring in some detail what he calls America's "origin myth," Bellah provides sociologists with a new realm of potential investigation. Of course, the upshot of his empirical narrative is that "paradise" lies at the beginning of America's great experiment, whereas for evolutionists like Parsons "paradise" is never at the beginning of history but always at the end. In conceptual terms, the gesture toward myth marks a fundamental advance. In his essay "Between Religion and Social Science," Bellah had outlined a program for what he called "symbolic realism," in which symbols and symbol systems were seen as having autonomy, as opposed to functioning solely in the service of other, more powerful interests. Symbolic realism suggested that symbolic patterns were themselves powerful determinants in their own right. This move is what allows Bellah to take things like myth and archetypes seriously for the first time in his work.

Once again, this change in content corresponds with, and is facilitated by, a change in form. Parsons's formal model is like a bronze Michelangelo: it could only stand and be admired, it could not take life and move. Parsons could posit, for example, what he called "constitutive myth" as the apex of the pattern-maintenance (i.e., cultural) subsystem of his social-system model, but he had no way of tangibly exploring it. In the more informal, more internal, hermeneutic style of Bellah, Michelangelo's cultural masterpiece can walk off the pedestal and look around. Bellah's style enables him to suggest how the empty box of Parsons's model can be filled in with the rich and full reality of American myth. Parsons's work provided the deep theoretical foundation for the later linguistic turn, for thinking about the relevance and importance of myth, ritual, and code, but his style precluded him, and anyone else who remained within his stylistic parameters, from demonstrating the *reality* of culture in terms of its feeling and form—that is, in terms of its internal structure. By contrast, Bellah's bold approach to the centrality of secular myth and symbol indicated the path that cultural sociology would take.

Bellah's move is from the analytical formalism of Parsons to narrative formalism, from the thin narrative of analysis to the thicker narrative of history. His historical narrative is a tragic one, and it comes with the requisite appurtenances of tragedy. There is the nostalgia for a paradise, made necessary by the need to compare the degenerate present (self-interested, corporate capitalist America) with the purer or pristine past (virtue-driven Puritan and Civil War America). There is a strong villain (the advent of corporate capitalism) and a helpless protagonist, the once-proud civil religion. While this move from analytic to historical formalism[29] ensures a thicker and more meaningful sociological narrative, Bellah's analysis also has become, as suggested above, thinner in significant ways. By stressing the tension between virtue and self-interest, Bellah reinstated the dichotomy that Parsons's pattern variable scheme and, indeed, *The Structure of Social Action* were designed to overcome. This reinstatement tended to obscure the important ways in which Bellah had moved to incorporate such cultural-sociological elements as myth, code, and ritual. Whereas these latter, theoretical innovations have been sustained by subsequent developments in cultural sociology, the empirical dichotomies that Bellah saw as endemic to capitalist democracy have not stood up nearly as well. The apocalypticism grounded in *The Broken Covenant*'s tragic narrative seems outdated. Was Bellah's conviction, echoing Melville, that America was facing the "Dark Ages of Democracy" borne out? Was America's covenant really "broken" by the mid-1970s? We do not believe that the answers to these questions are "yes." While *Broken Covenant* was successful as a cultural intervention, presaging the extraordinary resonance achieved by *Habits of the Heart,* the jeremiad is not social science. For us, it is Bellah's formal and substantive contributions to cultural sociology that constitute his most important legacy, not his rejection of the ethical traction of American civic culture or his "emplotment" of American history in a tragic frame.

CONCLUSION:
BELLAH'S DURKHEIM AND CULTURAL SOCIOLOGY

We have traced some highlights in the culturalist revolution that Bellah initiated vis-à-vis Parsons. It is not our place here to speak about the deep psychological, even spiritual, motives that compelled him to undertake this revolt. Such complex and personal issues properly could be approached only through biography—for which Bellah's life and work would make a richly rewarding subject. Yet, without delving into Bellah's motives for this revolution, we would proffer a few concluding words about the intellectual resources that allowed him to carry it out.

We would point to, above all, his special relationship with Durkheim. To be sure, Bellah had a profoundly original interpretation of Durkheim, but this was more than an intellectual link; it was a markedly personal relationship, one that had distinctly religious overtones. Whereas Parsons had appreciated Durkheim, it was Weber whom he considered the true father of his own sociology. For Bellah it was the reverse; he appreciated Weber's comparative genius, but it was Durkheim who truly inspired him. More to the point, increasingly it was the *late* Durkheim, the Durkheim of "religious sociology," who led Bellah to the promised land of cultural sociology in 1968. "Civil Religion in America" has been read as Weberian because of its emphasis on asceticism as a political ethic; its deep structure, however, derives from Durkheim's late masterwork, *The Elementary Forms of Religious Life.* Bellah's essay challenges the very foundation of Weber's thesis of demagicalization; it describes the organization of a secular society "religiously," interprets history as myth, and puts civil ritual at its very center. What Durkheim said about his study of Aboriginal religion could just as well have been said by Bellah about his study of civil religion in America:

> We are not going to study a very archaic religion simply for the pleasure of telling its peculiarities and its singularities. If we have taken it as the subject of

our research, it is because it has seemed to us better adapted than any other to lead to an understanding of the religious nature of man, that is to say, to show us an essential and permanent aspect of humanity.[30]

While the tragic moral vision of historical declension that informed Bellah's subsequent writings made this late-Durkheim framework less and less apparent, this framework had already made its way into the basic lexicon of cultural sociology, allowing the third stage in the development of this new field, cultural sociology, to be articulated in a particularly effective way. Bellah's students have been centrally involved in developing this third stage, even as they struggle among themselves about the proper relationship between virtue and interest in contemporary society, about the contingency of action versus the traditions of structure, and about exactly how the later Durkheim's contributions to the study of contemporary societies ought to be considered.

TWO

Social Differentiation and Moral Pluralism

Steven M. Tipton

Since Plato proposed a systematic sociology of moral ideas, sentiments, and practices to unify institutional life around *The Laws,* social thinkers have recognized in the mutual influence of moral and social difference a persistent problem.[1] As the long history of its exposition branches into modern philosophy and sociology, ethicists tend to flatten if not ignore the institutional contexts implied or suppressed by their models of moral meaning. Sociologists tend to do likewise with the different moral perspectives implied or suppressed by their institutional analyses. In both cases, the wide range of moral meaning embedded in our cultural traditions and social institutions is narrowed into oversimplified representations of "culture" or "social structure." Anglo-American sociologists most often assume utilitarian, contractarian, and emotive ethics based on individual desires and interests, rights and values. These generate strategic action as means aimed at the ends of social utilities and subjective satisfactions, channeled by cost-benefit calculations, contractual agreements, and procedural rules.[2] Such ethics provide the axiomatic categories to analyze all moral life in relation to social processes of "rational" exchange, association, and coordination peculiar to the modern market and bureaucracy, coupled with the affective self-fulfillment of private life.

The following analysis of social differentiation and moral pluralism seeks to incorporate such efforts into a broader sociology of morality built around descriptive ethics and interpretive sociology. It uses conceptual categories drawn from moral philosophy and religious ethics to analyze the chief moral traditions of American culture in terms of contrasting styles of ethical evaluation. It argues that these styles ring true to our experience of distinctive activities, practices, and relationships structurally arranged within the different institutional sectors of social life. In turn, these styles constitutively interpret that experience and justify the arrangement of these institutions as well as our moral action and character within them. The variable salience of contrasting modes of moral understanding and ideals of character within different institutions offers a framework for grasping moral disagreement in relation to social difference, conflict, and cultural change. Distinguishing modes of ethical argument that justify different institutions permits rethinking the problem, and the limits, of a complex society's moral integration.

ETHICAL STYLES AND CULTURAL TRADITIONS

Contrasting *styles* of ethical evaluation distinctively characterize the various moral traditions that underpin American culture. These include biblical religion, civic humanism, and two forms of modern individualism, one utilitarian and bourgeois, the other Romantic and bohemian.[3] Let us take Athens and Jerusalem first, as moral traditions passed on to us from Socrates and Moses through such all-American hands as those of Jefferson, John Winthrop, and Frederick Douglass.

The revealed tradition of biblical religion features an *authoritative* style of ethical evaluation, even as it defies modern moral construal of authority as authoritarian constraint set against the freedom of individuals to act by right and conscience on their interests and desires. This tradition poses the moral question, "What should I do?" by asking, "What does God command?" An act is right because divinely revealed authority commands it. A person is good because she is obedient.

No less fundamentally, this tradition asks, "What does God love?" and "What sort of persons seek and embody the love of their Creator?" A person is good because she loves God, and her neighbor as herself. (Dt 6.5, Lv 19. 18; Mt 19.19, Mt 22.37–40.) The same is true of a community, conceived as the people of God. Both are blessed if they "obey the voice of the Lord your God, being careful to do all his commands." (Dt 28.1–2)[4] To be dutiful in following the Law of God in its act-specific commands rests, more profoundly, on an ideal of growing holy and godly in "becoming" the Law through living the life of holiness it orders and engenders. So every specific moral and cultic injunction in Leviticus, for example, is prefaced by the general command to be holy: "You shall be holy; for I the Lord your God am holy." (Lv 19.2) Jesus likewise proclaims the Beatitudes and a universal law of love, linked to the call to "be perfect, as your Heavenly Father is perfect."(Mt 5.48) Every commandment of God set down in scripture marks the divine favor granting the faithful the privilege of serving their Creator by fulfilling God's will and joining in God's holiness.

This ethical style is oriented mainly to an authoritative source whose will and grace are revealed to us directly or via some scripture or institution, such as the Bible or the synagogue, discerned by literal exegesis and by faith. Moral disagreement is resolved by further exegesis, greater familiarity with scripture or institution, and, finally, by conversion. The authoritative style prescribes, forbids, and inspires particular acts and ways of life more specifically than does any other ethical style. It does so by means of fixed commandments and exemplary ideals of virtue applied directly to specific cases and situations through detailed narratives of virtue and through collective precedents of right action, which covenantal communities of faith seek to live by and live out in history, in order to "Do justice, to love kindness, and to walk humbly with your God." (Mic. 6.8) (The typology of styles of ethical evaluation described here is outlined in table 1.)

In its covenantal framework of testimony, advocacy, and dispute between a lawful, graceful God and a sinful, faithful people, biblical religion also includes a reasoned line of development consonant with classical republican humanism. It features a rule-governed or *regular* style of evaluation — although the complex substance of this republican tradition, too, resists reduction to modern moral construal, notably in terms of rational legal rules predicated on formal grounds of procedure and consistency. This tradition poses the question, "What should I do?" by asking, "What is the relevant rule, virtue, or principle?" An act is right not only because of its consequences, but because it conforms to principles of conduct defined by dialectical reason in accord with laws of nature. The regularity of nature conceived as a cosmos, to which human beings essentially belong, entails a telos inherent in human existence. What it means to do the right act and become a good person on the classical model of a *microcosmos* within the body of the polis, therefore, resembles biblical ideals of living a life of holiness within the body of God's people, or of imitating Christ to become a *microchristus* within the Pauline body of the church, by contrast to a modern view of individuals exercising their moral will, conscientious intuition, and rationality defined by Kantian canons of consistency and generalizability.

Classical ethics of virtue, which define both the goodness of persons and the civic body they compose as members, rest on substantive, naturally lawful ideals of justice that recall the Greeks' *dikaiosune*. Linked to the inner ordering of an individual's appetites with intellect in the virtue of moderation, justice unifies all the virtues of human excellence in the proper social ordering of persons' relations with one another for the common good of the civic body of the polis or the republic. This body is conceived to incorporate society as a whole, instead of distinguishing between the state and civil society in modern terms that set off the political authority of government from the free association of individuals.

Classically construed, the regular ethic relies on a rationality less like Kant's identification of reason at its highest with the moral will served by theoretical reason than like practical reason in Aristotle's sense of right

TABLE 1   Styles of Ethical Evaluation

		Dimension			
Style	Oriented to	Mode of Knowledge	Discourse	Right-making Characteristic	Virtue
Authoritative	Authority God	Faith Conscience	What does God love, command?	Commanded, beloved by God	Obedience Neighbor-love
Regular	Rules	Reason	What is the relevant rule, principle, practice?	Conforms to rules, embodies virtue	Rationality Justice
Consequential	Consequences	Cost-benefit calculation	What do I want? What will most satisfy wants?	Produces the most good consequences	Efficiency
Expressive	Self and situation	Intuition Feelings	What's happening? How do I feel?	Expresses self, responds to situation	Sensitivity

SOURCE: Adapted with permission from Ralph B. Potter, "The Structure of Certain Christian Responses to the Nuclear Dilemma, 1959–1963" (Th.D. thesis, Harvard Divinity School, 1965).

reason and true wisdom in practical matters, accompanied by a stable acquired habit of personality to do what one judges to be good and just. This ethical style stands opposed to reason as the Hobbesian reckoning of self-defining subjects, the purely technical alignment of strategic means to subjectively given ends, reasoning instead dialectically from specific problem to solution to general principle to counterexample, toward objective criteria of conduct and character in accord with nature. Thus it can resolve moral disagreement and prescribe acts and virtues more specifically than can any other ethical style but the authoritative.

Now let us move from Athens and Jerusalem to the early modern city, for example, Adam Smith's Glasgow, John Locke's London, or Benjamin Franklin's Philadelphia. Utilitarian individualism features a *consequential* style of evaluation. It begins with each person asking first, "What do I want?" and then, "Which act will yield the most of what I want?" *Wants* are taken as given in ways that define as the good such ends as happiness, pleasure, and self-preservation. Good consequences are those that most satisfy wants. Right acts are those that produce the most good consequences, as reckoned by a cost-benefit calculus. A person is good because she is efficient in satisfying her wants.

This ethical style is oriented to the wants of individual actors to define what is good, and the calculation of consequences to determine which act is right. Where moral disagreement cannot be resolved by rechecking the consequential facts, this style explains why different persons perceive the facts differently in terms of their different interests, values, and positions in society and history. The consequential style prescribes particular acts least specifically, since it judges all acts not in themselves but by their usefulness in producing given consequences. Biblical religion and classical humanism take the opposing view that right-making characteristics inhere in acts as well as in their consequences, and that the goodness of desires is itself open to evaluation. Utilitarianism holds to a consequential view: an act is right if and only if it will produce at least as great a balance of good over bad consequences as will any available alternative act.[5]

The Romantic tradition scorns Athens, Jerusalem, and the bottom line of the industrializing city and its offices for the grassy countryside of Wadsworth and Whitman. It begins with the individual not as an actor efficiently pursuing her own self-interest but as a personality which experiences, feels, and simply *is*. Self-expression, not self-preservation, is the touchstone of moral motives. Neither a logic of following rules nor a logic of maximizing consequences guides this ethic. What does is the idea that everyone ought to act in any given situation so as to fully express her inner feelings and her empathic experience of the situation and of others in it. This situational and *expressive* style of evaluation poses the question, "What should I do?" by asking, "What's happening? How do I feel?" An act is right because "it feels right." It expresses one's self and responds to the situation most appropriately. A person is good because she is sensitive, in touch with herself and the moment. The expressive style is oriented to an intuitive, affective awareness of self and situation, and to empathy with others. In this style moral disagreement is resolved, if at all, by exchanging discrepant intuitions during diffusely sustained social interaction, thereby reshaping the situation and the actors' consciousness of it. The expressive style prescribes acts less specifically than do ethics of authority or rules, yet more specifically than ethics of consequences, through the intuited and empathic moral sense of the relevant group or community regarding the most appropriate feeling about a given situation or the most fitting action in response to it.

In conceiving the relationship between styles of ethical evaluation and the moral traditions of American culture, it is important to note that the consequential and expressive styles of evaluation more adequately characterize the utilitarian and Romantic cultural traditions than the authoritative and regular styles capture the complexity of the biblical and republican traditions. For the specificity of these singular styles of ethical evaluation is itself a function of the same process of social and cultural differentiation that has produced the singular spheres of the modern market and private life. By contrast, the biblical and republican traditions span a wider range of less differentiated institutions over a much longer history, ancient and medieval as well as modern. They embrace more broadly mixed modes of moral discourse within narratives of virtue to define good persons in a good society, made in the image of God and harmonized in the order of the cosmos. These narratives resist reduction to modern notions of rational legal rules and coercive authority counterposed to the liberal freedom of individuals.[6]

THE SOCIAL SETTING OF ETHICAL STYLES

At this point, let us turn to the different social settings of these ethical styles. I describe the relation of settings to styles, including the authoritative and regular, primarily as it appears to persons within American society today, although such a taxonomy could be modified and extended to span premodern and modern cultures and societies, as Mary Douglas's account of cultural bias and Robert N. Bellah's exposition of religious evolution suggest.[7] For the sake of simplicity, I will proceed in ideal-typical fashion, as if particular institutional settings and ethical styles are neatly and exclusively paired. Because they are not, I will afterward qualify this account in terms of the mixed moral meaning of modern institutions.

Social conditions bear on the content and structure of the ethical outlook a person comes to hold. They help make one moral idea or logic more plausible than another to a given person; they help make a given idea more plausible to one person than to another. For example, the child being commanded to obey by her parent, the soldier by his officer, or the lawbreaker by police must heed the voice of an authoritative ethic; and authorities must respect the rights of persons on the modern model of citizens. The youngster learning the rules of games, the student learning the rules of disciplines, and those who make and interpret the law must face a rule ethic's demands for consistency and generalizability. Handling money and holding a job, or managing a private, corporate, or public household, bring adults into continual reliance on the cost-benefit calculus of consequential ethics. Working within a bureaucratic organization reinforces respect for its procedural rules and contractual structure. Private life with lovers and friends, especially as it flourishes in youth, apart from family and job, supports the free-form intimacy of the expressive ethic. (An outline of the social settings of ethical styles described below appears in table 2.)

1. Authoritative Ethics and Institutions

Seen reciprocally, each ethical style relies on a given social institution's structural arrangements, practices, and relationships to frame the moral activity and character it articulates, and each ethical style justifies the arrangement of social forms that embody its meaning. Each is necessary to constitute the other. So the authoritative ethical style does more than simply enjoy a loose "elective affinity" with parental institutions, with related *in loco parentis* political institutions such as the military, police, and prisons, and with *ex cathedra* religious institutions.[8] Its commanding mode of discourse and virtue of *obedience* presume organizations structured by chains of command, in which those above issue orders and those below obey them. It presupposes a set of social roles and relations that feature superordinate and subordinate members, whether parent and child, officer and soldier, foreman and laborer, or ruler and subject.

Ethics of authority that reach beyond act-specific commands, and underlie them, can be heard in biblical calls to "Love God and neighbor" as God loves us, not simply to do God's will. In its inspiring mode of discourse and its cardinal virtue of a caring love, compassion, and reverence, this profoundly anti-authoritarian dimension of an ethic of authority requires the generalized reciprocity and nurturance of parental care within the family, pastoral care within the church as "mater et magistra," and patriotic love of country as "patria" or motherland.

Thus Durkheim argues that the moral authority of God and society not only commands respect and submission to forms of thought and conduct individual persons neither made nor desired, by virtue of its transcendent power over them, but also inspires them from within, through the vivifying power of the effervescent rites and binding social practices persons share in becoming civilized.[9] This process begins, according to developmental

TABLE 2   The Social Setting of Ethical Styles

| | *Social Dimension* | | |
Style	Institutional Location	Organizational Structure	Social Roles and Relations
Authoritative	Parental, familial; military, police, penal; totalitarian state, theocracy; state church, totalist sect	Chains of command; bonds of love	Parent-child; officer-soldier; officer-suspect; foreman-laborer; ruler-subject
Regular	Legal-political; educational; scientific; constitutional republic; religious denominations	Assemblies for discussion and disciplinary debate; councils and hierarchies of expertise	Professional colleagues; citizen-representative; teacher-student
Consequential	Market economy; corporate economy; contractarian state; group-interest politics; therapeutic groups; religious associations	Individuals linked through exchange and contract; agencies linked through bureaucratic procedures and offices	Buyer-seller; investor-entrepreneur; bureaucratic allies; client-official
Expressive	Leisure; romance; arts; private life; organismic utopia; mystic-aesthetic cults	Couples in love; circles joined in intimacy and tastes; lifestyle-enclaves	Lovers, friends; artist-aesthete; entertainer-fan

psychologies, with the nurturing care parental figures give the needy, helpless infant.[10] This creates hope and trust as the first virtues of persons in social relationship, and thereby grounds in love subsequent forms of parental authority that come to constrain and command the active toddler. Seen in this light, love dramatized in parental nurture plants the seed of anti-authoritarian rebellion as well as loyalty. It underlies biblical commandments to love God and "Honor thy father and mother." But it also leads away from moral prescription toward Augustine's counsel to "Love and do what you will," which rings in modern ears at least with the freedom of the expressive style of ethical evaluation.

The authoritative style is *most* prescriptive given the strongest forms of social classification and group bonds, terms of an institutional analysis adapted here from Mary Douglas's grid/group theory.[11] Such classifications take the form of ascriptive statuses and highly role-specific commands, which together do more than prescribe interaction. They separate and rank

	Social Dimension	
Occupational and Educational Class	Degree of Presciptivity	
Unskilled labor; service workers; welfare clients	*Most:* A total institution or total community commanding acts via strong group bonds and strong social classification	
Knowledge workers; professionals; engineers; skilled crafts and trades	*More:* Schools and political-professional bodies ordering norms and values via weak group bonds and strong social classification	←——————— Political Economy: Rule-Utilitarian Bureaucracies in the Administrative State and in the Corporate Economy
Managers, merchants, capital investors, administrators; bureaucrats	*Least:* Competitive markets coordinating interests via weak group bonds and weak social classification	
		←———————
Leisured rich and youth; stylish consumers	*Less:* Freely chosen networks shaping feelings and tastes via strong group bonds and weak social classification	

persons by age, sex, and seniority, so that they behave uncompetitively and unmistakably like a "good" daughter or mother, soldier or officer. Persons thus classified ought to act differently, and they do, because they *are* different, as normative rites and ideals of character make dramatically clear.

Strong group bonds are defined by frequent, long-standing, and often affective interaction such as that between parents and children, and by the clear-cut boundaries and powerful personal incorporation of total institutions such as the military, on which members depend almost entirely for their lives' support. Tightly knit, strongly inclusive and exclusive, able to command allegiance and punish defection, these groups endure through time. Chains of command permit resources to be distributed unequally yet justly among their members, because subsets of members are ranked and identified as essentially unequal. These groups also permit internal conflict to be adjudicated by direct appeals to authority and to reciprocal duties and virtues specific to each person in a given relationship.

Direct commands issued by figures of political or religious authority require a differentiated polity typical of archaic kingdoms and empires. In "simple" pre-modern societies, which feature a low division of labor and conflate the institutions of politics, kinship, and religion, moral authority holds sway through the norm of reciprocity and the similarity of moral consciousness and sentiment within a collective conscience, as Durkheim puts it, albeit with leeway left for negotiation in the course of everyday life.[12] Moral authority finds expression in comprehensive, compelling narratives of virtue that embed reciprocal duties and responsibilities in stories played out by representatives of ascribed social roles and statuses.

Within this social order, space and time, roles and relationships, belong to the community, not the individual. They are defined by rites, customs, and practices that leave little to personal choice, selection, and contract. So everyone in such a community must take part in religiously anchored rites of celebration and play on fixed holy days, for example, instead of going their own leisurely way as modern individuals to do as they please with their own time on holiday vacations.[13]

Ethics of authority predominate in pre-modern societies that conjoin the institutions of politics and religion. To predominate in the whole of modern social life, such an ethical style requires dedifferentiated political and religious institutions that subsume family, economy, schooling, and law into the order of a totalitarian or theocratic state, a state church or totalistic sect.

2. Regular Ethics and Institutions

The regular style, by contrast, is socially rooted in distinct legal-political, educational, and scientific institutions. Its reason-giving debate and rational virtue presume the organizational structures of assemblies for disciplinary discussion and hierarchies of expertise, relying on roles and relations that feature professional colleagues, teachers and students, judicious political representatives and public-spirited citizens who elect them. The reflective reason of the regular style requires schooling in systematic knowledge, dialectical exercise in argument over particular issues and over the construal of moral tradition itself, and application of reasoned conclusions in policy and practice. The regular style is *more* prescriptive given the relatively strong social classification yet weak group bonds of communities of practice such as schools, law courts, legislative or professional bodies. Social roles are defined by obligatory rules of interaction and ideals of character such as those of a good physician or judge. Duties and virtues derive from principles rather than commands, and they fuse role and personality in consciously learned practices rather than ascribed statuses. Affective ties are weaker in such communities of practice than in the family. Group boundaries are usually lower than in total institutions, as is the degree of personal incorporation and dependency.

In contrast to the microcosm-to-macrocosm fusion of knowledge and faith anchored by the unity of religious and political authority, regular ethics arise in a society when political and educational institutions separate out from those of religion and kinship in response to the increased scale of social units and the increased heterogeneity of their members' experience within a higher division of labor. Assertions of authority and demarcations of duty-bound status no longer suffice to resolve social conflict. Religious and political differentiation leads to the moral universalism that makes dialectical argument both possible and necessary in a political community based on the city, as distinguished from one based on the extended household.[14]

When the experience of essential social practices can reproduce excellence in these practices without reasoned reflection or argument, along with the conviction that the order of nature, society, and divine authority necessarily and self-evidently coincide, then education remains diffuse and it yields the unanimity of *doxa,* of that which is taken for granted.[15] Institutionalized education arises when practical experience yields conflicting or incoherent meanings, when one culture encompasses contrary axioms and modes of discourse, and one society includes their carriers. Instead of a unitary, comprehensive tradition experienced as the natural world and taken for granted, tradition begins to diversify and its construal becomes the object of critical discourse and argument that move back and forth from problematic cases to first principles and cosmology. In this fashion orthodoxy must be distinguished from heterodoxy, and knowledge from opinion. The nature of things in themselves must be critically rediscovered in some form of natural law—Stoic or Thomist, for example—by which the institution of human laws can be consciously judged and justified.[16]

Increased social scale and heterogeneity, combined with property inalienably embedded in social relationships, underlie the classical republican premise that politics fundamentally constitutes society through the reasoned friendship of its members, rather than growing out of society's creation by divine authority or economic exchange. As such, politics becomes the highest form of the art of caring for souls. With the waning of feudal corporatism and of the hierarchy of its ancient antecedents, ideals of natural law and reason undergo radical reconstrual into early modern conceptions of natural rights. These check and transform traditional ethics of authority by extending to citizens—by contrast to political subjects—the moral logic of salvation religion, on the one hand, and on the other, by limiting them to the positivist moral knowledge of a mechanistic science. This affirms selves of infinite value and equality in constitutive relationship to a universal creator and cosmic order, for example, in the image of "Nature and Nature's God" that endow all persons with inalienable rights, in Jefferson's usage in the Declaration of Independence. But it also opens the door to political absolutism by dismissing classical reason and religious revelation from public justification, in favor of Hobbesian ethics of self-interest and collective security attuned to the rise of the nation state.

In modern society a constitutional republic comes closest to embodying the regular ethical style in political form, especially in its legislative and judicial functions. So do congregational and denominational types of religious organization that couple freedom of religious exercise and inquiry with regular patterns of religious understanding and practice to form the members of binding bodies of faith.

3. Consequential Ethics and Institutions

The consequential ethical style is socially rooted in economic institutions based on the market. Its organizational structure links free, equal, and self-interested individuals through exchange and contract, whether as buyers and sellers or investors and entrepreneurs. Its means–ends mode of discourse and criterion of efficiency presume the cost-effective organization of technological production and capitalist finance, which aim to maximize productivity and profitability. Its cost-benefit calculus and its quantified comparison of qualitatively different acts' consequences require a market and a money economy to provide the experience of a price or cost. Only in these terms can different items be quantified and compared, because they are all for sale and because one all-purpose utility—money—can acquire them all.[17]

Rule-utilitarian ethics extend this consequential style of evaluation from markets to bureaucracies. The rules and regulations that define and structure modern bureaucracies are procedural rules, justified by the collective consequences of their recognition, not by divine authority, dialectical reasoning, or first principles taken as laws of nature. Instead of asking which *act* will produce the greatest good consequences, rule utilitarian ethics ask which *rule* will do so. Rule utilitarianism holds to the principle of utility and its consequential logic, but uses them to evaluate rules instead of particular acts. It thereby tends to stabilize and strengthen rules by requiring the agent, once she has assessed which complete set of rules produces by its recognition the greatest balance of good consequences for everyone, to act according to the relevant rule of that set in any particular case, even when a given act contrary to the rule would seem to yield better consequences in that particular case. While moral rules must be justified by their consequences in this view, an act violating a moral rule cannot itself be so justified. Acts can only be justified by their compliance with the relevant rule.[18]

In bureaucratic social settings, such consequential ethics of rules interact with regular ethics of rules and principles socially rooted in legal political institutions. This interaction works to subsume regulations and laws into a procedural hybrid socially rooted in the bureaucratic institutions of a corporate economy and administrative state. In these social settings, organizational structures link self-interested yet cooperative individuals through bureaucratic offices and standardized operating procedures. As client-citizens of the welfare state, they contend for the benefits of its public provision, lobby for advantages in its regulatory policy, and seek the entitlements that multiplied and diversified rights convey to specific groups such as home owners and the elderly. As bureaucratic "team players," supervisors, and clients within a corporate economy, they "go along to get along," complying with procedural rules to maximize the collectivity's productive output, profits, or security, from which they draw a share of the utilitarian proceeds to purchase their own private pleasures.

The consequential style is *least* prescriptive given the weak social classification and group bonds of autonomous individuals. They are left free to choose and be chosen in a competitive market, depending on the contingent facts of supply and demand and reciprocity itself, for you should give only if you get. As individuals in a market freely choose their own deals and trading partners, their transactions cross the group boundaries and ascribed statuses of social hierarchy. Hierarchical ethics of authority are undercut in the apparently natural play of universal individual interests, in turn politically curbed and framed by universal individual rights.

Obeying fixed moral commands or following rules pre-establishing particular acts as right cannot guide conduct in a market. Markets prescribe, "Maximize benefit-cost ratios, returns on investment, and profitability," and they command, "Buy low, sell high." But such rules and imperatives are not morally act-specific. For all action becomes transaction in the market. Only results count, not buying and selling per se; even as the value of goods inheres in their exchange, not in the substance of the labor, land, materials, and technology that went into their production.[19] Markets require rules of transaction and contracts. These depend on noncontractual moral bases within the larger social order, as Durkheim argues, including more or less principled norms of commutative justice to define the equivalency of exchange. But in its own economistic terms, the market displaces regular moral principles and radically reinterprets their meaning in terms of interests, utility, and the procedural form of fair contracts.[20]

Thus social relationships are selected, not given, in a free market. They are open to negotiation to define social obligations, rights, and status by contractual agreement based on exchange between mutually disinterested agents.[21] Like money itself, time and space, roles and relationships, are resources open to the individual to use as he chooses, restricted only by the calculated costs of doing so and by the competition. Cost-effectiveness and economies of scale in a market encourage agents to innovate, specialize, and expand operations, and to treat all relationships instrumentally as allies or competitors in relation to these utilitarian ends. In the event of failure to deliver goods contracted for or to price effectively one's own services in the market, the individual can make no binding claims on others for support, although he may seek their sympathy.[22]

As market transactions and contracts increase their social range and complexity, procedural rules and bureaucratic institutions keep pace. In theory this enables each individual to receive a fair turn and an equal opportunity to pursue his own ends, while coordinating collective action to maximize its total utility—on the model, for example, of traffic laws. Such procedural regulation of the political economy separates individuals equal in their essence as citizens by the educational and occupational qualifications they earn, the offices they occupy, and the economic resources they possess or lack. By these criteria, corporate and state managers differentially distribute income, welfare benefits, and related opportunities to the more or less deserving members of an egalitarian, individualistic society made up of free citizens bearing equal legal and civil rights.

In bureaucratic social settings and rule-utilitarian ethics, the consequential style of evaluation becomes more prescriptive than in the act-utilitarianism of the market. Group bonds are still weak, but social classification is strengthened to restrict the scope of personal transactions. Persons remain individuals but now they are taxonomically or functionally subordinated to one another, their jurisdictions delimited, and their behavior coordinated by procedural regulation. Time, space, and social roles are compartmentalized and standardized. Relationships are no longer so open to negotiation, and individuals can gain benefits only by complying with the procedures governing their case or office.[23] Because the corporate units of rule-utilitarian ethics are often large, even society-wide, and its calculations are long-term or causally complex, those below the level of policy-making elites typically experience bureaucratic institutions as impersonal or anonymous. Within them, judgments are made and decisions reached with little of the face-to-face communication of empathic private life or market bargaining, of disciplinary debate or authoritative commands.

Consequential ethics come to the fore in a society when economic institutions separate out from political and religious ones. In Western history this takes the form of putatively self-regulating markets. They emerge from local political communities and empires to set their own prices for labor, land, and capital as well as goods through supply and demand, and to control production and distribution in turn by prices and profit. Now exchange occurs increasingly between strangers instead of neighbors, between entrepreneurs instead of landlord-rulers. Economic surplus is appropriated through increased productivity and exchange within a capitalist "world-economy," rather than by direct political appropriation in the form of imperial tribute or feudal rents. The early modern state stimulates such economic differentiation by breaking down feudal localism. In response to subsequent needs for procedural regulation of the market and taxonomic ordering of industrial production, more integrated political economies arise with the expansion of modern nation states on the constitutional model of Western liberal democracy and the development of large-scale bureaucratic institutions of corporate management. Government seeks to sponsor economic progress and stabilize the prices of labor, land, and capital without itself becoming the central economic enterprise. By taxes and other redistributive devices, it acts with more or less vigor and effect in the name of social justice to modify inequalities inherent in the market, where persons differ in what they have to offer and can thereby earn in exchange.[24]

Group-interest politics in a philosophically liberal, contractarian polity embodies the consequential ethical style, in tandem with the administrative activity of a bureaucratized welfare state. So do individualistic, interest-oriented and loose religious associations, ranging from nonconfessional, positive-thinking churches to human potential movements.

4. Expressive Ethics and Institutions

The expressive style is socially rooted in the leisure institutions of private life, where couples in love, circles of friends, and members of "lifestyle-enclaves" (whether polo players or punk rockers) are linked through shared tastes and experiences of intimacy.[25] Its intuitive, affective knowledge and virtue of *sensitivity* require sufficient leisure time for a person to gain fluency in feelings. Gaining fluency in feelings for their own sake also requires a measure of freedom from economic pressures to suppress or use one's feelings as strategic means to the end of success in the market or bureaucracy. Such sensitivity also stands apart from professional, educational, or other practices that capture and discipline emotions in regular fashion; and from religious or civic rites that bind them to authority. So expressive ethics flourish particularly among the rich and the youthful who do not work. Those who do, meanwhile, seek in the expressive warmth and intimacy of private life the ends that justify or at least compensate for instrumental relationships in the marketplace and office.

The expressive style is *less* prescriptive, given the weakly regulated social classification of its roles but the relatively strong if unstable group bonds it creates through sharing feelings or tastes and through interacting frequently. Because the lifestylish group maintains clear boundaries against outsiders and intuitively shares evaluative attitudes and self-images, it can influence individuals' moral behavior and judgment, working changes of heart through intimate interaction sustained and examples set among members and judged in forms akin to the "boo-rah" terms of emotivist and intuitionist theories of ethics.[26] "I like X," group members affirm, and so should you, by implication, even if we can't say why. However implicitly and aesthetically, the lifestylish group thus prescribes specific acts in themselves and for their own sake, and it likewise exemplifies certain modes of relationship and traits of character.

External boundaries and cohesive attitudes also enable lifestylish groups to withdraw sympathetic approval from deviants and expel the intransigent. But because such groups classify internal roles so weakly, relationships between individual members tend to be morally ambiguous, however enjoyable, and conflicts between them elude adjudication in terms of authority, duties and rights, or clearly calculable interests. Jealousies and conflicts unresolved by expulsion or changes of heart tend to go underground and lead to covert competition, factions, and eventually to group fission, making lifestylish groups relatively fluid and short-lived.[27]

Since the individual's role and relationships in this institutional context are left otherwise undefined in moral terms, expressive self-definition in the present moment becomes an essential and unending social practice. Moment by moment, an elusive yet intuitively shared sense of stylishness confirms a version of good character, as a sense of appropriateness defines right action. This attenuation of moral judgment and its criteria begins with the institutional effects of the market. Since its contingencies divorce intention from act from consequences, as Adam Smith argues, action can only be judged by its efficiency in producing certain consequences, *or* by the situational appropriateness and benevolence of the intentions that motivated it.[28] Moral responsibility shifts its frame of reference from communal virtues and duties to the conscience of individuals to complement their interests and contracts. Individuals can be held accountable only by themselves for their situationally appropriate, benevolent intentions and only by civil law for their contractual commitments to others, whom the market may nonetheless ruin or reward undeservedly.

The two-sided relationship of the economy to lifestylish social groups is evident in Smith's seminal formulation: Individuals will seek to win one another's sympathetic approval and identification by modulating their own attitudes and appearance, because their middle-class livelihood depends on such acceptance in a market-centered society. Just as honesty is the best policy for self-interested individuals, shared self-imagery is a social utility that serves to advance individual interests and coordinate collective exchange.[29] Persons pursue riches and avoid poverty to win social attention and approval. At the same time, in a society no longer centered around the ritualized moral authority and reasoned principles of religious and political institutions, essentially separate and equal selves must make the imaginative and moral effort to intuit each other's experience and sympathize with it in order to know themselves, harmonize their passions, and order the social world impartially and justly.[30]

Expressive and utilitarian forms of individualism arise side by side in a society when work, like politics before it, moves out of the family. Then intimate feelings go unchecked by the exigencies of economic production and the authority of those who head household and business alike.[31] When families no longer arrange marriage to maintain their productive property or political alliances, romance can flower between individuals who court and marry knowing their livelihood will depend mainly on their own success in school and at work. When the middle class can acquire through the market and the constitutional state a measure of economic independence without assuming the organic political responsibilities a landed aristocracy must bear, then leisure can grow up around aesthetic self-expression and lifestylish consumption freed from the rites of political and religious community.[32]

In political institutions, the expressive style points toward an organismic utopia of confluent feelings and wills to incarnate a communal moral consensus without authoritative commands, regular debate, or cost-benefit calculation. Expressive ethics also inform fluidly cultic religious organizations, in which initiates share the aesthetic or mystical experience of a gnostic truth.

SOCIAL DIFFERENCE AND MORAL DISAGREEMENT

Since Marx and Durkheim, sociological observers have asked how the division of labor in modern society carries over into the division of moral understanding in modern culture. Consider the moral differentiation of work itself. The unskilled laborer follows a foreman's orders, the skilled worker also refers to craft standards, the white-collar worker to bureaucratic regulations and interpersonal responses, the professional to disciplinary practices, canons, and collegial criticism. The varied length and quality of education anticipate the different occupational patterns of work and its rewards. Education distributes occupational opportunities and helps justify their inequality, and by extension the greater inequality of occupational rewards, since "school is fairer than life." The disciplinary demands and meritocratic grading of school are "fair," that is, in a more substantive, regular sense than are the consequential contingencies of success in the market or the purely procedural justice of getting one's bureaucratic due.[33] Class-specific socialization in the family transmits work-related moral differences from one generation to the next, typically stressing conformity to act-specific commands in the laborer's home, for example, and self-directive, empathic communication about attitudes and consequences in the manager's family.[34]

The social experience of women who work mainly within the family as mothers and homemakers supports a relational ethic of nurturant care, interdependence, and recognition of unequal needs as relevant to understanding moral desert.[35] Institutional situation, then, not only the gendered interplay of culture and nature, figures in findings in developmental psychology that women commonly emphasize this outlook over ethics of equal rights, even exchange, and procedural justice that guide the marketplace and bureaucracy, which are disproportionately filled and controlled by men. In Lawrence Kohlberg's sequence of moral stages, an ethic that stresses caring relationship to others and responsibility for them as interdependent members of a community is localized within the home and equated with conformity to convention. Kohlberg's "higher" stages of moral consciousness subordinate relationships to rules and rules to universal principles of justice (exemplified by John Rawls's concept of justice as fairness and Kant's categorical imperative) that serve autonomous selfhood, grounded in a liberal logic of equality and reciprocity. This view of morality favors men over women, Carol Gilligan and others point out.[36] Such criticism casts doubt on stage theories of morality that claim to represent sequential levels of cognitive development or human growth per se, but it supports sociological construal of such theories to reveal the institutional contexts they assume.

Insofar as they lack the independent income and bureaucratic power conferred by well-paid work in the world of the market and office, women are more liable than men to come under the authority of those who possess such utilities, to accept under duress uneven utilitarian exchanges with them, and to face unfairness within the moral drama of the family as "the first school of justice." Women are also more likely to sell their smiles, using self-expression to offset such exchanges or soften such authority.[37] Exclusion from work in the market and office also characterizes the class-bound situation of the structurally unemployed, undereducated, and impoverished. In return for welfare benefits doled out by the state, they are subject to the severest forms of its bureaucratic authority, which can approach the commanding authority of police or penal institutions. Apparently free of work's burdens with time on their hands for leisure, although, in fact, commonly working overtime to survive, the jobless poor lack the economic independence and occupational ties to enjoy leisure in middle-class moral fashion, as a reward for paid work and a sign of successful social standing.

Institutionalized differences in moral meaning do not exist only among persons of different classes, sexes, races, regions, and religious, ethnic, or cultural backgrounds. They also exist for each individual, because she experiences different moral norms, values, and attitudes in different sectors of her own social life, and within each sector at different times in her life. Both authority and self-expression are relatively strong for *any* individual as child, parent, and lover within the modern family. Consequentialism holds sway in business and bureaucratic life, but it is circumscribed by law, appeals to rights, and minimal obligations not to injure. Among friends and lovers expressive feelings are the norm, while duties and householding calculations arise between spouses.

Taken in terms of its own tradition, each ideal of moral character and its narratives of practical virtue extend to the whole of life and seek to capture our outlook on it. Each tradition is imperial. It wants to show and tell us, for example, how to love and obey God not just in worship but in business, politics, play, and family life, so that work and love and the rest all become worship in their fundamental meaning, and the synagogue or church becomes the central institution in the believer's life if not in the society's structure. Similarly, classical humanism asks us to reason with others toward the common good in a forum that reaches beyond the academy and polity to embrace all of life in dialogue. Utilitarian individualism asks us to calculate the costs and benefits of every social exchange, not only those in the marketplace, and to see ourselves producing and consuming political or cultural goods, accumulating and investing symbolic capital.[38] Expressive individualism asks the romantic to give her all for love, and the dandy to live all of his life as a work of art; it asks us to seek stylish self-expression in our every activity and acquisition so that food, clothing, shelter, householding, and transportation reveal the social image of our inner identity through our sensibilities.

On the one hand, the diversity of moral outlooks surrounding each individual in a modern society encourages her to distance herself from any single outlook and relativize all of them in order to enact each one in the social role and practices specific to it: efficient worker, expressive lover, law-abiding citizen, lifestylish consumer, authoritative yet caring parent, faithful believer, and so on. The institutional multiplication of moral ideals accounts for the apparently inconsistent and self-contradictory cosmologies modern individuals hold simultaneously, and the "eccentric" moral hybrids they compose from various traditions.[39]

On the other hand, a diversity of ethical outlooks triggers a countervailing tendency toward convergence through generalization and synthesis. This yields the sliver of social truth within such moral stereotypes as authoritarian soldiers, sensitive artists, rule-bound bureaucrats who go by the numbers, and calculating businessmen who cut corners to get to the bottom line. Social circumstances cannot determine but they can promote stereotypically autonomous men and caring women, the imperious rich, industrious middle class, and dependent poor. Such moral stereotypes rarely fit us, we rightly feel, because we experience *both* relativizing and generalizing impulses in response to multiple moral ideals and their institutional contexts.

The practical bases of this multiplicity underscore the need for institutionally nuanced ways of grasping the constitutive connections between social practices and moral character. Modern commonsense spots morality most readily in the form of rules. So it sees the good person who follows these rules as one possessed of traits or virtues defined as dispositions to act in accord with certain rules or laws in given social settings. But ideals of moral character more closely describe the sort of person who acts, feels, perceives, thinks, judges, and responds well in certain activities distinctively ordered *as practices* by given institutions, and distinctively interpreted by given cultural traditions, rather than uniformly regulated as exchanges or protocols.

Recognizing these institutional and cultural distinctions qualifies theories of social practices that conceive a unitary modern institutional order unquestionably reproducing itself through the uniform dispositions it habituates in those who inhabit it. It also qualifies theories of isomorphic modern institutions that conceive a unitary Western cultural account of individual human agency unquestionably belied by the sovereign structural power of institutionalized cultural rules to give uniform definition to the meaning and identity of the individual and to the patterns of appropriate economic, political, and cultural activity engaged in by individuals. The conjunction of contrasting ideals of moral character and distinctive arrangements of social institutions through specific practices enables us to grasp the social variability of character ideals, and moral conflicts among them, without privileging only a few forms of moral character and practice as islands of Aristotelian virtue in a Weberian sea of bureaucratic individualism that covers the modern world.[40]

PRACTICAL MORAL QUESTIONS AND ANSWERS

The preceding sections have argued that the institutional diversity of modern social activities and relationships in practice underlies diverse answers to questions of what life means, and how we should think out and live out the very answers that justify the structural arrangement of the institutions we inhabit. Tensions between these ways of understanding right and wrong accompany tensions between different sectors of social life, for example, between the market's bottom line and the family's loving authority. Each moral outlook seems more plausible in one social sector than in another. It rings truer to that particular form of social experience. And each institutional arrangement of social life seems more justifiable within that particular outlook. Greater involvement in one social institution than in another, and greater identification with it, favor holding the ethical style and cultural assumptions predominant in it.

Now let us begin to shade in this ideal-typical outline of a sociology of morality. Practically posed, moral questions are about one or another concrete social activity and setting. They are about learning, working, and loving, about familial, communal, or political relations. By themselves, "styles" or modal types of ethical evaluation are empty analytic categories. Granted, ethical evaluation occurs within institutional contexts, and it refers to cultural traditions. But it also takes in the peculiar social situation and biography of persons as moral actors and thinkers facing particular questions, posed in terms of specific strands of cultural traditions and set within specific sorts of social institutions. Traditions are not univocal, and institutions are not uniform across societies or monolithic within each society. In every society there exist family, polity, economy, religion, and education of more or less varied sorts,while in each society at each historical moment there exist certain sorts of familial, political, and economic ordering. In each case, a different ethical style may predominate, at once grounded in and justifying the practical activities, relationships, and roles specific to that set of institutional forms. Thus political ethics of authority tend to predominate in dictatorships, principled rules and virtues in republics, consequentialism in contractarian states, and expressive feelings in organismic utopian communities.

But diverse ethics and structural arrangements also coexist within a single social institution. Within the family, for example, parents nurture infants, restrain toddlers, and, as children age, reason with them, weigh their interests, and elicit their feelings. Within schools in the United States, for example, can be found aspects of a forum and academy to educate citizens of a democracy—a church of sorts to preach its rationale, catechize its tenets, and justify its social arrangements, including the meritocracy marked by the unequal occupational life-chances that schools hand out and certify. These elements coexist with the school as a "knowledge factory" to train students as human resources for technical work in a knowledge-intensive economy, as an office to coordinate their age-graded bureaucratic interaction, and as a studio to nurture their personal creativity and communication in forms linked to romantic love, leisure, and consumption as well as to the demands of emotional labor in the economy's service sector.

Similarly, the U.S. federal government includes courts that interpret the law on constitutional grounds that are both substantive and procedural. Congress debates legislation and policy on these grounds, and it also brokers and serves group interests. The executive branch commands the military; it also coordinates an administrative bureaucracy by reference to the utility of programs and procedures, the rule of law, the sovereignty of the people, and both the national interest and special interests.

A more pervasive moral ambiguity runs through the U.S. polity. It is a religiously resonant republic that depends on the participation of public-spirited citizens for its shared self-government, and a liberal constitutional state that pledges to protect the individual rights of self-interested citizens who pursue wealth and knowledge through free markets for economic and intellectual exchange.[41] The liberal tradition of public philosophy in America conceives persons as independent selves, unencumbered by moral or civic ties they have not chosen. Freedom consists in the very capacity of such persons to choose their own values and ends. The rival republican tradition conceives freedom as the fruit of sharing in self-government whose public-spirited character is cultivated by these very practices of deliberating together over common goods and sharing responsibility for the destiny of the political community.

Each tradition poses key questions of public life within a distinctive logic of moral argument. How can citizens become capable of self-government, asks the republican, who then seeks the social conditions and political arrangements needed to promote the civic virtue self-government requires and the liberty it breeds. The liberal first asks how government should treat its citizens, then seeks the principles and procedures of justice needed to treat persons fairly and equally as they pursue their own ends and interests. Fair procedures take priority over particular moral ends posed as public goods. Individual rights function as moral trump cards, played to insure the state's neutrality among competing conceptions of the good life, in order to respect persons as selves free to choose their own ends.

In a society divided by class, race, gender, region, and generation there also coexist corresponding structural and moral variants of a given social institution. Comparison of "pro-life" and "pro-choice" abortion activists, for example, shows how different patterns of arranging and living in practice the institution of marriage can shape the experience of two typically well-educated, mobile, religiously liberal, and late-marrying professionals into a pro-choice outlook on abortion at odds with the pro-life outlook that rings true to the experience of a small businessman and his homemaker wife, who married out of high school and remain religiously conservative.[42] Conversely, the two couples tend to define and justify the diverse arrangement of their marriages—conceived as a contract, covenant, or sacrament, for example—by drawing on different moral traditions, drawing out different strands of the same tradition, and construing traditional moral goods and norms in different styles of ethical evaluation.

The predominance of particular ethical styles and conceptual categories that persons use in posing and answering a concrete moral question can be coherently related to their culture's traditions, on the one hand, and to the institutional contexts and forms of their socially situated experience, on the other. Problematic moral issues such as abortion demonstrate this two-sided relationship. For Americans who identify themselves as pro-life or pro-choice, the problem of abortion characteristically centers around the ambiguous moral status of the fetus: is it a person or not?[43] But this question involves a binocularity of ethical styles and traditions tied to institutional ambiguity over the issue's social location and context. If the fetus is a person in its soulful or telic essence, and abortion take a person's life, then religious and political authorities, holy writ and criminal law should pro-scribe it. If the fetus will not become a person until it develops a personal-ity in the course of its psychological development over historical time, and if abortion is a function of utilitarian career and family planning or of expressive self-fulfillment, then pregnant individuals or couples expecting a baby should be free to consult their interests or get in touch with their feelings to decide whether to abort or give birth, without interference from church or state.

Note that each proposition unites perceived fact and cultural ontology, institutional definition and moral judgment. Both the pro-life and pro-choice sides of the abortion debate agree that the issue is located at least partly within the institutions of marriage and the family. But they disagree over the practical moral meaning of the marital bond and "family values." Is marriage primarily a romantic and contractual relationship between two autonomous individuals equally entitled to emotional and occupational self-fulfillment? Or is it primarily a sacramental and naturally lawful rela-tionship whose procreative ends necessitate different duties and forms of authority for male and female parents? Abortion is also a political issue. But is the state being called to act as a commanding authority to proscribe abor-tion as the arbitrary taking of a person's life contrary to criminal law, or is democratic self-government being called on to respect the autonomy of individual citizens to make their own choices in a personal matter? Both appeals can make a prima facie claim to plausibility because the American polity includes both of these ethical and institutional elements, just as American society includes groups whose diverse experience and axiomatic cultural assumptions support each of these ideals of marriage and family life.

The issue of abortion appears unique in the social-survey evidence it of-fers for polarization among Americans' social attitudes.[44] Yet ongoing liber-alization and fluctuation in quantifiable measures of Americans' attitudes toward abortion also appear consistent with the fact that most Americans do not identify themselves as unequivocally pro-life or pro-choice. For them abortion remains an object of moral confusion as much as absolute convic-tion. There is something wrong about it, or at least deeply troubling, but when you really need one, you should really be free to have one. What seems clearest to most Americans about the question of abortion, signifi-cantly, is that the answer to it finally rests with each individual and her con-science. In this conscientious decision making, whether or not it is seen as necessarily involving the divine, the state should be loath to intervene. Freedom of individual conscience, understood as a moral axiom extending across American culture and subject to diverse construal within distinctive traditions, at once underlies and reaches well beyond the legal right to pri-vacy and the freedom to choose abortion as defined by *Roe v. Wade.*

Consideration of concrete moral problems such as abortion helps clarify the sociology of morality in general. First, it indicates that matters of social fact and cultural ontology are joined together in moral understanding, and often prove as inseparable as the facts of fetal life and the ontological definition of persons in terms of an essential soul or a developmental personality. Second, the normative implications of agreed-on facts, such as the fetus's lack of independent viability, vary with the traditional assumptions and logic of argument into which these arguments are integrated, for example, on the moral status of the fetus bearing or lacking a right to life. Third, moral ideas such as freedom and justice, obligations and rights—including "the right to life" and "the right to choose" in the abortion debate—change their meaning by shifting their underlying style and logic of argument from the framework of one cultural tradition to another and by shifting their social referents and institutional context. Fourth, the moral and institutional ambiguity of issues such as abortion is tied to the varied social locations of those who face the issue and the varied social experience of the issue to which their contrary moral ideas ring true within specific institutional arrangements.

Responsibility for the common good of bearing and raising children, for example, seals the biblical covenant between God and the whole of God's people, including "the least of these." But the institutional arrangement of parenthood in relation to marriage, education, and work in the United States today concentrates responsibilities and sanctions for abortion decisions on individuals unevenly across gender and class lines, in effect counterposing individual legal rights and free market liberties to approve babies for those who can afford to pay for them and abortions for those who cannot.

TOWARD A SOCIOLOGY OF MORALITY

No fixed, exclusive, one-to-one correspondence obtains between each institution, tradition, and ethical style for everyone regardless of their place in society and history. The actual institutions in which we live, as opposed to ideal-typical ones, are both structurally and ideologically mixed. In each social situation and institution we actually experience, we have all these ethical styles and traditions in our heads, however fragmentarily or unevenly represented, ringing more or less true to the practical activities, roles, and relations of that situation and of our own history. The distinctions of ethical outlook we actually adopt, then, are rarely all-or-nothing, mutually exclusive matters. They are more nearly matters of mixture: Which ethical style will predominate in which situation? Which style will order the interrelation of other styles and the elements of tradition in a given situation, and for whom? Particular persons and groups combine and recombine moral traditions and styles in mixtures of meaning specific to particular social situations and problems.

This perspective rebuts ethical absolutism without confirming ethical relativism. For in each situation and with each problem, institutionally arranged and enacted as they are, persons frame practical moral questions and answers in search of alternative responses that are intelligible, justifiable, and therefore public in their cultural coherence. To guide my moral decisions, I am seeking criteria that I can communicate coherently and persuasively to others, not rationalizations I can use to mask my arbitrariness. I am seeking moral guidance not just for myself, but for anyone in my situation.[45] Institutionally embedded and dramatically enacted as it is, such guidance is not simply a matter of universalizing from each person to every rational subject or free citizen, abstractly conceived, but neither is it simply a statement of personal intent or group interest. For we cannot make the modes of moral discourse and the moral drama of institutions mean whatever we wish and still make sense to ourselves and others, which is what we must do in order to live as social beings.

Moral ideas can change meaning and social usage within a culture because every culture is intricately interwoven through reflection and practice rather than simply driven by interests or precipitated from ethics. Social facts and cultural axioms can be ordered and reordered in contrasting moral styles, in traditions that evolve as persons and groups peculiarly placed in society and history bring them to bear on institutionally problematic cases, such as abortion in the changing context of contemporary marriage, motherhood, and work. As soon as we consider any concrete moral question, we find styles of ethical evaluation existing in situ, ordering the other elements that make up moral thought: perceptions of facts, social loyalties, and axiomatic assumptions about the nature of reality.[46] Only thus do these analytic categories reveal a living ethic by which persons make particular judgments and groups articulate a moral consensus.

Without considering styles of ethical evaluation and moral traditions, on the other hand, we are left with nothing but the particular judgments persons make.[47] These appear as discrete opinions presumed to follow from the interests that their adherents' social conditions define and the values they espouse; when persons act contrary to their interests, it can only be because they have miscalculated them. This pragmatic view of moral behavior has practical drawbacks that a more interpretive approach can address by relating the process of evaluation to its outcome. How a person thinks about goodness, right, and wrong shapes what she judges to be right or wrong, and what she decides to do about it. How a person justifies his moral positions and actions influences how he may be persuaded to change them. Styles of ethical evaluation are the necessary links between social circumstances and cultural traditions (which give these styles plausibility and substance) and particular moral positions and actions (which these styles generate and defend). Without taking ethical styles and traditions into account, we cannot understand moral judgments, nor can we change them, except by coercion or the manipulation of interests. The same holds true of the social structures which moral judgments shape and by which they are shaped. This is because we think our way to moral action. Social and economic circumstances influence our thinking, but they do not do it for us. Recognizing this fact makes it possible to enrich research that neatly correlates social and economic data with discrete opinions on concrete issues by exposing the interlocking assumptions, arguments, and modes of discourse that hold together these particulars. It also makes it possible to honor the common-sense conviction we have of our own moral views—that they come from our understanding, not only our circumstances.

Social theories of morality that reduce it to individualist affirmation, or to institutionalist denial of subjects seeking to satisfy their freely chosen desires or socially determined interests, reflect from two sides a society whose economic exploitation of nature and bureaucratic organization of public affairs seem designed for the utility of individuals. They go along to get along, playing instrumentally required social roles while pursuing their own happiness. But social and moral life, seen in the complexity of its institutions and traditions, is subtler than such social scientific objectification. In fact, these theories themselves presuppose a subject of science whose regular understanding of truth and practice of inquiry they cannot account for. Such subjects—which is to say, you and I—remain angelic observers standing outside the consequentially objectified stream of social life.[48]

Instead of doing our thinking for us, social conditions intersect with culture to make moral sense of our lives, in the form of discourse about what is good, which acts are right, and who is virtuous. To weigh the raw evidence of cultural coherence, conflict, and change, therefore, we must get at the actual content of this discourse and know what to make of its logic as a living text, its back-and-forth flow as a cultural conversation that draws on multiple traditions to interpret the very experience that sustains or transforms tradition. Cultural transformation follows on social structural change and leads into it in ways that usually elude one-to-one correspondence or neat causal attribution. This makes it essential for scholars, especially social scientists, to learn to use ethical categories to build a thick conceptual model of culture, not just a "thick description" of social events, interests, and institutions.[49] We need to dissect cultural change and continuity using taxonomies of tradition, not just trend data. We need to trace cultural contrariety and conflict, overlap and order, along lines etched by tension and alliance among moral ideas, not just social interests. Only by such interlocking steps can we move from social to cultural analysis and back again, while keeping our feet on the ground of lived-out human meaning.

THREE

Saving the Self
Endowment versus Depletion
in American Institutions

Ann Swidler

As critics of simple secularization arguments know well, American religion is thriving. Not only has religious membership and participation not declined, but almost all Americans say that they believe in God, and a majority not only believe but join congregations, worship regularly, and even claim to have had a deeply moving religious experience.[1] Nonetheless, subtle changes in American religion signal a change in the contemporary landscape of the self. And new demands on the self reveal, in turn, a wider depletion of America's cultural and institutional infrastructure.

The changes in religion I want to point to are of two types, which may at first seem unrelated. One is the development of new religions and new forms of spirituality, some documented in *Habits of the Heart*.[2] The other is a reconfiguring of religious imagery within established, mainstream religious traditions.

GUILT

Guilt is going out of style. While such changes are hard to document with simple questions about doctrine or practice, I would argue that there has been a general shift in religious imagery away from sin, punishment, and damnation, toward a God who is, above all, the source of something like Abraham Maslow's "unconditional positive regard." This is embodied very well in one of the slogans of the (very mainstream, very main line) Marriage Encounter Movement, "God Does Not Make Junk"—since God made us, that is, we should remember that we are worthwhile, even if we sometimes feel like "junk." It is also expressed by gays and lesbians who claim the right to full membership in their churches, on grounds that God made them and that as children of God they have the right to religious "Dignity" (the actual name of the organization of gay and lesbian Catholics).[3]

Guilt and the threat of damnation have traditionally been among the most important psychological values religions offered. As an Evangelical Christian whom we interviewed for *Habits of the Heart* said, having a personal relationship with Christ "makes the fine line a little more black and white. Things which may have fallen in that gray area tend to sharpen up." He confessed, "I probably initially accepted Christ and the Christian faith partially out of love and partially out of fear—eternal damnation." His faith allowed him "get a grip" on his life and with "help from the other members of the congregation and with the help of the Holy Spirit . . . to do good to [my] fellow man, to refrain from immorality, to refrain from illegal things." God's love is important, but its importance is that it keeps one from sin: "I love God and He says we shouldn't do that."

In contrast, liberal Christians often emphasize a different aspect of their relationship with God or Jesus—not salvation from sin so much as salvation from debilitating self-doubt. In this second conception, God's love is what affirms us and gives us the strength to meet our obligations—in work, in love, to ourselves. The most dramatic example that arose in the *Habits of the Heart* interviews was with the liberal Presbyterian minister we called Art Townsend. He saw his pastoral mission as discovering, "How can I love them, how can I help these beautiful, special people to experience how absolutely wonderful they are?" He confessed that, although he believed in an afterlife, he couldn't accept the idea of hell or damnation: "If I thought God were such a being that he would waste a human soul on the basis of its mistakes, that would be a little limiting."[4]

Belief in heaven but not in hell or damnation may seem theologically illogical, but it is fairly widespread. General Social Survey data from 1991 and 1998 show that more than 85 percent of Americans believe in heaven, while only about 75 percent believe in hell.[5] The difference is greatest for mainline Protestants, among whom only 13 percent say there is probably or definitely no heaven, while 29 percent believe there is probably or definitely no hell. Even the apparent growth of fundamentalist and evangelical denominations at the expense of the mainline churches does not belie this interpretation,[6] for as Michael Hout, Andrew Greeley, and Melissa Wilde argue in a recent paper, although membership in "fundamentalist" denominations is increasing, "[d]octrinal 'fundamentalism' as represented by belief in the strict literal interpretation of the Bible is in decline. Literal interpretation of the Bible fell from 55 percent of Protestants to 40 percent while affiliation with fundamentalist denominations has increased from 40 percent to 60 percent" since 1984.[7]

There have been subtle but important changes in religious imagery, even among mainstream Protestants. The Old Testament God of Judgment, who weighs our deeds and punishes sinners, has been replaced to a significant extent by a God who is a source of affirmation, energy, and positive feelings about the self.

ENTER . . . EXHAUSTION

The sense of God as a powerful father, master, or judge, so central to American Protestantism, remains strong in many Americans' religious experience. But what has also entered is a sense of exhaustion and depletion, the remedy for which is not guilt and punishment but nurture and self-affirmation. Thus what people seek from religion is less salvation from sinfulness than help in recuperation. Rather than uncontrollable aggression and desire, the modern complaint is more often the inability to feel or to love and the related sense of exhaustion. We are mostly too tired to get into trouble.

The problem with guilt, from this point of view, is that it is potentially paralyzing. The liberal Protestant pastor Art Townsend made clear his understanding that an all-loving God could help people to love themselves and to forgive themselves, and thus to move beyond destructive or self-limiting behaviors. He cited the parable in which Jesus asks who, if his child asked for bread, would give a stone, if the child asked for a fish, would give a serpent. Pastor Townsend then offered his own paraphrase of Jesus:

> Now, you turkeys, now that you know that about yourselves who are evil, in the sense of world-bound, or whatever, how much more do you think your heavenly Father, who is not hung up with all this crap, is going to love you? Isn't it apparent to you even in the small, fragmentary, distorted way that you know how to love your children, you who do not have many tools, much skill, or much interest, that your heavenly Father, who's got it all at His command, is going to love you too? How is it possible to think otherwise?

Sustained by God's love, people are obliged, in Townsend's view, to act with "integrity and responsibility." He cites as a failure to act with integrity and responsibility a conflict in which "rather than deal with the issue and sort it out, what I did was to stomp around for a while saying, 'They can't do—*they*' (see already my shift) '*they* can't do this to us.'" This had the consequence of "wast[ing] about twenty minutes of energy stomping around, calling people up on the phone, and kicking asses, making them wrong. . . . What I experience now is, that wasn't necessary. It didn't move toward a resolution of the dilemma." Summing up, he says, "It was wasted energy. . . . It didn't do anything, and it started to break down very tender and somewhat fragile relationships I had." Thus acting with integrity and responsibility means tackling problems without resentment or guilt, which could only get in the way, slow one down. God's love, and the assurance that one makes mistakes only to learn from them and move on, can be a source of renewed energy.

These developments in mainstream religion are related, I believe, to broader changes in religion and culture. On the one hand, many of the new religions, from neo-Shamanism to Transcendental Meditation to Wicca, attempt to tap sources of energy within the self, or to remove "blockages" to a flow of energy.[8] Scientologists,[9] weekend Buddhists, trendy Kabbalists, meditators, and Goddess worshipers are united in attempting to find new sources of personal, psychic energy. (This was perhaps epitomized by the claim of *est* practitioners, at least during the early days, that they needed only three or four hours of sleep a night—making theirs an ideal religion for the perpetually overworked.)

Different in tone, but not in psychic thrust, is the contemporary pre-occupation with health and the body.[10] The proliferation of health foods, "alternative and complementary medicine," and the associated set of thera-peutic practices, herbal remedies, nutritional supplements, and books and lectures on health and wellness[11] reflects not only the crisis of medical au-thority, but the widespread conviction among ordinary people that they are not as energetic (megavitamins) or mentally sharp (ginkgo) as they ought to be, that they do not sleep as well as they need to (melatonin), and that they need to boost their immune systems to avoid getting colds or flu (echi-nacea). Health worries are certainly fostered by the increase in medical knowledge (in the Foucaultian sense of power/knowledge) that advises us, often with the backing of government authority, to eat fruits, grains, and vegetables, avoid fats, exercise, stop smoking, and so on, to reduce our risks of heart disease, cancer, osteoporosis, Alzheimer's, and a host of other maladies. This mildly paranoid "first-year-medical-student" syndrome, in which we imagine we have each disease we hear about, may be induced in part by the proliferation of medical and lifestyle advice. But this advice, and the pervasive reporting of medical news, is itself a response to widespread interest. Americans want any information that will increase "wellness" and prevent disease or debility.[12]

Whether the imagery is indebted to Freud (blocked energies, muscula-ture holding long-repressed emotions), reflects concerns with pollution and the boundaries of the self[13] (such as concerns to purge the body of poi-sons, fears about lead leeching from tooth fillings, worry over pesticides and hormones in food), or is an imagery of exhaustion requiring remedy from energy-boosting drinks, pills, and foods, all these experiences of the body suggest a self assailed, potentially unable to meet the demands on it.

Why do we suffer from this sense of vulnerability, of exhaustion and de-pletion? What is the source of our longing to be more energetic and alive, to function at hitherto unattainable levels of effectiveness?

ENDOWMENT VERSUS DEPLETION

Behind shifting social and psychological preoccupations is the logic of what I want to call "endowment versus depletion." Although we consume a great deal, both as individuals and as a society, Americans are undergoing a period of social, institutional, and cultural disinvestment. The effect is to place greater burdens on selves increasingly unsupported by institutions.

By "institutions," I mean those larger, more enduring structures that carry out collective purposes.[14] Institutions are repositories of resources and of the commitments of their members. They are upheld by collectively defined meanings and purposes—the shared identity and commitments that make a family, for instance—and they are sustained by rewards and sanctions, as in the legal entailments of marriage, parenthood, or, a very different kind of institution, corporate organization.

We are depleting rather than building the endowment of our cultural, institutional, and social infrastructure. The psychological and cultural themes of vitality versus vitiation, nurture versus deprivation, wholeness versus fragmentation, energy versus exhaustion are echoed at every level of our social experience.

Economic Institutions

Despite America's current long economic expansion, the past twenty-five years have been a period of intense economic pressure, both for middle-class couples, who have kept even only through women working many additional hours, and for the unmarried, the working class, and the poor, whose wages and share of national wealth have fallen. Americans work harder than ever, and often for less money (except at the very top where individuals work even harder, under yet more intense pressure, but for vastly more money). The increases in productivity and economic efficiency, which look so positive from an economist's point of view, represent intensified labor on the job, in fact; in a corporation that has downsized, those employees who take up the slack simply work harder. There is more to be done, so they do it; time for errands, chatting, and even daydreaming on the job is relentlessly reduced.

Even more important, this has been a period of heightened economic insecurity. While Robert Reich's estimate that every American can expect to have seven different careers in a working lifetime may turn out to be an exaggeration, most Americans cannot anticipate the single-line career that was the model, if not the modal, career path of earlier generations. For the working class, the unionized jobs that provided protections against termination or changes in work rules have diminished, in favor of jobs that are part-time, pay few benefits, and can be terminated at any moment. In a robust economy, workers may have reasonable certainty of getting a new job if they are downsized out of the current one, and workers whose skills are in demand may change jobs frequently to improve pay or opportunities to acquire new skills. Even this mobility in search of opportunity demands new understandings of the self.

The dynamism of the American economy has been purchased at the cost of massive institutional disinvestment. American corporations are downsizing for competitiveness, making the very concept of a bond of loyalty between company and worker, of a lifetime commitment to one job, anachronistic. Indeed, the individual corporation itself increasingly has no institutional identity, as mergers, buyouts, and reorganizations create a fluid corporate landscape. Public policy, by encouraging takeovers and buyouts, forces corporations to liquidate assets and convert them into profit for current shareholders—or risk takeover by those willing to sell off "underutilized" assets. This is "use it or lose it," writ large.[15] Firms have no economic room to squirrel away assets to build future productivity or to weather bad times.

Thus the core institution of our economy, the corporation, depletes its cumulated infrastructure of loyalty and commitment on the part of its workforce. It also necessarily undermines the institutional presence of the firm in the wider society, undermining the sense of continuity that would make its employees active members of their local communities and reducing their sense of "corporate citizenship."

Political Institutions

There has been a similar, if less obvious and even more pernicious, disinvestment in political institutions. California has led the way, first with its "taxpayers' revolt" and the property tax–slashing Proposition 13 and more recently with term limits for state legislators. These popular measures are direct disinvestments in political institutions, depleting the accumulated capital of political influence, reciprocal favors, and commitments, as well as of competence and knowledge, that allow the formal structures of government actually to operate.[16] In the view of term-limit promoters, greater access even to weakened institutions enhances democracy. But the democracy of media campaigns, ballot initiatives, and term-limited officials breeds voter cynicism when government proves unable to solve problems and citizen disillusionment when political institutions are unable to follow through on the promises office seekers have made.

At the national level as well, party politics has weakened and, with it, the partisan loyalties that traditionally sustained voting and other citizen involvement. Inside and outside the political arena, more "independent" voters are less likely to be politically engaged and less likely to vote, since they are detached from political institutions, neutral rather than committed.[17] The weakening of political institutions may indeed explain one of the puzzling paradoxes of contemporary political science: better-educated voters participate in politics more than the less educated, yet as levels of education have increased overall, voting has fallen off dramatically and some other forms of political participation have also declined.[18] Voting is a hollow exercise if no party can govern effectively.[19]

Weakened political institutions make it harder for collective purposes to emerge in the first place. It is, after all, through collective deliberation that shared ideas and purposes develop; and, as noted in *The Good Society*, many widely shared definitions of the common good are based on experiences of competent or effective government. Consensus develops around such values as clean air and water, publicly managed national parks, the exploration of outer space, and even the protection of civil rights partly because people have experienced effective government action that has made those goals plausible.[20] When weakened political institutions make it harder for government to enact collective purposes, it becomes harder for the public to hold collective purposes. Indeed, the very existence of a "public" implies a shared universe, an institutional arena in which citizens share concerns. This is why we do not usually think of ourselves as being in a "public" with those (citizens of other nations, for example) to whom we are not linked by common political institutions—even though we are certainly linked globally in a common fate.

Effective political institutions also work to transform powerful private interests into larger public ones.[21] This was Alexis de Tocqueville's point about the beneficial effects of political participation in developing "self-interest rightly understood." Robust political institutions create arenas (whether legislatures, conferences of stakeholders, or public meetings) where the parties know that significant decisions will be made; there, those who wish influence must come to terms with other interests, thereby generating a sense of a wider public interest. The depletion of political institutions, in contrast, empties out the very conception of a public interest as more than the sum of private goods. Political institutions enact, and thus create, communities of fate by making it possible for people to see and to act on their interdependence.[22]

Social Infrastructure

Weakened political institutions have also meant a reduction of (already meager) public spending and thus a massive depletion of social and physical infrastructure. Many analysts in and out of government have pointed to the large, unmet needs for investment in physical infrastructure—from highways and bridges to the air-traffic control system to the fiber-optic cable that is supposed to undergird the "information highway."

More damaging to the sense of membership in a wider social community has been the depletion of America's social infrastructure. Public provision—of parks, libraries, hospital services, social welfare, and much else—has declined. Many formerly public services have been privatized. On the one side, the middle class and business elites opt out of public systems: gated communities and private security guards replace public police forces; wealthy neighborhoods and business districts vote special assessments for garbage collection; middle-class parents opt out of the public school system. On the other side, the poor are forced out of public systems when "welfare reform" cuts off direct monetary aid and food stamps, or when the shift to for-profit hospitals throws more and more poor persons into an ever-smaller number of increasingly overwhelmed, underfunded public hospitals. The multiplication of user fees that now support such public amenities as parks, museums, and campgrounds also increasingly privatizes access to recreation or leisure activities.

Because education creates crucial social endowments for the future, depletion of educational infrastructure is especially costly. California provides a cautionary case study of how weakened political infrastructure undermines social endowments. California's weakened political system and the Proposition 13 taxpayer revolt it generated dramatically eroded the state's public school spending, tumbling its schools from among the best and best funded in the nation to among the very worst.[23] Nationwide, and especially in California, higher education spending slowed after the early 1970s, as spending on prison construction increased.[24] Currently in California, the budget for corrections threatens to overtake the budget for higher education as the number of California prison inmates tops the total enrollment of the University of California system, even though prisons arguably do nothing to create endowments for the future, while the future increasingly depends on investments in education.[25]

Culture also affects investments in education. Juliet Schor has shown that today's teenagers expect to consume—to buy clothes, eat out, pay for entertainment—requiring that they work during their high school as well as college years. Thus short-term consumption drives out longer-term investments in homework, grades, or development of intellectual interests and academic skills. Young people flip burgers for the minimum wage at McDonalds rather than reading or studying.[26]

Why are young adults so preoccupied with current consumption, even at the cost of preparing for the future? Why have expensive athletic shoes, fast food, and entertainment become necessities of life? Affluence alone cannot explain the priority many teenagers now give to acquiring the symbols of adult status. Young people want to feel independent, whether that means an after-school job, driving a car, or experimenting with drugs, sex, and al-cohol. Of course, many young people have to work because their families need the money. But many others see paid work as a way of showing that they have learned to cope with the real world, to be responsible, and to take care of themselves.

Aspirations for symbols of adulthood, including discretionary spending money, mean less time for "childhood" as a period of relative dependence, of preparation for, rather than assumption of, adult status. Of course, many factors—from greater gender equality in dating to the wide availability of inexpensive eating places—contribute to this shift in practical mores. But it is also plausible that the increased desire of young people for outward symbols of adult competence and freedom is in turn due to the increased pressures on youthful selves.

On the one hand, a more autonomous youth culture may be related to the greater economic pressures on families. When both parents work, chil-dren and young people inevitably spend a greater proportion of their time in the company of age-mates. The well-documented decline of the family dinner may be symptomatic of such a change. But even where the family din-ner has given way not to parents' work schedules but to the conflicting de-mands of gymnastics, soccer, piano lessons or drum practice, baseball, and debate team, the effect can be similar: children are expected to do and be more. While everyone regrets the harried schedules, no one dares forgo developing his or her child's talents. Between the demands of the youth cul-ture for the autonomy that pocket money brings and the pressures on (at least) middle-class children (and their parents) for an ever-wider array of accomplishments, activities, and interests, young people have little time to develop inner resources.

The Family as an Institution

Marriage and family have also suffered institutional depletion. But here we must make a crucial distinction between institutional change and individ-ual aspirations. There is little evidence that Americans, as individuals, are less committed to or less involved in their marriages or families. Indeed, about 90 percent of Americans still see marriage and family as central parts of a full life. But the acceptance of nonmarriage, divorce, premarital sex, cohabitation, and nontraditional sexual and family arrangements has also increased dramatically. In spite of the greater insecurity of marriages, or partly because of that insecurity, men and women work harder to make their own marriages succeed. But effort at the individual level does not add up to institutional strength at the societal level; indeed, in some ways the two are inversely related.[27]

As a society, we have disinvested in marriage—in the institution of marriage, not our particular marriages. This means that individual marriages now survive only insofar as they meet the needs of the partners, not because the marriage itself carries powerful institutional sanction. This may be good for many marriages. People expect more of their marriages in terms of companionship, intimacy, shared interests, and personal fulfillment, and, to some degree, they may get it. After all, if partners are continually aware of how fragile their marriages are, they may be less likely to take each other for granted, to indulge bad moods by sniping, to criticize each other harshly, or to let their appearance go. In interviews with middle-class adults, I heard again and again how important it was to communicate, to share feelings, not to neglect each other or the relationship. The theme that resonated most strongly was that a love relationship requires hard work. The question of whether love "lasts forever" was met with horrified denial: to say love lasts forever would imply that love endures without the partners having to work at it.

If many people value marriage and family, and if most marriages are happy[28]—perhaps happier than in the past—then in what sense has the institution of marriage weakened? First, the frequency and the relative ease of divorce weaken marriage as an institution.[29] However much particular individuals may believe in marriage as an institution, their marriages inescapably turn into personal choices. Thus the "divorce culture"[30] is not so much a matter of what people believe or want (which is still stable marriage, not divorce), but of the loss of social support for marriage as an institution. The irreducibly social nature of institutions means that they cannot be established and made authoritative by individual desires.

The social disestablishment of marriage, however, goes beyond the rise in divorce and the consequent fragility of marriage. Changes in law and mores have also changed the qualitative meaning of marriage. No-fault divorce, as Lenore Weitzman notes, changes marriage as an institution. Once unilateral divorce is effectively the law of the land, with property and child custody shared equally, spouses have only modest claims on each other. The message that such legal changes carry is that each individual must put her (or his) own welfare first.[31] A woman who sacrifices her career for the family is not a heroine or a martyr but, should the marriage not "work out," a fool. Society increasingly invests its hopes in the happiness and well-being of individuals and not in the strength of its institutions.

Children

In ways large and small, we as a society are also disinvesting in children. There are the big ways—the number of children in poverty, the growing number of children without health insurance, the decline in spending on schools as compared to spending on prisons.[32] But the small ways may matter more, as working parents in two-earner families spend less time with their children and as, in other families, the sole parent is, with "welfare reform" and no-fault divorce, expected to work full time outside the home. The kind of equality the women's movement initially aspired to, in which both men and women would take off time to be with their children, has, as Arlie Hochschild laments, been replaced by a competitive rush to the bottom, in which men and women alike find themselves too involved in downsized, sped-up workplaces to spend time with their children.[33] As Hochschild notes in *The Second Shift*, couples sacrifice time with each other and their children for immediate consumption—the barely affordable house with a brutal commute. Their skirmishes over equality lead each to insist on how busy and overworked she or he is, adopting a rhetoric in which the demands of the job, of business and busyness, are the only legitimate terms in which to adjudicate rights and privileges at home. Many women find they can be "equal" with their husbands only by being equally willing to subordinate home and family to work demands.

There is also disinvestment as parents decide that college-age children should work to pay for their education. I regularly teach college students who work twenty or thirty hours per week. Some cannot afford to be full-time students, but others work because neither they nor their families think of their education as an endowment worth collective sacrifice. A 1999 poll of first-year college students by the University of California, Los Angeles, reported in the *New York Times*, found students increasingly stressed (saying in growing numbers that they "often feel overwhelmed" by what they have to do) as they tried to balance academic demands while working, often at full-time jobs. Several studies have reported growing levels of psychological distress stress among students, even while levels of volunteer activity have been rising.[34]

Many students take pride in supporting themselves through college, without realizing that, while their efforts may speak well for their character, energy, and efficiency, they are forgoing the enduring benefits of a rich, full education and the self-development it permits. Many come to think of their education in purely instrumental terms, just as they may their work lives—an accumulation of credits toward a degree that will help them in the labor market. The idea that the college years allow time for the development of deeper understanding of history, cultures, and societies outside one's own, for deepened appreciation of one's own history and traditions, and for reflection on the meaning of one's life in society—the appropriation of a cultural endowment that is one's birthright, won through generations of those who came before—this conception of education is all but lost.

The Self

Finally—to come back to the *self*—we are, in some respects, also disinvesting in the individual self. This is an ambiguous phenomenon. On the one hand, we are enormously preoccupied with the "self." What Michel Foucault calls the "constitution of the modern subject" has become a full-time job.[35] We engage in a quest for identity, seeking to know "who we really are." In support groups and therapy groups we seek sympathetic others with whom to share difficulties and attempt to reshape our lives.[36] We also try to defend and protect the self against "unreasonable" emotional demands.

A new interpersonal ethics (perhaps best exemplified by *est* in its heyday)[37] emphatically denies that anyone can be responsible for another's problems. Avoiding "co-dependence," getting over the idea that one can solve others' problems, is recommended as a strategy of self-preservation. Hochschild, in an examination of advice books for women, has described a "cool modern" culture that encourages limiting one's emotional needs, investing emotions judiciously, searching for partners who do not make excessive emotional demands, and, most important, learning not to be too dependent, not to need anyone too much.[38] This is where, uncannily, preoccupation with the self and disinvestment in the self converge.

An unencumbered self, nimble enough to cope with an unpredictable economy and an insecure personal world, is deprived of fundamental sources of nurture.[39] Defining dependence as a sign of weakness; believing that persons find real identity "on their own," rather than with others with whom they share a life; forming interpersonal ties that do not create a community of fate in which what happens to one is of fundamental importance to others—these experiences necessarily undermine the self.

American culture provides one standard response to institutional, social, and cultural depletion: rely on the self. As the institution of marriage weakens, individuals respond by trying harder to make their own marriages succeed. Those who wind up single expect even more of themselves, as if a truly mature person should be so autonomous and self-reliant as not to need a partner. When the economy makes jobs insecure, individuals are advised to try harder to make themselves marketable. Although government is blamed for problems, leaders insist that government cannot solve problems, only individuals and communities can. Throwing people off welfare is packaged as moving them toward "independence"; the "family" is held responsible for youth violence; the right of moneyed interests to finance political campaigns is protected on grounds of "free speech." Our culture recommends independence, self-reliance, and learning to take care of one's own needs; success is a product of one's own prodigious effort, and failure is always personal failure.

One way, then, to think about the pressures on the contemporary self is to note not only the depletion of the social infrastructure but also the pressure on individuals to function at ever higher levels of personal integration and competence. When I teach today's undergraduates or sit on a graduate admissions committee, I note the number of eager, energetic, active students, some with long résumés listing their many volunteer activities, their leadership experience, and their work commitments along with their academic accomplishments. I am sometimes awestruck. But all this presumes, and, indeed, demands, a self that functions at a very high level, under constant pressure, and with very little time for reflection.

In our contemporary culture, where moral claims on others as seen as unenforceable, a strong, resilient self is a necessity. The modern, streamlined workforce with its expectation of low employer-employee loyalty rewards the worker who can take initiative, continually developing his or her skills. The advice to those downsized is to look carefully at themselves and ask what skills, interests, and abilities they have to offer another employer. Bitterness or resentment against the previous employer is regarded as completely out of place—just as community sanction against an unfaithful spouse is increasingly unlikely. Indeed, an upbeat sense of energetic optimism, the ability to find internal resources to face any difficulty, is the recommended frame of mind for those down on their luck in either love or work.

Nothing is wrong with the ideal that those who lose out in love or work, even perhaps those who have been wronged, will do better if they can "get over it" and "move on." But this attitude necessarily puts added demands on the self. Not only is the spouse who expected lifelong commitment, or the worker who saw employment as involving reciprocal obligations, supposed to reemerge from disappointment with a strong sense of self, ready and eager to go out on the market again. She or he is also supposed to harbor no resentments. This expectation may even extend to children, whom, Hochschild has argued, are being redefined to minimize their needs for parenting, nurture, and protection.[40]

Even the weakening of political institutions places new demands on the self. Weaker political parties and, in California, a plethora of "initiatives"—a symptom of weakened political institutions—means that voters, as individuals, have ever greater responsibility to make their own political choices, even if often among bad options. In our current political rhetoric, Americans are also expected, as individuals, to help solve pressing social problems. They volunteer to feed the homeless, to tutor poor children, to take meals to those living with AIDS, and to clean up public spaces.[41] But when political institutions fail, when hospitals in poor neighborhoods close or more homeless appear on the streets, Americans are reduced to feeling guilty and helpless as, on each block, they have to decide which, if any, of the outstretched hands receives some spare change.

Thus both the institutional depletion and the economic dynamism of our era create pressure to strengthen the self, make it more autonomous, more independent. The irony is that it is hard to develop stronger, more integrated, more genuinely autonomous selves in an institutionally depleted social world. So it is no wonder people feel a need for "support," for sustenance, whether from myriad "support groups" or from God.

But support for our selves, as individual selves, can never solve the problem. The support we seek requires reendowing our institutional and our cultural infrastructure. This means, at least in part, recognizing the connection between institutional endowment and personal wholeness. We do not create our own lives. What we are and what we can be depends upon an endowment—moral, intellectual, social, and institutional. We are not self-made. We depend on a culture and a set of social institutions that we did not make, and could not have made, for ourselves. Yes, surely there is individual responsibility. But it is only by recognizing the irreducibly collective nature of a cultural and institutional endowment that we can begin to take responsibility, not for our selves, but for beginning a process of social rebuilding.

I want to end with a passage from Isaiah 58:5–12, which is the Haftorah portion on Yom Kippur, the Jewish Day of Atonement. It is particularly appropriate here because it deals with guilt, that most debilitating if urgent prod to moral action. It argues that there are more and less worthy sacrifices, and that those that create a more just society are the sacrifices God requires. But what is most fascinating about the passage is the link it draws between justice, nurture, and the rebuilding of common structures on which our lives depend. Isaiah promises that those who reach out to help others will themselves be sustained and filled—The Lord "will refresh you in dry places, renewing your strength"—followed by the mysterious promise that as you are replenished you will yourself be a restorer or rebuilder of ruins: "And you shall be like a watered garden, like a never-failing spring. And you shall rebuild ancient ruins, restoring old foundations. You shall be known as the rebuilder of broken walls, the restorer of dwelling places."

> Is this the fast that I have chosen? Is this affliction of the soul? Is it to droop your head like a bullrush, to grovel in sackcloth and ashes? Is that what you call fasting, a fast that the Lord would accept?
>
> This is My chosen fast: to loosen all the bonds that bind men unfairly, to let the oppressed go free, to break every yoke. Share your bread with the hungry, take the homeless into your home. Clothe the naked when you see him, do not turn away from people in need. Then cleansing light shall break forth like the dawn, and your wounds shall soon be healed. Your triumph shall go before you and the Lord's glory shall be your rearguard. Then you shall call and the Lord will answer; you shall cry out and He will say, "Here I am."

If you remove from your midst the yoke of oppression, the finger of scorn and the tongue of malice, if you put yourself out for the hungry and relieve the wretched, then shall your light shine in the darkness, and your gloom shall be as noonday. And the Lord will guide you continually. He will refresh you in dry places, renewing your strength. And you shall be like a watered garden, like a never-failing spring. And you shall rebuild ancient ruins, restoring old foundations. You shall be known as the rebuilder of broken walls, the restorer of dwelling places.[42]

FOUR

Mirror-Image Modernities
Contrasting Religious Premises of Japanese and U.S. Modernity

S. N. Eisenstadt

Throughout his scholarly career Robert N. Bellah has focused on the analysis of two major societies and two cultural traditions—the Japanese and that of the United States—to the understanding of which he has made seminal contributions.[1] These analyses have been greatly inspired by his continuing concern with religious evolution, with respect to which these two societies stand at opposite extremes. The United States probably constitutes a crucial, if not *the crucial,* illustration of a fully modern development from within Axial civilizations, while Japan seemingly constitutes a very close approximation to an almost archaic religion. But, at the same time, Japan is not just a remnant or survival of an "old" or tribal religion but a dynamic modern society, constituting the great puzzle or paradox of a non-Axial modernization.[2] Hence the comparison between these two societies is of great interest from the point of view of the relations between religious evolution and the comparative analysis of modern societies or civilizations, and it is to such a comparison that I address myself in this work honoring Robert N. Bellah.

Such a comparison explicitly assumes the existence in the contemporary world of multiple modern civilizations. This view goes, to some extent, against both the "classical theories" of modernization of the 1950s and the classical sociological analyses of Marx, Durkheim, and even Weber (or at least one reading of him). These analyses have implicitly or explicitly conflated the different dimensions of modernity. They have assumed, if only implicitly, that the basic institutional constellations and the cultural program of European modernity, as it developed in the West, will "naturally" be ultimately taken over by all modernizing societies. Implicit in these approaches was the assumption that the modes of institutional integration attendant on the development of relatively autonomous, differentiated institutional spheres, which constitute the crucial core of modernity, would on the whole be similar in all modern societies.[3]

But the reality proved to be radically different, calling for a revision of at least some of these assumptions. Unresolved are the nature of the common core found in all modern societies and the range of variability of the different cultural and institutional patterns that may develop around this common core. It is the contention of this chapter that in the explanation of such variable dynamics two aspects of social order, closely related to the religious dimension, are of crucial importance. These aspects have not been fully enough worked out in the social sciences, especially in the analysis of modernization and modern societies. The first is the conceptions of basic premises of social and political order, including the accountability of authorities rooted in basic ontological conceptions; the second, the construction of patterns of collective identity in different modern societies. I shall analyze the importance of these aspects in two modern societies, one with a seemingly "bronze age" religion or symbolism and the other possibly the most modern in terms of religious evolution. I shall explore this problem by analyzing a central aspect of modern political dynamics—the structures and ideologies of movements of protest.

PROTEST AND MODERNITY

Protest is indeed a central component of modernity, of the modern political program as it crystallized in the aftermath of the Great Revolutions, incorporating the utopian component inherent in these revolutions. This utopian dimension was rooted in the strong eschatological orientations of the major sects or groups active in the revolutions, which attempted, as it were, to bring the Kingdom of God to earth.[4]

This utopian component gave rise in post-revolutionary modern societies to a far-reaching transformation in the symbolism and structure of modern political centers. The crux of this transformation was the charismatization of the center as the bearer of the transcendental visions inherent in the cultural program of modernity, along with the incorporation of themes and symbols of protest as core components of the premises of these centers and of their relations with the peripheries of their respective societies.[5]

In contrast to what had happened in almost every previous civilization, in post-revolutionary modern societies themes and symbols of equality, participation, and social justice became not only elements of protest against the existing center but also an important component of the political legitimation of *orderly* demands by peripheral groups on the political center.[6] Protest and the possibility of transforming some of society's institutional premises were no longer considered illegitimate or marginal aspects of the political process. They became central components of the transcendental vision that promulgated the autonomy of man and of reason. The incorporation of such themes into the centers of modern societies epitomized their status as central components of the transcendental vision of modernity. The sectarian utopian visions of earlier times were transformed into central components of the modern political and cultural program. Concomitantly, societal centers increasingly permeated the peripheries and the peripheries impinged more and more on the centers, often blurring the distinctions between center and periphery and incorporating the symbols and demands of protest into the central symbols of the society.

In Europe, where the first major constellations of modern protest crystallized, the revolutions and the numerous movements of protest that developed in post-revolutionary societies focused above all around the continual reconstruction of two poles that defined the centers of European societies: the tension between equality and hierarchy, most fully articulated by the various socialist movements; and the construction of the boundaries of collectivities, carried out by national movements.

Given that what can be called the drama of modernity was first played out in Europe, it has often been assumed (in line with the general emphasis on the convergence of modern societies) that these themes constituted the "natural" or inevitable types of protest—the yardstick against which protest in other societies should be measured. And yet these themes were not central in either Japan or the United States—the two modern societies that could be perceived as standing at the two poles of religious evolution. In a paradoxical way, most of the movements of protest that developed in the two countries shared, in comparison to those in Europe, a common characteristic: they rarely (with the exception of small groups of intellectuals or activists) challenged the basic premises of the centers and of the collective identities of their respective societies. Rather, they affirmed the basic premises of their respective societies—for different, indeed contrary reasons, constituting, as it were, mirror images of each other.

How can this fact be explained, and what can such an explanation tell us about the comparative analysis of modern societies and about the development or crystallization of multiple modernities? And what is the bearing of such an explanation on central problems of sociological analysis?

SOME DISTINCT CHARACTERISTICS
OF PROTEST IN THE UNITED STATES

Protest was built into the very premises and the institutional framework of the American political program, as promulgated in its "myth" or creed—in, to use Bellah's famous term, its "civil religion."[7] But the concrete movements of protest that developed in the United States differed greatly from those that developed elsewhere.

American protest movements differed from those of Europe (and, to some extent, of Japan). Unlike the two major types of social movements that developed in Europe in the nineteenth and twentieth centuries—the socialist one, with its very strong class symbolism, and the various nationalist movements—American protest movements did not (despite many attempts, especially by groups of intellectuals and, to some extent, by workers' groups) occupy the center stage of the political arena, as they did in Europe, or develop into full-fledged parties of the European type.

True, the development of American industrial capitalism gave rise to many movements of workers or farmers who saw themselves pushed out by the processes of industrialization and the development of national capital markets, and to continual intensive industrial conflict.[8] But these movements, as well as the socialist groups that mushroomed, especially after the Civil War, did not give rise to European-type "class movements." Although there developed a continuing alliance between union organizations and the Democratic Party, this was of a different nature than the almost total integration of unions in social democratic (and labor) parties in Europe and the promulgation of clear socialist programs by the latter.

Class consciousness did indeed develop among many sections of the working classes, but it did not become a central component of a full-fledged, countrywide political movement. Significantly, the numerous socialist programs or movements that developed in this period, especially among intellectuals, tended to promulgate the more "utopian," rather than class-oriented and/or social-democratic, type of socialism.[9] It was indeed this absence of a class-conscious socialism that constituted the central theme of Sombart's famous *Why Is There No Socialism in the United States?*[10]

In a parallel way, no national or nationalist movements developed in the United States. It is true that during the nineteenth and early twentieth century, a distinct American collective identity emerged, which can be designated national. A strong emphasis on American "manifest destiny," and later "the American way of life," was promulgated by the major socializing agencies—schools, churches, associations, and many agencies to "Americanize" immigrants. But these emphasized the *common* American identity; no potentially separatist national movement, the likes of which flourished in Europe, developed.

The late nineteenth century was a period of growing racial tension, reinforced by the industrialization of the South and the flow of black workers to the North, and accompanied by racist ideologies promulgated by the Ku Klux Klan and by fascist movements in the 1930s. At the same time, ethnic organizations and associations developed from the middle of the nineteenth century—possibly even before—and by the twentieth century were quite visible on the American scene. In several cases—as with the Irish, Italians, and Jews—the ethnic and religious dimensions coincided. But even these ethnic or ethnic-religious associations, however important in mobilizing support for any party or in influencing its policies, did not succeed in occupying the center stage of the American political scene, in creating a distinct political party, or in becoming a central and continuing organizational component of any party[11] (although such associations have been a continual component of, especially, the Democratic Party).

As against socialist, class-oriented, and national protest movements, a multiplicity of populist movements and political movements of reform developed in the United States, such as the Progressives (1890–1920), the Populists in the 1890s, and the Prohibitionists in the second and third decades of the twentieth century, as well as religious movements, out of which later developed the fundamentalist movements.[12]

PROTEST AND THE AMERICAN VISION

As in Europe, and in contrast to Japan, these populist and reform movements were imbued with strong transcendental and utopian orientations, according to which they measured social and political reality—and found it wanting. But, unlike in Europe, and seemingly as in Japan, these movements were not oriented to the reconstruction of the basic premises of American social order but rather to their purification—to the fuller realization of the basic utopian vision of the American community, especially the covenantal republican and communitarian components of the American political creed.

The major themes of protest that developed were set firmly within the basic parameters of American political and constitutional discourse. These parameters, and the tensions inherent in the American political tradition, also provided the basic framework of protest, with themes closely interwoven with the nation's central political discourse.[13]

The groups and individuals promulgating these themes saw themselves as the bearers of the pristine American vision, and thus the discourses of protest were continually imbued with highly moralistic themes. Most movements upheld the basic premises of the American cultural program: messianism, this-worldliness, emphasis on active participation in, and commitment to, the social order, and a strong future orientation.[14]

These movements were oriented against aspects of society seen as contaminating the purity of American life, against pollution by various evil forces, and particularly against possible pollution of the original vision of a utopian America. These movements epitomized, in Samuel Huntington's phrase, the "promise of disharmony"—the possibility that reality would not conform to a pristine vision of American community inherent in the American political system. Their most important common denominator was, as Richard Hofstadter and others have pointed out, that they did not espouse distinctive competing ideologies. They developed within the basic common American ideology, emphasizing different variants within it.

These movements perceived, as the two most important polluting forces, unbridled individualism and the concomitant corruption or dissolution of community life and the concentration of power and wealth that could exclude large sectors of American society from active and equal participation in political life. Thus the most prevalent theme in American reform discourse was the criticism of the extremes of selfish individualism, the perception of such individuals as amoral and as giving rise to the atomization of society. The other major outcry was against the concentration of power and wealth and the inequality generated by such concentration, with such inequality seen not in class terms but in moralistic terms such as "producers" against "parasites." Later, in the twentieth century, the attack on monopoly was framed in terms of denial of access to the possibilities of competition and to the fruits of a good life.

Such criticism did not deny the legitimacy of individual pursuit of wealth but rather described the corrupting effects of concentration of wealth or power on the possibility of such pursuit. The concentration of wealth and power was depicted in individual or organizational terms, not in society-wide structural ones, and denounced as special privilege. It was "bigness" (of business, of bureaucracy, and especially of government) that was the focus. Wealth, power, and bigness were the predominant focus of protest—in partial contrast to European political and social discourse, in which these categories, while fully recognized (for instance, by G. Mosca), were usually subsumed under such categories as class or, to a lesser extent, nation or ethnicity.[15]

These protest movements did not challenge the basic individualistic premises of the American ethos or of inequalities resulting from economic achievement. They only protested the excesses of such inequalities, the claims of the successful to be better than others. Hence their strong ambivalence to, but not negation of, differences in wealth or power. The critique of concentrated power and excessive inequality could develop from republican constitutional points of view, from a deeply conservative viewpoint, as well as from religious or communitarian outlooks, and could also become closely connected with populist themes.[16]

THE UTOPIAN COMPONENT IN PROTEST
MOVEMENTS IN THE UNITED STATES

Very significant for the specific development of themes of protest in the United States was the structure of utopian visions in the "classic" American literature of the nineteenth and early twentieth century—the works of Thoreau, Melville, Whitman, Emerson, and Henry Adams.[17]

Many of these works were inspired by an awareness—often acute—of the contradictions between the pristine religious or aesthetic ideals of Republican or Protestant individualism and the realities of the extension and growing autonomy of market relations since the Jacksonian era. "America" embodied the ideals of the American Way—independence, enterprise, opportunity, individualism, expansionism—as opposed to the "United States"—the mundane reality of nitty-gritty daily government. The anguished recognition of these contradictions permeated the works of these authors and gave rise to their search for a utopian "overcoming" of such contradiction. But these utopian visions did not postulate either a historical process or a metaphysical dimension through which contradictions could be resolved or transcended, as did most great works of European literature.

All these utopias came back to the basic premises of the American Way—to pristine republican communal visions of "America." This America has been analyzed in recent literary criticism as a highly ideological, middle-class ideal. But, significantly, this middle class was not fettered, as was the European bourgeoisie, by a confrontation with a strong feudal, aristocratic tradition. And it was this middle class that promulgated visions of the trans-historical fulfillment of a pristine utopia that could be portrayed as the bearer of "spiritual" forces in danger of contamination by the market and by community-eroding individualization. As Leo Marx has indicated, the vision of pastoralism that was central to this utopia contributed to its transhistorical conception.[18]

MOVEMENTS OF PROTEST IN THE UNITED STATES

These utopian themes, often couched in terms of the basic premises of the American creed and of American constitutional discourse, animated almost all the movements of protest that developed in the United States, with each movement naturally emphasizing different themes and combining them with different concrete social and economic issues, which in turn varied greatly over different periods. There developed, of course, many differences among these movements—differing symbolic credos oriented to upholding the utopian purity of the American community—often giving rise to highly acrimonious relations among them but not, until recently, questioning the image of purity, the basic utopian vision of America and the premises of the American order.

Especially in periods of great turbulence, the movements could develop strong utopian orientations, with strong totalistic absolutizing tendencies and potentially very strong restrictive orientations that could lead to witch hunting, which, of course, had a long tradition in America. These tendencies constituted a continual component of American political life that could flourish in many fundamentalist and populist movements.

MOVEMENTS OF PROTEST IN JAPAN—
A BRIEF COMPARISON WITH EUROPE

The movements of protest that developed in modern Japan under the impact of modernization were on the face of it very similar to those that developed in Europe. This was especially true of movements for citizens' rights to greater participation in the political arena, and of the labor and socialist movements. National or ethnic movements were of much less importance, due above all to the relative success of the Meiji state, building on previous developments under the Tokugawa, in promulgating and institutionalizing the conception of the Japanese nation as a national collectivity—a conception constructed in primordial terms. This was made easier by the relative—but only relative—ethnic homogeneity of large sectors of Japanese society.[19]

It was in the period after the Second World War that, with the democratization of the regime, numerous movements of protest emerged into the open. In this period, the various oppositional movements, especially the communist and socialist ones, which were illegal in the earlier periods, became fully legitimized and could openly participate in the political process. In this period, too, there emerged relatively strong connections between socialist politicians and intellectuals and working-class organizations. There was also a rise in class consciousness among large sectors of industrial workers, and political class movements developed, with some trade unions playing important roles.[20]

These movements and parties were more prominent than their counterparts in the United States. In Japan, the Marxist and socialist parties and a fairly radical communist party were able, throughout the postwar period, to mobilize about a third of the votes (36 percent in 1958 and 32 percent in 1992).[21] But events certainly did not follow the European pattern. Only in the 1993 elections did the Socialist Party emerge as a strong and potentially innovative force attempting to transform the center.[22]

The most intensive development of movements of protest took place in the late 1940s and early 1950s. It was also in this period that many movements, especially labor groups, became both radical and relatively widespread, in many ways reminiscent of European socialist and labor movements. In addition, at this time labor and socialist parties became fully legalized, signaling the possibility of a social-democratic, if not socialist, order emerging in Japan.[23]

Later, there developed many other movements on the local and, to some extent, the national scene, such as citizens' and ecological movements, women's movements, and movements of local opposition. Such movements have continued to sprout and have become an integral part of the Japanese political scene. Some of these movements were also connected with opposition political parties, often prominent locally.[24] In the late 1960s and early 1970s, the worldwide wave of student unrest swept through Japan, giving rise to intensive student radicalism.[25]

Within many of these movements, especially among student radicals and, later, among the extreme terrorist groups, there were sometimes violent confrontations with the authorities, as well as litigation, undermining the picture of a society of harmonious consensus. Such confrontational themes were usually expressed in terms of denial of the moral legitimacy of the authorities, with accusations that they had abandoned the trust with which they had been endowed.[26]

There also developed a wide range of critical social discourses and artistic activities—for instance, the new "proletarian" theater that developed especially after the war, or the many "critical" films. In many cases, intellectuals participated in protest movements, or in demonstrations such as those against the Japanese-American Security Treaty and those, much later, on the occasion of the death of the Shōwa emperor, when the Meiji Gakuin University initiated a series of open lectures and discussions on the emperor system and did not fly the flag at half-mast.[27]

However great the similarities among the political, labor, and social movements in Japan and Europe, there were some important differences. These can be identified both in the aims of these movements and in the nature of their impact on the broader society. The Japanese movements were not able to attain the prominent role in politics that such movements did in Europe. The socialist and communist movements were not able to form a government or, after 1955, even to participate in the government or in shaping its policies. These movements, especially the Socialist Party, did not undermine the hegemony of the Liberal Democratic Party (LDP), at least until 1993; even then, the LDP lost its majority through the defection of many internal groups, not through the challenge of the socialists.

After about the mid-1950s, the socialist and labor movements split, and their central core, the Socialist Party, lost its original impetus and became, seemingly, domesticated by the evolving Japanese political system. The same may be claimed for later movements.

These later movements could not restructure the premises of the center in terms of universalistic or transcendental principles, as socialist movements were able to do in Europe, where they imbued the center with their symbols, influenced its politics directly, and participated in the formulation and implementation of policies. Nor were they able to change the modes of decision making or give rise to a more autonomous civil society, even if they did broaden the range of public discourse.[28]

True, many intellectuals and leaders of these movements espoused such principles, but they were not very successful. Repression of course played a very important role in their lack of success, but repression was not unique to the Japanese state; it could be found in all modern capitalist constitutional regimes. What was more characteristic of Japan was how difficult many leaders found it to mobilize support for principled confrontation.

MOVEMENTS OF PROTEST IN JAPAN AND
THE CONSTRUCTION OF SOCIAL AND CULTURAL SPACES

As against their relative weakness in direct confrontations with the center, most of these movements were quite successful not only in achieving their concrete aims but above all in the creation of social and cultural spaces. They opened up new spaces of public discourse, new types of associations, and new lifestyle possibilities— for instance, for women in many middle and upper-middle sectors.[29] As had happened with Confucianism and Buddhism in Japan in earlier periods, there was success in constructing arenas of social action and cultural creativity in which the hegemonic rules were not predominant—even if these spaces were segregated from the central ones. Within these spaces, new types of sophisticated discourse and new levels of reflexivity emerged. Here many rebellious and subversive themes, like equality and commonality, were able to find expression, and many different new lifestyles with some liminal potentialities developed.

One of the most fascinating illustrations of this process is the development of the many new religions that have blossomed since the late Tokugawa period.[30] The New Religions were to some extent suppressed in the early Meiji period and during the military regime but again flowered after the Second World War. While many of these movements evinced very strong millenarian tendencies, utopian orientations were very weak, if present at all. The movements, even when engaged in politics, have rarely challenged the existing order. Their orientations have been strongly this-worldly, lacking critical stances rooted in transcendental universalistic visions or principles transcending the given order.[31]

These movements greatly broadened the scope of the political agenda and political discourse in Japan. Even when, in the Meiji and Taishō eras and in the mid-1950s, themes or demands were suppressed in the public arena, they did not sink into total oblivion. The fate of the themes promulgated by the Taishō liberals provides a good illustration. These themes had far-reaching impact, as shown by Sharon Nolte in her recent study of liberalism in Japan, and as even more fully illustrated in the recent collection, *Culture and Identity,* edited by T. Rimer, concerning Taishō intellectuals.[32] Themes of liberalism, freedom of the press, women's rights, and concern for social problems, as well as a general, if diffuse, emphasis on equality, remained on the public agenda in one way or another and were not entirely removed from political, literary, or ideological discourse.[33] Rather, they were discussed and debated orally and in specialized publications among intellectual groups as well as in more general publications. Thus very wide arenas of new discourse were generated in Japanese society.

In addition, many of these themes were incorporated into the predominant ideology, the carriers of which often portrayed themselves as having solved the relevant issues in the "proper" Japanese way. From the late Tokugawa period, new types of discourse and social consciousness continuously developed, including potentially subversive themes promulgated in the name of an "autonomous" mature anti-statist view. Some of these could merge with the romantic stances of the folklorists; others developed in a more "rational" or humanistic direction.

THE DOUBLE-PRONGED IMPACT
OF MOVEMENTS OF PROTEST IN JAPAN

The preceding analysis attests to the double-pronged impact of movements of protest and other movements of change in modern Japan. Such a process has generated new modes of discourse and has given rise to many "segregated" sectors of action and to a growing reflexivity. New types of cultural and social activities have flourished, and new social spaces have been created in which many new patterns of economic and social activities and new modes of cultural creativity could develop. Nonetheless, these movements were not able or willing to aim at reconstructing the basic premises of the Japanese collectivity in terms of universalistic principles transcending the given reality.

PROTEST IN THE UNITED STATES AND JAPAN—
COMPARATIVE INDICATIONS

We face thus a very complex result. In both Japan and the United States, there developed dynamics of protest markedly different from the "classical" European picture. In both—modern societies, at different poles of religious evolution—the intensive movements of protest were not oriented to reconstructing either their respective centers or the boundaries of their respective collectivities, although for almost entirely obverse reasons. In Japan, such limitations were rooted in the absence, or at least weakness, of utopian orientations. In the United States, where movements of protest were imbued, as in Europe, with strong utopian orientations, the limitation derived from the association of the utopian ideal with the core principles of the American cultural center and from the widespread belief that America constituted an already achieved utopia. Accordingly, despite their shared contrast to European societies—manifest in the lack of attempts at the reconstruction of the center—the modes of confrontation of these movements with their respective centers differed greatly.

These differences were of great importance for the dynamics of the political systems of these two societies. In Japan there developed, to use Michio Muramatsu's expression, "patterned pluralism,"[34] involving a relatively weak state that does not command but bases its functioning on continual consultations with various groups, with various consultative bodies playing a crucial role.[35] But such patterned pluralism and weak state did not entail an open public arena. One central aspect of this type of responsive decision making, which necessarily entails continuous negotiations between different participants in such networks, is that it is not easy to identify the one person or group responsible for a decision. Another aspect is that deliberations are not easily brought out into the open. The relation between any open discussions, for instance, in the parliament (Diet), and the considerations guiding decision making are tenuous, even more than in other modern political systems. Similarly, changes in policies, even when undertaken in response to demands, need not be directly connected with some broad, principled, political issues; they may more often be connected with breakdowns in relations between networks. As indicated by Gary Allinson, the process is based on a fragmented citizenry, on multiple consultative bodies, and on multiple contests between different groups and the authorities.[36]

In contrast, in the United States there developed political dynamics based, on the one hand, on a very strong and emphatic acceptance of the basic institutional, especially constitutional, framework, and, on the other, on a strong suspicion of those in authority and a distrust of government. This tension generated a very specific combination of moralism and pragmatism in political life. The overall community—the Republic or Commonwealth—and its basic institutional-symbolic frameworks could easily become the embodiment of the charismatic-utopian search for the pure unpolluted community, while the concrete political process, including both political institutions and officeholders, became the focus of mistrust. Such mistrust was closely connected to the very strong populist orientations prevalent in America and could give rise to a search for participatory politics undiluted by the political process, a theme promulgated for instance by Ross Perot, with his emphasis on symbolic electronic town meetings.

This attitude to authority was closely related to the great concern about distribution of power, manifest not only in the separation between the executive, the legislature, and the judiciary but also in discourse about the "spatial" locus of sovereignty—epitomized in the problem of federalism, of the relation between the central and the state governments. This problem, a continuous focus of American political discourse about "states' rights," has not really been about the appropriate technical arrangements for the distribution of resources and authority between a central, federal power and local government; it has basically been an argument about the locus of sovereignty, the nature and scope of political participation, and the nature of the national community.

The same attitude toward authority also related closely to a more general characteristic of American politics and political discourse—a continual oscillation between the pragmatic, "realistic" attitude epitomized in pork-barrel politics and in the unsentimental and sometimes brutal attitude to the "political game" and a highly moralistic, often missionary, self-justifying, and sanctimonious vision. Such a combination of absolutizing idealism with pragmatism and the oscillation between the two also characterized the conduct of foreign affairs and even of wars and attitudes toward them.

Thus, while the movements of protest that developed in the United States and in Japan shared the absence, or at least weakness, of attempts to reconstruct the centers and collective boundaries of their respective societies, they differed in a mirror-image way in their basic orientation to these centers and in their impact on them. The movements in the United States frequently confronted the center, in highly principled transcendental terms, by claiming that it did not live up to its basic premises but did not aim to reconstruct these premises or those of the American collective identity. In Japan it was not the attempt to confront the center but the creation of new cultural and social spaces that characterized most movements of protest.

PROTEST AND THE PRIMORDIAL COMPONENT IN COLLECTIVE IDENTITIES IN MODERN SOCIETIES—JAPAN

How can we explain the distinct characteristics of the movements of protest and their impact on the political dynamics that developed in the United States and Japan and account for their commonalities and differences, as well as their differences from protest movements in Europe?

Such an explanation can, as I have indicated, be found in two dimensions of the construction of social order, dimensions that are closely related, albeit in different ways, to central aspects of religion and of religious evolution. These are, first, the modes of construction of modern collective identities, especially the place of their primordial components, and, second, the basic premises of social and political order, especially the conceptions of equality and hierarchy, and of the accountability of authorities.

Such modes of construction of collective identities and such premises of social and political order are, in all societies, rooted in fundamental, religiously based cosmological and ontological conceptions. These conceptions differ greatly, perhaps above all between non-Axial and Axial religions, of which those of Japan and the United States constitute prime illustrations.

Contrary to the often implicit assumptions of theories of modernization, these dimensions of social order cannot be subsumed under the general category of structural differentiation. While always interwoven with structure, these dimensions exhibit strong autonomous tendencies that are of crucial importance in shaping the dynamics of modern societies. With respect to the place of primordial components of collective identity, conceptions of equality and hierarchy, and the accountability of authorities, Japan and the United States stand at two extreme poles closely related to their contrasting religious premises. In Japan the modes of construction of collective identity and of conceptions of authority have in common the weakness of any transcendental criteria or utopian visions according to which to judge existing reality. This weakness is rooted in the basic non-Axial ontological conceptions prevalent in Japan.

Japanese collective identity, as it became crystallized throughout Japanese history, was characterized by principled primordiality, in combination with certain weaker elements of civility. Such a conception of collective identity crystallized relatively early (probably in the eighth century C.E.) out of Japan's encounter with other civilizations, especially the Chinese but also the Korean, and with two Axial religions, Buddhism and Confucianism, with their universalistic premises. However, the outcome of these encounters was the construction of a mode of collective identity distinct from, for instance, the Korean or Vietnamese, which also came under heavy Buddhist and Confucian pressure. Unlike Korea or Vietnam, where the "local," "national" identities were—in principle at least—subsumed under the broader Confucian and Buddhist ones, Japan reacted to this encounter by a *principled* denial of universalistic orientations and a concomitant *principled* emphasis on primordial elements.

This conception of a nation under the protection of the deities differed from, for instance, the Jewish conception of a chosen nation and its later transformation in Christianity. The Japanese conception of a divine nation, while emphasizing the sacrality and uniqueness of the Japanese nation, did not characterize this uniqueness in terms of a transcendental and universalistic mission, as did the self-conceptions of the monotheistic civilizations. In Japan such particularity did not entail the conception of a responsibility to God to behave according to universalistic precepts or commitments.[37] That is, the Japanese conception of a particularistically sanctioned polity involved commitment to the existing divine order and its embodiment—the Emperor—but did not entail the possibility of a critical challenge of this order or of the authorities in the name of some transcendent criteria.

A closely related pattern developed regarding the relation of the Japanese collectivity to other collectivities. Many Japanese intellectuals and influential persons acutely sensed the need to define the relation of the Japanese nation to other Asian nations, especially the Chinese, and, later in the nineteenth and twentieth centuries, to Western civilizations. The conceptions of the Japanese collectivity that developed entailed intensive orientation to "others"—China, India, the West—and recognized that other encompassing civilizations claimed some universal validity. This awareness was a continual focus of Tokugawa Neo-Confucian discourse.[38] Such orientations to other civilizations, however, did not give rise to a conception of the Japanese collectivity as part of broader civilizational frameworks, structured according to universalistic premises. Japan was not seen as one component—even a central component—of such a universalistic framework. At most, the Japanese collectivity was held to embody the pristine values enunciated by other civilizations and wrongfully appropriated by, or attributed to, them.

Such claims about the superiority of Japan, as the embodiment of the pristine virtues proclaimed by "foreign" universalistic religions, were promulgated especially in the Meiji period, often together with claims for Japanese hegemony in East Asia. Again, these claims did not entertain the possibility that Japan was only one, if possibly the leading, country in terms of transcendental and universalistic orientations open to all. Rather, these claims were based on the assumption—already promulgated by the schools of nativistic learning under the Tokugawa—that the primordial Japanese collectivity itself represented these universal pristine values.[39]

Such a conception of particularity provided the background to the different "schools" of Japanese uniqueness in the modern period—for example, to the emphasis on the uniqueness of Japanese language, race, or culture in the later development of Nihonjinron literature. These "schools" veered between emphasis on the incomparable uniqueness of Japan, often taking the direction of rabid nationalism, and the claim that the Japanese people or culture embodied the pristine values promulgated by all humanity.[40]

CIVILITY IN THE CONSTRUCTION
OF COLLECTIVE IDENTITY IN JAPAN

Civility constituted the second major component of Japanese collective identity. This emphasis did not, however, entail the recognition of civility as an autonomous dimension of legitimation of the social order but rather stressed its contribution to the collectivity, defined mostly in primordial terms. The central focus of civility in Japan was that of loyalty. It was closely related to the legitimation of political authority, which entailed a far-reaching transformation of the "original" Confucian conceptions of political authority prevalent in China and later transferred to Korea and Vietnam.[41] Particularly in the Tokugawa period, Japanese intellectuals grappled with Chinese concepts of authority, especially with the concept of the "mandate of heaven," which became a focus of intensive intellectual and ideological discussion. Japanese interpreters minimized the principled accountability of rulers and the transcendental and universalistic principles of legitimation, emphasizing again loyalty to the Emperor.[42]

Such loyalty, focused on the "lord"—any personal superior up to the level of the Emperor—and on the group or collectivity of which individuals formed a part, could not be questioned. This was contrary to the case in China, where it was universalistic principles borne by a higher, transcendental authority that justified such loyalty or legitimated the lord's authority. The nativistic scholars saw the very possibility of such questioning as anathema to the Japanese spirit or culture.[43]

True enough, this reformulation of the concept of loyalty contained within itself the possibility of an extension of family loyalty beyond any given setting, potentially in a universalistic direction. But in fact such extension always took place within the confines of the Japanese collectivity, emphasizing strong particularistic orientations. In the Meiji state, this orientation developed in a distinctive restorative direction, focused around the concept of loyalty to the Emperor as the living embodiment of the Japanese collectivity. Such conceptions of loyalty negated, or at least marginalized, the confrontation between equality and hierarchy in terms of transcendental principles.

THE CONSTRUCTION OF COLLECTIVE IDENTITY IN THE UNITED STATES—POLITICAL IDEOLOGY

In contrast to these characteristics of Japanese conceptions of collectivity and authority, those that crystallized in the United States, strongly rooted in the potentialities of Axial civilizations, had weak primordial components. The United States was perhaps the first great civilization (with the possible very partial exception of the Roman Empire) to construct collective identity essentially without primordial ties. The premises of social order that developed were based on a conception of metaphysical equality that, in principle, negated the symbolic legitimacy of hierarchy and entailed the possibility of continual challenge to authority.

The American Revolution was alone among the Great Revolutions to create a new collectivity, a new republic, and a new nation; it was the "First New Nation."[44] But, paradoxically, it shared with the other revolutions a relative lack of interest in primordial symbols. Out of this paradox developed the unique way in which the modern American political and national community was constructed. The collective identity of this national society was not, as in Europe and later in the "third world," based on primordial components—common territory, history, (fictive) kinship, language, and the like. True, in the American creed, conceptions of territory and of peoplehood were strong, promulgated in biblical terms of "Promised Land" and "Chosen People." But, unlike the Jewish tradition or the Zionist movement, the American creed couched these conceptions mostly in religious-ideological and not in primordial terms. The new land was not the Land of the Fathers to which one returned. The very constitution of their new political order was conceived by the settlers as an innovative act of universal significance, not a continuation of the history of their countries of origin.

This new collective identity crystallized around a political ideology rooted in a combination of Puritan religious conceptions (especially that of the covenant) and the premises, especially the legal premises, of natural law and of common law, including the English tradition of Enlightenment rationalism and of the radical thought of the Commonwealth.[45] The crystallization of this ideology created a new collective identity and a new constitutional order, ultimately forming, as Bellah has shown, a distinct "civil religion." This transformation was at the crux of the American Revolution and distinguished it from other wars of independence, not only the later ones in Europe or Asia, but even the Latin American ones.

The American myth of political order proposed not only legal but metaphysical or ontological equality, even if de facto such equality had strong implicit, sometimes explicit, racial or "ethnic" undertones. In principle, it negated the legitimacy of hierarchy in the political order and any sort of "ex-toto" conception of social and political order. This picture was of course different in the South, where some conceptions of hierarchy and of aristocratic deference prevailed. There were strong hierarchical undertones in the republican components of the American political tradition, but they were transposed into the emphasis on virtue and obligations of citizenship that, in principle, if only in principle, was within the reach of all citizens. There also existed in America, as R. G. Smith has recently shown,[46] very strong hierarchical ascriptive orientations, based on conceptions of race, gender—or even of ability, insofar as the bases of ability could be explained in "biological" racial terms. But, however important these themes were in certain sectors of American society in different periods, they never attained fully legitimate, hegemonic standing. After sometimes prolonged struggles, these hierarchical themes were subsumed under the dominant more egalitarian-constitutional premises, and were usually justified and legitimated in terms of them.

It was the problem of race, especially of African-American slavery, that continuously loomed large on the American scene, challenging the myth of equality and constituting a continual negative reference point for the conception of citizenship.[47] But the very fact that it was seen by many sectors of American society as such a challenge or negative reference point attests to the strength of the myth of equality as the core of the new political order, even if this core was often subverted in practice and this emphasis on equality, as we shall see, also contained many intolerant or exclusivist components.

Closely related to the metaphysical emphasis on equality was the radical transformation of concepts of representation and of sovereignty. The transition from virtual to actual representation—that is, from citizenship manifested in the acclamation of rulers to an active participation in the political process—totally negated the vesting of representation in any hierarchically or ascriptively defined category of persons or groups,[48] even if there was sometimes a yearning for a "natural" aristocracy. Concomitantly, there took place the invention of "the people" as the bearers of sovereignty, a radical and potent new conception that transformed the very concept of sovereignty.[49] True, the conception of the sovereignty of God, rooted in sectarian Protestantism, was strong in many sectors of American society.[50] But as no specific institution, but rather the community of all believers, was seen as the locus of this sovereignty, the more religious conception joined with that of the sovereignty of the people to radically deny the legitimacy of any hierarchical or traditional authority.

In opposition to any such authority, Americans legitimized the free or spontaneous self-organization of society—even if often constructed along lines of power and hierarchy. Closely related was the strong emphasis on the dignity of labor—of "production" contrasted with aristocratic idleness—as an important component or "prerequisite" of citizenship,[51] even if such emphasis often served as a defense against the actual economic situation. All of these conceptions emphasized the idea of self-rule by the people. Such a transformation also took place, of course, in the French Revolution. But in contrast to the conception of the Republic or *Patrie* in the French Revolution, the conception of the people in the American Revolution and later American political tradition was markedly anti-statist and highly voluntaristic.

Many Europeans visiting the United States emphasized the "rudeness" and "vulgarity" of public life in America.[52] They remarked on the volatility and tumultuousness of new political activities there—the emphasis on self-government, the fragility of authority, and, above all, the lack of respect for authority.[53] Similarly, the distinctive conception of individualism that developed in the United States, embodied by such writers as Emerson, Thoreau, or Henry Adams even in their critical stances toward many aspects of American reality, was strongly oriented against restrictive *Stände,* or "estate-bound," European conceptions.[54] The foundations of this American individualism could already be found in the colonial period—in Puritan conceptions of individual conscience and of the individual as bearer of the obligation to glorify God on earth, in the Lockean emphasis on individual rights, and in widespread republican-contractual tenets.

These conceptions of equality and individualism shaped conceptions of the sovereignty of "the people," which in turn had institutional implications for the state. The most important implication has been the principled predominance, as Daniel Bell has emphasized, of civil society as against the state—and not just against bad or tyrannical or despotic government.[55] Indeed, it is significant that this anti-statist tradition did not develop a concept of the State—or rather, of the State as a distinct ontological entity. American egalitarianism and individualism made the European conception of the State, with its hierarchical overtones, a focal point for the break with European tradition.[56] In the American conception, to no small degree rooted in Protestant tenets, society was seen as continually re-created through the activism and moral commitment of the people.[57]

"NEWNESS" IN THE CONSTRUCTION
OF AMERICAN COLLECTIVE IDENTITY

The founding myth of the American political program as promulgated in the Revolution and the Constitution strongly emphasized discontinuity with the European past. The American creed transformed the premises of social and political order, especially conceptions of equality and individualism—and thus, also, concepts of sovereignty, attitude to the state, and relations between state and civil society.

This myth emphasized the "newness," the pristine purity of America, its sacredness. As Adam Seligman has stated, the mythical importance of American newness was felt not only in the symbolism inscribed in its political and social consciousness; it stretched back in time to the virgin new world, where humanity lived in a state of nature. The first settlers already saw America as such a pristine state, related to biblical imagery of Eden and paradise.[58] The conception of the new American "Adam" constituted a central component of the American ideology.[59] The American wilderness was viewed either as the "Promised Land," the "New Canaan," "paradise," or, as Bellah noted, in a more Hobbesian light, as an "unfruitful desert, abode of death."[60] In either case, the image of the land was tied to a paradigmatic image of the new American "Adam"[61]—a combination of individualism and millennial expectations that developed among many Protestant sects. The tension with the wilderness—the vision of its conquest but also of untamed nature as the setting for humanity's fall, reform, and redemption—became a profound cultural idiom in America.

Closely related was a firm belief, found already among many Protestant groups in the colonies, that the American settlers were a "chosen people," with a special mission. They thus imposed, in Sacvan Bercovitch's words, a "sacred telos on secular events."[62] By the end of the eighteenth century, the destiny of the American republic was firmly identified with "the course of redemptive history." America had become "the locus and instrument of the great consummation." This equation of the "Kingdom of God" with the "Nation" essentially replaced the idea of the Church with that of the Nation and became the central tenet of the "religion of the republic."

The emphasis on "newness," on breaking with the past and freeing oneself from its shackles, persisted as a central theme in many sectors of American society, for instance, as Joyce Appleby has shown, among many new economic entrepreneurs of the early nineteenth century[63] or, later, among the second generation of many immigrant groups.

CIVIL RELIGION IN THE UNITED STATES

Out of the fusion of these themes there developed what Bellah called the American "civil religion," in which "the nation emerged as the primary agent of God's meaningful activity in history." Civil religion interprets historical experience "in light of transcendent reality," seeking to transfigure reality so that it provides moral and spiritual meaning. It is this interpretation that forms the core of the American myth or creed.[64]

This interpretation, and its closely related conceptions of social and political order, contained a very strong utopian component derived from the combined heritage of the Enlightenment and of sectarian Protestantism. This utopian orientation was rooted in European eschatological traditions, but it became greatly transformed in the United States, where utopian orientations lost their historical rootedness, their connections with the unfolding of a historical process. Rather, utopian eschatological components became detemporalized and dehistoricized, relocated in a continually "future-oriented" present.

The combination of Protestant themes with those of the Enlightenment gave rise to the conception of a timeless, already historically achieved Utopia. Thus utopian orientations became embedded in the continual present, albeit with strong orientations to an open future in which the United States embodied either the Christian eschatological utopia or that of the Enlightenment. This attainment could be polluted, but there was no further unfolding, through actual historical process, of a future utopian end-point.

In the American civil religion, several conceptions of the social and political order coexisted, sometimes in complementary and sometimes in contradictory modes. These were the contractual conception, with its strong emphasis on rights and on the contractual relations between individual and society; the republican conception; and the covenantal conception. It was not only liberal and republican values that coexisted in continual tension in the American vision. The covenant, usually conceived in religious terms as binding together the members of the community,[65] constituted (as Bellah strongly emphasized) yet another component, in tension or harmony with the others.

Several far-reaching tensions among these different conceptions developed. One was between the republican and the liberal (Lockean) orientations; closely related was the tension between the contractual and the covenantal conceptions of social order. The Lockean emphasis on individual rights, very often with strong legalistic overtones, offered a vision of the common good, in which it grounded moral obligations. Opposed to, or in continual tension with, this Lockean view was the civic republican one, expressed either in constitutional terms—that is, in terms of the upholding of the constitution—or in religious terms, as the upholding of the community's covenant with God. Such visions could be promulgated in a religious way rooted in the country's Protestant heritage with a strong covenantal component, or in a more secular way, rooted in the "scientific" elements of the Enlightenment.

It was the continual tension among these different components of the American civil religion, especially as they became related to continually changing social and economic conditions, that made the "promise of disharmony" an inherent possibility and also shaped the specific orientations of movements of protest in the United States.

THE UNITED STATES AND JAPAN IN COMPARISON TO EUROPE

The two contrasting—yet often mirror-image—ways of constructing collective identity and social order that developed in the United States and in Japan can be briefly compared, in their broad outlines, with those that developed in Europe. One of the most important characteristics of the construction of collective identities in European historical experience has been the continual interweaving of primordial, civil, and universalistic components. (Obviously, European countries differ precisely in the mode in which such interweaving took place.)

In all modern European societies there developed a continual confrontation between the primordial components of collective identity, continuously reconstructed in such modern terms as nationalism and ethnicity, and modern universalistic and civil components. The mode of interweaving these different components of collective identity shaped the differing institutional dynamics of different European societies, especially the scope of pluralism within them. Those societies in which the primordial components were subsumed relatively successfully under the civil and universalistic ones—with all components "peacefully" interwoven into collective identities—could allow pluralism a relatively wide scope.

The contrary tendencies to absolutization of the major dimensions of human experience and social order and concomitant principled exclusivity encouraged the development of extreme movements with strong Jacobin tendencies, both leftist revolutionary and extreme nationalistic ones. But in Europe these movements were set within the framework of basic European conceptions of social order and collective identity, which differed greatly from both the American and the Japanese ones.

CONCLUSION

The preceding analysis of aspects of social and political dynamics in the United States and Japan sheds light on the more general problem of influences on the crystallization of different modernities. First, it shows that, however great the structural similarities among different modern societies, they nonetheless differ greatly in some crucial aspects of ideological and institutional dynamics. Second, it indicates that such differences are influenced by two basic dimensions of the construction of social order—the construction of collective identity and the premises of social order and authority—closely related to the basic aspects of religion and of religious evolution. In most of the social science literature, either these dimensions have been neglected or their specific European constellations have been taken for granted in analyzing modern societies. While these dimensions have, of course, always been closely interwoven with the structural elements that have been central in the development of modern societies, they exhibit strong autonomous tendencies. Their close relations to the religious dimensions of human life are of crucial importance in shaping the dynamics of modern societies, or indeed, in more general terms, of any pattern of social order.[66]

FIVE

Calvinism and Revolution
The Walzer Thesis Reconsidered

Philip S. Gorski

Among the various extensions of the "Weber thesis"—the thesis that the "Protestant Ethic" and the "Spirit of Capitalism" bore an "elective affinity" toward one another[1]—Michael Walzer's *Revolution of the Saints* surely ranks as one of the most important and influential.[2] For the most part, Walzer's book focuses on issues of interpretation—in particular, on the theo-logical and psycho-logical interconnections between the "Protestant Ethic" and the "Spirit of Revolution." At the same time, however, the book contains a causal argument regarding the divergent outcomes of the English Revolution (1642–58) and the French Wars of Religion (1562–1626). The reason the Puritans succeeded and the Huguenots failed, Walzer claims, is that the former were mobilized and urged on by a militant and well-organized body of clergymen, while the latter were not. The purpose of this essay is to take issue with this argument and suggest an alternative.

At first glance, the Walzer thesis seems compelling, according quite well with the cases in question. But its plausibility is diminished considerably when the scope of the comparison is extended to include the Dutch Revolt against Spain (1555–1609), a Calvinist-led revolutionary struggle that succeeded despite the absence of a militant and well-organized body of Reformed clergymen. It is diminished even further when one considers the role that Geneva-trained missionaries played in organizing the Huguenot Church—and fomenting the French Wars of Religion.[3] Indeed, one could plausibly argue that France had a more radical and better-organized group of Calvinist clergymen during these years than did the Netherlands.

But if the presence or absence of a militant clergy was not the key determinant of how revolutionary a particular Calvinist movement became, what was? Given the small number of relevant cases and the subtle and not-so-subtle differences among them, one cannot really distinguish between "general" or "essential" causes, on the one hand, and "contingent" or "nonessential" causes, on the other. Nonetheless, it is possible to detect certain patterns. Specifically: (1) Calvinist movements seem to have taken a revolutionary turn only when and insofar as they (a) had a popular base and (b) faced a Catholic monarch; and (2) they appear to have succeeded in overthrowing the monarchy and attaining religious "liberty" (and denying such liberties to other confessions) only in countries that had strong national parliaments with well-established fiscal powers. Such, at least, is the argument that I will try to defend here.

But before turning to a detailed analysis of the individual cases, it may be useful to outline Walzer's argument in greater detail and to present a bit more of the evidence against it.

REFORMED CLERGYMEN AS REVOLUTIONARY CADRES?

It should be said at the outset that *The Revolution of the Saints* is a rich and multifaceted work that defies easy summary. Nonetheless, it is possible—albeit at the risk of oversimplification—to distinguish two central strands of argumentation in Walzer's book.

The first strand is interpretive. It consists of a close reading of religious and political tracts written by Calvinist pastors and propagandists from France and England, and seeks to trace the various "affinities" and connections between Reformed theology and revolutionary politics.

The second strand is explanatory. It consists of a (somewhat cursory) comparison of the milieus in which French Calvinism and English Puritanism took shape, and seeks to account for variations in the dynamics and outcomes of the French Wars of Religion and the English Civil War. In France, Walzer contends, Calvinism was an "aristocratic movement" in which clergymen played a subordinate role. As a result, "the French Civil Wars were never transformed into a revolutionary struggle."[4] In England, by contrast, Calvinism—rather, Puritanism—grew up in exile, in the refugee congregations established on the Continent during the reign of the Catholic Queen Mary (1553–58). In this context, Walzer argues, it was the clergy rather than the aristocracy who played the leading role in the Calvinist movement, and who, in turn, formulated the Puritan program. The English Revolution, he concludes,

> can only be explained in terms of the impact of the Puritan ministers and their ideology upon the gentry and the new merchant and professional classes. Had that impact . . . never been made social, economic forces might have produced many different forms of conflict and even of civil war in England; they would not have produced a revolution.[5]

In other words, Walzer is arguing that the Puritan struggle escalated into a revolution due to the presence of strong clerical leadership and that the

Huguenot conflict remained a mere civil war due to the absence of such leadership.

Now, this argument is quite plausible if one considers the French and English cases in isolation: the Calvinist clergy in (sixteenth-century) France was certainly much weaker and less militant than the Puritan clergy in (seventeenth-century) England, and there can be little doubt that Condé's struggle was ultimately less successful and less radical than Cromwell's. But it is less convincing when one considers the Dutch case, because the clergy of the Dutch Reformed Church was neither stronger nor more radical than its French counterpart; indeed, it may have been less so. Consider the following evidence. During the years leading up to the Dutch Revolt, much of the missionary work was by laymen who "had almost no pastoral training whatsoever."[6] Even as late as 1600, only a few of the approximately eleven hundred Reformed pastors active in the Netherlands had received any formal training.[7] In most areas, the shortage of qualified clergymen continued until well into the seventeenth century.[8] It should be added that the Dutch clergy was deeply divided during the latter decades of the Revolt as a result of the "Arminian controversy," a bitter dispute over the nature of divine grace and predestination that broke out in Leiden in the 1590s and lasted for nearly thirty years.[9] The Dutch Reformed clergy, then, was hardly a large, well-trained, and cohesive body during the decisive years of the struggle against Spain. In France, by contrast, the first Reformed missionaries were not only trained, they were trained by Calvin himself at the newly established Genevan Academy.[10] Moreover, the majority had received some education before arriving in Geneva.[11] The French Protestants were also quicker to train their own clergy. The first Reformed seminaries were established in 1561, almost fifteen years before similar institutions were founded in the Netherlands. There are no reliable figures on the total number of Reformed pastors in France during this period, but it seems likely that the absolute and per capita totals were at least as high as in the Netherlands, particularly during the 1570s and 1580s, the decisive decades for both the Wars of Religion and the Dutch Revolt. Moreover, the French clergy remained relatively untouched by the Arminian controversy until 1635, long after the fate of the Huguenots had already been effectively decided.[12] Thus, it seems unlikely that the "failure" of the Huguenot struggle and the "success" of the Dutch Revolt had much to do with differences in clerical organization or militancy.

There are also good reasons to question Walzer's claim that the French Wars of Religion were "nonrevolutionary" in character. It is certainly true that the Puritans went somewhat further than the Huguenots in both word and deed. But it is also true that the English Revolution occurred a full half century after the French Wars of Religion and that the former even built on and extended the latter in certain respects: if the English Roundheads were the first to sentence their king to death, the French Monarchomachs were the first to outline the conditions under which this act could be legitimate. This difference in timing may also explain the greater militancy and coherence of the Puritan clergy; they had much longer to develop and organize. Thus, in assessing whether the Wars of Religion may be justly called a revolution, it is perhaps more appropriate to compare them with other, more contemporaneous events, such as the Dutch Revolt against Spain or the "Executionist" Movement (1550–1609) in Poland. Compared with the latter, the Huguenot struggle looks quite revolutionary indeed. For while the Executionists did oppose the expansion of monarchical power and demanded freedom of (Protestant) worship, they did not advocate regicide or establish an alternative state. In fact, the Executionist Movement never progressed beyond the stage of a noble uprising. Conversely, the French Wars of Religion were every bit as radical and violent as the Dutch Revolt against Spain, which is often regarded as "the first modern revolution."[13] Until the 1580s, the arguments espoused by Huguenot ideologues were virtually identical to those propagated by the French Calvinists. In both instances, the rebellion against monarchical authority was defended through an appeal to "popular sovereignty" as embodied in the "ancient constitution"— hardly surprising, given the personal acquaintance of the French and Dutch leaders (Coligny and William of Orange) and the shared background of the key propagandists (legal studies and Reformed theology).[14] There are also striking parallels in the dynamics of the two struggles. Both, as shall become clear, began as noble uprisings, escalated into popular rebellions, and culminated in the division of the country into two competing polities, one Catholic, the other Calvinist. The key difference between the two cases lay in their outcomes: while the Calvinist Republic of the northern Netherlands survived, the Reformed polity of southern France did not.

Rather than draw a sharp line between revolutionary and nonrevolutionary events, as Walzer does, I find it more useful to distinguish between "revolutionary situations" and "revolutionary outcomes."[15] By "revolutionary situation," I mean the emergence of two rival blocs that establish rival governments and vie with each other for control over a given territory. By "revolutionary outcome," I mean the victory of the insurgent bloc—the monopolization of control over the contested territory by the rival government. Seen in this way, there are many forms of collective violence that do not qualify as revolutionary (e.g., most *charivaris*, food riots, peasant revolts, noble uprisings). Similarly, there are many types of power shifts, some violent, that are not the result of revolutions (e.g, coups, assassinations, wars of succession). Combining these distinctions, it is possible to distinguish between episodes of political violence that are nonrevolutionary in dynamic and outcome (the Executionist Movement), revolutionary in dynamic but nonrevolutionary in outcome (the French Wars of Religion), and revolutionary in dynamic and outcome (the Dutch Revolt, the English Revolution). In other words, it is possible to construct a (more or less) continuous scale of political violence along which cases of (early modern) political struggle can be arrayed.

How can these variations be explained? Let me emphasize that I do not believe one can develop a "general theory" of revolution that will be valid for all times and places—unless, of course, one defines revolution in a way that is so restrictive as to eliminate all but a handful of cases.[16] The conditions under which revolutions are likely to occur depend, among other things, upon the structures of social classes and political institutions and are thus historically specific. Moreover, the dynamics and outcome of any particular revolution will be affected by "contingent" and "accidental" factors—the fate of a particular leader, the outcome of a particular battle, the geography of a particular region—in ways that no reasonably parsimonious model can possibly predict. With these caveats, revolutionary situations generally (if not exclusively) emerged during the period in question (ca. 1550–1650) when and to the degree that the Calvinist movement (1) had a strong popular base and (2) faced strong resistance from a Catholic monarch. Where one or both of these conditions were absent, Calvinist movements were more likely to remain politically moderate and to strike a separate peace with the monarchy. In turn, these revolutionary situations generally had revolutionary outcomes when and to the degree that the polity in question had strong traditions of representative government, particularly at the national level.

To understand why these particular factors were so important, it is necessary to place them within their historicopolitical context, the Renaissance *Ständestaat.*

THE CRISIS OF THE RENAISSANCE *STÄNDESTAAT*[17]

The typical Renaissance state was a *Ständestaat,* a dualistic system of rule in which the monarch shared power with councils or assemblies representing his or her most powerful subjects. The membership, organization, and prerogatives of these representative bodies varied enormously, both geographically and over time. While members of the nobility and, until the Reformation, the clergy were virtually always present, many councils or assemblies also included representatives from the cities and sometimes even from the peasantry.[18] The most common organizational models were the "tricurial," in which each Estate met independently, and the "bicameral," in which the Estates were divided into upper and lower houses comprising, respectively, the high nobility and clergy and the lower nobility and/or commoners.[19]

Such representative bodies might exist solely at the provincial or national level, or at both. In theory, the "liberties" and "privileges" of the Estates were rooted in common law or written charters and usually involved judicial and financial immunities as well as consultative rights in important matters such as war and taxation. In practice, the Crown and the Estates were engaged in a continual tug-of-war. In times of national duress or under weak monarchs, the powers of the Estates might wax considerably. In times of economic prosperity or under strong monarchs, they might be substantially reduced. Generally, however, neither the Crown nor the Estates were interested in scoring a "knockout blow." The monarch could not easily govern or defend a kingdom without the support of powerful vassals and subjects. And the Estates were generally unable to manage their disputes or act effectively without the unifying impulse of the monarchy.

But social and political changes that occurred during the first half of the sixteenth century threatened the internal balance of this system of *dominium politicum et regale*. Rapid economic growth generated centrifugal social strains. In many cities, particularly in western Europe, the expansion of world commerce gave rise to a new stratum of rich merchants, who, often with the backing of disgruntled artisans, challenged the monopoly of political power held by the established, patrician oligarchies. In the countryside, especially in eastern Europe, the growth of the international grain trade engendered a powerful class of landed magnates and threatened the livelihood of the lower nobility. These cleavages were often further deepened by the dependence of the upper nobility and urban patriciate on the Crown for political patronage and military protection. At the same time, the ongoing warfare sparked by the Reformation strengthened the hand of the princes and—with the onset of the military revolution and the growth of standing armies[20]—dramatically increased monarchs' appetites for material resources. As a consequence, the "privileges and liberties" of the Estates, particularly their consultative rights with regard to taxation, came under increasing attack.

But, explosive as it was, the crisis of the *Ständestaat* did not automatically give rise to a revolutionary movement opposed to monarchy. This occurred most frequently (though by no means exclusively) where anti-monarchical opposition became entwined with radical Calvinism.

RELUCTANT REVOLUTIONARIES:
THE RISE OF CALVINIST RADICALISM

It should be emphasized at the outset that there was nothing inherently radical about Calvinism qua doctrine, at least not in comparison with other versions of Protestant theology. Theologically, Calvin's teachings generally followed Luther's, and where they did not, as in his interpretation of predestination and his understanding of the Eucharist, they diverged only slightly.[21] And while Calvin, again following Luther, allowed that "lower magistrates" (nobles and patricians) might resist an unjust and ungodly ruler, he generally stressed the duty of the people to obedience.[22]

Nonetheless, it is clear that Calvinism could *become* quite radical, especially when its adherents faced violent and sustained oppression. Under these circumstances, the Calvinist emphasis on congregational autonomy, communal discipline, and lay participation could give rise to proto-republican arguments that melded easily with a constitutionalist defense of traditional "privileges and liberties." In Weber's phrase, there was an "elective affinity" between Calvinism and republicanism.[23]

But, strong as this affinity was, it did not always take hold. This is particularly evident in the Polish example, where Calvinism never became fully politicized. The only instances in which Calvinism developed in a genuinely revolutionary direction were ones in which it had a broad popular following, because it was the popular classes who were most willing to engage in the acts of religious violence that transformed religious dissent into political rebellion, and it was their representatives—the leaders of the "third estate"—who were most likely to seize on the (potentially) radical elements of Calvin's thought and develop them into an ideology of anti-monarchical resistance.

Let us now take a closer look at the Dutch, French, and Polish cases, their dynamics and outcomes, and the role of Calvinism in them.

THE NETHERLANDS: FROM REVOLT TO REVOLUTION (1566–1589)[24]

During the first half of the sixteenth century, the Spanish Habsburgs worked diligently to consolidate their control over the Low Countries, the seventeen provinces comprising what is now Belgium and the Netherlands.[25] Under Emperor Charles V (1506–55), the central administration in Brussels was reorganized and the powers of the national and territorial assemblies—the "States General" and the provincial "Estates"—were gradually curtailed. Charles's son, Philip II (1555–98), sought to shift the balance of power even further; in desperate need of resources to finance his campaign against the French, he proclaimed new taxes without the consent of the States General. Tensions heightened in 1559, when Philip announced plans to reorganize the Church and create a number of new bishoprics,[26] thereby sparking the ire of the upper nobility, which tended to view Church offices as their private patrimony.

There was nothing particularly unusual about these conflicts. Relations between Renaissance monarchs and representative assemblies were often tense. But in this case, as in others, long-standing constitutional conflict intersected with a precipitous Protestant upsurge. Itinerant Calvinist preachers began crossing into the Low Countries from France during the early 1550s,[27] and by the early 1560s the Calvinist movement had a national following and was actively calling for freedom of worship. Philip II responded by renewing the old anti-Protestant edicts and expanding the activity of the Inquisition Courts.

In spring 1566 a large group of noblemen forced their way into the chambers of the Spanish governess, Margaret of Parma, and presented her with a letter demanding the retraction of the anti-Protestant edicts.[28] She responded with an act of moderation that was widely interpreted by the Calvinists as a proclamation of religious freedom. The following summer, open-air religious services, or "hedge sermons," were held outside many Dutch towns, attracting thousands of worshipers. And in August, the Netherlands were swept by the "iconoclastic fury," a wave of Calvinist-led image-breaking.[29] Then, in the fall, a group of rebellious nobles under the Duke of Brederode took up arms against the king; however, they failed to muster widespread support and were easily defeated by royal troops under the Duke of Alva, who succeeded Margaret as governor.

Retribution was swift and brutal. A special tribunal was established to try "heretics" and "rebels."[30] Thousands were executed and many more were driven into exile, including William of Orange, the future leader of the rebel movement.[31] At the same time, native nobles were dismissed from many top administrative posts in Brussels and replaced with Spaniards, the "new bishoprics" plan was revived, and a series of unpopular taxes were unilaterally proclaimed.[32]

Meanwhile, the Calvinist refugees began organizing popular resistance to the Spanish inside and outside the Low Countries, and William of Orange desperately worked to enlist foreign support for military intervention. The next round of conflict began in 1572, when the undefended coastal town of Brill was stormed by the "Sea Beggars," a ragtag band of eleven hundred Calvinist desperadoes.[33] With the help of local sympathizers, this group soon "liberated" much of the northern Netherlands, "opening" churches to Calvinist worship and replacing uncooperative magistrates with rulers more sympathetic to their cause.[34] William of Orange followed up with a hastily organized invasion from the south. But his troops were thin on the ground, and he was soon forced to beat a hasty retreat northward, where a Calvinist-dominated republican regime had been established by the provincial Estates of Holland and Zeeland.[35]

A financial crisis in Castile soon stalled the Spanish campaign, however, and Philip II was forced to sue for peace. But negotiations quickly broke down over the religious question. Philip II refused to make any concessions to the "heretics," and William of Orange proved equally unwilling to give ground. Following the breakdown of the peace talks, the Spanish launched another assault on the north. The Imperial armies, under the command of the new governor-general, Don Louis Requesens, made rapid progress. But, once again, the offensive was brought to a standstill by the fiscal woes of the Spanish Crown.

The death of Requesens the following spring created an opportunity for moderates and *"politiques"* who yearned for religious peace. For, with his passing, power reverted to the Council of State, the central organ of the territorial administration, dominated by moderates under the (Catholic) Duke of Aerschot. Under Aerschot's leadership, the Council hammered out an agreement with Holland and Zeeland that "solved"—or rather, devolved—the religious question by turning it over to the provincial Estates—the so-called Pacification of Gent.[36] When Requesens's successor, Don Juan of Austria, finally arrived in the Low Countries in 1577, the States General made their recognition of him as governor contingent upon acceptance of the Pacification of Gent. In the so-called Perpetual Edict, he reluctantly assented.

But the peacemakers were soon overtaken by events, as revolt gave way to revolution. This time it was the urban *popoli* who took the lead, demanding freedom of worship and an end to oligarchy. In some towns, most notably Gent and Bruges, Calvinist-dominated republics were proclaimed.[37] The southern provinces were now in open rebellion against Spain.[38]

During these same years, William of Orange steadily consolidated his control over the northern cities, and in 1579, the seven northern provinces signed a treaty of mutual defense, the Union of Utrecht.[39] In 1581, after another round of fruitless peace talks, the northern provinces did in the letter what they had already done in fact; they renounced Philip II as their "lord and sovereign."[40] The stage was now set for a war between the seven "United Provinces" and the king of Spain.

In October 1578, Don Juan died of the plague and was replaced by Alexander Farnese, Duke of Parma, a shrewd diplomat, a brilliant military tactician, and a convinced Catholic, who was determined to put down what he saw as a heretic rebellion. Through a sustained campaign of siege warfare, Parma reconquered most of the southern Netherlands.[41] By 1585, only Holland, Zeeland, and parts of the surrounding provinces remained under rebel control.

To alleviate this increasingly desperate situation, the States General began searching for a powerful protector who could muster needed military leadership and foreign assistance. They first turned to Francis Hercules, Duke of Anjou and brother of Henry III, King of France, but dismissed him after an abortive coup. Then they turned to Robert Dudley, Earl of Leicester, a protégé of Queen Elizabeth of England.[42] He, too, was dismissed following an attempted coup. Thereafter, the States General quietly neglected to name a successor. The provinces of the north were now a republic, in fact if not yet in name.

Throughout these years, the military situation in the United Provinces had grown increasingly desperate. But the sinking of the Spanish Armada in August 1588 brought a temporary respite, allowing the Dutch to recoup politically and militarily. The fiscal and administrative system was put onto more solid footing by Johan van Oldenbarnevelt, the "Grand Pensionary of Holland" and de facto leader of the States General.[43] Meanwhile, the army was instilled with new discipline and order by William the Silent's son, Maurice of Nassau, with the assistance of Simon Stevin, a gifted mathematician and engineer.[44] While the war against Spain would continue until 1609, by 1600 the independence of the United Provinces was a fait accompli.

This war had given birth to a new state: the Dutch Republic. Geographically, the Republic consisted of the seven northern provinces of the Low Countries (Holland, Zeeland, Utrecht, Friesland, Drente, and Overijssel), together with small pieces of Flanders and Limburg. Politically, it had a federalist constitution, in which ultimate authority was vested in the States General but was limited, in law and in practice, by the powers of the *Stadholder,* the provincial estates and the city magistrates.[45] Religiously, it was a multiconfessional society, in which the Reformed Church enjoyed special legal and financial privileges and eventually secured the allegiance of most of the population, but in which other creeds, including Catholicism, were, in the end, grudgingly tolerated.[46] It was, in short, a state in which republicans and Calvinists, the core of the anti-Habsburg coalition, had obtained much, but not all, of what they wanted.

The Revolt had no single or "essential" cause. In part, it was rooted in resentments—of the Dutch grandees against the Spanish Court, of the lesser nobles against their social superiors, and of the urban *popoli* against the ruling oligarchs. More immediately, it was precipitated by the proto-absolutist policies of Philip II, in his attempts to centralize power in Brussels, impose taxes without the consent of the Estates General, and rationalize the administration of the Church. And it was fanned into revolutionary conflagration by the militancy of the Calvinists and the intransigence of the Catholics— by religious violence and counterviolence. What transformed the Revolt into a revolution was not simply the conjunction of these three sources of discontent but the way they interacted and eventually fused. Social, political, and religious grievances reinforced one another, gradually became focused on the king, and served to bridge (and obscure) the diverging interests of the various wings of the anti-Spanish alliance—republicans and Calvinists, conservatives and revolutionaries, merchants and artisans. What emerged, in stages, was a groundswell of anti-Spanish sentiment, a religious "party" led by William of Orange, and, ultimately, a republican regime under the States General.

There was nothing inevitable about this outcome. The (partial) success of the Revolt was due to numerous factors, some quite "contingent" (e.g., the role of the weather in the sinking of the Spanish Armada and the role of the Rhine and Maas Deltas as natural lines of defense for the provinces of Holland and Zeeland) and some largely "external" to the situation (e.g., the ups-and-downs of silver production in the New World and the vicissitudes of Spanish royal finance).[47] But, insofar as the success of the Revolt was due to noncontingent (i.e., social and "internal") causes, one factor clearly stands out: a strong system of representative government. At the base of this system stood the towns, ruled by mayors, aldermen, and magistrates elected (or co-opted) from the ranks of the powerful and well-to-do citizens. At the next level were the provincial estates, composed of delegates from the larger towns, the nobility, and, in some cases, the clergy. And at the apex was the States General, which consisted of delegates elected by the provincial Estates. Of course, the decentralized constitution of the Republic could just as easily have produced discord and particularism, and there were times during the middle decades of the Revolt when this was precisely what happened. But, drawing on historical traditions and personal experience, Oldenbarnevelt and other Dutch leaders eventually developed techniques for taming these "centrifugal forces,"[48] including patronage, partisanship, and pork-barrel spending—the classic tools of legislative politics. Another danger was lethargy and inefficiency, a problem that is inherent to representative government and particularly grave during war, when rapid responses and quick decisions are essential. Here, too, the response of the States' leaders was creative and resourceful: the day-to-day administration of the Republic's affairs was placed in the hands of small, parliamentary committees, while final responsibility for wartime strategy and logistics was vested in the *Stadholders*. Perhaps the greatest achievement of the Republic's leaders, however, was the establishment of a sophisticated system of public finance that exploited Amsterdam's growing importance as a world financial center and enabled the States to mobilize vast sums of money at comparatively low cost.[49] A strong system of representative government was therefore essential to the success of the Revolt—just how essential becomes clear in considering a less successful attempt at revolt, the French Wars of Religion.

FRANCE: FROM REVOLT TO REINTEGRATION (1559–1598)[50]

Like the Dutch Revolt, the French Wars of Religion had a political as well as a religious background.[51] The political background had three elements.

The first was fiscal. To finance his military engagements in Italy, Francis I (1515–47) had been forced to employ various financial expedients: he repeatedly increased the *taille*, took loans from foreign bankers, extracted "contributions" from the clergy, and, most fatefully, began the systematic sale of offices. The second concerned the declining power of representative assemblies. In contrast to their predecessors, Francis I and Henri II rarely consulted the representative bodies of the realm, a fact that sparked considerable anger and resentment among the Estates. (However, it should be emphasized that the provincial Estates remained active during these years, particularly in the south. This would be of some consequence during the Wars of Religion).[52] The third element concerned the increasing power of, and rivalry between, the Guise and Montmorency clans, which controlled far-flung patronage networks and served as key intermediaries for the monarchy.[53] By the middle of the sixteenth century, political stability was threatened by a volatile mixture of financial insolvency, noble unrest, and clan rivalry.

The catalyst that ignited this mixture was religion.[54] Like the Netherlands, France had escaped — or rather, repressed — the first wave of Protestantism, only to be inundated by the second, Calvinism.[55] Calvinism found supporters everywhere, but it scored its greatest successes in the south, or *Midi,* where traditions of representative government were strongest and the sirens of Geneva closest.[56] There, the Calvinist movement not only included a majority of the nobility (as in Normandy, Brie, and Champagne) but also embraced urban artisans (as in Lyons) and even peasants (as in Languedoc).[57]

The twin currents of political and religious discontent were channeled together by the unexpected death of Henry II in 1559. Henry's successor was Francis II, a protégé of the Guises, and the Guises seized the opportunity to exclude the Montmorency and Bourbon clans from power. Because the Guises were Catholic, and the Montmorencys and Bourbons were Protestants, the conflict between the clans became entangled with conflict between the confessions.

Francis II died in December 1560. He was succeeded by Charles IX. Since Charles was a minor, power fell to his mother, Catherine of Medici, who was determined to bring the Guises to heel. Accordingly, she sought reconciliation with the Protestants and urged them to make peace with the Catholics. She faced an uphill battle. Protestant and Catholic nobles were busily mobilizing for war. In the cities, meanwhile, religious riots and interconfessional violence thoroughly poisoned relations between the competing faiths.[58] Catherine's efforts to broker a religious peace ultimately met with little success.

The first war of religion broke out in spring 1562. It was quickly followed by two more. The Guises and the Catholics won most of the wars, but it was Coligny and the Protestants who won the peace: the Edict of Saint Germain (1570) granted them full liberty of conscience, partial liberty of worship, and four "safe havens" (*plâces de sureté*), cities where the governor and garrison had to be Protestant. In effect, this transformed the French Protestants into a sort of Fourth Estate, with its own set of "privileges" and "liberties."

This situation was intolerable for Catherine and the Catholic radicals of Paris. When the Protestant nobility assembled in Paris in summer 1572 to celebrate the marriage of Henri of Navarre (a Calvinist and head of the House of Bourbon) to Marguerite of France (Catherine's youngest daughter), someone saw an opportunity to eliminate Coligny—perhaps Guise, perhaps Catherine, perhaps someone else (there is little evidence and no consensus on this point). In any event, the assassination attempt failed. For some reason, Coligny bent down at the decisive moment, and the ball struck his arm rather than his vitals. Placing his trust in Catherine and the king, he elected to stay in Paris, as did the rest of the Huguenot leadership. The trust was misplaced. Fearing the inevitable reprisals, the king and his mother elected the *fuite en avant,* ordering the execution of the entire Protestant nobility; only the princes of the blood, the young Condé and Henry of Navarre, were to be spared. But events soon slipped beyond the control of the court, as Catholic radicals and militia embarked on a ten-day killing spree that ultimately claimed at least three thousand lives—the St. Bartholomew's Day Massacre. Over the next several months, the violence spread to the provinces, claiming as many as ten thousand lives.

While the Massacre did not destroy French Protestantism, it did fundamentally alter its character. The Calvinist movement was stripped of its "natural" leadership and, with the onset of a wave of apostasy, of many of its followers as well. The effects were particularly devastating in the central and northern regions of France, where Calvinism had never sunk deep roots, but less pronounced in the provinces of the Midi, where the Reformed faith possessed a wider following. With the decapitation of the movement, moreover, the initiative increasingly shifted to the Third Estate, bringing about a democratization—and radicalization—of French Protestantism. At the same time, the atrocities committed in the name of the monarchy served to alienate many moderate Catholics from the Crown, creating new possibilities for a sort of "center-left alliance."

This is precisely what took shape in the southern provinces of Languedoc, Dauphiné, Provence, and Guyenne, where Protestants and Catholics banded together to form a "defensive league." All of these provinces had strong traditions of representative self-government—they were among the so-called *pays d'état,* which had retained control over taxation—and their estates had continued to meet throughout the 1560s.[59] Angered by the ruinous incursions of royal troops and the Crown's ceaseless demands for new "contributions," they voted to "withhold" tax revenues from the king and mustered a "defensive" force.[60] A Calvinist and republican regime also emerged in northern France in the city of La Rochelle, where a popular uprising had swept the Catholic oligarchy from power.[61] The Protestant Estate was evolving into a Protestant state. The result was increasing polarization and continued fighting that dragged on into the 1580s.

In June 1584, the political constellation was suddenly and dramatically altered by the death of Henry III's brother, the Duke of Anjou. By the terms of the Salic Law governing monarchical succession in France, the Protestant Henry of Navarre was next in line for the throne. The possibility that the leader of the French Protestant movement should inherit the title of *roi très chrétien*, which required its bearer to extirpate all heresy, provoked anger and disbelief among the Catholic population.

Scenting the political opportunity, a group of Catholic noblemen, led by Henry of Guise, established a Holy and Sacred Catholic League, put forth their own candidate for the throne, and concluded an alliance with the Spanish Crown. In Paris and throughout France, Catholics began rallying to the League and establishing local "councils" that monitored and often usurped the activities of the municipal government. Under increasing pressure from radical Leaguers, Henry III revoked the various edicts protecting the Protestants. And in September, the pope issued a bull declaring Henry of Navarre unfit to assume the throne.

The military successes of the League pushed Guise's popularity to new heights. It was even rumored that he had personal aspirations to the throne. Meanwhile, the League was developing in an increasingly radical direction, particularly in Paris. To its main religious goal, recognition of the Articles of Trent, it now added a catalog of political demands: restoration of the ancient privileges of the nobility and the towns, abolition of all venal offices, expulsion of Protestants from the courts, and tax relief for the populace.[62]

The stability of the monarchy was again threatened, this time by the Catholics, and the course was determined for a confrontation between Henry III and the League. The first set went to Guise, who seized control of Paris and forced the king to sign a humiliating truce. But the match went to Henry III, who revenged himself on Guise with an assassin's knife. It was a short-lived victory. The next year, Henry III was also assassinated.

Now began Henry of Navarre's long march to power. Although he was the legitimate heir to the throne, many Catholic royalists initially hesitated to support him. But the radicalism of the urban Leaguers, combined with the continued meddling of the Spanish and the Pope, helped turn the tide in Henry's favor after 1590, and in 1593, he formally converted (back) to Catholicism, clearing the way for the restoration of royal power. While it cost him some Protestant backing and failed to convince hard-line Catholics, Henry IV's apostasy brought royalists and moderates of both confessions firmly behind him, and in February 1594 he was anointed king of France. The League was put down and the kingdom gradually pacified. In 1598, Henry IV signed the Edict of Nantes, codifying the political and religious rights of the French Protestants.

Although the Edict of Nantes brought the religious wars to a close, it did not represent a lasting solution to the religious problem. The Protestants were officially reintegrated into the monarchy, but their privileges—urban safe havens, independent political assemblies, special courts—institutionalized their status as a sort of Fourth Estate and provoked great resentment among Catholics. The Protestants, for their part, jealously guarded their special position and did not hesitate to take up arms to defend it. This fragile political and religious symbiosis could be sustained only by a skillful and tolerant king, such as Henry IV, who stood above the confessional fray. But with the assassination of Henry IV in 1610 and Louis XIII's accession to the throne, the Protestants came under political, and then military, attack by the Crown, signaling the start of an anti-Protestant war of attrition that would culminate in the revocation of the Edict of Nantes in 1685. This gradual reduction of the Protestants' political privileges went hand in hand—indeed, was a critical precondition of—the dismantling of constitutional limits on monarchical authority and the establishment of royal absolutism in France.

The Huguenot struggle ended in "failure": unlike their Dutch counterparts, the French Calvinists never succeeded in establishing a fully sovereign and independent state and were forcefully reintegrated into the French monarchy—and, in most cases, into the Catholic Church as well. This "failure" is even more striking when one considers the parallels between the two cases. Both began as noble rebellions that were largely (though not entirely) motivated by political discontent. Both then developed into popular uprisings whose chief background was religious, leading to the formation of opposing, confessional parties. And both witnessed the emergence of a Protestant "party" grounded in the representative institutions of the Estates. In short, both gave rise to a revolutionary dynamic.

So what explains the differing outcomes? Much has been made of the role of historical accident and political violence in the French Wars of Religion. What if Coligny had not bent over and the assassin's bullet had found its mark? What if the Huguenot nobility had fled Paris and the St. Bartholomew's Massacre had never happened? Without doubt, the struggle would have evolved differently. But it is worth remembering that the Dutch rebels also lost some of their most important leaders—two (Egmont and Hoorn) to the executioner's block and one (William of Orange) to an assassin's bullet. So it is not immediately evident that the difference in outcomes can be attributed to historical accident. In the end, two factors seem of greater importance to the failure of the Huguenot struggle.

The first was the relative weakness of representative institutions. This weakness had a number of sources. The most important, certainly, was the Estates General's lack of fiscal authority. Without the power to tax and spend, the Estates could not raise an army, and without an army, they could not mount any serious or sustained opposition to the king. Consequently, their only real means of resistance was passive, the refusal to grant supply. Given the independent revenue base possessed by the French monarchy, this was a weak weapon indeed. There were other factors as well. The Estates General could not assemble without the permission of the king, and could also be dissolved by him. And once it was in session, consensus-building was extraordinarily tedious. In contrast to the Dutch States General, where delegates assembled and deliberated in one chamber, the three Estates of the French Estates General met separately and consulted by means of missives and messengers.[63] Moreover, once an agreement *was* reached, in the form of a *cahier général*, it still had no force of law; the king was free to refuse the Estates' requests, and those he granted still had to be registered by the Parlement of Paris. The Estates, in short, were a consultative body, without real legislative powers.

This point should not be overstated. It must be remembered that traditions of representative government were still quite strong at the regional level, especially in the *pays d'élections* of southern and western France. There, the provincial Estates retained broad powers, including, in most cases, the rights to collect taxes and to assemble at regular intervals. Not coincidentally, perhaps, this was also the region in which Reformed Protestantism achieved the widest following and the deepest implantation.[64] And it was in this "fertile crescent," stretching from Guyenne through Languedoc to the Dauphiné, that Huguenot resistance assumed its most resilient form—a Protestant proto-state, with its own assemblies, taxes, and troops, sometimes referred to as the "United Provinces of the *Midi*."[65] And yet, in 1620, the year the Netherlands were gearing up to defend their independence from Spain, the "United Provinces of the *Midi*" were effectively defunct. Why?

The critical factor, it seems to me, was the appearance of a Protestant pretender to the French throne in the person of Henry of Navarre. I think it would be hard to overstate the impact that this event had on subsequent developments. Like a sudden change of polarity in a magnetic field, it immediately reversed the lines of political attraction and repulsion that had shaped the course of events for over two decades: French Protestants, who were on the verge of seceding from the kingdom, were drawn back into the arms of the monarchy, and French Catholics, who had styled themselves as loyal defenders of the Crown, were suddenly pushed to the brink of revolution. Had Henry of Navarre continued down this path, the Wars of Religion would have raged on, perhaps for decades, and might have culminated in the Protestantization or division of France; but he did not. Placing duty above conviction, he converted to Catholicism, hoping to secure the allegiance of moderate Catholics without entirely alienating his Huguenot followers. He succeeded. After several years of tortuous negotiations, Henry IV patched together the peace party of the 1570s and pushed through the Edict of Nantes (1598), which provided the Huguenots with various legal protections but stripped them of their political armor—the independent assemblies of the South. Over the next three quarters of a century, the privileges and protections enjoyed by the French Protestants were gradually withdrawn, and in 1685 the Edict of Nantes was formally revoked. The circle was now complete; revolution culminated in reintegration. If contingency and chance played a role in the Wars of Religion, it was here.

In the foregoing account, the failure of the Huguenot revolution has been traced to a conjunction of two factors, the weakness of representative government at the "national" level and the appearance of a Protestant pretender to the French throne. At the beginning of this essay, however, it was claimed that yet another factor influenced the development of the Calvinist movement: the presence or absence of a popular base. To vindicate this claim, it would be necessary to show that there was at least one case in which traditions of representative government were strong and the king was Catholic, but in which the Calvinist movement was limited to the upper classes and in which neither a revolt nor a revolution occurred. Poland-Lithuania was precisely such a case.

REFORM WITHOUT REVOLUTION: THE REFORMATION AND THE REPUBLIC OF NOBLES IN POLAND-LITHUANIA (1548–1607)[66]

In 1550, the constitutional system of the Kingdom of Poland-Lithuania differed markedly from the systems of both France and the Netherlands in several respects.[67] First, like most other representative assemblies in east-central Europe[68]—and the English Parliament—the territorial estates (Sejm) of Poland-Lithuania were organized along bicameral (rather than tricurial) lines; that is, they were divided into two chambers, the upper house or "Senate," composed of the great nobles and clerics (who generally came from the same families), and the lower house or "Chamber of Deputies," made up of representatives of the lower nobility, or "gentry." Second, except for token delegations from the cities of Krakow and Vilno, the Third Estate was not formally represented in the Sejm—or the *sejmiks*. This situation was mitigated somewhat by the structure of the Polish nobility, which was unusually (indeed uniquely) large—it encompassed somewhere between 8 percent and 10 percent of the population, compared to less than 1 percent in most countries—and included a fair number of lawyers, professors, and other middle-class professionals who had been elevated into its ranks through a generous policy of ennoblement. But the "bourgeoisie," in the strict sense of the term, was completely excluded from the political nation, and town dwellers were widely looked down upon. Third, and most unusual, the Polish monarchy was elective rather than hereditary. In contrast to the Holy Roman Empire, with which the Polish-Lithuanian Empire is sometimes compared, the monarchs were not chosen by a small group of princely "electors" but by an open-air assembly of the entire nobility.

In Poland-Lithuania, then, the balance of power clearly favored the Estates, and the proceedings of the Estates, in turn, were dominated by the nobility. Representative government was clearly strong.

Still, by the late fifteenth century there were increasing signs of discontent, particularly among the lesser nobles. This discontent was directed not against the monarchy but against the great nobles or "magnates." By pleading their case with the king, who desperately needed their financial and military support, the gentry were able to obtain several important concessions, including the establishment of a lower house in the Sejm, the House of Deputies (1501), and a written guarantee of their political power, known as *Nihil Novi* (1505). But the gentry remained unhappy with the quality of royal justice and administration, and during the 1520s and 1530s, they began calling for a speedier and more conscientious "execution of the laws."[69] Initially, the demands of the "Executionists" were limited: a quicker dispensation of justice in the king's courts and a fairer distribution of rights to the king's domains. By the 1560s, however, "Execution" had come to stand for a broader and more far-reaching program of financial and political reform, of which the most important planks were the recovery of royal domains, alienated to members of the (upper) nobility; the election of special tribunals, charged with investigating charges of fraud and corruption; the annulment of royal grants and pensions dispensed without the approval of the Estates; and annual meetings of the Sejm.[70]

The growth of the Executionist movement coincided with—and was stimulated by—the diffusion of Reformed Protestantism. To understand the social and geographic pattern that this diffusion took, and the political impact it was to have, it is necessary to trace the development of Polish Protestantism in greater detail.[71] The Reformation came to Poland in four distinct waves and from four different directions. The first wave, Lutheranism, came during the 1510s and 1520s and emanated from Germany. Its impact was greatest in the cities, particularly those of the north and west, such as Danzig and Elbing, which had large populations of ethnic Germans. The second wave of reformation ideas, Reformed Protestantism, reached Poland during the 1540s and 1550s; it emanated from Switzerland, especially Zurich and Basel. Its impact was greatest in the south (Little Poland) and the east (Lithuania), where it attracted a following among, respectively, the lesser nobles and the great magnates. The third wave came in 1548, when members of the "Bohemian Brethren" stopped in western Poland (Great Poland) on their way to East Prussia. The Brethren were an ascetic off-shoot of the Hussites, whose theology, liturgy, and ecclesiastical government strongly resembled those of the Calvinists.[72] The two movements explored the possibility of a merger during the early 1550s and signed an official statement of unity in 1555, in which they agreed to hold common synods and pledged to work toward a more perfect union. The fourth wave, anti-Trinitarianism, arrived in Poland during the 1550s and 1560s; it came from Italy by way of Geneva.[73] Its earliest exponent had been Michel Servetus, an Italian refugee, who was burned at the stake in Geneva at Calvin's behest in 1546, and its most important leader was Faustus Socinius, who arrived in Poland in 1579. The anti-Trinitarians were eventually excluded from the Reformed Church, and their influence was most pronounced in Great Poland and Lithuania. By 1570, then, there were four Protestant Churches competing for members in the Polish-Lithuanian Republic.

In Holland, Scotland and France, it was opposition to the king that first drove Calvinists and constitutionalists into each other's arms. In Poland, it was opposition to the Church, for it was the Catholic clergy who took the lead in persecuting the Protestants. While the Polish kings did issue a number of anti-Protestant edicts, they rarely enforced them. The only serious effort to suppress Protestantism in this period came from the (Catholic) ec-clesiastical courts, which executed many "heretics," most of them renegade priests or underground booksellers, during the 1520s, 1530s and 1540s. The actions of the ecclesiastical courts excited opposition not only among Protestants but also within the nobility, which had always resented the pre-rogatives of the clergy.

The political and religious currents of discontent first merged in 1550, when Stanislaw Orzechowski, a Polish nobleman and Catholic priest who had denounced the rule of celibacy and taken a wife, was excommunicated and ordered deprived of his land, title, and honor by his superior, the Bishop of Przemsyl. Orzechowski appealed to the Diet, which readily agreed to hear his case. No consensus was ever reached, but the Orzechowski affair quickly became a lightning rod for anti-clerical sentiment within the nobil-ity and helped to knit together a loose coalition between Protestants and Executionists, which would dominate the Diet for over two decades.

Meanwhile, the Catholic Church began to mobilize its supporters. In 1555, the pope dispatched a seasoned diplomat, Aloysius Lippomani, to serve as his Nuncio in Poland, and the following year he sent long missives to Sigismund II and various noblemen, berating them for their Protestant sympathies and their failure to defend the Church. The Polish Synod, for its part, passed a long resolution acknowledging that "the beginning of the troubles has been caused by the carelessness of the parochial as well as the higher clergy" and calling for a restoration of clerical discipline and for execution of the anti-Protestant edicts.[74] And in 1558, the Society of Jesus sent one of its members on a fact-finding trip, thus initiating the Jesuit mission to Poland.

But, while the king did what he could to gird up the Catholic cause, he doggedly refused to embark on a policy of anti-Protestant persecution, despite continued pressure from the Apostolic See and the Polish clergy. This restraint may have been inspired to some degree by a humanist respect for the liberty of individual conscience. But political necessity was probably more important; faced with a stream of onslaughts from the south (the Tatars) and the east (the Russians), Sigismund II could hardly afford to alienate the Protestant leaders of the Sejm, who ultimately controlled the pursestrings. In any event, the king chose to enter into a series of pragmatic quid pro quos, in which he accommodated the political demands of the Sejm and the Sejm accommodated the fiscal needs of the Crown. The result of this pact was a steady erosion in the power of the Church—and a steady increase in the power of the gentry. The potentially explosive mixture of religious and political tensions that emerged after 1550 was thus defused for nearly two decades by the accommodationist policies of the Crown.

Storm clouds first appeared in 1570, following the conclusion of the Livonian Wars. With the fiscal burdens of war lifted, the king was free to pursue a political policy more in line with his religious convictions. The political climate grew more ominous still, following the king's death in 1572. For Sigismund II was the last member of the Jagiellonian line, and the Diet was now able to choose a new monarch without regard for dynastic considerations. At first, it appeared that the Sejm might split along purely confessional lines. Members of the Calvinist gentry sought to have the fiery John Firley elected interim king (*interrex*). Meanwhile, a Catholic cabal centered around the Papal legate, John Francis Commendone, hatched a plot to have Archduke Ernest of Habsburg proclaimed Grand Duke of Lithuania and then raise an army to force the Sejm to recognize him as king of Poland. But events unfolded quite differently. The vote for *interrex* fell on the Primate of Poland, Jacob Uchaski, a moderate Catholic who opposed religious persecution. And the vote for king favored the Duke of Anjou, who swore to uphold the rights of Polish Protestants. More significantly, perhaps, the Diet enacted a legal framework for ensuring peaceful coexistence between the confessions—the so-called Confederation of Warsaw. Drafted by an ad hoc committee of three Protestants and three Catholics, it applied the tried and tested principle of *cuius regio, eius religio* to the political unit of the manor. Each noble was henceforth free to practice the religion of his or her choosing—*and* to impose (or not) these beliefs on his or her subjects. Not surprisingly, Protestant and Catholic radicals were unhappy with this agreement and with the elections. Commendone tried to persuade Anjou that his oath to protect the Polish Protestants was not legally binding, and Firley and his supporters threatened to take up arms if they were not provided with clear guarantees for their religious freedom. But a confrontation was avoided through the skillful diplomacy of Jan Zamoyski, a moderate Catholic noble who had emerged as the leader of the "centrist" alliance within the Sejm. Anjou agreed to uphold the articles of the Confederation.

The reign, however, was brief. Anjou arrived in Cracow on February 18, 1574, and was coronated three days later. His brother, Charles IX, died on May 30, leaving the French throne vacant. Anjou was next in line, and on June 18, he departed for Paris under cover of darkness. Anjou had been king for less than four months.

The second interregnum was essentially a replay of the first, albeit slightly more turbulent. Again, the threat of confessional confrontation loomed large. "Right-wing" Catholics came out in favor of a Habsburg successor, and this time were backed by the magnates in the Senate, who saw the Austrian connection as a vital counterbalance to the Russian threat. "Left-wing" Calvinists and gentry, meanwhile, favored the election of a native noble, who would be more apt to respect their political and religious liberties. At the Convocation Diet in November of 1575, members of the Senate came out strongly in favor of Maximillian II, while members of the House of Deputies expressed their continued desire for a Polish candidate. The delegates had come heavily armed, and a confrontation ensued. Civil war appeared imminent. But again, the centrists succeeded in defusing the conflict and brokering a compromise. Andrew Zborowski, a powerful Protestant magnate, declared his support for Stephen Bathory, the Protestant prince of Transylvania, and Jan Zamoyski, the moderate Catholic leader of the gentry, agreed to support Bathory's candidacy, provided that he consent to marry Princess Anne, a Catholic and the last surviving member of the Jagiellon line. The deal was struck, the vote was cast, and Bathory was anointed king of Poland on May 1, 1576. When it was learned that Bathory had converted to Catholicism shortly after his election, the specter of civil war briefly reared its head again. But the new king promptly declared his determination to uphold the terms of the Confederation, and Zamoyski, now vice-chancellor, was able to cool the tempers of the would-be rebels.

The path toward peaceful coexistence between the confessions thus appeared to be cleared. And indeed Bathory was careful to respect the rights of the Protestant nobles and went so far as to abolish the Church courts. But he also did whatever he could to promote the Catholic cause, and was particularly supportive of the Jesuits, who referred to him as *"pater et patronus noster."*[75] The Polish Jesuits had already established four colleges and a number of missions before Bathory took the throne, and by the end of his reign, had 360 members, twelve colleges, and missionary stations reaching into all corners of the kingdom.[76] They continued to grow under Bathory's successor, Sigismund III of Vasa. Of particular importance was the network of Jesuit preparatory schools, which educated hundreds of noblemen and won many back to the old faith, a development strongly encouraged by the new king, who systematically excluded Protestant nobles from royal appointments. As a result, the number of Protestant delegates in the Sejm declined precipitously, from 58 members in the Senate and a clear majority in the House of Envoys in 1569[77] to 17 members in the Senate and less than 30 percent in the House of Envoys by 1606.[78] And it seems likely that the proportion of Protestants within the nobility as a whole, probably somewhat lower to begin with, underwent an even more substantial drop.

Nor was the Catholic resurgence confined to the upper reaches of society. Protestantism had never put down very deep roots within the popular classes, except in the German-dominated cities of Ducal Prussia. Elsewhere, Catholic mobs attacked individual Protestants and churches with growing frequency from the mid-1570s onward. The Reformed Church of Cracow was pillaged three times between 1574 and 1591 and was razed during the final attack.[79] Similar incidents occurred in Vilna, Lublin, and other large cities.[80] Much of the violence seems to have been committed with the tacit approval of the local authorities.

Meanwhile, the Protestant movement was being torn apart by doctrinal conflicts and denominational schisms. The Reformed Church had been plagued by inner strife, particularly over the doctrine of the Holy Trinity, almost from its inception, and in 1565 the Polish synod excluded a group of anti-Trinitarian ministers from its ranks. This group, known as the "minor church," soon became embroiled in disputes of its own, regarding the sacrament of baptism (infant vs. adult) and the person of Christ (divine or human), which were not stilled until the early 1580s, when the unitarian or "Arian" faction won. Nor was this the end of the schisms. The Lutherans had never seen eye-to-eye with the Polish Calvinists and the Czech Brethren, and during the 1580s, they gradually distanced themselves from the Consensus of Sandomierz, eventually withdrawing from it altogether. These internecine disputes made it virtually impossible for the Protestants to form a common front against the Catholics—indeed, the Calvinists and Lutherans were wont to ally with the Catholics against the Arians—and probably enhanced the popular appeal of Catholicism. By 1600, Polish Protestantism was well down the road toward extinction.

Still, the Protestant nobility had not entirely lost its fighting spirit and in 1606 rose up against the king. The nobles were not alone. Through his continual flouting of the constitution and his unflagging support for the Jesuits, Sigismund III had succeeded in alienating a great many nobles, Catholic as well, including, in the end, his trusted chancellor, Jan Zamoyski, and in 1606 fifty thousand of them signed an Act of Confederation threatening an

armed rebellion, or *rokosz*, unless the king addressed a long list of grievances. "Our ancestors," they complained, "knew that they were born nobles
rather than Catholics . . . and that Poland is a political kingdom, not a clerical one. . . . They did not mix holy religion with politics, and did not submit
either to priests to gluttons."[81]

Armed conflict ensued, and despite superior numbers, the confederates
went down to defeat. The *rokosz* of 1606–7 did not spell the end of the Polish constitution; indeed, it is generally regarded as the beginning of the
"Golden Freedom" or "Polish Anarchy." But it did mark the last gasp of militant Protestantism in Poland; henceforth, the Calvinist gentry ceased to play
an important role in Polish politics.

Nonetheless, it would be too simple to dismiss the gentry's movement of
the 1550s and 1560s as a "failure." At a time when "new monarchs" in other
parts of Europe were circumventing the Estates, taxing without consent,
and establishing standing armies, the Polish nobility succeeded in defend-
ing and even expanding its role in territorial government, and in securing
freedom of worship—at least for itself. These were no mean accomplishments, and they must be attributed, in large measure, to the efforts of the
Protestant gentry.

Still, it would be an exaggeration to characterize these changes as "revolutionary," for they were achieved mainly by peaceful means and they realized, more than changed, existing constitutional principles. Compared to
events elsewhere in Europe—in Scotland, France, the Netherlands, Bohemia, England, even Hungary—developments in Poland were actually quite
"moderate." Resistance to monarchical authority was limited to a few noble
uprisings and lacked ideological stridency. And the ultimate result was not
a popular dictatorship, as in England, or even an oligarchic republic, as in
the Netherlands, but a sort of neofeudal *Ständestaat*, in which the power
of central institutions were severely limited, the "liberties" of the individual
noble were essentially unchecked, and the rights of the common people
were virtually nonexistent. Its watchwords were not national representation
and popular sovereignty but *"rex non regnat sed gubernat"* (the king governs
but he does not rule), and *"Nierzadem Polska stoi"* (It is by unrule that Poland
stands).

Why did the gentry's movement culminate in conservative reform rather
than full-blown revolution?

At first glance, two factors might seem decisive. The first was the accommodationist policies of the Polish kings. Sigismund II, Henry of Anjou, and
Stephen Bathory all refrained from open attacks on the Protestants and
made many concessions to the gentry. Partly for this reason, much of the religious and political discontent that crystallized around the Executionist
program came to be focused on the Church—and not on the Crown. The

second was the "centrist" alliance between moderate Catholics and Protestants that dominated the Sejm. Although tendencies toward confessional
polarization were evident, especially during the *interregna,* and although
there were militant Catholics and Protestants, such as Hosius and Firley,
who clearly sought to accentuate such tendencies, it was the *politiques* rather
than the radicals who ultimately gained the upper hand. In a more Walzer-
ian vein, one might also point to a third factor, the relatively "apolitical" and
"undisciplined" character of the Protestant clergy in Poland-Lithuania. For,
while there was no shortage of "radicalism" within the Polish churches, it
was primarily of an intellectual and "otherworldly" sort, focused more on
theological and moral issues than on political and social ones. And this situation was due, in part, to the lack of central institutions, such as a Protestant university or a powerful synod, capable of imposing order.

But these were only proximate causes for the "failure" of revolution in
Poland. The underlying cause becomes immediately clear when we place
the gentry's movement within a larger context—the lack of a popular base,
the fact that the gentry's movement was a *gentry's* movement. It was the
actions of the common people—iconoclastic violence, civic coups, and so
on—that served to radicalize the religious struggles in the Netherlands,
France, and other parts of Europe, and it was the absence of such actions
that explains the "pragmatic" stance of the king and the Estates in Poland
and the "moderate" character of the changes demanded by the gentry.[82]
Without the pressure of popular disorder, there was no need to "appease
the masses" and no reason to question the established order. The upper-
class character of Polish Protestantism may also help to explain the character of the Reformed clergy, for the Polish ministers, like their followers,
were drawn mainly from the ranks of the nobility—in stark contrast to the
situation in other Reformed countries, where the clergy was overwhelmingly "middle class" in origins.

But this conclusion raises another question: why did Reformed Protestantism fail to attract a popular following in Poland? Part of the answer is
that Reformed Protestantism was preempted by Lutheranism in those areas
of the kingdom most susceptible to the Calvinist message—the commercial
cities of the Baltic and the Vistula. Another part was Poland's "economic
backwardness." Whether in the city (as in Holland or Flanders) or in the
country (as in Scotland or the Cevenne), Reformed Protestantism tended
to attract those who engaged in manufacture or commerce of one kind or
another—people likely to be literate and to be part of transregional networks and, so, likely to be exposed to and capable of assimilating the evangelical creed of Biblicist Christianity.

But this is not yet the whole answer. For, as we have seen, the Jesuits
proved quite capable of organizing the popular classes in Cracow, Vilna,

and other parts of Poland, and their followers, in turn, showed little hesita-
tion about committing acts of religious violence. If Polish Protestantism remained a head without a body, a movement without arms and legs, this was
due, at least in part, to the lack of a militant and disciplined clergy willing and able to undertake the twin tasks of proselytizing the populace and
building up the Church.

SUMMARY AND CONCLUSIONS

The main purpose of this essay has been to refine Walzer's analysis of Calvinism and revolution and in particular to identify the complex social and
political conditions under which the revolutionary energies of sixteenth-
century Calvinism became activated and effective. The argument, to reiter-
ate, is (1) that Calvinism tended to develop in a revolutionary direction only
when it (a) had a popular base and (b) faced monarchical opposition; and
(2) that Calvinist-led insurgent movements tended to succeed only when,
and to the degree, that they could draw on strong traditions of representative government, especially at the "national" level. In the Netherlands, all of
these conditions were present. There, attempts at religiopolitical compromise were repeatedly undermined by the violence of the Calvinist *popoli,* on
the one hand, and the intransigence of a Catholic monarch, on the other,
setting in motion an upward spiral of mobilization and countermobilization
that culminated in the formation of two opposing religious "parties" and
two rival governments. Despite superior resources and manpower, Spain
was unable to reconquer the northern Netherlands and topple the revolutionary government, primarily because of the presence of strong representative institutions that rebel leaders could use to mobilize the manpower
and resources necessary to defend their claims to independence. In France,
on the other hand, only the first two factors were present—a popular base
and monarchical opposition. The third—traditions of representative government—was less strongly developed than in the Netherlands. Nonetheless, a rival government did emerge at the provincial level in the *pays d'états*
of the Midi, and it might have survived had a Protestant pretender to the
throne not appeared in the person of Henry of Navarre. But Navarre's claim
to succession brought about a demobilization of the Huguenots and a radicalization of the Catholics (the League), and thereby set the stage for the
gradual suppression of the French Calvinists. In Poland-Lithuania, finally,
the first two conditions were absent and the third was present. There, the
early decades of the Calvinist movement were marked by a spirit of compromise, made possible by the lack of popular violence, on the one hand,
and the king's policy of accommodation, on the other. The more aggressive
and pro-Catholic policies of Sigismund III did eventually spark a noble up-

rising in 1607, but it lacked popular support and was quickly suppressed. While the Polish gentry succeeded in blocking the rise of absolutism, they did not articulate a coherent theory of republican government and failed to establish an effective set of representative institutions, such as occurred in the Netherlands—and in England.

Although it has only been possible to examine three instances of Calvinist-led insurgency in this essay, I believe that the foregoing model could be applied to a number of other, more or less contemporaneous, cases of early modern revolt, including the rebellions of the Scottish Covenanters, the Bohemian Uprising, and the anti-Habsburg revolts in Hungary—as well as the English Civil War. This, however, is a task that must be left to someone better qualified (and more ambitious) than I.

Yet it is important not to lose sight of the larger point raised by Walzer's analysis, the broader connection between Calvinism and revolution. As we have seen, there was nothing automatic about this connection; the rise of Calvinism did not always culminate in the outbreak of revolution, and in some cases, particularly in Germany, Calvinism became an ideology of absolutism and "counterrevolution." Moreover, many "revolutionary situations" that arose during the early modern period had little or nothing to do with Calvinism, or with religion more generally—the French Fronde or the Revolt of the Castilian *communeros,* for instance. Still, a connection existed; all the *successful* revolutions of the early modern era, from the Dutch Revolt through the English Civil War, were inspired at least partly by Calvinism. It is Walzer who first recognized the two strands of this connection: the ideology (or rather, the cosmology) of radical Calvinism and the organization of the Reformed Church, for it was by means of Calvinist ideology and organization that the "masses" or "popular classes" were mobilized and routine uprisings of the nobility transformed into broad-based struggles for control over the state—revolutions. If there is a fault in Walzer's analysis, it lies mainly in exaggerating the significance of the clergy in this process, for the threads that bound together the causes of Calvinism and revolution were spun, not only by ministers, but also by lawyers, merchants, and even the occasional artisan; and the tension in this thread that made it possible to stitch the pieces of the old order into something genuinely new came less from the pens of militant clerics than from the hammers of popular iconoclasts and the swords of uncompromising gentry. It was these persons, as much as the ministers, who pushed religious opposition over the brink of violent revolution. In a word, revolutionary Calvinism had not one "carrier" but many.

The foregoing analysis does not purport to be a "general theory of revolution" from which testable "predictions" may be deduced. Rather, it seeks to identify, through induction, the most important preconditions for revolutionary situations and outcomes within a specific historical context, early modern Europe. Put differently, it uses the prism of comparison to refract the stream of revolutionary events into its constituent elements. Were these elements wholly specific to a particular time and place, they could teach little; but they are not. In fact, there are striking similarities between early modern and modern revolutions: the literal and figurative "Puritanism" of revolutionary leaders from Cromwell to Robespierre to Malcolm X; the Manichaeanism of revolutionary ideologies from Beza to Saint-Just to Lenin; and the vision of a "city on the hill" from Geneva to Paris to Moscow. These parallels are not the result of accident, for in many ways it was the Calvinists and their allies who first invented revolution—its "personality," its tropes, and its utopias. If Calvinism placed the modern subject within an "iron cage," as Weber said, it also supplied the tools for springing the locks.

SIX

Comparative Cosmopolis
Discovering Different Paths to Moral Integration in the Modern Ecumene

Richard Madsen

One could apply to Robert N. Bellah the words he used to describe Emile Durkheim: "[His] work reflects the great preoccupations of his predecessors: religion, law, morality, and education—in short, the various ways in which social and individual action are ordered and controlled. And many of his central problems are classical as well: how to reconcile freedom and authority, rational choice and the weight of tradition, individual autonomy and social cohesion. But his answers, though indebted to many influences, were new."[1] Like Durkheim, Bellah has devoted his career to exploring the possibilities of moral order in modern societies. In truly ecumenical fashion, Bellah has pursued these questions by drawing inspiration from an extraordinarily wide circle of diverse theorists. Unlike his mentor Talcott Parsons, however, he has not attempted to organize the work of these theorists into a formal system. His career, indeed, follows a trajectory that is almost the obverse of Parsons's. Parsons's began with *The Structure of Social Action,*[2] grounded in a close reading of texts (albeit texts about theory), and culminated, in books like *The Social System,*[3] with an elaborate, logically interconnected system of ideas spun from his own analytic imagination. Bellah, by contrast, began with Parsons's abstract theories and, although guided and inspired by such theories, culminated in a close reading of texts, notably the interview transcripts and historical works that formed the stuff of *Habits of the Heart*[4] and *The Good Society.*[5]

In his famous essay from 1963 on religious evolution, for example,[6] Bellah argues that religious symbol systems tend over time to get more differentiated and comprehensive and that these changes are connected with more complex, open, and changeable forms of society. Modern societies—in Bellah's definition the most complex, open, and changeable forms of society—are characterized by modern religion. The United States, with its broad middle classes, tends to be seen by Bellah at this stage of his career as the most modern of societies and the natural home of the most modern kind of religion, a kind that maximizes the freedom of personality and society relative to environing conditions and that gives rise to endlessly revisable forms of culture and personality.

But, by the 1980s, in *Habits of the Heart* and *The Good Society,* Bellah and his coauthors[7] give a more complex portrait. The openness and fluidity of American society is seen as based on an extreme individualism that is undermining its social integuments. That American society retains what coherence it has, depends to a significant degree on historic legacies of premodern or early modern religion.

Between "Religious Evolution" and *Habits of the Heart,* then, Bellah moved from theory to history. The essay on religious evolution outlines a majestic, tidy pattern of religious change from archaic times to the present. But works like *Habits* portray a messier, more contingent social reality, the product of historical accident as much as systemic change—a tension-filled blend of old and new cultural languages and moral norms. In this vision, there is no inexorable movement to a new state, only an array of more or less dire possibilities that will be realized in accordance with the capacity of a citizenry to creatively meet their challenges. This vision was, I believe, a realistic view of the moral conditions of America and other Western middle-class industrial societies by the last decade of the twentieth century.

The move from theory to history helped Bellah's work gain widespread public influence. In contrast, as Parsons's work progressed, it became increasingly abstruse and jargon ridden, inaccessible to the general public and mimicking the style of scientific discourse. Bellah's writing became, rather, increasingly resonant and allusive; thoroughly blending theoretical inquiry with empirical research and moral passion, it took on the qualities of humanistic literature and gained a wide audience.

This turn from theory to history is not without costs, however. One of the most attractive qualities of Bellah's later work has been the closeness of the mesh between theory and data. But precisely because of the consequent difficulty in disentangling theory from data, it is difficult to use this work as a basis for comparative research into the bases for moral order in different kinds of societies. This is frustrating, because books like *Habits of the Heart* and *The Good Society* have been seen as so suggestive in insights about the challenges of modernity in different cultures as to have been translated into many languages and read around the world.[8] Most comparative social science uses positivistic frameworks to compare the consequences of structures of wealth and power in the international world system. But there seems to be a felt need among humanist intellectuals for frameworks that can compare the social effects of patterns of meaning and morality in different kinds of modern cultures. There is a need for a comparative sociology not only of the modern world system, but of the modern ecumene, the interdependent global fabric of moral orders as distinguished from the global structure of counterbalancing centers of wealth and power. My aim in this essay is to show how Bellah's perspective can be applied to comparative research on moral order. I will unpack some major theoretical themes in Bellah's work that might be relevant to projects in comparative sociology and discuss how they might best be formulated to give a clear picture of similarities and differences of cultures in the modern ecumene.

INTELLECTUAL CONCERNS

The main theoretical questions driving the work that culminated in *Habits of the Heart* and *The Good Society* came from Durkheim. It is a revelation to reread Bellah's introduction[9] to the volume he edited on Durkheim's discussion of morality and society. Published in 1973, this introduction draws from Durkheim's writing most of the main themes that shape Bellah's subsequent work (and also reveals a main source of inspiration for much of his earlier work). In Bellah's account, "society" is, for Durkheim, an immensely complicated, multilayered reality. Sometimes "society" refers to specific social groups, but other times it is, in Durkheim's words, "a composition of ideas, beliefs, and sentiments of all sorts which realize themselves through individuals. Foremost of these ideas is the moral ideal which is its principal raison d'etre." In Bellah's words, "Not only is society not identical with an external 'material entity,' it is something deeply inner, since for Durkheim it is the source of morality, personality, and life itself at the human level. . . . Durkheim uses the word 'society' in ways closer to classical theology than empirical science."[10]

Bellah uses the idea of society in a similarly wide and deep range of senses. He tends not to focus on specific social groups but, rather, seeks to explicate the moral sinews at the base of social relations. In Bellah's work (and work deeply influenced by him)—unlike work more centrally influenced by Marxist and Weberian traditions—one seldom sees interest groups in zero-sum conflict. Instead, there are persons misunderstanding or failing to understand (in part, because they hold more or less wealth or power but also because they simply do not have a requisite conceptual vocabulary) their fundamental interdependence. Like Durkheim, Bellah's aim is to deepen this common understanding of interdependence and to awaken the sense of mutual responsibility that this entails. Bellah's vocation combines the role of research with that of moralist—and takes on something of the burden of a prophet as well.

The fundamental problem for Bellah, as for Durkheim, stems from the division of labor in modern societies. Such societies are vast assemblages of individuals performing myriad roles. This circumstance leads to tremendous differences among individuals, while making it difficult for them to see their connection to the whole. Durkheim believed that this advanced division of labor required, indeed gave rise, to a new form of moral solidarity—"organic solidarity." In Bellah's exegesis, the meaning of this term for Durkheim is complicated and difficult. Bellah's interpretation stresses the connection between "justice" and "the cult of the individual." The moral solidarity of modern societies must be based on a common respect for the dignity, even sacredness, of each individual, and it also requires "an institutionalized system of enforcing good faith and the avoidance of force and fraud in contract . . . in a word, justice."[11] This moral vision sees a society of diverse individuals who each celebrate the other in their very differences and reconcile conflicts to their mutual benefit by commonly accepted norms of justice.

But how is this vision to be realized? The modern focus on the individual leads to a competition for wealth and power that all too often leads to the denial of the dignity of rivals and to a blindness to the requirements of justice. Following the later Durkheim, Bellah looks especially to religion as the source of the moral energy to create and sustain moral solidarity. As he said in "Religious Evolution," modern society will require (and probably call forth) a modern form of religion, one that maximizes the freedom of the individual personality while still offering a sense of connection to a transcendent ground of being.

Bellah's approach to studying America, then, is, first, to see American society not as an assemblage of interest groups but as an interdependent social whole driven by fundamental principles arising from its division of labor. These fundamental principles are embedded in the story with which *Habits of the Heart* begins—the account of Brian Palmer, a hard-charging business manager who has risen from humble beginnings to relative affluence, ruining his first marriage in the process.[12] Palmer is an individualist whose identity is defined by endless possibilities for mobility among jobs and families and social statuses and by the variety of "values" he chooses, at each step, to express his individual uniqueness. This is Durkheim's modern division of labor, leading to great individual differences but also to difficulties in discerning responsibilities to a larger society.

Nonetheless, this is not a simple Durkheimian picture. Bellah and his colleagues see considerable "lumpiness" in American society. Not everyone has the same opportunities for mobility. There is a wonderful variety of ethnic communities, working-class communities, regional communities, all partially but not completely assimilated into an "American Way" defined by the best-educated and most successful members of the middle class. There are different forms of individualism (and combinations of these forms), deriving from the particular history and circumstances of the nation. Bellah and his colleagues rely heavily on Tocqueville as a guide to thinking about these particularities.

Having developed a complicated portrait of the principles underlying that multilayered, complicated entity called "American society," Bellah asks what kinds of problems of moral order arise from such an entity. He finds the incoherence and anomie that Durkheim would have predicted, but these take on particular American characteristics. He then asks what role religion has played and can play in overcoming this society's moral incoherence. Unlike Durkheim, who believed that established churches, especially the traditionalist Roman Catholic Church in France, could not provide the sacral basis for a modern moral order, Bellah stresses the possibilities of America's traditional denominations resolving the country's spiritual crisis. Finally, like Durkheim, Bellah employs his research to attempt to morally educate. Social science, he and his colleagues write in the appendix to *Habits of the Heart,* should be a kind of public philosophy.[13]

If one were to apply Bellah's line of inquiry to other contemporary societies, one would start with the basic Durkheimian questions, find a way to conceive of a society as a social whole based on principles implicit in its modern division of labor, show how basic challenges to moral order arise from these principles, and look for some religious, or quasi-religious, sources of a new moral order. What are the limitations of this kind of research, and what are the boundary conditions within which it might be fruitfully carried out? What framework can be used to compare one kind of "lumpy" society with another and show what difference that kind of lumpiness makes to the moral challenges faced by each? Where does one look for the sacred in different kinds of societies? And what implications will these differences have for efforts to bring about effective moral education in different contexts?

THE MIDDLE CLASSES AND MODERNITY

Not only *Habits of the Heart* and *The Good Society* but most of Bellah's work for the past thirty years has been grounded in observations of the American middle classes. Although some critics faulted *Habits of the Heart* for focusing on this class to the exclusion of the poor and the very rich, the focus was completely consistent with the theoretical concerns of Bellah's life's work. Bellah seeks to explicate the fundamental principles shaping the social relations of American society as a whole. To find such principles, he naturally looks to that part of society that dominates its culture and defines the moral aspirations of the rest. What was distinctive about advanced industrial societies in the second half of the twentieth century was the emergence of broad middle classes, large and self-confident enough to determine their nations' political culture. Nowhere was this more true than in the United States, which, as Tocqueville had described it, had been predominantly middle class since its inception, and which had been able to extend the material and social conditions of middle-class life throughout its citizenry to an unprecedented degree after World War II. As Bellah began his academic career in the 1950s, the dynamics of such middle-class societies, models for aspiration the world over, were posing new problems of moral order. A study of such societies, especially of the United States, could call forth new answers to classical problems of social philosophy.

Since Bellah has been interested in society in the Durkheimian sense— as a complex, multilayered, fundamentally moral entity—he would not define the middle classes primarily as a collection of groups with interests in wealth or prestige (as they are usually defined, for instance, by contemporary political sociologists, or even by a sociologist of culture like Pierre Bourdieu, who sees the middle classes as an agglomeration of class fractions competing over symbols of distinction).[14] Instead, Bellah has turned to Tocqueville for his primary sense of what a middle class is. *Habits of the Heart* is "explicitly and implicitly, a detailed reading of, and commentary on, Tocqueville, the predecessor who has influenced us most profoundly in thinking about life in America." Tocqueville uses the term "middle class" only once in the two volumes of *Democracy in America,* but central to his argument is that it is crucially important that America is dominated by "people who though neither rich nor powerful enough to have much hold over others, have gained or kept enough wealth and enough understanding to look after their own needs."[15] Such persons owe their position to the "equality of conditions" that defines American democratic culture, and they are the most passionate advocates of this equality. But it is precisely this class that generates the individualism that ultimately threatens the freedoms of Americans. "Such folk owe no man anything and hardly expect anything from anybody. They form the habit of thinking of themselves in isolation and imagine that their whole destiny is in their own hands. . . . Each man is forever thrown back on himself alone, and there is danger that he may be shut up in the solitude of his own heart."[16] Tocqueville claimed that he studied America because developments there were harbingers of changes that would sweep the whole world. In the late twentieth century, theorists like Seymour Martin Lipset have followed him in arguing that a middle class is a necessary condition for the development of modern liberal democracies.[17]

Other late-twentieth-century theorists emphasize different aspects of modernization. Following Weber, many assume that rationalization, in the form of dominance by large bureaucratic organizations, is the primary characteristic. One might have a society that is highly rationalized in this sense without having a large middle class. Other theorists emphasize the production of skeptical, critical thinking under the impact of modern education; still others emphasize the evocation of new desires constantly expanding under the impact of consumer culture. However, societies with these characteristics of modernity are not necessarily—and often are *not*—democratic societies. And Bellah (and his colleagues) are passionately concerned with preservation of a certain kind of moral society, one based on democratic values. It is natural that Bellah focused on that social formation—the middle classes—that seems most crucial to a democratic modernity.

If one were to use comparative sociological research to test and extend the ideas of *Habits of the Heart,* and, indeed, of most later writings of Bellah's career, one would have to confine the comparisons to middle-class societies. And even when comparing these, one would have to be more reflexive and precise in defining middle classes than were Bellah and his colleagues in the 1980s.

Although the middle classes are central to the analysis of *Habits of the Heart,* the term is not precisely defined, at least in its economic or statistical sense. In *Habits,* "middle class" is seen (as for Tocqueville) more in terms of state of mind than of socioeconomic condition. "In the true sense of the term, the middle class is defined not merely by the desire for material betterment but by a conscious, calculating effort to move up the ladder of success. David Schneider and Raymond Smith usefully define the middle class as a 'broad but not undifferentiated category which includes those who have certain attitudes, aspirations, and expectations toward status mobility, and who shape their actions accordingly.'"[18] Of course, a middle-class mentality is dependent on a socioeconomic status that gives people a realistic chance to attain success—enough income to get on at least the lower rungs of the ladder, enough resources to obtain the education and training necessary, in the current world, to climb farther. A middle-class mentality is also dependent on an institutional context that allows people to climb—that allows them to switch jobs and residences in pursuit of success and does not erect barriers to qualified people based on race or ethnicity, for example. Since this mentality is the aspect of middle-class status that Bellah and his colleagues focus on, it is natural that their interviews and observations are carried out mostly with persons in the upper levels of the middle classes, successful professionals like Brian Palmer rather than struggling workers. Insofar as the middle classes are defined by a mentality, the Brian Palmers must be at the moral (though not the statistical) center of the middle class, because they are blessed with just those prospects of mobility that inspire the strongest middle-class mentality. To the extent that struggling workers can realistically dream that they, too, can have such mobility, they will also develop part of this middle-class mentality. Unlike Marxian or Weberian theorists, who would define social class in terms of common economic interests, Bellah sees the middle classes as possessing common interests without seeing interests in common. Their common interest is precisely the maintenance of the conditions for individualistic status competition and makes it difficult for them to perceive extensive solidarity with others.

If a society is so economically polarized that it has only a very small middle class and if such a society is dominated by a zero-sum struggle between the very rich and the masses of the poor, it makes no sense to apply Bellah's perspective. The vision suggested in books like *Habits of the Heart* and *The Good Society* is probably not applicable to most third world countries or to many post-socialist societies like contemporary Russia. Sociologists studying such societies would do well to take their primary lessons from Weber or Marx.

But the Bellah perspective should be broadly applicable to European and Asian industrialized societies that have developed large middle classes. It could be fruitful to compare such societies in terms of Bellah's concerns. Throughout his career, Bellah has been concerned (as were Tocqueville and, later, Durkheim) by the tendency for the middle-class mentality to end in an extreme individualism that blinds people to their interdependence; however, not all middle-class societies exhibit this tendency to the same degree. It would be worthwhile to compare how and why middle-class societies may differ in their individualisms.

To carry out a meaningful comparison, one would have carefully to consider the ways in which the social ecology of middle classes in different countries might make them more or less conducive to individualism. The key factor would be the prospects for mobility afforded middle-class persons. To the extent that such prospects are relatively open or relatively constricted, one would expect differences in a society's forms of individualism. In comparing middle-class societies, one would have to consider the breadth of the middle classes relative to other segments of the societies— for example, through a standard social stratification analysis—and the extent to which their middle classes are increasing or decreasing. One would also need to look at the different institutional configurations of the countries to determine the pattern of mobility that each sustains. The middle classes in Japan, for instance, are much less mobile than the middle classes in the United States. (And the possibilities for mobility among the middle classes in the United States at the beginning of the twenty-first century are different from those of the 1980s, giving rise perhaps to conflicts between an "overclass" of increasingly affluent educated professionals like Brian Palmer and an anxious class of less educated workers that finds itself falling behind—conflicts that force modifications in the analysis attempted in *Habits of the Heart*.) One might hypothesize that, in general, the more mobile a middle class (the more opportunities its members have to rise or fall, as individuals, on the ladder of success), the more individualistic its members will be and the more problematic that they may develop a sense of moral solidarity.

GRID, GROUP, AND MORAL ORDER

To carry out such comparative research as I have outlined, we may need a more abstract frame of reference than that provided in *Habits of the Heart* or *The Good Society*—a frame of reference that can encompass societies that differ widely in history and culture yet have at least roughly comparable patterns of social mobility and comparable problems of moral regulation.

In her book *Natural Symbols,*[19] the English anthropologist Mary Douglas draws on Durkheim to develop a framework for comparative study of the relationship among social structure, moral order, and religious cosmology. Although he did not directly use this framework in *Habits of the Heart* or *The Good Society,* Bellah has explicitly cited Douglas and used her ideas in various talks extending and applying concepts from his works of the 1980s. For Douglas, the structure of a society's moral order, the forms of its cosmologies, its understanding of grace and sin, the meaningfulness of its rituals, all depend on two main characteristics of social structure, which she calls (in somewhat infelicitous terminology) "grid" and "group."

"Grid" refers to the system of classification used in a society to determine roles and statuses, rights and responsibilities. A society with "strong grid" is highly regulated, with strong institutions. Its system of rules and distinctions is comprehensive in scope and highly coherent in form. Everyone has a specified place and faces clearly defined regulations. A society with "weak grid" is one in which the rules and classifications are indistinct and/or in which clearly defined rules only apply to limited sectors of life.

By "group," Douglas refers to the capacity of a society to put social pressure on its members. This capacity is strongest, obviously, when persons are confined to small groups with strong boundaries, so that they cannot escape scrutiny from and interaction with other group members. This is what Douglas calls "strong group." In contrast, the capacity to exert social pressure is weakest when people live in large, open, mobile societies where they can voluntarily choose associates. This is "weak group."[20]

Different combinations of grid and group—for instance, strong grid and strong group, weak grid and strong group—lead to different patterns of moral practices and different kinds of religious belief. Douglas's mode of analysis gives us tools for considering how differences in the structure of middle-class societies might lead to important differences in moral and religious culture.

Applying Douglas's mode of analysis, middle-class American society in the late nineteenth century, especially on the frontiers, may be seen as weak in both grid and group. There were none of the fixed status distinctions of the Old World. Persons could aspire to any social position to which talent impelled them. There was great opportunity to remake oneself, to take up new occupations, assume new identities. At the same time, society, especially in emerging urban areas on the frontiers, was anonymous and fluid. According to Douglas's theory, under these circumstances one would expect a rugged moral individualism that downplayed external ritual formality, rejected the importance of strong religious institutions, and left each individual free to relate to others through the logic of individualism.

But modern American middle-class society differs in important respects. It is characterized by what Douglas would call strong grid but weak group. The strong grid is provided by distant, impersonal bureaucratic organizations, those of modern corporations and the modern state. The modern citizen is confronted with a vast lattice of impersonal categories that powerfully determine social standing—for instance, categories that define his or her intelligence and therefore his or her capacity for the schooling that makes possible a wide array of credentials that give access to occupations that qualify him or her to buy a dwelling in a more or less prestigious community, and so forth. At the same time, middle-class society remains open and mobile. Persons can choose friends and lifestyles, within the constraints provided by levels of income and job security. It is what Alasdair MacIntyre would have called a society of "bureaucratic individualism."[21]

All modern industrial societies with large mobile middle classes are structured according to this strong grid, weak group pattern. But this pattern is not, according to Douglas, exclusively confined to such societies. It is, for example, also found in the "Big Man" systems of certain post-colonial societies.[22] Wherever it is found, she argues, it leads to an opposition between what, in *Habits of the Heart,* are called utilitarian individualism and expressive individualism. This, in turn, leads to an oscillation between an "extremely pragmatic, unspeculative, and materialist belief system" and "a tendency, alternately repressed and breaking out, to millennialism."[23] Douglas interprets the American and European countercultural social movements of the 1960s as examples of the millennialism that alternates with the pragmatic materialism of modern bureaucratically dominated societies. "Students . . . protest against bureaucracy, against exaggerated compartmentalism of study, discontinuous and truncated understanding and loss of personal attachment to the worth of study as a humanistic enterprise." But the tragedy of such movements is that "they do not usually lead to a better society. . . . Anyone who tries to correct the unfeelingness of the bureaucratic machine with a revolution of feeling gives up control of the situation to natural symbols. After attacking definition as such, differentiation as such, ritual as such, it is very difficult to turn about and seek the new definitions, differentiations and rituals which will remedy the case."[24]

Douglas has a sociolinguistic theory to explain how these social structural characteristics lead to cultural outcomes. People socialized under conditions of strong grid and group use a "restricted" speech code. They utilize multilayered, metaphorical symbols that condense many meanings gained through the common experience of relatively closed groups. Some of these "condensed" symbols are felt to be so intrinsically powerful that in the very act of being expressed, they bring about what they signify. Such speech codes are the basis for sacramental religions, based, in turn, on a strong sense of the sacredness of religious institutions.

People socialized under conditions of strong grid and weak group use "elaborated" speech codes. These are, first, based on symbols with specific, clearly defined meanings, which each individual can use to communicate his or her unique interests and feelings with the hope of reaching agreement with someone with complementary interests or feelings. Second, they allow for many fine distinctions classifying the degrees, occupations, and ranks that define the bureaucratic ladders of success. This kind of speech code is the basis for a "positional" moral code that relies heavily on reference to clearly defined expectations based on age, sex, and patterns of relationship. It also leads to a religion of inner experience rather than external form and to a critical consciousness that frees individuals from habitual following of authority, even as it allows them to calculate ahead in a complexly organized world. The elaborated code is obviously the mode of expression and communication of the "symbol manipulators" who comprise the new middle classes.[25]

Following Douglas, we could expect the elaborated speech code to dominate every modern "post-industrial" middle-class society. However, such societies differ in the degree to which they correspond to Douglas's sleek "strong grid, weak group" model. Each society is "lumpy" but in different ways. Consider contemporary Japan. Like all modern societies, it is characterized by strong grid—comprehensive systems of classification and regulation that ensure the coordination and control of a complex industrial society. But, in contrast to the United States, it also has relatively strong group. Though Japan has a strong middle class (there is indeed considerably less of a gap between rich and poor there than in the United States), the Japanese middle classes are not as mobile as in America. Though the Japanese system is in the midst of change, "salarymen" are still for the most part constrained in job mobility. Group pressures bear down more heavily and more obviously on the Japanese than on Americans. There is still a great emphasis on rituals of social deference and loyalty. There is, as well, a greater sense of social solidarity in Japan than in the United States, and thus the religious and moral challenges faced by Japan are different than in America.[26]

Douglas's framework might help us better categorize differences in structure among middle classes. The United States, on the one hand, could be seen as a relatively extreme example of a high grid, low group, modern industrial society. On the other hand, northern European countries could be seen as high in grid and moderately high in group, and Japan as relatively high in both grid and group. These differences lead to systematic differences in patterns of moral discourse: different blends of utilitarian and expressive individualism, on the one hand, and webs of loyalty and responsibility, on the other—and they differ in their patterns of public debate about how to create a proper blend. A systematic mapping of such differences could then provide a way to extend the framework of *Habits* and *The Good Society* to comparative sociology.

RELIGION AND MORAL ORDER

It was Durkheim's hope that modern individualism would not be egoistic, materialistic, and purely pragmatic but grounded in a common consensus that each individual had an inviolable dignity, a consensus leading to a responsibility to affirm that dignity in every member of society. This commitment to individual dignity had to be grounded in a sense of the sacred, achieved through religious ritual and practice. Following this line of thought, Bellah and his colleagues have looked to religion as one of the most important sources for redeeming modern society from its moral disorder. The portrait these authors draw is of a profound interconnection between religion and the conditions of middle-class American life. In this they also reflect Tocqueville's second volume of *Democracy in America*.

According to Tocqueville, American religion is distinctive in the sparsity and the simplicity of its symbolism. It does not use numerous elaborate rituals, it does not have a rich array of mysterious doctrines. Rather, its teachings are logical celebrations of a relatively few fundamental ideas. Moreover, it downplays complex external observances in favor of pure internal intention. Finally, its institutional structures are relatively simple, with an emphasis on congregational leadership rather than on elaborate hierarchies. As Tocqueville put it:

> I have seen no country in which Christianity is less clothed in forms, symbols, and observances than it is in the United States, or where the mind is fed with clearer, simpler, or more comprehensive conceptions. Though American Christians are divided into very many sects, they all see their religion in the same light. This is true of Roman Catholics as well as of other beliefs. Nowhere else do Catholic priests show so little taste for petty individual observances, for extraordinary and peculiar ways to salvation, and nowhere else do they care so much for the spirit and so little for the letter of the law. Nowhere else is that doctrine of the church which forbids offering to saints the worship due to God alone more clearly taught or more generally obeyed.[27]

He notes the congregational style of governance followed by many Protestant sects. This sometimes leads to such fragmentation that the Catholic Church, with its emphasis on an authoritarian unity, appeals to many Americans. But even the Catholic style of leadership is less formal than in traditional Europe.

According to Tocqueville, the reason American religion is less clothed with external forms, symbols, and observances, and its beliefs relatively clear, simple, and comprehensive, is American "democratic instincts." These are based on an "equality of condition" that does away with ascribed aristocratic statuses, removes barriers to individual advancement, and demands that all citizens be treated with equal dignity. The individualism engendered by this condition makes persons suspicious of anyone claiming special privilege as mediator between God and humanity. Thus:

> the more the barriers separating the nations within the bosom of humanity and those separating citizen from citizen within each people began to disappear, by so much the more did the spirit of humanity, as if of its own accord, turn toward the idea of a unique and all-powerful Being who dispensed the same laws equally and in the same way to all men. In democratic ages, therefore, it is particularly important not to confuse the honor due to secondary agents with the worship belonging to the Creator alone.[28]

This attitude leads to clear, simple, and comprehensive beliefs. It also leads people to value independence of mind and to distrust any doctrine that is based simply on tradition or the pronouncement of an external authority. Finally, in a time of equality, "nothing is more repugnant to the human spirit than the idea of submitting to formalities. Men living at such times are impatient of figures of speech; symbols appear to them as childish artifices used to hide or dress up truths which could more naturally be shown to them naked and in broad daylight. Ceremonies leave them cold, and their natural tendency is to attach but secondary importance to the details of worship."[29] An extreme but not uncommon form of this religion in contemporary America is the faith that one of our interviewees named after herself. "Sheila Larson . . . describes her faith as 'Sheilaism.' 'I believe in God. I'm not a religious fanatic. I can't remember the last time I went to church. My faith has carried me a long way. It's Sheilaism. Just my own little voice.'"[30]

For Tocqueville, it is the conditions of American middle-class society that primarily give rise to such symbolically and institutionally spare, individualistic religion—the same conditions that lead to individualism in general. Following his reasoning, we could expect that everywhere one finds the development of a broad, fluid, mobile middle class, one will see the development of relatively individualistic religious practices. And there is indeed empirical evidence for this. However, there remain important variations in the extent to which individualistic forms of religion prevail in middle-class societies and in the influence that religion has on the public life of such societies. We must look to other social forces to explain these variations.

Tocqueville himself gives hints, which are pursued in *Habits of the Heart.* He discusses the movement of a middle-class society toward individualistic religion in the second volume of *Democracy in America.* In the first volume, which is more descriptive and less of an explicitly theoretical, systematic philosophical meditation on the logical tendencies generated by an ideal-typical American society, he writes about the capacity of American religion to counteract some of the atomizing tendencies of American society. Here, religion is more of an independent variable. The particular kinds of Protestantism and Catholicism that were brought to the United States and the ways in which religion has been separated from state power render religion a strong resource for instilling the moral discipline that is essential to the health of a democratic republic. Thus, it is the contingent accidents of American history, not the inexorable logic of democratic society, that has given religion its particular role in America.

As historians and ethnographers of American society, Bellah and his collaborators were attracted to this form of argument. While acknowledging that the character of religion in American society has been profoundly shaped by the fluidity of its middle-class society, Bellah also wanted to show how the heritage of certain religious traditions has helped to overcome some of the more alienating forms of individualism encouraged by the mobility of the middle classes.

He is especially impressed with the possibilities of those religious institutions that retain a strong sense of church—that see themselves as the Body of Christ, as an objective reality not only expressed but actualized by the powerful, condensed symbols of the sacraments. His understanding of this is based on a theory of moral language based directly on the work of Jürgen Habermas and indirectly on theorists like Douglas.

Habermas says that modernization is accompanied by a "linguistification of the sacred." This is equivalent to, in Douglas's terms, a replacement of condensed symbols by the elaborated speech code. According to Habermas:

> the socially integrative and expressive functions that were at first fulfilled by ritual practice pass over to communicative action; the authority of the holy is gradually replaced by the authority of an achieved consensus. This means a freeing of communicative action from sacrally protected normative contexts. The disenchantment and disempowering of the domain of the sacred takes place by way of a linguistification of the ritually secured, basic normative agreement; going along with this is a release of the rationality potential in communicative action.[31]

In Habermas's critical theory, rational subjects create and maintain a "lifeworld" based on normative agreement to critique the "systems" based on the rational pursuit of money and power. Yet, in Habermas's vision, this lifeworld is "linguistified," based on rational argument, not on religious premises.

For Bellah, a completely linguistified lifeworld would not be much of a lifeworld at all. Paraphrasing Habermas, he calls it a "liquefied" world, a form of life not viscous enough to resist the overwhelming "systems" of wealth and power.[32] Douglas would agree, and Bellah calls on her theory to bolster his case.

Douglas believes that a society that uses only elaborated codes is a symbolically impoverished society.

> No one would deliberately choose the elaborated code . . . who is aware of the seeds of alienation it contains. . . . There is no person whose life does not need to unfold in a coherent symbolic system. The less organized the way of life, the less articulated the symbolic system may be. But social responsibility is no substitute for symbolic forms and indeed depends upon them. When ritualism is openly despised the philanthropic impulse is in danger of defeating itself . . . Those who despise ritual, even at its most magical, are cherishing in the name of reason a very irrational concept of communication.[33]

Douglas wants us to choose to retain at least some of the restricted codes and the rituals and sacramental religious institutions they make possible.

Bellah affirmed this position by citing Douglas's ideas in a speech to Catholic school administrators in 1992.

> In a society where group boundaries are weak, where families are often incoherent, where individuals lack a clear sense of positional identity, which is to say that they do not feel innerly connected to their roles, and where the elaborated code of feelings and reasons is much more pervasive than the condensed code of symbol and meaning, then it is hard for people to understand the very idea of the church. I will argue that without a strong sense of what it is to be the church, it is very hard for people to understand the faith, the liturgy and, ultimately, what we are called on to be and to do as disciples of the crucified Christ.[34]

Here Bellah is encouraging Catholic educators to be true to their traditions, and especially to maintain in their students a strong sense of the liturgical life and of the institutional church as the Body of Christ. He thinks that certain "anachronistic" religious institutions, such as the Catholic Church, have an important modern role to play precisely as carriers of restricted codes that help convey respect for the transcendent institutional order that makes society possible.

Nonetheless, he recognizes that, given those individualizing tendencies to which Tocqueville referred, it is often difficult even for Americans who have grown up with a faith like Catholicism, which traditionally has had a strong sense of church, to see themselves as part of an institution that transcends them. Moreover, Bellah recognizes that some main currents of American religion were based on dissenting Protestant traditions that rejected the idea of a transcendent institutional church. He thus does not have a sociological reason for hoping that the idea of the church will continue to act as a counterforce to the atomizing tendencies of American individualism. Instead, at this point he tends to take off his sociological hat and don the robes of a prophet, exhorting cultural and religious leaders to reappropriate those traditions that give a strong sense of the church in spite of everything in modern society that conspires to make such a sense difficult.

His prophecy is courageous, eloquent, and certainly necessary, but could, I believe, be complemented and rendered more persuasive by further comparative sociology. Different societies, with different institutional histories, rely on different sources of symbolic grounding. Douglas's ideas about grid and group may help point out where to look for such grounding.

In all modern societies, the conditions of middle-class life, reinforced by the global market economy and globalized mass media, are generating a spirit of individualism. In each society, however, various social forces place moral limits on that individualism and encourage a sense of social solidarity for the common good. In different kinds of modern societies, the predominant forces for placing moral limits on individualism differ. In a society with strong group like Japan, the forces counteracting individualism come from the family and the corporate work group, rather than from religious institutions; religious practices and rituals celebrate and reinforce the pressures of relatively closed corporate groups. In northern Europe, the welfare state and its attendant institutions provide the limitations on individualism; religious symbols help to enhance the moral authority of the welfare state, but most people do not regularly attend church or ordinarily pay much attention to religion. In the United States, there is little to place moral limits on individualism except religion; thus, people attend church in greater numbers than anywhere in the world, seeking a deeply needed (if not necessarily widely heeded) source of moral rules and a venue for community life. But American religion itself has been deeply individualized and requires prophetic voices like Bellah's to recover sufficient robustness to counterbalance the forces of anomie. Because many people in the United States take religion seriously, however, they may be more willing than their coreligionists in other parts of the world to listen to religiously prophetic voices.

Thus, if one were to look cross-culturally for answers to how to establish a coherent moral order in the face of the atomizing tendencies of individualism, one should not assume that religious institutions would be as crucial to this moral order as they are in the United States. If one were trying to promote a moral education that would instill a stronger sense of solidarity in the face of market-driven individualism in these societies, one might not give highest priority to prophetic witness toward religious institutions.

TERMS OF PEACE AMONG WARRING GODS

Besides comparing societies with relatively strong or weak levels of grid and group with regard to sources of social solidarity, we may compare the societies with respect to the configurations of their institutional grids. If we examine societies with comparably strong grid—comparably high levels of classifications and rules—we may find that different strong grid societies have different *kinds* of classifications and rules. A Weberian analysis may help us in this. Modern persons, said Max Weber, live in a world of "warring gods" that preside, as it were, over highly organized but incompatible value spheres. The demands of kinship, economics, politics, art, erotic love, and science are extraordinarily powerful but inconsistent. The prophets of the great salvation religions tried to dethrone this polytheism by making all spheres of life subservient to an ethic of universal brotherliness (or sisterhood), of "world-denying love." But this project had come to an end with the beginning of the modern era. Now, "the individual has to decide which is God for him, and which is the devil."[35] Weber's is a bleak picture of the moral fragmentation that Bellah strove to overcome through his search for the social bases of moral integration. Yet Bellah came back to Weber's ideas in the last paper he wrote before his formal retirement from the University of California, Berkeley.[36] In this essay, Bellah accepts the realism of Weber's view. "We can imagine that much of the last eighty years of history would only have confirmed Weber in his darkest predictions: 'Not summer's bloom lies ahead of us, but rather a polar night of icy darkness and hardness. . . .'"[37]

Yet Bellah refuses to be as completely pessimistic as Weber.

> At least in the figures of Mohandas Gandhi and Martin Luther King, Jr., we have seen leaders exemplifying the ethic of Jesus, the Buddha and Francis on the public stage and with significant, if not unambiguous, political achievements. Equally if not more significant, we have seen in the years after World War II an effort in Western Europe, usually under some combined effort of Christian Democrats and Social Democrats, to create what has come to be called a welfare state, one that would embody in impersonal legal and bureaucratic structures something of the ethic of brotherly love. Even in the United States there was a half-hearted and inadequate effort in this direction during the middle years of this century.[38]

So it may still be possible to broker a truce between the warring gods—to make the gods of the market economy and the bureaucratic state, especially, respectful toward family life and the life of the mind and heart—to achieve at least partially a social and moral wholeness. It is significant that Bellah looks to two paths toward such wholeness: the charismatic leadership of deeply religious political figures like Gandhi and King, or the creation of a welfare state. Although one could argue that the impersonal legal and bureaucratic structures of the welfare state spring ultimately from religious roots, their establishment and maintenance may in places like Scandinavia owe little in the near term to religious institutions—and the security and solidarity that they provide may undermine the sources of religious devotion.

To determine how people in different societies might enable "an ethic of solidarity and normative standards of social justice to take priority over the pure incentives of profit- and power-maximization," one would have to be attentive to the institutional legacies of these societies, to the ways these societies have, in the past, worked out a balance among value spheres. Comparative research can help us see how and why one society (in northern Europe, for example) will fall back on law and on welfare bureaucracies to civilize the forces of money and power, while another (in Asia, perhaps) will fall back on networks of extended family and kin, and yet a third (possibly in North America) will respond to prophetic leadership from churches. For people committed to the need for creating transnational institutions to bring a moral order to a Hobbesian clash of nations and to the global polarization between rich and poor nations, it would be especially useful to recognize that different societies can rely on different resources to engender their own moral order and that different societies can have different contributions to make to a global moral order.

A comparative study of the institutional sources of moral order would have to be confined, of course, to societies with strong institutions in the first place, for another threat to moral order today comes from the total breakdown of all social institutions, usually because of political or economic collapse. The societies of the former Soviet Union often fall into the "breakdown" category, and there is danger of institutional breakdown from economic crisis in parts of Africa and even parts of Asia. In Douglas's terminology, societies like these have weak grid; there is no stable system of statuses and roles, no agreed-upon rules and responsibilities. Such social circumstances are conducive to the rise of social movements led by charismatic figures, often drawing upon religious symbols. This symbolism helps to create strong groups. But the religious effervescence creating such groups does not sanctify the dignity of the individual, as Durkheim had hoped might happen. Instead, it often divides the world into saints and demons and fosters a war of all against all. Bellah's work, however, does not really provide tools to study this. His (and his colleagues') gaze has been directed toward societies with enough grid, enough functioning, even if fragmented, institutional order, to offer some foundation for the reconstruction of moral order.

Bellah eloquently warns of the consequences of so neglecting repair of social institutions that there is a general collapse. But he has always wanted to repair and to rebuild, not to contemplate the torments of a total system failure.

SEVEN

Mammon and the Culture of the Market
A Socio-Theological Critique

Harvey Cox

Just as a truly global market has emerged for the first time in human history, that market is functioning without moral guideposts and restraints, and it has become the most powerful institution of our age. Even nation-states can often do little to restrain or regulate it. More and more, the idea of "the market" is construed, not as a creation of culture ("made by human hands," as the Bible says about idols), but as the "natural" way things happen. For this reason, the "religion" the market generates often escapes criticism and evaluation or even notice. It becomes as invisible to those who live by it as was the religion of the preliterate Australians whom Durkheim studied, who described it as just "the way things are."[1] My thesis is that the emerging global market culture—despite those who do not, or choose not, to see it— is generating an identifiable value-laden, "religious" worldview. I would also hold that a truly critical theology should make people aware of these religious values and of how they coincide with or contradict Christian values.

There is much disagreement today about the global world market and its culture. But these also display some characteristics about which both advocates and critics agree. For example:

1. Global market culture uproots traditional forms of work, family, and community. In doing so, it also undermines traditional belief systems and moral norms. Some welcome these changes as contributing to "progress." Others lament the erosion of "traditional values." But all agree that the process is universal and apparently inevitable wherever global market culture spreads. Indeed, such changes are often believed to be prerequisite to the development of a genuinely market-oriented culture.

2. Global market culture produces enormous new wealth but tends to polarize populations between a relatively small group who reap the benefits

of this wealth and a much larger group who are excluded from its bounty. For example, in June 1996 the U.S. Census Bureau reported that the gap between affluent Americans and everyone else in the nation was wider than at any time since the end of World War II, and steadily increasing. On a global scale, the disparity was even wider. The result is that as we begin the twenty-first century, in Central America as well as in Africa the "quality of life" levels today are lower than those experienced by the indigenous peoples of Central America and Africa five hundred years ago. There are many who consider this to be *the* scandal of our age. More than 70 percent of the people of Central America live in poverty, 50 percent in economic misery, and these percentages continue to rise each year.

There is relatively little disagreement about the scope of this disparity. But advocates and opponents of the global market economy tend to disagree on how long the polarization will last and how best to overcome it. Advocates claim it is only a temporary phase and that at some future point everyone will be drawn into the benefits. Opponents say this is a false promise, that an unregulated, "free" market economy will always produce enormous inequalities that will only grow worse over time. They also warn that if the entire population of the earth, now about six billion people, were in fact to reach the level of consumption enjoyed today by the elites in industrially developed countries, the planet's resources would be exhausted even faster than they are being depleted now.

3. All agree that an economy is closely related to the possibilities of political democracy. But the nature of the relationship is a highly disputed point. Its advocates say that by dissolving traditional, semifeudal, and corporate-state structures and command economies, the "free market" makes political freedom possible as well. Others claim that when the market becomes this powerful it "marketizes" politics, with the result that the democratic idea of "one person one vote" is replaced by "one dollar one vote." Then, what appears to be a democracy becomes in fact a plutocracy, where the wealthiest groups exert undue influence on the electoral process.

The recurrent debate over campaign finance reform in the United States highlights this dispute. Some defend virtually unlimited contributions as a constitutionally protected exercise of free speech. Others disagree and point out that although theoretically anyone can be elected to the Senate, in actuality only people with private fortunes or who are financially supported by special interest groups with considerable financial resources have much of a chance. Consequently, a majority of U.S. senators are millionaires.

These are all complex debates that will undoubtedly continue for some time. My goal in this essay, however, is to explore the *mainly* implicit value-and-meaning system that market capitalism engenders, sustains, and, in fact, requires. My contention is that, however these debates proceed, the discourse *within which* they are argued (a highly value-laden one) is rarely probed and that the myths that carry these values are scarcely examined at all.[2]

Although, as will soon become evident, I am highly critical of many (not all) of the values of market culture, I do not use the term "myth" here in a polemical sense. I use it, as phenomenologists of religion have for decades, to characterize the empirically nonverifiable assumptions—often stated in narrative fashion—that constitute the worldview of market culture. I realize that others have done this before. What I wish to add is that this worldview is itself grounded in a system of beliefs—sometimes, but not often, stated—that add up to a functioning religion grounded in a doctrine of God.

THE GOD OF THE MARKET AND THE MARKET AS GOD

The religion of market culture exhibits all the qualities of a more classical religion. It has:

A story ("myth") about the origin and course of the human enterprise. The current worldwide "Market Revolution" is seen as the culmination of this history.

An interpretation, often quite explicit, of the inner meaning of human history. It is the story of freedom, with human freedom of choice as its climax.

A doctrine of sin and redemption—what is wrong and how to fix it. More about this will be said below.

An array of sacraments—that is, rituals for delivering the salvific power to those in need of it. This sacramental system focuses on the central act of exercising the freedom to choose by making market decisions: "I shop therefore I am."[3]

A vast catechetical network by which to convey teachings to those who require enlightenment. Advertising is the systematic self-explication of the market faith.

An eschatology (a teaching about the "last things"). This was recently described by Fukuyama in his book *The End of History and the Last Man.*[4]

A pantheon of exemplary heroes—the risk-taking, informal, relaxed, but tough and realistic new breed of entrepreneurs—who inspire emulation as did the saints and martyrs of old.

Most important, the market culture's "god," under whose benevolent, if sometimes mysterious guidance, all things eventually work together for the good. These divine qualities the market culture attributes to the *Market itself* (which I shall, from here on, capitalize to indicate its "divine" status).

THE MARKET GOD

Different religions have, of course, somewhat different—although sometimes quite similar—views of the formal qualities of God. In Christianity, God has traditionally been seen as omnipotent, omnipresent, and omniscient, although these characteristics are partially hidden from human eyes by sin and by the transcendent mystery of the Divine. The Market God also exhibits all these "divine attributes," but, analogously, they are also not always completely evident and must often be affirmed by faith.

1. The Market Is Omnipotent

From the earliest stages of human history there have been markets. But in previous eras the Market was not "God" because there were other centers of value, other "gods." The market functioned within a complex set of traditions and institutions that restrained and guided it. As Karl Polanyi has demonstrated in his classical *The Great Transformation,* only in the past two centuries has the Market been cut loose from these social and ethical restraints and allowed to become the culturally determinative institution it is today.[5]

At first, the Market's ascent to Olympic supremacy replicated the gradual emergence of Zeus above all the other divinities of the ancient Greek pantheon.[6] But recently the Market has become more like the Yahweh of the Old Testament, not just one superior deity contending with others, but the Supreme Being, the only "true" deity, a "jealous God" whose reign must be universally recognized and who brooks no rivals.

In the American school of "process theology" advocated by followers of Alfred North Whitehead, God is *not yet* fully omnipotent but wills to be and is *becoming* so. This would seem true for the Market God. The true, accomplished omnipotence of the Market God would mean that everything was for sale. This is not quite the case. Not yet. But in the logic of the Market, there is no humanly conceivable limit to the infinite reach of consumer choice, the profit motive, and the transformation of creation into commodities. Land is the key example. For millennia of human history, land has held multiple meanings for human beings—as soil, resting place of the ancestors, holy mountain or enchanted forest, tribal homeland, aesthetic inspiration, sacred turf. The Market transforms all these complex meanings into one: land becomes real estate; there is no land that is not theoretically for sale, at the right price. This change radically alters the human relationship to land. The same, of course, is true of water and air and presumably of space and the heavenly bodies. In theological terms, this process appears to be similar to the miracle of transubstantiation in which the ordinary bread and wine of the Eucharist are changed into vehicles of sacred power—only in reverse. Sacred elements are now transformed into saleable products.

The human body itself is the latest, but surely not the last, object of this reverse transubstantiation by the Market. Beginning with blood, but now all organs—including kidneys, skin, bone marrow, eyes, and the heart itself—are being moved into the expanding realm of the commodity. Fathers' sperm cells and mothers' wombs are for sale and rent. But this transformation is not proceeding without opposition. A considerable battle is shaping up in the United States about the effort to market human genes. For the first time in memory, virtually every religious institution in the country, including so-called conservative and liberal ones, have banded together to oppose this new extension of the power of the Market God into the human body that persons of faith believe was created "in the image of God." Many nonreligious people also oppose this extension of the Market, on other grounds.

Occasionally some people try to bite the hand of the deity that allegedly feeds them. On October 26, 1996, the German government, with no previous notice to its 350 residents, ran an advertisement offering the entire village of Liebenberg—in what was previously East Germany—for sale. Its citizens—many of them elderly and retired or unemployed—loudly protested. They had certainly not liked communism, but when they opted for the market economy that reunification would bring, they had hardly expected this. The town, however, includes a thirteenth-century church, a baroque castle, a lake, a hunting lodge, two restaurants, and three thousand acres of meadow and forest. Once a favorite site for boar hunting by the old German nobility, it was obviously entirely too valuable a piece of real estate to overlook. Besides, having once been expropriated by the former East German communist government, it was now legally eligible for sale under the terms of German reunification. The outraged *burghers* of Liebenberg were finally granted a postponement. But everyone realized that in the long run theirs was a losing battle. The Market may lose a skirmish, but, *sub specia aeternitatis*, it always wins.

Lakes, meadows, church buildings—everything now carries its sticker price. But this practice exacts a cost. As everything in creation is transformed into a commodity, human beings inevitably internalize this cultural ethos and look upon the world, nature, each other, and themselves as bearing a colored tag with numbers on it. The inherent worth of things and persons disappears as their sale value defines them. Money and income become the determinants of worth. According to the inscrutable logic of the Market God, if a child is born severely handicapped, and has little to contribute to the gross national product, there is no logical reason to expend valuable resources to keep him alive, unless the value derived from sale of medicines, leg braces, and the CAT scan equipment is figured into the equation. A careful cost analysis might conceivably conclude that it would be economically worthwhile to keep the child alive, but the inherent value of the child's life is not part of the calculation. The same costing out is applicable to older people who have lost their productive utility, but might become customers for nursing homes and geriatric medical suppliers. Health and life itself change before our eyes on the Market altar, and once the God of the Market's rule is complete, everything will be for sale and nothing will be sacred.

In fact, it seems that already not even the sacred is sacred. Recently a sharp controversy erupted in Great Britain when a Railway Pension Fund that had owned the small jeweled casket in which the remains of Saint Thomas à Becket are said to have rested decided to auction it off through Sotheby's. The casket dates from the twelfth century and is thought of both as a sacred relic and as a national treasure. A bid by the British Museum was not high enough, however, and the casket was sold to a Canadian. Only feverish last minute measures by the British government prevented the removal of a national relic from the U.K. In principle, however, and according to the logic of the Market God, there is no reason why any relic, coffin, body, or other national monument—including the Statue of Liberty or Westminster Abbey—should not be for sale.

2. The Market Is Omniscient

Current thinking about the global "free market" attributes to it a comprehensive wisdom that in the past only the gods have known. The Market, it is alleged, is able to determine not just how much things should sell for but also what genuine human needs are, what raw materials and capital should cost, and how much workers should be paid. In days of old, seers entered a trance state and then informed seekers what mood the gods were in and whether it was advisable to begin a journey or enter into a marriage. The prophets of Israel repaired to the desert and then returned to announce whether Yahweh was feeling benevolent or wrathful. Today, the Market God's fickle will is clarified by the daily reports that emanate from Wall Street and by the other sensory organs of finance. Thus we can learn on a day-to-day basis that the Market was "apprehensive," "relieved," "nervous," or even at times "jubilant." On the basis of this information, the faithful make critical decisions about whether to buy or sell. Like one of the devouring gods of old, the Market—aptly personified as a bull or a bear—must be fed and kept happy under all circumstances.

The prophets and seers of the Market God's whims and moods are the high priests of the Market religion. To act against their admonitions is to risk excommunication and possibly damnation. Today, for example, if any government's policy displeases the Market God, those responsible for such irreverence will be made to suffer. The fact that the Market is not at all displeased by rising unemployment or a decline in the living standards of workers, or can be gleeful about the expansion of cigarette sales to Asian young people, does not cause anyone to question the Market's unfathomable omniscience. Like Calvin's inscrutable God, the Market's ways may be mysterious but It knows best.

But the Market God's omniscience seeks further knowledge. The traditional God of Christianity is described as One "unto whom all hearts are open, all desires known, and from whom no secrets are hid." The Market God too wants to see the deepest secrets and darkest desires of our hearts. By knowing our fears and desires, and then by offering commodities-for-sale as the remedy, the reach of the Market can be extended infinitely. Like the gods of the past, whose priests offered up the prayers and petitions of the people, the Market God relies on its own intermediaries: market researchers. Trained in the advanced arts of psychology, which has replaced theology as the true "science of the soul," market researchers—like the confessors of the medieval Catholic Church—probe the fears and fantasies, the insecurities and hopes, of the populace. They are also the Market's soothsayers. But instead of examining bird entrails, they rely on thematic perception profiles, depth interviews, field surveys, and focus groups. Then, by devising powerful images (once mainly the artifacts of the priests, now the favored medium of the marketeers), they link whatever deep human aspiration they uncover to a commodity that has the power, they assure us, to assuage it.[7]

Advertising is both the catechumenate and the confessional of the Market Religion. The penitent is first urged to become aware of his or her failure. Is someone lonely, unattractive, insecure, in need of love and respect? The cure of the soul can heal the most painful flaw. This new item of apparel, houseware, jewelry, software, perfume, tobacco, food, or drink will restore both body and spirit. The proof that the product for sale does provide satisfaction is that we see it replete with icons of carefree, healthy, vigorous people—young, nubile, joyously interracial, and almost always at the beach—and so can be sure of its universal redemptive properties. Now, go and buy, and sin no more.

In the cold light of day it may seem like sheer nonsense to claim that a perfume can bring anyone serenity, that a laundry detergent can solidify anyone's family ties, or that swallowing a mixture of carbonated water, sweetener, and synthetic flavoring can initiate you as a full member of the rollicking fellowship of those who live life to the hilt. But to dare to question the omniscience of the Market is to question the inscrutable wisdom of God. People continue to buy these things, it is argued, and so it is clear they are exercising sovereign consumer choice. Consequently, even things that seem patently absurd must be believed—if only to make sure the mechanism keeps rolling. As the early Christian theologian Tertullian once remarked, "Credo quia absurdum est" (I believe because it is absurd). It seems that the real venue of the *sacrificium intellectum* today is not the church but the mall. It is no longer God but the Market that—by definition—knows all and knows best.

3. The Market Is Omnipresent

The latest trend in Market economics is the attempt to apply market principles to areas that once appeared to be exempt, such as courtship, family life, marital relations, and child rearing. Henri Lepage, an enthusiastic advocate of the world market culture, speaks now about a "total market." Just as Saint Paul reminded the Corinthians that their own poets sang of a God "in whom we live and move and have our being," so now the Market is not only around us but inside us, informing our senses and our feelings. There seems nowhere left to flee from Its insatiable maw. Like the Hound of Heaven, It now pursues us home from the marketplace itself and into the nursery and the bedroom. Once Zeus becomes supreme, he can bear no rivals. Once the logic of the Market is enthroned as omniscient, it demands our devotion in all realms of life. Finding a wife or husband becomes just another example of comparing what is in the showcase and engaging in some carefully calculated shopping. Of course, like other consumer choices, if the customer is not satisfied, then—since there is nothing intrinsic or unique about the item sold—a return-and-exchange policy must be understood as part of the original transaction. Perhaps soon every marriage, not just some, will be preceded by a documented prenuptial agreement—the not-to-be-mislaid sales slip required with returned or exchanged goods.

It used to be thought that at least the inward, or spiritual, dimension of life was resistant to market values. But as the markets for material goods become increasingly glutted, such previously nonmarketable phenomena as adventure, serenity, personal growth, and spirituality are appearing in the catalogs. Since buyers already have all the wardrobe, automotive, and audiovisual gear they can absorb, the eternally creative Market offers personal growth, exotic experiences in unspoiled regions, ecstasy, and "spirituality"—now available in a convenient generic form. In this way, the Market makes available the religious benefits that used to come from prayer and fasting but can now be acquired without the awkward particularity that once limited their accessibility. All can be handily purchased, without unrealistic demand on one's time, as a weekend workshop package on an island resort (with a psychological consultant taking the place of a retreat master).

Advertising is both the basic catechism and the mass evangelism of the religion of the Market God. It is the medium through which the Market shows us what to think and feel about ourselves, and what the Market tells us to do to become what it tells us to be. Like any Christian evangelist, the advertiser is not content with making the message known. He or she presses for a decision. "Act now . . . tomorrow this offer may be over." I believe that theologians should study the images and messages of advertising with great care. These images spell out just what the Market God, the main rival to Christianity in our time, wills and wants. Advertising tells us what is wrong with us (sin) and what we need to do to correct it (redemption). The reason we do not recognize the catechetical evangelism of the Market God for what it is, is that it surrounds us every day. It envelops us so completely in its omnipresent messages that we fail to identify the values, worldviews, and ways of life it promotes.[8]

CHRISTIANITY AND THE GOD OF GLOBAL MARKET CULTURE

The early Christians lived within a complex relationship to the global culture of their time, just as we do today. On the one hand, they took advantage of the *pax romana* to carry the Gospel across the empire. They wrote in *koine* Greek, the lingua franca of the day. But they also found themselves in conflict with the imperial religion and the market culture of their time. This is why they caused such a "a great disturbance," as the Bible reports, at Ephesus. An "idol" is any human creation made into a value that displaces the preeminence of God. Also, an idol, in the biblical view, is hollow. It poses as something it is not. It makes promises it cannot possibly fulfill. The first-century Christians exposed the false promises of the idols. They saw that the idols of their time were promising people life and community, salvation and well-being, but that those idols were in reality completely powerless. They were "not gods at all." So Paul and his followers proclaimed, in the name of the God revealed in Jesus Christ, that gods made of human hands could not deliver on their promises. There was bound to be a great disturbance.

Today the relationship between the now much larger Christian movement and the Global Market God with all its promises is even more complex. One could argue that the emergence of a global technological culture has made a truly global Christian movement possible for the first time. Christians use the hardware and software of the global culture to make the Gospel known. Just as Paul made use of ships, letters, and his Roman citizenship to travel with the good news, so Christians benefit from the worldwide travel and communications technologies of today. Just as the *pax romana* guaranteed by the emperor cult and by the Roman legions provided the space for the expansion of the early church, so today's global village makes possible a global church.

But while the first-century Christians said both "yes" and "no" to the global culture of their time, today's Christians mainly just say "yes."[9] Occasionally, however, here and there Christians challenge the hegemony of the Global Market God. The churches of the United States of America have insisted that human genes should not be marketed. Christians have advocated a simplification of lifestyle so that the goods of the Earth can be shared more equitably. Christians in Latin America and elsewhere have strenuously opposed imposition of an international market economy on their more traditional ways of living. Both the World Council of Churches and the pope have issued statements reminding Christians that there are important virtues the market does not nurture—indeed, mostly discourages—virtues Christians value such as compassion, cooperation, and tenderness. In many churches pastors warn their people against being swept away by the empty promises of consumerism and acquisition.

But frequently Christian churches are reluctant to cause any "disturbance" about the Market God, and even contribute to its growing power. Most often, they do this by simply trying to ignore the Market God and all Its patently non-Christian values. They concentrate on the "spiritual" and leave the "material" to others. What they forget is that Christianity is a radically embodied, and even in one sense "material," faith. God created the material world and found it originally good. Also, the Bible has much to say about economics. The Jewish law protects the poor and those without families from the cruelty of the rich. The prophets issue stern warnings against the privileged and powerful. In Jesus Christ, God actually enters the material world and clearly casts his lot with those on the bottom of the social and economic hierarchy. The Bible is anything but a merely "spiritual" book. It repeatedly warns against the terrible dangers of following after the gods of the market. There may be some religions in which it would be acceptable to ignore the economy, the ways in which the goods of the Earth are produced and distributed; or there may be religions in which one might not take any interest in the culture spawned by an economy, that is, the values it celebrates and the worldviews it promotes. But Christianity cannot ignore these things and remain true to the Bible.[10]

At worst, certain Christian movements actually promote and even sacralize the false values of the Market. In a church in America, I once heard a minister tell people that if they were rich and successful it meant that God had looked with favor on them, and that poor people were poor because they lacked sufficient faith. In a church in Brazil, I once heard a woman give a testimony in which she thanked God that although she once did not have a color television, now she owned one. Rather than help her to question the consumer way of life, which is the main rival of Christian faith today, her church seemed to strengthen and undergird consumerism's values. It is hard to reconcile this woman's testimony, however sincere, with the values announced by Jesus in the Sermon on the Mount.

Christianity and the religion of the global Market also have different views of nature. For Christians, "the earth is the Lord's and the fullness thereof, the sea and all that is therein." God is the only real owner of the earth, the sea, the sky. God makes human beings his stewards and gardeners. But God, as it were, retains title to the Earth. The logic of the Market religion is quite different. Human beings, more particularly those with the money to do so, own anything they buy (and everything is for sale), and they can dispose of it as they choose. But a terrible collision awaits the human race if the religion of the Market God continues to go unchallenged, a future quite different from the rosy one predicted in the promises of the global market forecasts. There is an absolute contradiction when an economic system whose inner logic is based on infinite growth continues to dominate a finite planet. The Market God literally knows no limits. But the Earth's supply of clean air, drinkable water, arable soil, and minerals and fossil fuel is limited. Infected by the pathology of the Market logic, which celebrates "growth" above all else, some Christian groups point to their growth, rather than their faithfulness to the Gospel, as the hallmark of their success.

The Market God strongly prefers individualism and mobility. It needs to be able to move people wherever production requires. It is only hampered when individuals have deep ties to families, local traditions, particular places. Therefore, It wishes to dissolve these ties. In the Market's eyes, all places—and indeed all persons—are interchangeable. The Market prefers a uniform, homogenized world culture with as few inconvenient particularities as possible. We can discern a foreshadowing of what the Market God has in store for us in the indistinguishable airports, luxury hotels, and glistening downtown business areas of the major cities of the global culture. Even food and music and dress, which used to exhibit distinct local cultural qualities, are becoming uniform. Where particularities survive, they are rapidly becoming merely folkloristic, exotic reminders of what used to be. Parodies of local custom are preserved to lend a pseudo-"authentic" flavor to places that have been transformed into commodities in the world travel market.

But Christianity need not become a mere acolyte in the temple of the Global Market God. The early Christians did not shrink from telling the Ephesians that their gods were no gods at all. They did not hesitate to announce and demonstrate a way of life based on sharing, not vicious competition. Acts 4:32 to 5:12 describes the common purse Christians required, and the sorry fate of Ananias and Sapphira, who preferred to accumulate rather than share. In a blow against all leveling and homogenizing, the descent of the Spirit at Pentecost in Acts showed how people could respect and affirm cultural particularities, including different languages, and still live together in a vibrant Spirit-filled community. Although they were not always completely consistent, they were usually unwilling to make compromises with the corrupt religious culture of their day. Paul and Peter and many others died rather than allow Christianity to become yet one more subcult in the imperial religious system, which at that time spanned the known globe. The result of this early Christian resistance was that when the global culture of Rome cracked and fell, Christians were ready to build a new culture to replace it.

Christians are not against a world culture as such. The vision of a single world family stems from the biblical teaching that we are all descended from the same ancestors, and that Jesus Christ died to redeem the whole world, not just one class or nation or race. Christianity, however, envisions a world culture built from the bottom up by the gentle action of the Holy Spirit, not a culture imposed from the top down by an imperial religion or a wealthy elite. The Gospel clearly requires a "preferential option for the poor," not an economic system that rewards the few and excludes the many. Christianity is not against markets, but it is unalterably opposed to allowing the Market ethic to dictate the meaning of life; and the Gospel stands in dramatic opposition to the dominant values of the currently reigning Market Religion.

But will Christians in this global economy manage to resist it as the early Christians resisted theirs? The question is still an open one. If Christians ignore the obvious fact that the global economy has spawned not just a new kind of society but a new Market culture with its characteristic religion, then Christianity will fail in its prophetic task. But Jesus said, "You cannot serve God and Mammon." And what is "Mammon" but Money (as it is translated in the New English Bible) that is growth and productivity and consumption raised to the level of a religious system?

In this new century, Christians will have to develop ways of living marked by communal sharing, not by individualistic accumulation. Christians will have to speak out for the integrity of the Creation against its despoilers. And we will have to expose the false claims of the "gods that are no gods," in the religion of the global market. If we can be faithful to this calling, God may permit us to create something new, just, and beautiful in place of the religious culture of the present world age, when it finally collapses, as it one day surely will.

EIGHT

Selling God in America

American Commercial Culture as a Climate of Hospitality to Religion

John A. Coleman, S.J.

Even schoolchildren might be likely to remember the first *noun* that characterizes Alexis de Tocqueville's two-volume classic. They could easily enough know the work is about *Democracy in America*. Rare, however, would be the student who could correctly guess the pervasive *adjective* that Tocqueville uses to typify that democracy. He calls it a *mercantile* or *commercial* democracy and takes some pains to show how a free market both in ideas and in trade bolsters freedom and equality and staves off serious dangers of revolution.[1]

I want to borrow more from Tocqueville's adjective than from his noun to talk about the climate of receptivity to religion in American culture. I want to connect religion in America to the pervasive free play our culture gives to the market and to market imagery, even beyond the realm of economics. Indeed, some have referred—correctly, it seems to me—to a kind of "market imperialism" to capture this promiscuous American free sway of market logic.[2] At least since the Jacksonian revolution, politics in America has obeyed a market mechanism of trade-offs and interest balancing rather than substantive statesmanship. The culture itself has also followed, by and large, a dominant market logic of commodification and consumerism. Inasmuch as religion is an ingredient of culture, not surprisingly, it too conforms to this dominant market-driven logic.

Democracy, the Tocquevillian noun, to be sure, has important necessary religious corollaries about disestablishment and free exercise of religion. Tocqueville even claims that religion is the first of America's *political* institutions. For one thing, religion creates an independently virtuous citizenry, without which no democratic republic can survive. It becomes the main engine in such a republic by which crass self-interest becomes "self-interest rightly understood"—that is, becomes tamed by a broader communitarianism and some semblance of altruism. It stays the hand of rampant individualism, the *rust*—as Tocqueville, who coined the word "individualism," piquantly calls it—that erodes any democratic republic.

Further, religion generates free associations in the common interest that overcome mere mass mobocracy.[3] This generalization still generally holds true, if we take our cue from the work of the Princeton sociologist Robert Wuthnow on voluntarism in America. Religiously inspired voluntarism is more likely to be communitarian in its motives than is voluntarism that flows from a purely secular, more individualistic, source.[4] And, in America, religion continues to spawn vast associations for service and moral reform. Disproportionately to any other institution, it creates what the Harvard political scientist Robert Putnam calls *social capital*—the networks of trust, mutuality, and cooperation that undergird and fuel democracies.[5] Finally, as Robert Bellah and his associates have argued in *Habits of the Heart* (itself a title lifted from Tocqueville) religion still provides our best cultural language to tame and correct the excesses of the dominant expressive and utilitarian individualism of our society.[6]

But the special nature of religion in America cannot be laid entirely at the feet of democracy's disestablishment. The market, or the vigorous entwining of religion with it in a commercial culture, also partially explains why, in historian Jon Butler's phrase, America is *Awash in a Sea of Faith*.[7] America easily stands out, among industrial nations, in the percentage of its population (over 90 percent, by recent Gallup Poll data) who believe in God and regularly (approximately 40–50 percent) attend public worship. Compare this fact to statistics for Europe, which run as high as 40 percent of the population claiming *not* to believe in God, and national European rates that show as few as 10 percent who regularly go to church. R. Lawrence Moore captures this sense of religious vitality in America:

> In 1991, 90 percent of all Americans identified themselves as religious. Most Americans go to church—in percentage terms as many as a hundred years ago, and vastly more than contemporary Europeans. National leaders lace their public statements with religious sentiments with a frequency surpassed perhaps only in Middle Eastern countries. Religious symbols and references crowd into our marketplaces, our commercial media, our sporting arenas, and our places of entertainment.[8]

Or, as the sociologist Seymour Martin Lipset once put it:

> With the exception of a few agrarian states, such as Ireland and Poland, the United States has been the most God-believing and religion adhering, fundamentalist and religiously traditional country in Christendom, as well as the most religiously fecund country where more new religions have been born than in any another country.[9]

Indeed, it is only by remaining awash in the sea of an unverified a priori theory unrelated to any data (a theory called *secularization,* which has very little relevance for explaining the American cultural situation) that some historians, social scientists, and members of the media elite can be surprised that in America, far from a tale of declension, it is a story of religious *ascension,* such that religion in America flourishes more today than at the time of the American War of Independence or on the eve of the Civil War.[10] Drawing on careful data supplied both by the Gallup organization and by the National Opinion Research Organization in Chicago, the sociologist Andrew Greeley has shown that in the United States there has been no net religious change in practice, attitudes, or beliefs in the last fifty years.[11] What religious change there has been represents less a decline than a *switching,* a kind of musical chairs: if some mainline Protestant churches have experienced serious declines, these have been more than offset by the growth of the evangelical churches.[12] Americans give seven times more money to religious organizations than to political parties. As the political scientists Sidney Verba, Kay Schlozmann, and Henry Brady show in their careful comparative study of civic voluntarism in America, *Voice and Equality,* church-generated associations are more likely than secular civil organizations or business to inculcate democratic principles and to further equal voice in our democracy.[13]

Three relatively recent important interpretations of religion in America may help to probe how, by becoming a full part of commercial culture and accepting the market, religion came to flourish in America. The first is the Cornell University historian R. Lawrence Moore's 1994 book, *Selling God: American Religion and the Marketplace of Culture;* the second is the award-winning 1993 *American Journal of Sociology* article, "A New Paradigm for the Sociological Study of Religion," by Stephen Warner of the University of Illinois, Chicago; the third is the 1995 *Material Christianity,* by Colleen McDannell, a historian who uses anthropological methods. I will use these three sources to ask both how America's commercialization of culture has furthered religion and what ironic price American religion may have had to pay for the resultant comparative vigor.[14]

I. SELLING GOD

One problem of overstressing disestablishment as the only variable to describe American religious vitality is that this variable does not emphasize enough the strenuous religious entrepreneurship that has characterized American religion. Vigorous religious activists and innovators went out and churched the frontiers, built the country's ethnic churches, created new forms and reformed the old. Nor does such a description explain how it came about that only decades *after* disestablishment did religion finally spurt in growth. Once it lost legal privilege, "religion had to sell itself not only in the competitive church market but also in a general market of other cultural commodities that were trying, in many cases, to break free of religious disapproval rooted mainly in Protestant animosities."[15] Moore's first great law on religion and the market reads, "If you do not commodify your religion yourself, someone else will do it for you."[16] The pop singer Madonna's successful musical videos exemplify his point for Catholics.

Soon after disestablishment, with the expansion of the print medium into a burgeoning market, popular novels and newspapers began to compete with churches for time and ideas. The first reaction of the churches—and here we get something like a second law from Moore—was to oppose the new commercialized form of the novel as inimical to religion. Soon, however, they saw that if they could not beat it, they could join it, by sponsoring new forms of the uplifting and edifying novel, for example, Pastor Mason Locke Weems's often prurient looks into the worlds of sin, *The Bad Wife's Looking Glass, God's Revenge Against Gambling, The Drunkard's Looking Glass.*[17] The churches also began publishing their own newspapers and journals with a vengeance (and severe competition for readership). Their strategy was to fight fire with fire.

In a later era, as migration proliferated across the frontier, Baptists and Methodists outstripped the old-line Episcopalians, Presbyterians, and Congregationalists on the frontier because, through revivals with their panoply of play, celebration, and noise, they made going to church seem fun and exciting in a period when leisure was increasing and secular forms of entertainment (e.g., P. T. Barnum's circus) provided competition. Here again, a first phase of opposition on moralistic grounds yielded to a second stage in which the churches fought fire with fire by entering the world of commercial culture. One form this took consisted of public showings of the Hudson River painters' nature canvasses (a distinctly, indeed *the,* distinctly Protestant American form of religious art), such as Frederick Church's display of his massive painting of Niagara Falls, which attracted one hundred thousand viewers in two weeks in 1857 and for which "[t]he admission price of twenty-five cents was affordable and yielded a substantial return."[18] Besides making money, Church emulated his teacher, Thomas Cole, in seeing his nature paintings as a "triumph for religion." Another form of religion's attention to the market was a move to oppose music hall entertainment by support for family entertainment in *legitimate* midtown Broadway theaters. The churches in the nineteenth century did not, in short, eschew entering the world of popular culture and entertainment, any less than Pat Robertson, in the twentieth, has shrunk from the new commercial world of television.

Nor did the churches shy away from the gimmicks of self-promotion—the use of handbills, newspaper ads, and the telegraph—to sell their wares. With the rise of popular entertainment, the church again entered the lists, so that, even as the secular lyceum performances became more commercialized and dependent on advertising, preachers used the new medium and new marketing techniques to attempt to improve standards of public discourse. The success of the churches in competing with commerical entertainment was poignantly clear in Frances Trollope's narration of her discomforting visit to the city of Cincinnati. There she saw an immensely populated hall (with an equally immense ticket take) filled with persons who came to hear Robert Owen, the utopian socialist, and Alexander Campbell, founder of the Disciples of Christ, debate the truth of Christianity, with Owen taking the role of the village atheist. Trollope found Cincinnati a city where the theater, balls, and other entertainment she had known in London languished for want of patronage, while these debates drew a thousand people. Reflecting on "the triste little town" of Cincinnati, she noted, "A stranger from the continent of Europe would be inclined, on first reconnoitering the city, to suppose that the places of worship were the theatres of the place." The cultural life of London had not prepared her to imagine that religion might be fun. The groanings and shrieks that she heard at camp meetings and revivals, which she interpreted as a form of debased theater, made her "sick with horror," and she noted, "The coarsest comedy ever written would be a less detestable exhibition for the eyes of youth than the sight of violent hysterics and convulsions, seizing young girls who fell on their faces exclaiming 'O Lord Jesus, Help me Jesus,' and the like."[19]

The same churches that used market models to compete with secular entertainment also created a new form of "muscular Christianity" to gain young men for God through the YMCA. We should never forget that this church-based organization created the quintessential American institutions of basketball and volleyball (in, respectively, 1891 and 1895), just as earlier religious revivals suggested the form and characteristic hoopla of political party conventions (a later arrrival). These churches also quickly moved into new forms of commercial leisure, especially summer bible camps for families, predecessors of the vacation spas of the twentieth century. Moore remarks on a "frank combining of religious revivalism with sea bathing, vacations and commercialism" in Methodist summer camps—such as California's famous Pacific Grove on Monterey Bay. Andrew Dixon White, the first president of Cornell University, "a man whose stiffness had nothing to do with theological conservatism," wrote sneeringly that he was "repulsed by the sight of young people roller skating with arms around each other to a waltz version of 'Nearer My God to Thee.'"[20]

Few rivaled Dwight Moody in his astute use of business methods, methodical canvassing of urban markets for revivals and placing of ads for these (not, it should be noted, on religion pages but in newspaper entertainment sections). But if Moody knew how to massage the market, he also contributed to it. New York City had to build a new streetcar line to Brooklyn to accommodate the crowds who went out to his revivals there. Moody was strongly supported by the Philadelphia department store entrepreneur

John Wannamaker, a stalwart national officer of the YMCA, whose article, "Bringing Business Efficiency Into Christian Service," had a strong impact on the third great awakening of urban religious revivals.

Bruce Barton, cofounder of one of the nation's largest advertising agencies, in his phenomenally best-selling 1925 book, *The Man Nobody Knows,* pictured Christ as a canny businessman, a kind of Rotarian glad-hander. As Barton put it, "Christ picked up twelve men from the bottom ranks of business and forged them into an organization that conquered the world."[21] Nor could anyone in Los Angeles forget how Aimée Semple McPherson became, quintessentially, the best show in town—her life recounted in at least four movies and made-for-TV productions.

The Salvation Army, too, knew how to tap into the resources of America's burgeoning commercial culture. Barton helped, with advertising slogans ("A man may be down but he's never out!"). Wannamaker advised Salvationists on their retail enterprises (including a "Commander's day" sale). However, these commercial trappings could not totally transform the Salvationists' religious impulses of compassion. Late-nineteenth-century philanthropists were appalled that the Salvation Army did not require more in the way of sobriety, industry, and grooming from their beneficiaries. Religion only went so far in embracing commercial propriety.[22]

Protestants were not alone in recognizing religious entrepreneurship. As Robert Orsi notes in his important study of Catholic popular religiosity, *Thank You, St. Jude: Women's Devotion to the Patron Saint of Hopeless Causes,* "There was a striking convergence in those years [i.e., the 1920s] between novel forms and methods of devotional promotion and the new American advertising industry. Both were using ever more extravagant language to sell their products to a new national market that they were simultaneously constituting and exploiting and both were directed mainly at women."[23] Orsi's study provides an important nuance to my discussion of religion and commercial culture. While the clerics who promulgated devotion to Saint Jude sought, in Orsi's view, mainly to raise money and employed openly commercial methods to do so, devotees of Saint Jude, paradoxically, found through such devotion means to act quite counterculturally. They opposed, with the saint's help, male domestic violence and found their own voice to suborn the passive consumer role that the growing commercialization of American medical practice fostered. This example, like that of the Salvation Army, attests that religion, so entwined with commercial culture, nevertheless need not simply mirror it.

Televangelism and Christian Retailing

This marriage of religion and the market shines forth in the generous share of religious broadcasting appearing on radio and television. As Moore notes of televangelists, theirs is an arena "in which everything is up for sale, in-cluding an assortment of Armageddons seeming to exceed in number all the varieties of dog foods, canned soups and ribbed condoms in an upstate New York grocery store."[24] The same market mechanism drove door-to-door bible selling in the nineteenth century and the prodigious Christian retailing by Christian bookstores today. Indeed, Christian retailing—the selling of Christian goods and services—is a significant aspect of contem-porary American religious life; sales of Christian products in Christian bookstores exceed three billion dollars annually. As Colleen McDannell notes, "The trade show where Christian bookstore buyers come to order new books, necklaces, note pads, CD's, bibles and Bible paraphernalia ranks in the top 3 percent (in terms of square footage) of the almost 6000 annual trade shows in the United States."[25]

Again, the intertwining of religion and the market can be seen in the Church-Growth movement, where, in new tracts, "[d]enominational lead-ers read maps with an intensity that challenged land speculators and pro-spective settlers as they gauged a region's hope and development."[26] More-over, the new megachurches, such as the Vineyard Ministry and Calvary Chapel—a movement that the University of Southern California professor Donald Miller claims is virtually redefining American Protestantism—care-fully study census tracts and market data and appeal in their worship styles to the upbeat music and entertainment values found among their prime tar-get audience of consumers, age eighteen to fifty.[27] Jon Butler even suggests that religion may have led the way in creating national markets:

> A comparison with American economic development reveals how the growth of denominational institutions after 1790 created national "spiritual econo-mies" that preceded their material counterparts. By all accounts, national markets developed very slowly and erratically after 1776. . . . Indeed, in eco-nomic life, the Civil War may not have shattered the national economic sys-tem so much as it fully exposed the long failure to achieve one. Many denom-inations, in contrast, had shaped their spiritual markets at least by 1820 and perhaps earlier.[28]

Lest, like Andrew Dixon White, we throw up our hands or hold our noses at something so crass as an economic model for understanding religion in America, we need to hear the following two nuances from Moore:

> Religion is not clearly worse off or less "spiritual" than it once was. After all, if religion is to be culturally central, it must learn to work with other things that are also central. Previously, that might have been feudalism, kings or Platonic philosophy. More recently it has been market capitalism responsive to con-sumers with spare time and a bit of money to spend. If contemporary religion in America seems to lack anything suggesting transcendence, it may be be-

cause it has not had much to work with. Religion by itself never made any age great.[29]

What religious leaders did early in national history, they continued to do later. They opposed many new forms of commercial culture as these came along; they also tried to set up attractive, alternative diversions under church sponsorship. These efforts gave American religious life a distinctive quality. For one thing, most committed religious leaders to popularization. These leaders had to attract people to what they were doing. Whether trying to clamp controls on the marketplace of culture or not, they found themselves using the language of selling and commodification. We need to remember this: the word "spiritual" is a culturally constructed, highly problematic concept. Whatever its subjective import, its visible manifestations change over time. For what people call the spiritual to have any worldly or public importance, it has to be recognizable as something tangible—some institution, set of legal privileges, or anointed group of officials. In the United States, the tangible form of the spiritual lay in the proselytizing that made churches resemble *non*religious offerings in the marketplace of culture. Spirituality lay in hard-sell church campaigns and in the efforts of religious leaders to decide how culture was marketed, in what formats, with what claims, to which audiences. Without these campaigns, we might not be talking about spirit at all. In American life, religion had to become a commodity, but that did not make it peanut butter.[30]

II. THE NEW PARADIGM FOR THE SOCIOLOGICAL STUDY OF RELIGION IN THE UNITED STATES

Steve Warner's new paradigm for the sociological study of religion opts straightforwardly for an economic model that speaks of religious markets, supply-side entrepreneurs, and consumer demand for religious goods and services. It speaks of winners and losers in the religious market. This new paradigm drops all preoccupation with secularization (certainly in the case of the United States, where secularization does not readily apply) and asks more why religion flourishes here and which forms of religion are likely to garner large market shares than why the expected decline of religion has not eventuated. It turns away from older paradigms, which mainly looked to religion as a property of *whole* societies, to emphasize instead that religion more typically fits *subcultures* and smaller niches; religion, according to this paradigm, is more the vital expression of subgroups than some wan civil religion of an entire nation. Warner postulates five things about religion in the United States: (1) it is disestablished; (2) it is culturally pluralistic; (3) it is structurally adaptable; (4) it empowers people, especially marginalized groups; and (5) it is voluntaristic.

Culturally Pluralistic

Pluralism, itself, has a market character. The greater the pluralism of religions (the greater the competition in the religious market), the greater the religious mobilization of the population. Countries with monopoly religions do not generally flourish religiously. But there is more to this evocation of pluralism. Warner uses this subhead for a section of his article: "The Master Function of Religion in the United States: Social Space for Pluralism."[31]

In pluralist and multicultural societies, issues of identity and boundary become more acute. Who am I, and where do I fit in? are questions that are harder to answer there. But religion is better placed than most other sociological vehicles (e.g., race, gender, ethnicity, moral worldviews), both for setting *boundaries* and building *bridges*.[32] As Warner notes, "In the United States, religion mediates difference. Religion is the institutional area where U.S. culture has best tolerated difference. Meanwhile, religion is one area of difference that in the United States is experienced by most communities as authentically expressed rather than illegitimately imposed."[33] American religion legitimates sanctuaries and refuges for cultural particularities.

Warner is here suggesting that in a country like the United States, where there has been massive denial (perhaps never more than now) over social class differences, near-paranoia about boundaries based on linguistic differences (sparking, for example, the passion to impose English as the nation's single official language), and disapproval of hyphenated names that try to keep ethnic identities alive, religion has the advantage of providing identity markers, while allowing bridges across race, language, sexual identity, and ethnicity. The pluralism that helps religions to flourish also creates climates of religious toleration. As Moore states, "When people think of religion as something to be sold rather than something imposed—something advanced in the prospect of a mutually beneficial contract—which parties are free at all times to accept or reject—religious toleration advances."[34]

Structurally Adaptable

Religion in America, moreover, has shown itself structurally adaptable. Jewish synagogues somehow found ways here to seat women and men together. In general, immigrants took their Old World religion and gave it new shapes. Indeed, "[b]ecause religion in the United States is an accepted mode. . .of establishing distinct identity and intercommunal negotiation and because migration itself is often a theologizing experience, religious association may be more salient for both individuals and the group after immigration than it had been before immigration."[35] For evidence of this, one might visit a Vietnamese Catholic parish or a Korean Presbyterian congregation or explore why the modal Asian in America is a Christian. Warner gives a striking example of this structural adaptability:

> Among immigrant Muslims, the mosque, established in Islamic countries as a place for prayer, has become an educational and service center to meet the needs of the Muslim community, a congregation, in other words, with adult classes, potlucks and coffee hours. The iman, who, according to Sunni Islamic practice, is simply the prayer leader, has become in America a religious professional who celebrates marriages, counsels families, visits the sick, conducts funerals and represents his people among the local clergy, modeling himself, in the process, on pastors, priests and rabbis.[36]

Empowering

Religion in America, Warner argues, flourishes because it empowers individuals and groups. In his empirical work on the significance of the Metropolitan Community Church among gay Christians and in ethnic parishes across the country, Warner notes, "[T]he special potency of religious institutions comes from answers they give to a group's need for faith in the justice of their cause and the inevitability of triumph. Such faith depends on the conviction, misleadingly called 'other-worldliness,' of the existence of religious reality."[37]

Religion as Voluntarist

Finally, religion in America is voluntarist. One joins or leaves at will. And a great deal of switching does take place. One in three Americans now belongs to a church other than the one into which he or she was born. But there is a sociological truism: "For those who shift from one faith community to another, it also means greater religious involvement—contributing money to the church, greater prayer and bible reading[,] . . . searching for more meaning in religious participation."[38] Further, religion in America is voluntarist in several ways. De facto congregationalism occurs even in hierarchical churches such as Roman Catholicism; people vote with their feet and identify with the parish of their choice. Voluntarism is attitudinal as well; 80 percent of Americans, according to Gallup Poll data, agree that an individual "should arrive at his or her religious beliefs independent of any church or synagogue."[39] Growing churches such as the Vineyard are inherently churches of converts. Warner comments, "Taken for granted, traditional religion is passe. Born again, return to the fold, neotraditional religion is all the rage," not only among evangelicals but also among Jews.[40]

Warner is not heavily judgmental of this trend. Religious mobility and switching are facilitated by several social facts:

> including aggressive proselytization; the emphasis on loyalty to God over institutions that is part of the evangelical—and hence, mainline Protestant—

tradition; members' intermittent involvement, such that some who are formally church members may not feel committed and therefore not disloyal
when they leave; life-cycle events such as marriage, particularly religious in-
termarriage; children, for whom one may want to choose an appropriate Sunday school; and geographic mobility. Geographic mobility requires people to
choose a church. Since denominations are not homogeneous, a church of
one's former denomination in the new location may not "feel right." Denominations themselves change, and the switcher may well perceive that it is not
she or he who left the fold.[41]

Something like this list helps me, at any rate, to locate and understand
the members of my Irish Catholic family who are now Lutheran, Jewish, or
evangelical.

Yet a more careful parsing of this denominational-switching behavior
forces us to appeal to a sociological "something" other than Warner's market mechanism. The distribution of religious switching needs to be looked
at more closely than is usually done in surveys that break worshipers down
into the categories of liberal versus conservative Protestants, Catholics, and
Jews; it is necessary to pay attention to who is switching and where they
are going. Eighty-three percent of those raised in Catholic families still
self-report themselves as Catholic. Those who switch out of Catholicism between birth and age sixteen are 6 percent nonreligious; 4 percent evangelical; 2 percent fundamentalist; 2 percent mainline Protestant; 3 percent liberal Protestant. Seventy-eight percent of those raised Evangelical remain in
the fold. Fifty-seven percent of those who are Fundamentalist, 51 percent
of mainline Protestants, and 57 percent of liberal Protestants remain in the
faith in which they were born. Catholics pick up 14 percent of these former
Protestants, and 16 percent join the nonreligious.[42] Clearly, a mere appeal
to a market mechanism to explain this religious switching does not do justice to cultural and institutional realities. Presumably, the religious market
should be equally open to invade the niches of Catholics and Evangelicals,
yet these hold on to members better than do mainline or liberal Protestants.
Some factors that a market mechanism cannot catch—loyalty, commitment, institutional and communal sensibilities—need to be evoked to truly
explain this phenomenon of religious switching. No evidence exists, for
example, that Catholics do a better job of marketing than evangelicals, yet
Catholic retention rates are higher. The sociologist will not find the market
analogy sufficient to explain these data.

III. MATERIAL CHRISTIANITY

I will be more brief in my response to Colleen McDannell's brilliant and
groundbreaking study, *Material Christianity*. McDannell's thesis is both simple and breathtaking. People want to feel, touch, and smell their religion.

They use artifacts, ranging from home altars to bumper stickers, to create a material Christianity that may speak louder and clearer than sermons, pastoral letters, or hymns—a fact with implications for the cultural receptivity to religion. The market in religious goods (call it *kitsch* perhaps) mainly drives the profits of religious bookstores. McDannell ranges widely in her book from the temple undergarments worn against the naked skin by Mormons, to wall plaques with biblical citations that adorn kitchens, to religious pictures in front rooms, and from metal biblical verses affixed to refrigerator doors to baseball caps with the caption (aping the Coke ad) "Jesus, the real thing." She displays pictures of T-shirts advertising "I will not be here when the Rapture arrives" and of coffee mugs proclaiming "I love Jesus." During the last papal visit in 1987, entrepreneurs even sold little popes on a rope of soap. Next to my sink is a small souvenir fan with a picture of John Paul II, sold to fan oneself if it became too hot in Candlestick Part where he said mass.

Material Christianity in America breaks down rigid walls between the sacred and profane and brings religion into the everyday. Statues of Saint Francis adorn front gardens, and medals of Saint Christopher are found on dashboards. Not only does attention to material Christianity uncover the ubiquity and pluralism of religion in America, but it reminds us that religions that embody their truth in material artifacts tend to flourish better and more readily find ways to negotiate the chasm between belief and everyday life. Delivering the H. Paul Douglas Lecture at the national meeting of the Religious Research Association several years ago, Barbara Wheeler of the mainline Presbyterian Auburn Seminary in New York recounted her sojourn in the world of evangelicals. She talked about the enormous variety of Bible cozies—brightly colored knitted covers, sometimes purselike, for Bibles—and the world of religious knickknacks and bric-a-brac adorning evangelical bedrooms, kitchens, bumper stickers, and gardens. She lamented the absence of anything tangibly material in mainline Protestant church culture and suggested that the absence of a richer material Christianity may help explain the slow decline and impending death of many mainline Protestant liberal churches.[43] Selling the ubiquitous artifacts of material Christianity clearly takes religion, once again, into the market place.

IV. LIMITATIONS IN THE MARKET PARADIGM

Lest my apparent mania for the market mechanism to explain the effervescence of American religion be taken without nuance, let me add that there are very important things no market can produce for us. First, markets are not very good at tradition. Markets thrive on innovation, on the "new"—at their worst, on ephemeral fads and fashions. They itch for new products. There is irony in the fact that, in America, religion—which is inherently traditional and deals with the passing on of values and beliefs across generations—leans so heavily on a mechanism that undermines and disvalues tradition. A community of memory, such as a religious tradition, has to sometimes run counter to market individualism to survive. Its logic as a community of memory and commitment must undermine rather than reinforce market logic.

Second, markets do not encourage loyalties or commitment. Economic competition entails a search for the best product and the abandonment of older, less efficient, or more costly, forms. Again, this mechanism seems unpropitious for religion, which roots itself in commitment and loyalty. Third, most markets are content-blind. They push process and packaging more than truth. But religion depends, somewhere, on an appeal to something as old-fashioned as truth.

Notoriously, the consumer needs a great deal of genuine information (rarely supplied in a commercial democracy) to be a truly rational economic chooser; lacking such information, *caveat emptor.* America is such a good market for religion because it combines, across the land, the heady mix of spiritual hunger and identity-seeking with massive spiritual illiteracy. When New Age channelers are placed on the same supermarket shelf as Zen Buddhism or Catholic mysticism, in the presence of massive illiteracy about authentic religion, America may need a very large dose indeed of *caveat emptor.*[44] The tragedies of Jim Jones's People's Temple, Waco, and the Bo-Peep Hip-Hop and Rashneesh cults are object lessons of the dangers of letting the market determine what will sell. No foreign visitor since Tocqueville's time has missed the ubiquity and effervescence of American religion. G. K. Chesterton once said that this is a nation with the soul of a church. But most such visitors also remarked that they did not find this flourishing religion terribly deep. Markets, after all, are totally blind to the good, the true, the beautiful. So religious entrepreneurs need to monitor carefully the ways a culture of market individualism depletes the very substance of their message—lest, instead of the Weberian "elective affinity" between religion and material forces, sheer mimesis wins the day. As Randall Balmer notes, some thoughtful evangelicals are raising their voices against a vulgar "prosperity theology" that distorts scripture to make it palatable to middle-class kids wishing to go out in the corporate world and rise to the top for Jesus.[45]

Finally, markets do not encourage prophets. Not only is a prophet without honor among her countrywomen, but rarely do prophets bring in or make a profit. Moore ends his book sounding rather like the wisdom of Solomon in Ecclesiastes:

> Where are the real religious prophets? Can there be any in a country whose self-image rests on fast, friendly and guiltless consumption? It is not the taste

of the Big Mac that sells it; it is the way it feeds the low-down common desire to be democratically unpretentious. Would-be religious prophets have to learn the ways of Disneyland in order to find their audience, but even that popular touch cannot give them the capacity to reach the many Americans who would feel perfectly comfortable at a prayer breakfast held under McDonald's generous golden arches. How can the prophets among us terrify those people with an apocalyptic vision of a planet left desolate by careless stewards who have used up its fields, wasted its energy and blackened its air and waters? How can they make them understand that when Adam and Eve broke a commandment against a forbidden consumption in the Garden of Eden, forbidden because it was need-less, they were pointing humankind toward its final agony? Probably they cannot. So we are left with nothing new under an unforgiving sun whose burning rays carry cancer and God knows what else through an ozone depleted atmosphere.[46]

To know why American religion flourishes and what forms are likely to garner a large slice of the market (indeed, to know some of the cultural forms almost every religion will take in our culture), one may indeed turn to sociology of religion and its new paradigm for the study of religion. The economic model does go a long way toward explaining what needs explaining. But there is an important caveat here. Appeal to a market analogy must be uncoupled from a sometimes-cognate resort to the rational-choice model of the human actor derived from economics. The latter is inimical for any truly nonreductionist view of religion. Because the model of the human person used in rational choice models is so truncated, it does not allow for a model of a person as truly religious.[47]

But to answer Moore's last question, one must look elsewhere. The answer one finds may not sell in Peoria, but it may just be what is true. And the answer will have to take us beyond the "new paradigm" of Warner to older institutional and phenomenological paradigms that insist, with Durkheim, that religion (even as a social phenomenon) is sui generis, irreducible to markets, politics, and opinion poll data. Robert Bellah has, for one, always insisted, in what he refers to as "symbolic realism," on some variant of this notion.[48] What the Warner paradigm does seem to miss are sociological models of culture and of social institutions that stress conflict, moral contrariety, and even countercultural reactions. The religious traditions are not simply in polite competitive conversation in a free-market polity. They also stand for some truths that do not derive at all from markets, even if the best religious entrepreneurs have always used the ubiquitous American market mechanisms—sometimes to the peril of authenticity—to sell their wares.

NINE

In Search of Common Ground
Howard Thurman and Religious Community

Albert J. Raboteau

In 1929 Louis Armstrong recorded a version of a Fats Waller song, "(What Did I Do to Be So) Black and Blue." In this classic blues, Armstrong's voice and horn probe the existential pain of racism:

> Cold empty bed, springs hard as lead,
> Feel like old men, wished I was dead.
> What did I do—to be so black and blue?
> Even the mouse ran from my house.
> They laugh at you and scorn you too.
> What did I do—to be so black and blue?
> I'm white inside, but that don't help my case.
> Cause I can't hide what's in my face.
> How will it end?
> Ain't got a friend.
> My only sin is in my skin.
> What did I do—to be so black and blue?[1]

"What did I do—to be so black and blue?" This is not the Louis Armstrong most white Americans usually see or hear, the smiling face of good-time Dixieland jazz. Armstrong reveals a different face in this old blues, a different face of black people.

Do we know each other? Do we *really* know each other? Or are we, blacks and whites, "a country of strangers," as David Shipler's 1997 book of that title argues? The ongoing issue of race in this country remains the paradigmatic test of civic community. More than three decades after the passage of the landmark Civil Rights and Voting Rights Acts of 1964 and 1965, we are still a segregated society—not de jure, but de facto. And this fact creates distrust, dissension, unease, and fundamental disagreement about the character of race relations in the nation, with black Americans expressing much more pessimism than white Americans on this issue. (Meanwhile entrenched poverty in the inner cities constitutes an obstinate obstacle to opportunity and equal access for masses of black youth, especially young black males.)

To be sure, the two peoples, black and white, do meet; we meet in the workplace and, to some extent and in some places, in the schools (though schools reflecting the pattern of residential separation continue to be largely segregated, with devastating effect, as Jonathan Kozol demonstrates in *Savage Inequalities*). Yet we remain separate; we do not know each other's lives, we do not hear each other's stories, and we do not worship in each other's churches. The churches—the major sources of values, ideals, symbols, and identity for much of this nation's history—have failed, with few exceptions, to sustain meaningful interracial community. Nor have the symbols and institutions of the civil religion of the nation succeeded in maintaining lasting interracial community.

There have been moments, two in particular, when it seemed as if powerful revival movements within Christianity might bridge the racial divide and bring black and white Christians into a fellowship of aims and attitudes. Both occurred at the turn of centuries. The end of the eighteenth and the beginning of the nineteenth century was a time of evangelical awakening when the Methodists and Baptists briefly opened a door that seemed to reveal the possibility of equality and biracial fellowship. The antislavery witness of the Methodists and of some Baptists in the 1770s; their willingness to permit black men and women to pray, exhort, and preach in public; and especially their willingness to ordain black men as pastors verged on a gospel of equality. But this door to religious equality was rapidly slammed shut by the intransigence of slavery in the South, and the persistence of racism everywhere. And so black churches sprang up, wherever possible, and the "invisible institution" of the slaves developed so that the "real preachin'" of authentic Christianity, uncompromised by the heresy of slavery, could be heard and celebrated in the land.

A century later, the Holiness-Pentecostal movement seemed poised to develop a truly interracial Christianity. The great three-year-long Azusa Street Revival, begun in Los Angeles in 1906, involved interracial leadership and included participation of Asian- and Mexican- as well as European- and African-Americans. Early Pentecostals understood the interracial character of their movement as a sign of its authenticity—a new Pentecostal outpouring of the spirit upon diverse races and diverse tongues. For a time, black Pentecostal leaders ordained whites to the ministry and involved themselves in interracial revivals. But once again race emerged to constrain the movement's flow and turn it aside into the well-worn paths of discrimination.

Two mid-nineteenth- and mid-twentieth-century civil religion movements each brought whites and blacks together to cooperate in the black freedom struggle: the antislavery movement of the 1830s, 1840s, and 1850s and the civil rights movement of the 1950s and 1960s. Collaboration, co-operation, and fellowship characterized both movements, and yet the fit of interests and attitudes kept slipping as black antislavery activists became disillusioned with the patronizing attitudes of even the most outspoken white abolitionists and, a century later, as white veterans of the civil rights campaigns came to feel rejected and deeply hurt at the turn toward separatism of some black colleagues in the late 1960s and in the 1970s.

Today, the question asked by the Kerner Commission in 1968 still awaits an answer. Are we two nations, or one?

There was a visionary whose prophetic voice attempted to bring this issue to the fore of the national consciousness and conscience. He not only described a vision of interracial religious community, he succeeded in creating it. In looking at the life and thought of this mystic, poet, ecumenist, and preacher, Howard Thurman, perhaps we may gain a measure of hope and wisdom for our own situation, if we, like him, are truly committed to the search for common ground.[2]

Howard Thurman was born in 1900 in Daytona, Florida, and died in 1981 in San Francisco, California—moving from one ocean to the other, from the ocean that brought his slave ancestors in the Middle Passage to the ocean that faced Asia and defined the Pacific Rim. Thurman's life span of eighty-one years witnessed a sea change in the conditions of black people in this country. Race relations in the years surrounding his birth were such as to have led historians to call the period from 1877 to 1918 the "nadir"— with good cause. Forty years after slavery the erosion of the civil rights obtained during Reconstruction, the disfranchisement of black Southerners by intimidation, violence, and legal subterfuge, the spread of Jim Crow laws across the South, the *Plessy v. Ferguson* Supreme Court decision that rendered the principle of "separate but equal" the law of the land (four years before Thurman's birth), the depiction of black people by popular culture and by new pseudoscientific racial theories as a beast or a child, the gruesome mounting incidents of lynching—all seemed to demonstrate that race relations were getting worse, not better, as a new century dawned. Thurman was born into a society structured by rigid rules of segregation, a society in which a black person could never be sure when and where he or she might have to face humiliation and danger.[3]

Thurman was fortunate to have a strong, nurturing family. He grew up with the integrity of his personality supported by the loving care of his mother, Alice, and his grandmother Nancy Ambrose, both sensitive to his spiritual gifts. He experienced the additional support of the Mt. Bethel Baptist Church congregation, and of the wider black community of his neighborhood. His grandmother Nancy, a former slave and a highly revered woman, took Howard and other neighborhood black children in charge whenever she felt their self-esteem damaged by the racism of the larger society. She would gather them and repeat the story of an old slave preacher who was allowed to hold prayer meetings on her plantation during the closing years of slavery. After preaching a lengthy and emotionally exhausting sermon, he would always conclude, she remembered, by gazing intently into the face of each member of his congregation and, with as much forcefulness as he could muster, telling them, "Remember, you aren't slaves, you aren't niggers, you are God's children."[4] Early on Thurman derived from African-American spirituality a sense of self-worth and affirmation.

But Thurman was also well aware of the divisive tendencies within the organized church—his early memory of the death of his father, Saul Solomon Thurman, seared the experience of broken community into his life. Saul had not been a churchgoing man, and when he died the local Baptist pastor refused to bury him from the church. Grandma Nancy convinced the Board of Deacons to allow a church funeral, but the minister refused to preach. Finally, a substitute preacher was found who agreed to give the funeral sermon. On that day, the seven-year-old Thurman, sitting with his mother and grandmother on the front pew, was first amazed and then outraged as the preacher proceeded to preach his father into hell. Turning to his mother, he whispered, "He didn't know Papa, did he? Did he?" On the sad drive home, he resolved never to have anything to do with the church.[5]

In his childhood Thurman also experienced a profound mystical intuition into the unity of all being, which provided a powerful focal point for his vision of community. As he remembered the experience, much later:

> As a boy in Florida, I walked along the beach of the Atlantic in the quiet stillness that can only be completely felt when the murmur of the ocean is stilled and the tides move stealthily along the shore. I held my breath against the night and watched the stars etch their brightness on the face of the darkened canopy of the heavens. I had the sense that all things, the sand, the sea, the stars, the night, and I were *one* lung through which all of life breathed. Not only was I aware of a vast rhythm enveloping all, but I was a part of it and it was a part of me.[6]

He later spoke of this experience as one of the primary, defining moments of his life. Thurman does not identify the cultural antecedents to his experience, but the African-American religious tradition, both in its folk (extra-ecclesial) and its ecclesial dimensions, supported an intuitive understanding of the unity of all created being. Individual black folk artists have depicted such integral spiritual visions in painting, sculpture, and mixed media. And in the narratives of their conversion experiences, generations of black Christians typically spoke of arriving at an ecstatic state that filled them with an intense love for everything and everybody.

With assistance from local whites and blacks, Thurman went to a Baptist academy in Jacksonville for high school, as there were only three public high schools for black children in the entire state of Florida at the time. In 1919 he entered Morehouse College. (Martin Luther King, Sr., was a fellow student, although in a different class.) There, Thurman encountered Benjamin Mays and John Hope, who by their intellectual standards and commitment to social activism exemplified for him and generations of black students the finest qualities of black leadership.

In his senior year, having abandoned his childhood resolution to have nothing to do with the church, Thurman applied to Newton Theological Seminary in Newton, Massachusetts, an institution he had read about from high school days. He received a cordial letter from the seminary president who expressed regret that the school did not admit black men and referred him to a southern black seminary, Virginia Union, where he might secure the kind of training best suited for him to provide religious leadership for his people.

In 1926 Thurman applied to Rochester Theological Seminary (now Colgate-Rochester) in Rochester, New York. (He knew that it was the policy of the administration to accept two and only two black students in residence at the same time.) A number of racial incidents occurred at Rochester—and sometimes amused, sometimes hurt, sometimes angered him—but he persevered. After graduation, he accepted his first call to pastor—at a black Baptist Church in Oberlin, Ohio. His preaching began to attract a steady stream of white visitors, Oberlin College professors, and students—a mixed congregation of auditors—but they did not become members. Thurman decided that he needed to cultivate an inner life of prayer and meditation, hoping to connect on an experiential level his needs with those of his congregation.

One Sunday an incident occurred that revealed to Thurman the possibilities of the way that he had intuitively stumbled upon. A Chinese Buddhist, who had been attending the church Sunday after Sunday, came to say good-bye: "When I close my eyes and listen with my spirit I am in my Buddhist temple experiencing the renewing of my own spirit."[7] Thurman sensed that barriers were crumbling, that he was breaking new ground.

Returning south in 1928, Thurman took up a position as Professor of Religion and Director of Religious Life at Morehouse and Spelman Colleges. In spring 1929, he took a leave of absence from his pastoral and teaching duties and began a program of independent study at Haverford College with the Quaker teacher and mystic Rufus Jones. With Jones, Thurman read widely on mystical experience and developed a special interest in Meister Eckhart and Francis of Assisi. Thurman's own mystical experience resonated with Eckhart's idea of a still point at the heart of each person as the presence of God within, and also with the Dominican preacher's emphasis on God as the *ground* of all being. Surely, too, Thurman found in the nature

mysticism of Francis, in Francis's profound compassion for all of God's creatures, a spirit akin to his own. In 1932 Thurman's career took a new and
significantly public turn when Howard University, under the presidency of
Mordecai Johnson, appointed him Dean of Rankin Chapel. From this position, Thurman began to establish a national reputation as a preacher and
teacher of extraordinary talent and sensitivity.

Three years later, Thurman and his wife, Sue Bailey Thurman, accepted
an invitation to travel to India on a goodwill visit sponsored by the Christian
Student Movement of India and Burma. The trip proved to be a catalyst for
the Thurmans' future vocations. After his very first lecture, Thurman's ideas
about religion and race were challenged by an Indian lawyer, a Hindu, who
asked one of those questions that haunts a person for years, "How can you
be a Christian after all that Christians have done to your people for centuries and continue to do to them today?"[8] Thurman's answer, elaborated
most fully in his classic *Jesus and the Disinherited* (1949) and *The Luminous
Darkness* (1965), distinguished between Christianity, with its history of discrimination and prejudice, and the religion of Jesus, which supported the
needs and demands of the disinherited. Black Americans, he argued, had
recognized the religion of Jesus in the Christianity presented to them and
had appropriated it as their own. In effect, he claimed, "By some amazing gift of spiritual creativity, the slave undertook to redeem the religion
the master had profaned in his midst." Jesus, Thurman argued, had been a
member of an oppressed and rejected minority. And he offered and continues to offer to those who suffer the realization that they are of infinite
value as children of God. Moreover, the test of any religion "turns on what
word" it has "to share about God with men who are the disinherited, the
outsiders, the fringe dwellers removed from the citadels of power and control in the society."[9]

Like African-Americans before them, the Thurmans made the pilgrim-
age to visit Gandhi, who questioned them closely about the racial discrimination that divided American Christians. At the end of their meeting, Gandhi asked them to sing for him the slave spiritual "Were you there when they
crucified my Lord?" He admired it, he said, because "it got at the universal
human experience under the healing wings of suffering."[10] Thurman would
later mine the riches of spirituals in *Deep River* (1945) and *The Negro Spiritual Speaks of Life and Death* (1947). Important as the visit to Gandhi was for
the Thurmans, it was the experience of India that pushed them toward a
deeper and clearer perception of the interrelatedness of all peoples. The
occasion for this vision was a visit to the Khyber Pass:

> We saw clearly what we must do somehow when we returned to America. We
> knew that we must test whether a religious fellowship could be developed in
> America that was capable of cutting across all racial barriers, with a carry-over

into the common life, a fellowship that would alter the behavior patterns of those involved. It became imperative now to find out if experiences of spiritual unity among people could be more compelling than the experiences which divide them.[11]

It would take several years for this inner vision to take external shape, but the Indian journey, especially the epiphany at the Khyber Pass, had crystallized for Thurman ideas and experiences that had been developing since childhood. Returning to Howard University, Thurman received a letter of inquiry from Alfred Fisk, a Presbyterian minister in San Francisco. Fisk, a philosophy professor at San Francisco State College, was looking for a black ministerial student or young minister who could take a part-time position as copastor of a church in a black neighborhood in San Francisco. Thurman had no candidate to suggest—until he began to consider that the letter might be a call to him personally. Taking leave of his position at Howard University, he faced the pressing questions posed by its president: "How can you support your family? How will you manage? How will you live?" "I don't know," he responded. "I don't know. All I know is, God will take care of us."[12] To start on such a venture in 1944 required a leap of faith. American society was unthinkingly and unapologetically segregated: discrimination prevailed in housing, in labor unions, in the armed forces, and in churches. Nonetheless, Fisk and Thurman, white Presbyterian and black Baptist, became cofounders and copastors of the Church for the Fellowship of All Peoples—the only church integrated in both leadership and membership in the country. Significantly, it first met in the house of a Japanese family, vacated by their forced displacement during World War II to a "relocation" camp. For the next nine years, Thurman worked to create a new kind of community, committed to an ideal: "Religious experience must unite rather than divide men. There must be made available experiences by which the sense of separateness will be transcended and unity expressed, experiences that are deeper than all diversity but at the same time are enriched by diversity."

The community's worship and general church life concentrated on celebrating the variety of cultures represented in the congregation, with special focus on educating the children about one another's ethnic and cultural background through the church's summer camp. Thurman experimented with the Sunday worship service, incorporating a weekly period of guided meditation and reflective silence. Eventually the community developed a statement of commitment to which all members pledged themselves. The church decided to become independent rather than place itself under the authority of any one denomination, whose creedal and doctrinal definitions might restrict its ideal of inclusive fellowship. A nationwide network of affiliate or associate members was formed of visitors and supporters of the Fellowship ideal.

Thurman traveled extensively, lecturing and preaching to support the church and to spread news of its mission. He was a mesmerizing preacher whose voice and presence powerfully articulated his vision of interracial religious community. Many of these sermons and meditations formed the basis for books, including *The Search for Common Ground* (1971)—whose title is used for this essay. After nine years in San Francisco, Thurman accepted a call to Boston University as Dean of Marsh Chapel, where he continued to work to build community until his retirement in 1965. Returning to San Francisco, he chaired the Howard Thurman Educational Trust, a charitable and educational foundation, until his death in 1981.

At the time of his death, Thurman's institutional legacy consisted of the Church for the Fellowship of All Peoples (still in existence) and his Educational Trust, which granted scholarship assistance for needy students, assisted in educational and religious causes, and distributed books and tapes of Thurman's sermons worldwide. Admirers of Thurman established more than one hundred Howard Thurman Listening Rooms in America, Asia, Africa, and Europe to disseminate his message aurally. The form and effectiveness of Thurman's influence on the social and political movements of his day, both during his lifetime and since his death, have puzzled observers of his life. Some critics have questioned the liberal character of Thurman's theology and his privileging of religious experience over doctrinal formulations. Traditionalists have criticized the boldness of his ecumenical liturgical experiments at Howard University's Rankin Chapel and at Fellowship Church. Others felt disappointed that he did not emerge as a leader in the style of Gandhi or Martin Luther King, Jr. Thurman was well aware of this criticism and delighted in commenting on it by repeating a story related to him by Reinhold Niebuhr. Niebuhr, he said, had mentioned Thurman's name in a lecture one day, and a black student had responded, "I'm glad you mentioned that man. He is the great betrayer of us all. We were sure that he had the makings of a Moses and then he turned mystic on us."

Thurman had chosen, however, to exercise leadership behind the scenes, by force of his personal presence and pastoral counsel. He served, for example, on the boards of several major "movement" organizations, including those of the Fellowship of Reconciliation, the Congress of Racial Equality (CORE), and the National Association for the Advancement of Colored People (NAACP). He acted as a regular adviser to some more visible leaders of the Civil Rights movement, such as James Farmer, Bayard Rustin, Vernon Jordan, and Martin Luther King, Jr. When asked point blank why he himself had not led a movement for nonviolent change in American society, Thurman replied, "I have never considered myself as any kind of

leader . . . I'm not a movement man. It's not my way. I work at giving witness
in the external aspect of my life to my experience of the truth. That's my
way—the way the grain in my wood moves. I don't prescribe for anybody
else, and I'm willing to make available any resources I have to help people
who have other ideas. But I have to follow my way, because it's the only thing
I have to respect."[13]

Influence is difficult to measure. But an amazing number of people from
a variety of religious, ethnic, and political backgrounds claim to have been
affected by Thurman personally or through his writings and taped sermons.
Most of his books have been reprinted, and a three-volume edition of his
papers will soon be published. Articles, dissertations, and monographs
on Thurman's thought have mounted steadily since the 1980s, as a new
generation seeks to discover this thinker's significance for confronting
America's ongoing racial dilemma. That significance lies, as Thurman
noted, primarily in the authenticity of his spiritual experience as conveyed
to others through the spoken and written word. Thurman believed—as did
another twentieth-century activist contemplative, Thomas Merton—that
true social change must be grounded in spiritual experience and personal
transformation.

Thurman's vision of community was based on his profound awareness of
the interrelatedness of all created being. For Thurman, community must
extend to all life, since the search for community is *embedded* in the very fabric or structure of Life itself. Thurman equates the drive toward community
with the drive toward completion or wholeness, a drive as fundamental
as the physical drive for food: "The tendency toward whole-feeling . . . is
one with the endless search for nourishment, inherent in even the simplest
forms of life." That is, wholeness or completion, in Thurman's conception,
is the goal toward which all forms of life, from the simplest to the most complex, struggle.

And completion consists in community. Community consists, first, in
the integrity of the organism itself—in what may be called the community
within, the community of cells, tissues, organs, and systems, which are self-
regulating and organically ordered. This inner organic unity is the foundation for external or outer unity. Outer unity, necessary for the fulfillment of
the individual, is life in community; to actualize his or her potential, an individual must achieve community. Thurman puts this more strongly: "To
actualize potential is to achieve community." Community, then, is a goal
of life, a *telos* or end of life intended by Life's author. Life, in all its forms,
seeks to realize itself, and to realize itself consists in achieving inner and
outer community.

In the widespread myths of creation and origin, Thurman observes, human societies over the ages have expressed longings for a lost communion
within and without—with the self, the other, and the created world. Within

the myths of origin something deep resides, a latent memory of the soul, a memory of a lost harmony, a reminder "that the intent of the Creator of life . . . is that men must live in harmony within themselves and with one another and perhaps with all of life."[14] If accounts of the world's beginning reflect memories of a lost past, utopian stories and prophecies of a time to come when the lion shall lay down with the lamb, when people shall live free of conflict and hatred, project a profound "hope about the human situation and about the future."[15]

Both memory and hope, myths of origin and utopian prophecies, illustrate the internal drive for what Thurman calls "whole-making"—an important concept for him. "As long as I can recall reacting to the experiences of life, I have observed in myself . . . an inner demand . . . for 'whole-making,' a feel for completion in and of things, for inclusive consummation. Experiences must somehow fit together; they must make sense to the mind."[16] He goes on to identify the intellectual drive for coherence and order with the demand of Life for unity. "The tendency of the mind for whole-making or 'seeing whole,' for seeking harmony, for community is rooted in the experience of the body that in turn is grounded in all life." Life as it expresses itself in human consciousness seeks wholeness no less than when it expresses itself "instinctually in so-called subhuman forms of life."[17] So the human search for "making whole" stands on a continuum with the drive of Life for community in its myriad forms. We fail to see this interconnection at our own peril, Thurman warns.

> One of the deceptive aspects of mind in man is to give him the illusion of being distinct from and over against but not a part of nature. It is but a single leap thus to regard nature as being so completely other than himself that he may exploit it, plunder it, and rape it with impunity. . . . This we see all around us in the modern world. Our atmosphere is polluted, our streams are poisoned, our hills are denuded, wild life is increasingly exterminated, while more and more man becomes an alien on the earth and a fouler of his own nest. The price that is being exacted for this is a deep sense of isolation of being rootless and a vagabond. Often I have surmised that this condition is more responsible for what seems to be the phenomenal increase in mental and emotional disturbances in modern life than the pressures—economic, social, and political—that abound on every hand. The collective psyche shrieks with the agony that it feels as a part of the death cry of a pillaged nature.[18]

Note the radical connection that Thurman posits between the mental health or sickness of persons and the health or sickness of the environment.

Thurman not only connects humans' psychic condition to the condition of the environment but also argues that there is an "affinity" between human consciousness and the other forms of consciousness that surround us. The more aware we become of these other forms, the more our sense of self becomes enlarged, and the more all of life seems a part of us and we a part of it. In this, Thurman probably has in mind particularly the connection of consciousness between humans and animals. He recalled a childhood experience in his book, *The Search for Common Ground,* published in 1971, as an illustration. One day when he was a little boy, Thurman ran over to visit a neighborhood playmate. Passing in front of his friend's house to run around to the backyard, he was halted by a knock at the front window. His friend's father was motioning him in. Inside, Thurman was led by the father to a side window and saw, outside, his friend's baby sister, a child not yet two years old, sitting in the dirt of the yard holding a rattlesnake. She released the snake, and it would crawl away and then crawl back. She would pick it up and put it down, and it would again crawl away and then back. Eventually she tired of the game, put the snake down, and crawled, herself, to the back steps. At this point, the snake moved away. Clearly, the child and the snake were playing.[19]

Thurman posits a ground of unity between animals and humans that makes nonverbal communication between them possible. In this interspecies bonding, "the mind temporarily gives up its sense of individuality and drops back into an original creative continuum in which boundaries of the human self are temporarily transcended" and consciousness enlarged.[20] Communion between persons and animals is based upon life seeking to realize itself in all its forms.

Finally, community between humans is the source of identity for each person, according to Thurman, because, within each of us, the inner law of life ineluctably searches for wholeness and fulfillment. The fact that persons "need to be loved, to be understood, to be cared for is the essential stuff of community."[21] The primary place of human community is the family. But the nation also constitutes a community, a community not only of rights and responsibilities but of rites or rituals of belonging. When minority groups, such as African Americans, Native Americans, Hispanic Americans, or Asian Americans, find themselves outside the national community, excluded by those who are within, this exclusion has a devastating effect, both on them and on the nation.

> [W]herever citizens are denied the freedom of access to the resources that make for a sense of belonging, a sense of being totally dealt with, the environment closes in around them, resulting in the schizophrenic dilemma of being inside and outside at one and the same time. Or worse still, they are subject to the acute trauma of not knowing at any given moment whether they are outsiders or insiders.[22]

Such a denial of access assails persons "at the very foundation of their sense of belonging," affecting what goes on even in the primary place of community, the family. They become "outsiders" living in the midst of "insiders." This denial of community cuts deeply into the total life of the nation, too, creating a "condition of guilt in the general society that has to be absorbed in order to keep life tolerable within the body politic," a kind of low-level infection that periodically breaks out in virulent reactions. Historically in the United States, the drive for wholeness and community of black people has suffered sustained attack from the residual awareness "that always and under any and all circumstances," black persons' lives "were utterly at the mercy of the white world." This history of threatened and enacted racial violence has not been faced fully, Thurman wrote in 1973.

> The heartrending years when hundreds of Negroes were lynched, burned, and butchered by white men whose women and children were often special spectators of the inhuman ceremony are conveniently forgotten. It is scarcely remembered how long it took to pass anti-lynch legislation. The *bodies* of Negroes remember, and their psyches can never forget this vast desecration of personality. The boundaries of any sense of community, the effectiveness of one's life as a person, the breakdown of the instinctual tendency toward whole-making, the personality violence from aggression, thwarted and turned in on one's self[,] . . . the guilt inspired by anonymous fears that live in the environment—these are some of the shadows, the unconscious reaction to which must be understood as we try to find community in the presence of the . . . confrontation facing American society.[23]

When discrimination and racism intervene to destroy community, they frustrate the very thrust of life itself. And, just as any living organism when attacked will counteract in self-defense, so will a person or persons react if attacked by the destruction or denial of community. The move toward black separatism in the late 1960s and early 1970s was, according to Thurman, just such a stage of reaction. Eventually, however, the consciousness of racial separateness must be caught up in the realization of human community. Thurman had no doubts about his own black identity and valued the history and culture of his people, but he was also certain of the common ground of the human spirit.

Thurman described the situation between the races twenty-five years ago as a confrontation. We still face a confrontation insofar as we still fail to see each other face-to-face. Invisibility remains a quality of our inner eyes, the eyes with which we look out upon reality, as Ralph Ellison noted in his 1952 *Invisible Man.* Faces must be shown and seen before interracial community is possible. This confrontation—without the mask of evasion, the mask of fear, the mask of discomfort, the mask of false civility—must occur between white and black, painful and difficult though this may be, if we are to continue the search for common ground, the search that is the very manifestation of Life within.

"What if," Thurman asked, "in American life there had been imbedded in Christian orthodoxy a judgement which said that racial prejudice would bar a person from salvation? What if it had been taught and maintained all down the years that racial prejudice separates a Christian from God and his Christ? What might that have done for the search for common ground?" What if, today, the churches, the synagogues, the mosques, the temples, and—dare one hope?—the schools fostered sustained confrontation (face-to-face) of black and white persons, letting their masks drop, telling their own stories, listening to one another's—hard, frustrating, but necessary work.

In 1962 Howard Thurman accepted an invitation to attend a lecture at a gathering of Canadian Indian leaders in Saskatchewan. As he was being introduced, he spontaneously decided to forgo the use of a translator in spite of objections that no one would understand him.

> At first the atmosphere was tense and disconcerting. It was quite clear that the men didn't understand my words and were puzzled by the unusual procedure. My words went forth, but they seemed to strike an invisible wall, only to fall back to meet other words flowing from my mouth. The tension was almost unbearable. Then, suddenly, as if by some kind of magic, the wall vanished and I had the experience of sensing an organic flow of meaning passing between them and me. It was as if together we had dropped into a continuum of communication that existed a priori long before human speech was formed into sounds and symbols. . . . When I finished, there was a long breath of silence as if together we were recovering our separate rhythms.[24]

It is to the possibility of such spiritual communication, beyond—or rather, beneath—differences of speech and culture, that Thurman suggests we attend.

The world of music is the most accessible example for most of us of this type of communication. The music of jazz offers a prime example of a particular group's music crossing racial and national boundaries to speak to peoples around the world. I began with a musical text from that jazz tradition, a query by the incomparable Louis Armstrong, "What did I do to be so black and blue?" Perhaps the contrapuntal answer is another question: "What did I do to be so white and blue?"[25]

TEN

Reassembling the Civic Church
The Changing Role of Congregations in American Civil Society

Robert Wuthnow

In recent years, much interest has been expressed in the civic role of American churches. Some of this interest has been generated by debates concerning the Religious Right, with proponents pointing to moral decay and calling on churches to take a more active role in fighting it and critics raising questions about the apparently declining ability of theologically moderate or liberal churches to articulate alternative positions on social issues.[1] Some interest has arisen as a result of the sweeping reforms of the welfare system over the past decade; as government funding for social programs has been reduced, leaders of both major political parties have called on churches to do more to mobilize volunteers and to organize private initiatives to assist the poor.[2] The call for churches to engage more actively in social ministries has been voiced especially by social observers who believe that other sources of private support for civic activities may be waning. In their view, churches may need to take up the slack in mobilizing middle-class people who otherwise might spend their time watching television rather than joining service clubs such as Kiwanis or Junior League.[3] Churches are also thought to be one of the few civic organizations that can effectively draw together African Americans, Hispanic Americans, and white Anglos living in impoverished inner-city neighborhoods.[4] Interest in churches' civic activities also stems from questions rooted in historical observations. As historians consider the significant role that churches played in major social and political movements in the past (e.g., abolitionism, temperance, and the civil rights movement), their observations raise questions about the likelihood that churches can play such a role again in the future.[5]

The backdrop for the present expression of interest in churches' civic role is a perception that social and cultural conditions are making it harder for churches to mobilize genuine civic-spirited efforts than may have been the case only a few decades ago. This perception is widespread, even though church membership and attendance in the United States remain high compared to that in most other advanced industrial democracies and although there is little evidence of decline in religious commitment when measured in surveys asking about church attendance or belief in God.[6] But it is the *quality* of religious commitment, and its ability to sustain civic engagement in the face of enormous social obstacles, that has been the focus of most concern.

Some discussions point especially to corrosive cultural assumptions as a central problem. These assumptions include an apparent absorption with achieving individual goals at the expense of maintaining civic attachments and with focusing on the expression of inward impulses and feelings rather than demonstrating commitment to conceptions of truth and morality that are grounded in communal deliberations. For example, the authors of *Habits of the Heart* point to an excessive language of self-interest that makes it difficult for well-meaning individuals even to give adequate reasons for their behavior.[7] Other writers emphasize the moral relativism that may be an important aspect of contemporary culture or the incivility that has come to typify public discussions of politics or the treatment of subjects on television and in films.[8]

In other discussions, the changing character of social institutions has received greater attention.[9] Without necessarily denying the importance of cultural assumptions, these discussions often emphasize the ways in which economic conditions and other social arrangements are changing. Some writers point to the central role of capitalism, for instance, as a system of international competition that erodes individuals' ties to their local communities or their families.[10] Other writers point to the cumulative effects of changing family patterns on children.[11] In still other analyses, the failure of political structures that might have enforced better family-leave policies or health-reform initiatives receives greater emphasis.[12]

Although the connections between cultural assumptions or institutional changes and churches remain unspecified in many of these analyses, religious leaders often express concern about the difficulties either of ministering to or of mobilizing the commitments of people who are geographically mobile, overburdened with concerns about work and money, fearful of losing jobs, poorly integrated into their communities, and subjected to a constant barrage of appeals from advertisers and the entertainment industry.[13]

In this chapter, I focus on the interplay between the cultural assumptions that have been featured in some discussions and the institutional factors that have been emphasized in other accounts. I extend an argument, which I have developed elsewhere, about "porous" institutions, outlining some reasons why the United States has come increasingly to be characterized by institutions that often discourage long-term commitments or fail to undergird the authority of local communities, families, or civic organizations.[14] I then examine how these changes in the social environment have affected religious congregations and how such congregations have responded. *Porousness*, I suggest, does not result only in people dropping out of congregations or adopting a more individualistic language to describe their faith (although this is an important part of the story), but also sets in motion a process of *reassembling*. As has often happened in the past, unsettled social conditions dislodge individuals from their religious moorings, but they then use this dislocation as an opportunity to come together in new ways.[15] At present the civic church—those aspects of religious congregations through which their members relate individually and corporately to the needs of the wider community—is being reassembled. To make clear the nature of this reassembling, and its consequences for civil society, I shall begin by considering an example that illustrates the social conditions in which reassembly is rooted.[16]

THE DYNAMICS OF A POROUS SOCIETY

Bill Hartwig is a baby boomer who grew up in a small town in western Pennsylvania. The community in which he was raised was composed mostly of working-class families who earned their livings in a nearby steel mill. Like most of their neighbors, Bill's parents saw little hope that their children would secure steady, well-paying employment at the mill. They encouraged Bill to go to college and were able to save enough money to send him to a state university that was several hundred miles away but relatively inexpensive. Bill hoped to earn a degree in accounting that would allow him to return to his hometown and set up his own office. The university he attended drew students from across the state and was a good bargain for some from other states. It prided itself on the diversity of its student body and advertised that it had students from nearly every state and from a number of foreign countries. Bill made friends with students from other areas and by his senior year had fallen in love with a girl from the Midwest. He had also switched his major to political science and now planned to become a lawyer. After graduation he and his wife, Sharon, relocated to another state where he could attend law school. Sharon worked to support them until after their son was born and returned to work a few months later. She and Bill made friends with other young parents they met through potluck dinners at the day-care center where Sharon left the baby each morning on her way to work.

After finishing law school, Bill applied for jobs at several firms and received offers from three, all within the state. He took the one that paid the most, eager to have enough money to repay his loans and disappointed only that their new community was far from both his and Sharon's families. With Bill working, Sharon stayed home with their son. She also had more time to read and took courses toward a master's degree in social work. But she and Bill also began to grow apart in their outlooks on life, and three years later they divorced. Both remarried. Bill and his new wife have a son and a daughter; Bill still works as a lawyer but has changed firms several times.

As this example suggests, individuals in American society often move across social boundaries with relative frequency; they move geographically and educationally, change interests, switch employers, and sometimes separate from marriage partners and remarry. Goods and information, also, flow with relative ease and rapidity. A society that permits people, goods, and information to flow easily and rapidly across social boundaries can be termed a *porous* society. The increasing porousness of American society over the past three or four decades is evident not only in the lives of individuals like Bill Hartwig but also in the ways in which virtually all social institutions are currently arranged. Indeed, the concept of porousness permits a view of the similarities in these arrangements across a variety of social spheres. For example, the divorce that Bill and Sharon experienced is a phenomenon that has become common.[17] The rising divorce rate can be regarded as an indication of one kind of porousness: people disengage from the legal, religious, and emotional bonds defining married couples with greater ease, or greater rapidity, than in the past. In a different sphere, the downsizing by corporations and their increasing reliance on outsourcing and temporary workers is another example of porousness;[18] rather than attempt to retain labor and cultivate workers' loyalty over a long period, corporations opt for flexible, short-term arrangements. In neither of these cases does the change necessarily mean that family or business has become less valued; indeed, virtually everyone continues to name having a family and a job among the highest priorities; but a change has nevertheless occurred in the social arrangements by which these values are pursued. Individuals learn to expect that marriage may be difficult to sustain and that they may have to change jobs or even careers several times. Even if they themselves do not experience these changes, they realize that friends and neighbors may.

In other spheres, porousness is also evident. Neighborhoods no longer serve much as geographically enclosed places in which people live, socialize, make friends, raise children, shop, or engage in civic activities. Rather, individuals pursue many of these activities by flowing easily across neighborhood boundaries: traveling to visit friends and relatives, making long-distance telephone calls, using the Internet, commuting to work, shopping at malls, and sending children to regional schools.[19] At a wider level of social organization, national boundaries are also crossed with increasing frequency. Greater numbers have crossed them in recent decades to establish permanent residence in the United States. Many new immigrants have become part of a transient population that moves back and forth over borders as working conditions or financial needs dictate. Like local neighborhoods, national boundaries are also more easily permeated by long-distance telephone calls, by live television broadcasts, and by the integration of international markets.[20] Not only is it easier to exchange goods across national boundaries, but currency, capital investments, and stock ownership also increasingly transcend these boundaries.

The porousness of American life is thus a condition that influences the ways in which individuals lead their personal lives and the ways in which organizations conduct their activities. At the personal level, people like Bill Hartwig spend more of their days commuting to work, making trips outside their neighborhoods to shop or run errands, and interacting with others who live outside their neighborhood. Many spend time taking evening classes to prepare for new careers, or seek counseling out of the fear of losing a job or spouse. Their domestic schedules have become complicated by the fact that both spouses travel to work or by the fact that one spouse resides elsewhere. Gatherings for weddings and funerals may be emblematic of this porousness of family life, bringing together geographically far-flung relatives, spouses and ex-spouses, siblings and stepsiblings. At the organizational level, corporate leaders rely less on clear hierarchies of authority and more on networking, hiring subcontractors, and dealing with consultants. Politicians spend more time campaigning, interacting with foreign delegations, and forming multisectoral task forces. Civic leaders and educators forge loose ties with fellow professionals, spend more time writing grant applications to solicit funds from external sources, recruit more volunteers, and struggle to respond to an ethnically diverse population.

The image that someone like Bill Hartwig may conjure up is of a porous society composed mainly of people who move around a lot, make frequent changes in their lives, and are loosely related to one another through a casual contact here, a friend there, an organization somewhere else. But the movement of people, goods, and information that is characteristic of American society is only the *symptom* of porousness. Thus, it is on the underlying social conditions giving rise to this movement that attention needs to focus.

In Bill Hartwig's case, it is clear that *economic pressures* are an important aspect of the underlying social conditions that have influenced his decisions. The steel mill where his father worked started to lose business as a result of foreign competition; by the time Bill finished law school, it had closed. Later, his decision about which job offer to take was largely dictated by economic concerns. Like other members of the baby boom generation, he found that there were too many people his age for the jobs available in his hometown or in his preferred place of employment; he had to move on to move up. But his decisions were also influenced by *cultural pressures.* Although his parents hoped that he would remain nearby, they also encouraged him to get a good education and to pursue his own interests. Their expectations were transmitted to him through stories of friends and relatives who had encouraged their children to do the same.[21] In college, Bill learned that professionals such as accountants or lawyers could expect to lead a certain lifestyle but that they needed to be willing to leave friends behind to succeed.

Other social arrangements may work against these pressures (and thus be termed *social controls*). Bill's father worked at the steel mill most of his adult life because the deals his labor union struck with management gave him sufficient incentive; nor were the ethnic customs that bound his extended family together easy for Bill to leave behind. And when Bill first met Sharon, she was not thinking of a career; she had learned a woman's place was in the home. More generally, the factors that work against porousness include the pressure of an external threat (such as war), a lack of attractive alternatives, and a supervisory agent with high capacity to monitor what people do. These factors are particularly apparent in such examples as concentration camps, tribal villages, and one-company towns. But it is also clear that many controls that restrict movement across social boundaries have weakened. Norms that made it hard for African Americans to move out of segregated neighborhoods, or for women to enter traditionally male occupations, have changed. The gradual easing of superpower rivalries and the collapse of the Soviet Union helped to encourage greater exchange across national borders. Transportation and computing technologies have made easier the exchange of information.

The most interesting aspect of porous social conditions, however, comprises what might be called the *brokering mechanisms* that make it possible for people, goods, and information to be exchanged. The classic historical examples of a brokering mechanism are the barriers (often large chains) that German nobles in the late Middle Ages stretched across the Rhine to levy a toll on commerce moving up and down the river. Although a barrier of this kind may now seem only an impediment to trade, it was the prototype for the modern market-oriented economy. It interposed, as it were, a "middle man" who could make money from the exchange of goods: a feudal lord who could provide "value added" in the form of protection from brigands and smugglers.

Our own brokering mechanisms have become far more complex. They include travel agencies that assist people in planning trips and family lawyers who assist people in planning divorces. In Bill Hartwig's case, the most significant brokering mechanism was the university he attended. It drew the surplus youth who could not find attractive opportunities in local labor markets and provided credentials to help them find employment in other markets. Other brokering mechanisms played subsequent roles in Bill's experience: the standardized test that made it possible for him to be recruited by a distant law school, the placement officer who helped him find his first job, the day-care center that substituted for an extended family and that provided a chance to make friends, the head hunter who recruited him to a new job, and the lawyer who assisted with his divorce.[22]

Such brokering mechanisms not only respond to transactions that are already taking place; they encourage them. Indeed, like any other market activity, brokering mechanisms can further their position primarily in two ways: by competing effectively for a larger share of the market and by encouraging the whole market to expand. Thus, a travel agency can offer deals that are better than those offered by its competitors, or it can advertise exotic vacations that encourage more people to travel. In Bill Hartwig's case, the university he attended was able to expand because more baby boomers were going to college. It also competed for funds and faculty by trying to recruit the best students; expanding its potential pool to other states and abroad helped this recruitment. As these examples suggest, brokering mechanisms also become interwoven with the larger social fabric: advertisers do business with travel agents, who in turn do business with airlines, who in turn encourage college students to fly to exotic spots for spring vacations.

A porous society, then, is not one in which people simply move around, change jobs, get divorced, or consume information because they are forced or choose to do so (although both are true). It is also a society in which social arrangements encourage individuals to follow certain courses of action and to broker these transactions. This means that the likelihood of continuing porousness is high; it also means that individuals who break ties with groups or traditions are not left simply to fend for themselves—a point that is especially important for understanding the changing role of congregations.

POROUSNESS AND AMERICAN PROTESTANTISM

Bill Hartwig's story includes a dynamic saga that he refers to as his "spiritual journey." It began in the Latvian Lutheran church in which he was later confirmed. During most of his childhood, he attended this church regularly with his family and with other neighborhood families. In college he periodically attended meetings of the Inter-Varsity Christian Fellowship and went to worship services at an interfaith chapel on campus. This is where he met Sharon. Reared in a devout Methodist family, she found the chapel a good way to retain some of her religious upbringing. During law school, Bill did not attend church and Sharon broadened her interests in spirituality through reading and by participating in a women's discussion group. After Bill finished law school, the couple joined a United Church of Christ congregation that offered activities for their son. During their separation and divorce proceedings, Bill quit going to church and Sharon became more active in one of its support groups.

Spiritual journeys like this are not unusual. In fact, life changes such as Bill Hartwig's are especially conducive to dropping out of congregations. In a national survey I conducted in 1997, I found that the odds of being a church member were about 20 percent lower among persons who had ever divorced than among those who had not. The odds of being a church member were about a third lower among people who had worked at their present job only a year than among those employed in the same situation longer. Other factors had even stronger effects: having moved to one's current address in the past year reduced the chances of being a church member by half, as did knowing few or none of one's neighbors. Individuals who had been reared in environments that may have predisposed them to lead a more fluid life (e.g., having grown up in a city or suburb and having college-educated parents and thus more opportunities for exposure to new ideas) also showed lower rates of church membership.[23] Other studies have shown similar patterns. Baby boomers who have attended college and moved considerably have dropped out of churches, temporarily or permanently, in large numbers.[24] People of other generations and socioeconomic groups have often dropped or switched memberships for similar reasons.[25]

But the experience of a change in life, such as moving to a new community, going to college, or changing jobs, also gives individuals an opportunity to attach themselves to new congregations.[26] Bill Hartwig and his second wife, Roxanne, now live in an upper-middle-class suburb about fifteen miles from the center of a large city. They attend a Presbyterian church of thirteen hundred members. Like many other families at the church, they chose it because it was nearby—only several miles from their house—and because it seemed to attract people like themselves. They enjoyed the music, agreed with the preaching, and took comfort in the schedule of activities in which their children could become involved. The church sponsored a class for newcomers that helped them get acquainted, but it did not pressure them to join and said nothing about theological requirements that might give a former Lutheran pause.

Among the Protestant church members in my survey, Bill Hartwig's trajectory is not unusual. Members of large churches (memberships exceeding one thousand) differ from members of medium-sized or small congregations. Specifically, in large congregations, there are higher proportions of persons who were raised in suburbs or cities, attended college, moved around considerably, have lived a fairly short time at their current residence, and know few neighbors. Also, large churches are more likely than small congregations to be populated by individuals whose work contacts are mostly outside their own neighborhood, to be located in a suburban or urban area, and to be outside their members' immediate neighborhood. Whereas the members of small congregations are more likely to define "community" in terms of their neighborhood, those of large congregations are more likely to define it in terms of the larger region where they live.[27]

Several points about these patterns are worth emphasizing. The large Protestant congregation has become the home of persons who have experienced the porousness of contemporary life.[28] Of course, we do not know from the survey what their spiritual journeys may have included. But personal interviews with individuals like Bill Hartwig indicate that his story is not uncommon. Having had opportunities to experience a variety of activities—college, in particular—and having been dislocated from their communities of origin, these persons left behind the smaller churches in which they were raised and, after having shopped around for a while, relocated at a church that was substantially larger or growing. Others, who were already members of large congregations, stayed with the same congregation or joined a different church of similar size when they moved; for them, the size of the new church was important, permitting it to offer attractive programs that in some ways also made it easier for newcomers to assimilate. In short, the large congregation became a new place to assemble.

Large churches run the danger of being places where anonymous individuals sit passively and never become acquainted. But the evidence suggests that members actually do reassemble in ways that reinforce involvement and social relationships. In my 1997 survey, it became clear that members of large Protestant churches are at least as likely as members of small churches to say they attend worship services every week, to attend a Sunday school class regularly, and to participate in a Bible study or fellowship group and to say they have close friends in the congregation.[29] Nor is it the case that large churches show these patterns of involvement because their members are more theologically conservative; although some of the largest "megachurches" in the nation are regarded as evangelical or fundamentalist churches, in the survey under discussion, the likelihood of large-church members being religiously conservative was actually somewhat lower than it was of small-church members (most of whom said they were moderates).[30]

Large churches, then, appear to be places in which persons otherwise disposed to drop out of church entirely can reassemble. Thus, the question of immediate interest is whether these churches can also mobilize civic involvement. Judging from the social characteristics of their members, we might anticipate that these would be people who were not well enough integrated into their communities to be involved in civic activities. Yet we would hope that their church involvement might translate into other forms of voluntary service, as it has for many in the past.[31]

This does appear to be the case. Members of large churches are somewhat *more* likely than members of medium-sized or small churches to have done some volunteering during the previous year.[32] They are also more likely to have engaged in several specific types of volunteering: helping with youth or school service programs, volunteering for political or environmental activities, distributing food to the needy, and participating in neighborhood or home owners' associations. Several other kinds of volunteering, however, are *not* more common among members of any particular size church: informal volunteering, community organizing, violence prevention, community development corporation activities, building low-income housing, or AIDS-related activities.

On the whole, members of large churches are more likely than members of smaller churches to have volunteered for at least two different activities during the past year, and the average large-church volunteer devotes 4.6 hours per week to his or her activities, compared with 3.6 hours per week among small-church members and only 2.1 hours for members of medium-sized churches. Large-church members are also more likely to have done volunteer work in a poor, inner-city area and to have attended meetings about community issues.[33]

Other ways of measuring civic involvement help to put these patterns in perspective. In addition to being volunteers for service activities, the members of large congregations are *joiners*. They contradict the image presented by the Harvard political scientist Robert Putnam, who describes baby boomers as persons who disproportionately stay home and watch television rather than join civic organizations.[34] Members of large churches are more likely than members of smaller churches to belong both to civic or service organizations and to church-affiliated groups (in addition to the church). Although they are slightly *less likely* to be members of fraternal orders (a fact probably consistent with Putnam's observation that orders such as Elks and Moose are losing members), they are *more likely* than persons from smaller churches to participate in organizations that have attracted the middle class in recent years: health and fitness clubs, hobby or garden organizations, literary groups, discussion groups, and professional organizations.[35]

Although the civic activities of persons who belong to large churches vary, we can make sense of them by considering how they are influenced by the porous social conditions to which these persons have been exposed. Consider the apparent lack of interest in fraternal orders. These are organizations that emphasize long-term loyalties rather than the fluid coming and going that characterizes porous settings. Elks and Moose, for example, have secret initiation rituals that erect boundaries between members and nonmembers and are part of a large national bureaucracy that establishes guidelines for local chapters and maintains a hierarchy of ranks that take years of commitment to ascend. Some of the organizations have histories of discrimination against African Americans or other minorities, and many have remained male-only or female-only until recent years. These are characteristics that members of large congregations do not find appealing. Indeed, it is significantly more likely in large congregations than in smaller ones to find individuals saying that they would be very unlikely to join an organization that has a history of racial discrimination, that uses secret rituals, or that is part of a large national bureaucracy.

Not only the members, but the large congregations themselves, have tended to eschew these characteristics. Although some large congregations are run by fundamentalist ministers who erect high walls between members and nonmembers, it is more common for the congregations to be loosely evangelical, mainline, or moderate in orientation. Although many remain affiliated with denominations (and are thus part of national bureaucracies), independent and nondenominational churches with large memberships have become increasingly common; in other cases, denominational affiliations have been deemphasized. In many of these churches, standards of membership are relatively loose, permitting people like Bill Hartwig who may have been reared in different traditions to join with relative ease. Small group events and other social activities also break the large congregation into units where more intimate friendships can be made.

The volunteering that characterizes members of large congregations is another reflection of the porousness of these members' lives. These persons are more likely than those in smaller congregations to have volunteered for several *different* organizations and to have attended community meetings in several different settings. In other words, their contacts and relationships are more diverse or link them to a broader variety of networks. This is especially evident in the contacts that they state they have actually experienced in conjunction with volunteering. They are more likely than are members of smaller churches to have had contact with a wide range of organizations and specialists: teachers, lawyers, nonprofit organizations, service clubs, banks, social workers, political officials, and the like.

The reason for many of these differences is not size of congregation alone. It is rather, as I have suggested, that large congregations attract persons of a particular background. Thus, an important reason that members of large congregations volunteer and belong to clubs more than do members of smaller congregations is that the former are better educated, live in different sorts of communities, and earn higher incomes.[36] (These are also among the reasons these members have greater contact with lawyers, teachers, doctors, and other professionals when they volunteer.)

Bill Hartwig is an illustration of such connections. By serving on committees at his church, he became acquainted with a doctor, the pastor, and a couple of other lawyers. One of these acquaintances asked him to serve on the board of a local hospital. Through that involvement, someone asked him to chair the annual fund-raising drive for a long-term care facility. More recently, he started helping with a committee that supervises the construction of a low-income housing project; in this capacity, he has become acquainted with prominent men and women from other large churches in the area. But the differences in levels of volunteering are not only a function of church members' education. Size is also a factor. A larger church can help to sponsor a wider variety of programs than a smaller congregation.[37] Members of large churches are thus more likely to hear about, and have the opportunity to participate in, a wider variety of volunteer activities than members of smaller churches.[38] Indeed, virtually any service program is more common in large congregations than in smaller ones: day care, tutoring, help to low-income families, AIDS-related programs, shelter for the homeless, food distribution, alcohol recovery programs, employment help, counseling, inner-city ministries, and programs for prisoners. And that these programs are more common is not simply because larger churches can operate them alone and smaller churches may have to cooperate with other congregations to sponsor them; even when "helping to sponsor" is key, members of large churches indicate in far higher proportions than do members of smaller churches that their congregations are involved.[39]

More generally, one important way in which Americans have adapted to more porous conditions in recent decades has been to form complex interorganizational networks of the kinds suggested by these data. For instance, members of large congregations are significantly more likely than those in small congregations to say that their churches participate in interchurch coalitions and are active in service efforts that involve other, nonreligious nonprofit organizations.[40] Such "partnerships," as they are often called, mean that loose, short-term, or functionally specialized relationships can be established to accomplish a specific task. One partnership may be especially effective at curbing misunderstandings among people from different faiths; a different partnership may do better in helping to construct low-income housing.

A good example of how a congregation can participate in a large network involving other organizations is the low-income housing project in which Bill Hartwig has recently become involved. His pastor began talking with other influential clergy in the community and learned that they shared an interest in helping the poor. They pooled enough money from their discretionary budgets to invite a speaker from the Industrial Areas Foundation in Chicago to come and give them some ideas on how to get started. One of the pastors had a contact with the mayor, who happened to know about an attractive inner-city housing program in another city. When Bill Hartwig became involved, there was already an infrastructure in place that included representatives from banks, construction companies, and the municipal government.

The reason that members of large congregations are more likely to be involved in a wide range of volunteer activities and to experience wider contacts through these activities than do members of smaller congregations is thus twofold: first, these congregations draw persons who are better-educated, middle-class baby boomers and whose experiences have encouraged them to leave behind loyalties to neighborhoods, communities, or congregations of origin; second, these congregations provide a diverse menu of activities within the church, as well as in partnership with other organizations, so that interested members can become involved.

None of this implies that the members of large congregations are somehow more altruistic than those of small congregations. Indeed, the lifestyles of people in large congregations also predispose them to say no to civic involvement. Substantially more than in small congregations, for instance, say they have too much to do, and when asked why they do not volunteer more than they do, they are disproportionately likely to say they simply do not have time. Their self-interestedness is often evident as well. Their favorite volunteer activities are ones that help their own children, and they are prone to join self-help groups that focus attention on their own needs. They also are reluctant to say they admire persons who join service clubs or who take an active part in politics; instead, they are more likely to admire those who take an unpopular stand on issues or who can get things done. It is notable, nevertheless, given the social circumstances that predispose these members to disengage from civic activities, that they are as actively involved in volunteer work and other civic commitments as they are.

These considerations suggest that large congregations may be a place in which persons exposed to porous social conditions can reassemble—not only for their own sake but also for others'. Large congregations offer the diversity of programs and the richness of social contacts that many well-educated, middle-class, suburban residents appreciate. The limitations of these congregations are nevertheless important to emphasize as well. Much of their volunteer activity is sporadic: individuals fit in an hour or two a month, according to how busy they are and how much energy they have left after working long hours and commuting. By participating in interchurch coalitions and by working with secular agencies, such churches play at least a token role in their communities. But for their size, this role is often smaller than it might be and in many cases probably smaller than among churches in the past. Some of the largest churches, particularly those with a conservative theological orientation, also limit their involvement in wider community activities because they believe resources should be devoted to building the programs of the church itself.[41] Another limitation of large churches is that their programs require a multiperson professional staff and often a commitment to building and maintaining expensive facilities.[42] Large congregations are able to sustain these programs because their members give more generously than do members of smaller churches, both per capita and as a proportion of members' incomes.[43] It is nevertheless unclear whether large churches pass a significant share of their revenue to social ministries or keep most for their own programs.[44]

RELIGIOUS DIVERSITY

The large Protestant church is of course but one of the increasingly diverse ways in which Americans worship and translate their faith into civic engagement. By most indications, the patterns that characterize Protestants in terms of congregation size also pertain to Catholics.[45] Although Catholic parishes are, on the whole, larger than Protestant congregations because of the geographic definition of membership historically, it has become increasingly common in the past three decades for Catholics to choose the parishes they attend rather than let geography determine their membership. Parishes also vary in size with the growth or decline of communities. Just as among Protestants, college-educated, mobile, and suburban Catholics have gravitated toward larger parishes, and these parishes also appear to be mobilizing members to engage in civic activities. Individual Catholics volunteer for a larger number of activities if they belong to large parishes than if they belong to small parishes, and larger parishes support a wider variety of volunteer programs and activities than do smaller parishes.[46]

Smaller Protestant and Catholic congregations are quite diverse, and their patterns of civic activity need to be distinguished according to the characteristics of their members. In general, religious commitment remains one factor that reinforces civic engagement. That it does so in large congregations is of interest, given the porous lives that many of the members lead. In small congregations, close-knit social relationships are often still present to a greater degree, yet the resources that these congregations have for mobilizing their members varies considerably.

The small or medium-sized congregation that is located in an older, ethnically homogeneous, working-class community is especially interesting. Many of these communities, such as the one in which Bill Hartwig was raised, have declined as a result of factory closings or layoffs, or because younger people have left to live in newer and more heterogeneous suburbs. But congregations in these communities often remain important as centers of local civic activity.[47] Studies of such congregations suggest that volunteering tends to be focused more on the community and less on the wider region. This volunteer activity focuses more explicitly on helping others or on reciprocating kindnesses than in other areas where personal gratification may be the primary motivation. Ethnic ties, too, sometimes shape the character of civic activity, causing it to focus on, for example, Latvian nationalism, as in the case of Bill Hartwig's parents. Volunteering at local fire companies and attending functions at lodges or American Legion halls is also more common in these communities.[48]

The small congregation in rural communities has had to adapt to a declining or aging population, in many cases; in others, it is increasingly exposed to community issues such as confronting an influx of commuters or new housing developments, concerns about environmental protection, or struggles with large chain stores and outlet malls. In some cases, these congregations are also faced with growing competition from a "megachurch," which may be drawing new residents as well as some members of established churches.[49] Interviews with pastors and lay members suggest that small churches in rural areas and villages are beginning to experiment more, as large churches have, with forming coalitions to meet community needs, even when resources may be declining.

The other kind of small congregation that has been of particular interest in recent years is the inner-city church. Many of these churches are populated predominantly by African Americans, but a growing number are congregations of Hispanics or of recent immigrants of other ethnic backgrounds. These churches often experience the effects of porousness, as they are where those who have been left behind or who have fallen through the crevices of diverse institutions seek help: the homeless or hungry, single-parent families, and families that include victims of joblessness or drug abuse. Such problems mean that mistrust is sometimes a prevailing characteristic of members. These members may mistrust not only the outside world but also neighbors and fellow congregants, to the point that cooperative activities become difficult.[50]

With limited resources, inner-city congregations typically adopt one or more of several prevailing strategies. One is to maintain or cultivate ties with suburban residents as a way of attracting resources. African American churches that have experienced suburban flight of some middle-class members have sometimes been able to retain ties with these members through their family loyalties.[51] In other cases, partnerships have been established between suburban and inner-city churches; these partnerships provide a way for suburban residents to give donations or to occasionally volunteer without having to compromise the lifestyles to which they have grown accustomed.

A different strategy is to specialize in addressing particular problems that are especially acute in the inner city. For example, an African American church in Philadelphia sends its members up and down the streets in a low-income, high-crime neighborhood seeking homeless addicts to whom it can minister; it then provides a home in which a dozen or more of these persons can live and undergo an intensive recovery program for as long as a year, during which time other members help them find jobs. The church maintains itself entirely from the contributions of its own members, most of whom are former addicts.

Inner-city churches are also being drawn increasingly to participate in loosely structured networks of social service providers. The low-income housing effort in which Bill Hartwig is involved, for example, has solicited input from inner-city pastors, who are in a better position than members of large suburban churches to understand the needs and concerns of families in need of housing. Another example is an independent nonprofit agency in New York that, although working mostly through schools and with police to combat violence, has also tried to enlist the help of churches. Because inner-city churches are one of the few private organizations to which any significant number of their neighborhood residents may belong, they have strong potential for efforts to mobilize civic involvement. Yet they are often so weak financially that it is difficult for them to do much without help from other sources.[52]

TOWARD THE FUTURE

Although the evidence considered here is more suggestive than conclusive, it points toward a possibility that has broad implications for understanding the future of civil society in the United States. The porousness of social institutions is likely to increase in coming decades, but this increase need not lead only to further fragmentation of the society or to withdrawal from civic life. That porousness is likely to increase is primarily because the brokering mechanisms that have been established are well institutionalized and function reasonably well to prevent the worst kinds of fragmentation to which porousness might otherwise lead. In addition, markets are likely to become increasingly organized around international trade, and computing technologies are capable of processing large quantities of information; thus, people, goods, and information can move rapidly through social locations with the brokering help of travel agencies, relocation services, divorce lawyers, and support groups.[53]

The attendant human costs are not to be minimized and especially in low-income areas, where resources and access to supportive brokering mechanisms are not available, are very high. Yet most people who experience the dislocations of porous institutions do not decide simply to fend for themselves. They more typically reach out to one another, perhaps knowing instinctively that social relationships are both possible and desirable even in a porous society.

The dislocations in religion that accompany porous institutions are considerable and are likely to remain so in the foreseeable future. Some estimates suggest that as many as 40 percent of local congregations have fallen

below the size necessary to maintain attractive programs for a new generation of members.[54] The idea of spiritual seeking has become widely accepted, encouraging millions of Americans to piece together spiritual identities from a wide variety of sources, and even those who identify mainly
with Christianity or Judaism are often influenced by school courses on other
world religions, by television programs about mysterious spiritual encounters, and through access to books, tapes, and retreat centers. Searching of
this kind depends on, and elevates, the priority that individuals attach to
their own experiences of spirituality. Yet it also appears that Americans who
have experienced social and spiritual dislocations are reassembling in sufficient numbers to maintain overall memberships and attendance at religious services at nearly constant levels.

It should not be surprising that congregations have become places where
people can reassemble. They have repeatedly played this role in the past.
Despite belief regimens or rigid hierarchies of authority that sometimes
worked against adapting to new conditions, American congregations have
been part of a competitive environment that has encouraged them to innovate and to seek new adherents. Thoroughly Americanized congregations often became, for instance, the places in which new immigrants could
reassemble; in recent decades, new immigrant congregations have again
become important, not only as a source of religious vitality, but also as
places for assembling new identities and social relationships.[55] The large,
perhaps predominantly white Anglo American, suburban church is also an
important place of reassembling.

The large church is distinctive less for its size than for the kinds of relationships it reinforces. Many of these relationships are loosely structured.
They are not unimportant to their participants, but they are likely to be in-
tentional and thus changeable as needs and interests shift. They are often
focused on accomplishing a specific task. In many instances, their effectiveness depends less on long-term commitment and more on creating linkages
among individuals and organizations. In a complex social environment,
these linkages play an important role in holding civil society together. Congregations provide leadership and places to assemble, and, in turn, members become linked through friendships, small groups, and volunteer efforts to the wider community.

The shape of civil society is thus changing. Although it will continue to
depend on the long-term commitments that many people are able to make
to their families, careers, neighbors, and fellow congregants, it is increasingly held together by connections between congregations, among volunteers, and between these and secular nonprofit agencies. Many of these
connections are anchored in weekly worship services or in other enduring
civic organizations. But these civic organizations also serve as brokering

mechanisms, helping to solicit the occasional volunteer, putting together strategic planning committees, networking with other agencies, and appealing for funds from a variety of sources.

The complexity of these arrangements means that no simple solutions to present concerns about civil society are likely to be entirely compelling. Welfare reforms may require churches and other voluntary organizations to play a more active role in helping the needy, but these efforts will only be effective if there is continuing support from public agencies and a greater public commitment to social justice as well.[56] Working alone, churches may overcome some of the social isolation that results from living in a porous society, and they may help their members learn civic skills, but church membership alone cannot make up for being poor or disadvantaged in other ways.[57] Thus, the social relationships that churches can nurture must be viewed in a larger perspective. As valuable as these relationships may be, they can contribute only so much to the revitalization of civil society. This is why churches that cooperate with other religious organizations and with nonprofit agencies, government, and corporations hold special promise for the future.

ELEVEN

Democracy, Inclusive and Exclusive

Charles Taylor

Democracy, particularly liberal democracy, is a great philosophy of inclusion. Rule of the people, by the people, for the people, where "people" is supposed to mean (unlike in earlier days) everybody, without the unspoken restrictions of yesteryear (peasants, women, slaves, etc.): this offers the spectacle of the most inclusive politics of human history.

And yet there is also something in the dynamic of democracy that pushes to exclusion. This was allowed full rein in earlier forms of this regime, as among the ancient *poleis* and republics; but today it is a great cause of malaise. Worse, contemporary liberal theory tends to be unaware of this dynamic, or to misidentify its source—and this just to the extent that liberal theory has turned its back on its classical sources and relegated the goods of participatory self-rule to a twilight zone, overshadowed by those of equality and individual rights. Only those who, like Robert Bellah, have fought hard to restore a sense of the continuing importance of citizen rule, are in a position to understand fully the dynamic of democracy as something both immensely valuable and potentially dangerous.

I want in this essay first to explore this dynamic and then to make a few sketchy remarks about possible ways of compensating for or minimizing it.

THE DYNAMICS OF EXCLUSION

What makes the thrust to exclusion? We might put it this way: what makes democracy inclusive is that it is the government of *all* the people; what makes for exclusion is that it is the *government* of all the people. The exclusion is a by-product of something else—of the need, in self-governing societies, of a high degree of cohesion. Democratic states need something like a common identity.

We can see why as soon as we ponder what is involved in self-government, what is implied in the basic mode of legitimation of democratic states, that they are founded on popular sovereignty. Now, for the people to be sovereign, it needs to form an entity and have a personality. This need can be expressed in the following way: the people are supposed to rule, and this means that the members of this "people" make up a decision-making unit, a body that takes joint decisions. Moreover, this "people" is supposed to take its decisions through a consensus, or at least a majority, of agents who are deemed equal and autonomous. It is not "democratic" for some citizens to be under the control of others; it might facilitate decision making, but it is not democratically legitimate.

In addition, to form a decision-making unit of the type demanded here, it is not enough for a vote to record the fully formed opinions of all the agents. These units must not only decide together, but deliberate together. A democratic state is constantly facing new questions and in addition aspires to form a consensus on the questions it must decide, not merely reflect the outcome of diffuse opinions. However, a joint decision emerging from joint deliberation does not merely require everybody to vote according to his or her opinion; it also requires that each person's opinion should have been able to take shape or be re-formed in the light of discussion—that is to say, by exchange with others.

This necessarily implies a degree of cohesion. To some extent, the members must know one another, listen to one another, and understand one another. If they are not acquainted, or if they cannot really understand one another, how can they engage in joint deliberation? This is a matter that concerns the very conditions of legitimacy of democratic states.

If, for example, a subgroup of the "nation" considers that it is not being listened to by the rest, or that this rest cannot understand its point of view, it will immediately consider itself excluded from joint deliberation. Popular sovereignty demands that one should live under laws that derive from such deliberation. Anyone who is excluded can have no part in the decisions that emerge; consequently, these lose their legitimacy for him or her. A subgroup that is not listened to is in some respects excluded from the "nation," but, by this same token, it is no longer bound by the will of that nation.

Thus, to function legitimately, a people must be so constituted that its members are capable of listening to one another, and to listen effectively— or, at least, that it come close enough to this condition to ward off possible challenges to its democratic legitimacy from subgroups. In practice, still more is normally required. It is not enough for us to be able *now* to listen to one another. Our states aim to last, so we want assurance that we shall be able to listen to one another *in the future*. This demands a certain reciprocal commitment. In practice, a nation can only ensure the stability of its legitimacy if its members are strongly committed to one another by common allegiance to the political community. Moreover, it is the shared consciousness of this commitment that creates confidence in the various subgroups that they will indeed be heard, despite the possible causes for suspicion that are implicit in differences among subgroups.

In other words, a modern democratic state demands a "people" with a strong collective identity. Democracy obliges much more solidarity and much more commitment to one another in the joint political project than was demanded by the hierarchical and authoritarian societies of yesteryear. In the good old days of the Austro-Hungarian Empire, the Polish peasant in Galicia could be altogether oblivious of the Hungarian country squire, the bourgeois in Prague of the Viennese worker, without this in the slightest threatening the stability of the state. On the contrary. This condition of things only becomes untenable when ideas about popular government start to circulate; this is the moment when subgroups that will not or cannot be bound together start to demand their own states. This is the era of nationalism, of the breakup of empires.

I have been discussing the political necessity of a strong common identity for modern democratic states in terms of the requirement of forming a *people,* a deliberative unit. But this political necessity can also be made evident in other ways. Thinkers in the civic humanist tradition, from Aristotle to Arendt, have noted that free societies require a higher level of commitment and participation than despotic or authoritarian ones. Citizens have to do for themselves, as it were, what otherwise the rulers do for them. But this commitment will happen only if these citizens feel a strong bond of identification with their political community, and hence with those who share it with them.

From another angle: because these societies require strong commitment to do the common work, and because a situation in which some carried the burdens of participation and others enjoyed the benefits would be intolerable, free societies require a high level of mutual trust. In other words, free societies are extremely vulnerable to mistrust on the part of some citizens that others might not really be assuming their commitments—for example, that others are not paying their taxes, or are cheating on welfare, or as employers are benefiting from a good labor market without assuming any of the social costs. This kind of mistrust creates extreme tension and threatens to unravel the whole skein of the mores of commitment that democratic societies require to operate. A continuing and constantly renewed mutual commitment is essential for taking the measures needed to renew this trust.

The relation between nation and state is often considered from a unilateral point of view, as if it were always the nation that sought to provide itself with a state. But there is also the opposite process. To remain viable, states sometimes seek to create a feeling of common belonging. (This is an important theme in the history of Canada, for example.) To form a state, in the democratic era, a society is forced to undertake the difficult and never-to-be-completed task of defining its collective identity.

So there is a need for common identity. How does this generate exclusion? In a host of possible ways, which we can see illustrated in different circumstances. First, there is the phenomenon sometimes seen in societies with a high degree of historic ethnic unity. The sense of common bond and common commitment has been for so long bound up with a common language, culture, history, ancestry, and so on, that it is difficult to adjust to a situation in which the citizen body includes many people of other origins. People feel a certain discomfort with this situation, and this discomfort can be reflected in a number of ways.

In one kind of case, the homogeneous society is reluctant to concede citizenship to the outsiders. Germany is the best-known example of this, with its third-generation Turkish "Gastarbeiter," whose only fluent language may be German, whose only familial home is in Frankfurt, but who are still resident aliens. But there are subtler, more ambivalent ways in which this discomfort can play out. Perhaps the outsiders automatically acquire citizenship after a standard period of waiting; there even may be an official policy of integrating them, widely agreed on by the members of the "old stock" population. But these "old stock" citizens are still so used to functioning politically among themselves that they find it difficult to adjust. Perhaps one might better put it that they don't quite know how to adjust yet; the new reflexes are difficult to find. For instance, they still discuss policy questions among themselves, in their electronic media and newspapers, as though immigrants were not a party to the debate. They discuss, for instance, how to gain the best advantage for their society of the new arrivals, or how to avoid certain possible negative consequences, but the newcomers are spoken of as "them," as though not potential partners in the debate.

This is not to claim that democracy unfailingly leads to exclusion. That would be a counsel of despair, and the situation is far from desperate. Indeed, there is a drive in modern democracy toward inclusion, in its implication that government should be by *all* the people. Nevertheless, alongside this, there is a standing temptation to exclusion, which arises from the fact that democracies work well when people know each other, trust each other, and feel a sense of commitment toward each other.

The coming of new kinds of people into the country, or into active citizenship, poses a challenge. The exact content of the mutual understanding, the bases of the mutual trust, and the shape of the mutual commitment—all have to be redefined, reinvented. This is not easy, and there is an understandable temptation to fall back on the old ways and deny the problem, either by straight exclusion from citizenship (Germany) or by the perpetuation of "us and them" ways of talking, thinking, doing politics.

So much for societies that have historically been ethnically homogeneous. But there are analogous phenomena in mixed societies. Think of the
history of the United States, how successive waves of immigrants were perceived by many Americans of longer standing as a threat to democracy
and the American way of life. This was first the fate of the Irish beginning
in the 1840s. Then immigrants from southern and eastern Europe were
looked askance at in the last decades of the century. And, of course, one
old-established population, the blacks, when given citizen rights for the first
time after the Civil War, were in effect excluded from voting through much
of the Old South until the civil rights legislation of the 1960s.

Some of this was blind prejudice. But not all. In fact, the early Irish, and
later European, immigrants could not integrate immediately into America's
WASP political culture. The new immigrants often formed "vote banks" for
bosses and machines in the cities, and this was strongly resented and opposed by old-established Progressives and others who were concerned for
what they understood as citizen democracy.

Here again, a transition was successfully navigated, and a new democracy
emerged, in which a fairly high level of mutual understanding, trust, and
commitment (with the tragic exception of the black/white divide) was re-
created—although arguably at the price of the fading of the early ideals of
a citizen republic and the triumph of the "procedural republic," in Michael
Sandel's phrase.[1] But the temptation to exclusion was very strong for a time,
and some was motivated by the commitment to democracy itself.

The cases so far considered are characterized by the arrival from abroad,
or the entry into active citizenship, of new groups who have not shared the
host society's ethnic-linguistic, or else its political, culture. But exclusion
can also operate along another axis. Just because of the importance of cohesion, and of a common understanding of political culture, democracies
have sometimes attempted to force their citizens into a single mold. The
"Jacobin" tradition of the French Republic provides the best-known example of this.

In this situation, the strategy is, from the very beginning, to make people
over in a rigorous and uncompromising way. Common understanding is
reached—and supposedly forever maintained—by a clear definition of
what politics is about, and what citizenship entails; and these together define the primary allegiance of citizens. This complex is then vigorously defended against all comers, ideological enemies, slackers, and, when the case
arises, immigrants.

The exclusion operates here, not first against certain people already
defined as outsiders, but against other ways of being. This formula forbids
other ways of living modern citizenship; it castigates as unpatriotic any way
of living that would not subordinate other facets of identity to citizenship.

In the particular case of France, for instance, a certain solution to the problem of religion in public life—extrusion—was adopted by radical Republicans, and they have had immense difficulty even imagining that there might be other ways to safeguard the neutrality and comprehensiveness of the French state. Hence the French overreaction to Muslim adolescents wearing the veil in school.

But the strength of this "Jacobin" formula is that it managed for a long time to avoid, or at least minimize, the other sort of exclusion, that of new arrivals. It still surprises the French, and others, when they learn from Gérard Noiriel[2] that one French person in four today has at least one grandparent born outside the country. France in the twentieth century has been an immigrant country, without regarding itself as such. The policy of assimilation has hit a barrier with recent waves of Maghrébains, but it worked totally with the Italians, Poles, Czechs, who came between the wars; these people were never offered the choice and became indistinguishable from *les Français de souche.*

It has been argued that another dimension of such inner exclusion has operated along gender lines; and this not only in Jacobin societies, but in all liberal democracies, where without exception women received voting rights later than men. The argument is that the style of politics, the modes and tone of public debate, and the like, have been set by a political society that was exclusively male and that this bias has still to be modified to include women. If one looks at the behavior of some male-dominated legislatures at question time—resembling, as they sometimes do, a boisterous boys' school during recess—it is clear there is truth to this point. The culture of politics cannot fully include women without changing.

UNSTOPPABLE DIVERSITY

I hope I have made somewhat clear what I mean by the dynamic of exclusion in democracy. We might describe this dynamic as a temptation to exclude, beyond that which people may feel from narrowed sympathies or historic prejudice: a temptation that arises from the very requirement of democratic rule for a high degree of mutual understanding, trust, and commitment. This necessity can make it hard to integrate outsiders, and tempt citizens to draw a line around the original community. It can also tempt to what I have called "inner exclusion," the creation of a common identity around a rigid formula of politics and citizenship, which refuses to accommodate any alternatives and imperiously demands the subordination of other aspects of citizens' identities.

It is clear that these two modes are not mutually exclusive. Societies based on inner exclusion may come to turn away outsiders as well, as the strength of the Front National unfortunately well illustrates; conversely, societies whose main historical challenge has been the integration of outsiders may have recourse to inner exclusion in an attempt to create some unity amid diversity.

Now, the obvious fact about our era is that, first, the challenge of the new arrival is becoming generalized and multiplied in every democratic society. The scope and rate of international migration is making all societies increasingly "multicultural"; while second, the "Jacobin" response to this challenge—a rigorous assimilation to a formula involving fairly intense inner exclusion—is becoming less and less sustainable.

This last point is not easy to explain, but it seems an undeniable fact. There has been a subtle switch in mind-set in our civilization, probably starting in the 1960s. The idea that one ought to suppress one's difference for the sake of fitting in to a dominant mold, defined as the established "way" in one's society, has been considerably eroded. Feminists, cultural minorities, homosexuals, religious groups—all demand that the reigning formula be modified to accommodate them, rather than the other way around.

At the same time, possibly connected to this first change but certainly having its own roots, has come another change, equally subtle and hard to pin down. Migrants, in the same way, no longer feel the imperative to assimilate. One must not misidentify this switch. Most migrants want to assimilate substantively to the societies they have entered; and they certainly want to be accepted as full members. But they frequently want, now, to do this at their own pace and in their own way, and, in the process, they reserve the right to alter the society even as they assimilate to it.

The case of Hispanics in the United States is very telling in this regard. It is not that they do not want to become anglophone Americans. They see obvious advantages in doing so, and they have no intention of depriving themselves of these. But they frequently demand schools and services in Spanish, because they want to make the process as painless as they can and because they welcome such retention of the original culture as may fall out of this process. And something like this is obviously in the cards; they will all eventually learn English, but they will also alter somewhat the going sense of what it means to be an American, even as did earlier waves of immigrants. The difference now is that Hispanics seem to be operating with a sense of their eventual role in codetermining the culture rather than having this sense arise only retrospectively, as with earlier immigrants.

The difference between the earlier near-total success of France in assimilating eastern Europeans and others (who ever thought of Yves Montand as Italian?) and the present great difficulty with Maghrébains, while it reflects other factors—for example, greater cultural-religious difference, the collapse of full employment—nevertheless must also reflect the new attitude among migrants. The earlier sense of unalloyed gratitude toward the new countries of refuge and opportunity, which seemed to make any revindication of difference quite unjustified and out of place, has been replaced by something harder to define. One is almost tempted to say, by something resembling the old doctrine that is central to many religions, that the earth has been given to the human species in common. A given space does not unqualifiedly belong to the people born in it, so is not simply theirs to give. In return for entry, one is not morally bound to accept just any condition the inhabitants impose.

Two new features arise from this shift. First, the notion attributed above to Hispanics in the United States has become widespread—the idea that the culture immigrants are joining is something in continual evolution and that they have a chance to codetermine its future. This, instead of one-way assimilation, is more and more becoming the often unspoken understanding behind the act of immigration.

Second, there is an intensification of a long-established phenomenon, which now seems fully "normal"—the phenomenon that certain immigrant groups still function morally, culturally, and politically as a "diaspora" in relation to their home country. This has been going on for a long time; think, for instance, of the "Polonia" in all the countries of exile. But whereas it was frowned on, or looked askance at, by many in the receiving society, with toleration for it depending often on sympathy for the cause of the home country (the Poles were lucky in this respect); whereas people muttered darkly in the past about "double allegiance," now this kind of behavior is coming to be seen as normal. Of course, there are extreme variants that still arouse strong opposition, as when terrorists use the receiving countries as a base of operations. But such opposition arises because these manifestations shock the dominant political ethic, not because of the intense involvement with the country of origin. It is becoming more and more normal and unchallenged to think of oneself and be thought of as, say, a Canadian in good standing, while also being heavily involved in the fate of some country of origin.

REINVENTING DEMOCRACY

If all this is true, then democratic societies are going to have to engage in a constant process of self-reinvention in the coming century: redefining their common understandings to include new groups of people; and revising their traditional political culture to accommodate varied identities, both homegrown and newly arrived.

How should we go about this? There is not much that can usefully be said in general terms, and perhaps even less in philosophical terms. At this point, this essay might prudently end wishing the best of luck to people of goodwill everywhere in their endeavors. But because I have an irrepressible tendency to push the limits of philosophy farther than they perhaps ought to go, I should like to make a few general remarks about this process.

In face of a democratic society's having to bring together so many differences of culture, origin, political experience, and identity, the temptation is natural to define the common understanding more in terms of "liberalism" than of self-rule; that is, more in terms of individual rights and democratic and legal procedures and less in terms of definitions of civic virtue. In short, the temptation is to go for what Sandel calls the "procedural republic."

This move seems to have good pragmatic grounds. But it also has deep philosophical roots. Before going at the question of the practical merits, I want to bring out the philosophical roots, because inadequate views on this level cloud any vision of the pragmatic options.

The alternative is often put in this way: do we want a democracy focused on choice, on individual freedom, or one centering on participation and shared self-government? Both have existed throughout the past two centuries of liberal democracy; and are there even today. Only the balance has shifted so strongly in one direction that the civic definition risks being forgotten altogether.

What has the focus on choice had going for it? A number of things, including tendencies in our philosophical tradition that may, for the purposes of this essay, be put as the drift away from ethics of the good life toward ethics based on something else, allegedly less contentious and easier to carry general agreement. This partly explains the popularity of both utilitarianism and Kantian-derived deontological theories. Both manage to abstract from issues of what life is more worthy, more admirable, more human, and to fall back on what seems more solid ground. In one case, we count all the preferences, regardless of the supposed quality of the goals sought; in the other, we can abstract from the preferences and focus on the rights of the preferring agent.

This act of abstraction benefits from three important considerations. First, in an age of (menacing, if not actual) skepticism about moral views, it retreats from the terrain where the arguments seem the most dependent on our interpretations, the most contentious and incapable of winning universal assent; whereas we can presumably all agree that, other things being equal, it is better to let people have what they want, or to respect their freedom to choose. Second, this refusal to adopt a particular view of the good life leaves it to the individual to make the choice, and hence it fits with the anti-paternalism of the modern age; it enshrines a kind of freedom. Third, in face of the tremendous differences of outlook in modern society, utilitarianism and Kantian deontology seem to promise a way of deciding the common issues we face without having to espouse the views of some against others.

Now, the first two considerations are based on philosophical arguments—about what can and cannot be known and proved and about the nature of freedom, respectively. They have been much discussed and debated and often refuted by philosophers. But the third is a political argument. Regardless of who is ultimately right in the battle between procedural ethics and those of the good life, we could conceivably be convinced on political grounds that the best political formula for democratic government of a complex society was a kind of neutral liberalism. And this is where the argument has mainly gone today. The shift between Rawls I and Rawls II is a clear example. His theory of justice is now presented as "political, not metaphysical." This shift perhaps comes in part from the difficulties the purely philosophical arguments run into. But it also corresponds to the universal perception that diversity is a more important and crucial dimension of contemporary society. This comes, as I argued above, partly from the actual growth in diversity in the population and partly from the growing demand that age-old diversities be taken seriously.

So the issue now could be: what conceptions of freedom, of equality, of fairness, and of the basis for social coexistence are, not right in the abstract, but feasible for modern democratic societies? How can people live together in difference, in a democratic regime, under conditions of fairness and equality?

The procedural republic starts right off with a big advantage. If in your understanding of the citizen's roles and rights, you abstract from any view of the good life, then you avoid endorsing the views of some at the expense of others. Moreover, you find an immediate common terrain on which all can gather: Respect me, and accord me rights, simply in virtue of my being a citizen, not in virtue of my character, outlook, or the ends I espouse, not to speak of my gender, race, sexual orientation, and so on.

Now, no one in his or her right mind today would deny that this acceptance is an important dimension of any liberal society. The right to vote, for instance, is accorded unconditionally, or on condition of certain bases of citizenship, but certainly in a way that is blind to such differences as race, gender, and so on. The question is, however, whether this can be the *only* basis for living together in a democratic state, whether this is the valid approach in *all* contexts, whether our liberalism approaches perfection the more we can treat people in ways that abstract from what they stand for and that others do not.

Now, it can appear that, whatever other reasons there might be for treating people this way, at least it facilitates our coming together, feeling ourselves part of a common enterprise. What we all have in common is that we make choices, opt for some things rather than others, want to be helped and not hindered in pursuing the ends that flow from these choices. So an enterprise that promises to further everyone's plans, on some fair basis, seems the ideal common ground. Indeed, it is hard to see what else could be.

Here I think we suffer in modern philosophy from an absence of alternative models: models of how people can associate and be bonded together in difference, without abstracting from these differences. But there is another important such model, which I myself adhere to, and I should like to spell it out a bit more here. It has been invoked, among others, by Herder and Durkheim, thinkers who were rather divergent in other respects. The crucial idea is that people can also bond not in spite of but because of difference. They can sense, that is, that the difference enriches each party, that their lives are narrower and less full alone than in association with each other. In this sense, the difference defines a complementarity.

This concept can be the basis of a powerful theory of individual freedom, as in Humboldt's *On the Limits of State Action*. Humboldt's is not the classical negative libertarian argument that freedom is a right, in virtue of an inalienable claim on the part of each person to choose his or her ends or goals. Rather, Humboldt argues the crucial moral interest that each person has in the authentic development of the other. Since each life can only accomplish some small part of the human potential—Humboldt accepts Goethe's principle that we have to narrow ourselves to achieve anything—we can only benefit from the full range of human achievement and capacity if we live in close association with people who have taken other paths. To attempt to force conformity is to condemn ourselves to a narrower and poorer life.

One of the historical sources of this view is a certain theological understanding of human life, emerging particularly from Christianity. Humboldt probably no longer drew on this directly, although I would argue that Herder clearly did. This is the idea of humanity as something to be realized, not in each individual human being, but rather in communion among all humans. The essence of humanity is not something that, even in principle, a single person could realize in his or her life. And this is not because of the finitude and limitation of this life—since we cannot make up for the limitation of one life by laying other lives, as it were, alongside it, until human variety is exhausted. The fullness of humanity comes not from the adding of differences but from the exchange and communion between them. Persons' lives achieve fullness not separately but together. The image Herder used was of a chorus—or, we might say, an orchestra. The ultimate richness comes when all the different voices or instruments come together; it is something they create in the space between them. (The theology behind all this finds its sources in certain crucial Christian doctrines, e.g., the Trinity, and the Communion of Saints.)

Now, my claim is that if you look at the issue of what kind of common understanding we want to aim for, the procedural republic or the civic republic, against this background, it ceases to appear so self-evident that our choice must go to the procedural one. If we lay out these two models of what it is to create an associative bond, then my claim would be that, while the difference-blind, or procedural, model sometimes seems the obvious one, even the only one, in fact this may not be the case, and it may in the end be more of a source of discord. To avoid misunderstanding: it is not my purpose to deny that this model is ever appropriate. On the contrary, it often is. What I am pleading for is a more complex and many-stranded version of liberalism.

This will emerge if we look at some pervasive differences in the way the two models encourage us to respond to difference. The procedural model asks us to abstract from difference in our political-legal dealings with others, on two types of grounds. On the political level, it is because taking account of difference would be invidious, or divisive, or unfair, or some combination of these. On the basis of the underlying philosophical anthropology—for instance, Kantian—it may be because what is really important about the person is what he or she shares with everyone else—namely, the power to choose one's own ends and direct one's own life: one's autonomy. This model does not encourage us to learn about others' outlooks. Indeed, it may sometimes seem that the less we know, the easier it may be to treat people equitably, because their actual views are so offensive to us that it is hard to ignore these once known in all their repulsive detail.

Hate the sin, love the sinner. The Kantian saint will look away from the not very edifying outlooks that most people build for themselves, and keep firmly in view the autonomous agent ultimately responsible for them.

To the extent that we are operating out of the other model, however, there is a strong incentive to learn about the other. This is the powerful impulse, for example, behind Gadamerian hermeneutics, which in this respect is very Herderian. One principle of this hermeneutics is that there is no achieving understanding of the other that does not at the same time alter one's understanding of oneself. This is because what is preventing us from understanding the other initially is precisely the implicit, and hence unwitting, hold of our own too narrow horizon, of the undisputed terms in which we understand our lives. The attempt to understand leads, if successful, to a "fusion of horizons," a broader set of basic terms in which the other's way of being can figure undistortedly as one possibility among many. And this means that *our* way, too, figures as one possibility among many, and this precisely constitutes the revolution in self-understanding.

Now this decentering could be seen as a loss, of course. It is most emphatically not seen as such by Gadamer—testimony, I think, to the way he stands in this Herder-Humboldt tradition. Put baldly, teleologically: we are meant to understand each other. This mutual understanding is growth, completion.

Now, I have talked about two models here. But models are not people. Most of us operate to some extent on each. We treat different differences differently. No one is such a pure Kantian moral agent that he or she does not see some differences as complementarities, and act accordingly. So the issue is how we should respond to certain concrete cases. And here the different models of the associative bond, seen as overarching political formulas, dictate very different approaches.

But in what way does this discussion of the two models show that the procedural route may not be the best for overarching difference? Here, it is necessary to bring in the obvious point that no one has yet devised a procedure that is seen as neutral by everyone. The point about procedures, or charters of rights, or distributive principles, is that they are meant *not* to enter into the knotty terrain of substantive difference in way of life. But there is no way, in practice, of ensuring that this will be so.

The American case is eloquent in this regard. What is meant to be a procedural move, neutral between all parties—the separation of church and state—turns out to be open to different interpretations, some seen as far from neutral by important actors in the society. The school prayer dispute is a case in point. One could argue that insistence on a procedural solution—in this case, a winner-take-all constitutional adjudication—is exactly what will maximally inflame the division; which, indeed, it seems to have done.

Moreover, in comparison to a political solution, based on negotiation and compromise between competing demands, this constitutional adjudication provides no opportunity for each side to look into the substance of the other's case. Worse, by having their demand declared unconstitutional, the losers' program is delegitimated in a way that has deep resonance in American society. Not only can we not give you what you want, but you are primitive and un-American to want it.

In short, I would argue that the current American *Kulturkampf* has been exacerbated rather than reconciled by the heavy recourse in that polity to judicial resolution on the basis of the Constitution. But the issue is not to show for certain that the procedural approach has been bad in any given case but only to show how it could be, so as to reintroduce a certain healthy empiricism in this debate.

Because we are going to need all the flexibility of mind and imagination that we can muster. The struggle to redefine our political life, in order to counteract the dangers and temptations of democratic exclusion, will if anything intensify as the century goes on. There are no easy solutions, no universal formulas for success in this struggle. But at least we can avoid the handicaps of too rosy a self-perception and of inadequate philosophical views. This means, first, that it is important to see the drive to exclusion—as well as the vocation of inclusion—that democratic politics contains; and second, that we need to fight free of some of the powerful philosophical illusions of our age. This essay is an attempt to push our thought a bit ahead in both of these directions.

TWELVE

Raising Good Citizens in a Bad Society
Moral Education and Political Avoidance in Civic America

Nina Eliasoph

Many Americans who participate in civic groups say they are involved "for the children." Getting involved for and with children and community is Americans' sign of hope, trust that the world will continue, and faith that our actions matter. We assume that reaching toward children and community, with trust and faith, with voluntary goodness and solidarity, requires turning our backs on global problems and politics, on knowledge and critique, on institutions and deliberation. In this way, a nostalgic language of children and community suffocates public dialogue as surely as does any univocal language.

This metaphor of "the children" is the magnetic center of Americans' nostalgic understanding of community; and all symbols are right in their own way. This language of "children and community" contains our longings for solidarity and "generativity"[1]—our drive to pass along a cherished culture to future generations. Every adult, says Erik Erikson, "*needs* to teach . . . because facts are kept alive by being told, logic by being demonstrated, truth by being professed."[2] Adults can give world-sustaining hope to children; children, to adults. As Hannah Arendt puts it, raising children forces adults to "the point at which we decide whether we love the world enough to assume responsibility for it and by the same token save it from that ruin which, except for renewal, except for the coming of the new and young, would be inevitable."[3]

Concern for children could become a rich source of political energy at the center of community, home, and the moral self; indeed, this might be the source of the "politics of generativity" that Bellah and his coauthors propose in *The Good Society*.[4] The puzzle is that it is hard to know how to connect children to something as disturbing as current politics. If American democracy is "broken,"[5] how can adults communicate any faith in it to the next generation? As Hegel quips, "To a father who asked how he might best bring up his son [the answer is given,] 'By making him the citizen of a state with good laws.'"[6] But in the meantime, we still raise actual children in very imperfect societies. How do adults try to teach children to be good citizens in such states?

Traditions live by connecting one generation to the next; then, how can we pass down a faith in democracy when we are not even sure we live in a democracy? Raising children is an undebatable responsibility; we inevitably communicate some political culture to children. At best, we somehow have to teach them to have faith in spite of themselves, and ourselves—to keep walking on grounds we are not sure exist.

This essay will first show how difficult it is for volunteers and activists to imagine children's connection to politics—how Americans often inadvertently reproduce a politics of blocked generativity. Second, the essay will ask where, if at all, Americans try to embrace the wider world and children simultaneously—where, if at all, facing children does not seem to require turning away from politics.

The first set of portraits comes from a larger ethnographic study of civic life in a "post-suburban region"[7] I will call Amargo.[8] The first stories from Amargo show how a one-sided reach toward "community" made sense for a *volunteer* group that worked on school issues, the Parent League, a group of about fifteen parents of high school students that met monthly, organized frequent events, and gathered at school sports events to sell snacks. The second set of Amargo stories shows how difficult it was for an anti-toxics *activist* group to express concern for children and politics simultaneously. "For the children" was a phrase both groups used often, and it usually worked to stop conversation, as if we all already know what kind of community and society children need. Both groups rarely spoke about children in the same breath as national and international institutions—avoiding, that is, the "invisible complexity" that the authors of *Habits of the Heart* say Americans have such difficulty imagining. In retreating to a small, cozy, nostalgic understanding of children and community, the groups managed to avert any collision between their hopes for children and their desperate fears for the wider world.

After describing the Parent League and the anti-toxics group in Amargo, I search for situations of everyday life in which citizens might cultivate, in discussion, a more expansive understanding of the connection between childhood, community, and politics. This kind of discussion might happen any time, anywhere, where there are children and the adults who care for them. I have just begun a hunt for such interaction in a sprawling midwestern city that I will call "Snowy Prairie," and I am hearing this thoughtful political conversation springing up in surprising places, in contexts that our theories of civil society would not notice. Adults who gather together through children—at playgrounds or parks, for example, or in schools, day-care facilities, or play groups, at library story-reading hours or school-bus stops—do not necessarily debate foreign policy (though I have heard them do so) but do endlessly puzzle about what makes a good person, and what kinds of communities, institutions, and societies children need to become good people.

If adults would not otherwise carry on these conversations, children would force them to, by asking hard questions. The more areas of life that become potentially "political," the more potentially political seem the questions children ask—about gender, food, consumption, race, competition, discipline, marriage, television; adults might consider all sorts of issues worth subjecting to political deliberation. When "politics" expands, the fields in which people may deliberate expand, too. Where such discussions take place may be either more private (in that people attend them primarily as members of families) or more public (in that state and nonprofit agencies may help organize them) than theories of civil society lead us to expect.

Let me peel apart just one example, which confounds all prevalent definitions of civil society. In public library–sponsored story hours for pre-schoolers, parents often debate the politics and morality of the stories, sometimes in whispers, hoping that the children will not overhear, thus implicitly teaching them how and what is appropriate to discuss. A frequent topic is the gender relations in the stories, for example. These conversations—whether in story hours, or on playgrounds, or over the plastic plates at a day-care center's little lunch tables—are not being held in the after-hours bowling leagues and other voluntary associations that scholars of civil society like Robert Putnam describe.[9] They are more closely tied to the intimate sphere and are often also tied to the market and/or state. Part of what they do is child care, one of the most involuntary activities of all. In most of these sites, the adult participants—teachers and leaders—are paid, sometimes by the state. And they are paid to take care of the other participants—the children who are not full citizens and need some shelter from direct exposure to the market, state, and civil society.

But these differences from "civil society" as imagined by scholars—as well as from "community" as imagined by popular wisdom—make sites like these all the more interesting. Indeed, for most Americans who participate in any civic life at all, participation revolves around children. It is quite remarkable that scholars of civic culture have not theorized the specifically child-focused content of our civic life—as if it does not matter what the contents of our civic groups are. Situations like the library story hour are ones that many Americans *are in already;* we need to understand how these incessant, semipublic conversations for and with children might open the door to public discussion about the connection between deep, personal moral and political education and wide, global conditions.

NOSTALGIC COMMUNITY AND INDIVIDUALISM:
A PRAGMATIC CASE FOR THEIR CONFLUENCE

What suffocates public conversation in the United States? Robert Bellah and his coauthors of *Habits of the Heart* and *The Good Society* convincingly argue that the prevalent American language of individualism is one culprit. Some critics of Bellah[10] incorrectly assume that if he is "against" individualism, he must be "for" a kind of sweet, unconflictive community; these critics slip into a groove that is worn deep in our culture, dichotomizing between cold individualism and warm, sticky community, as if they are the only two possibilities.[11] But Bellah and his colleagues say that these two seemingly opposed ways of talking work together;[12] like the language of individualism, nostalgia avoids entanglement with the invisible complexity of large-scale political and economic institutions.[13] Proclaiming "self-interest" is a way of stopping the public conversation; no one can argue with a person who simply states "this is in my interest." Similarly, in the nostalgically conceived community, no one needs to talk, because all important ends are already given; since we already know what we should want together ("community"), public deliberation seems unnecessary and everyone can go home.

That is, people are "doing things with words"[14] together when they invoke these two common languages; ironically, the two seemingly opposed languages both often do the same thing—stop public conversation and evacuate political, moral debate from public life. But perhaps any language that automatically offers only one unambivalent, obvious answer does. I want to push this pragmatic—as opposed to thematic—case for the two languages' similarity further. Instead of focusing on inner beliefs and the logic stringing these together (as a standard sociological study of values and attitudes might), and in addition to focusing on citizens' "languages," as Bellah and coauthors do, I suggest paying close attention to the meanings that participants attribute, in practice, to the very act of speaking, in the actual, everyday situations in which conversations among citizens take place. This elusive, subtle etiquette for public life is meaningful in itself.

The meanings citizens attribute to the very act of speaking in everyday situations are a key to understanding how they imagine community and politics. For example, in *Avoiding Politics,* I found, paradoxically, that American volunteers and activists could speak in a public-spirited way in behind-the-scenes, "backstage"[15] situations but that front stage, in public meetings, people sounded far less public-spirited. The more public the context, the less public-spirited the language. The problem was not that people lacked access to public-spirited languages but that they lacked access to them in public contexts.[16] Here, I am asking how and where people collectively create contexts for thoughtful discussion of children, community, and politics. Do Americans create any everyday, ongoing contexts that allow speakers to

honor the protective feelings that the language of "children and community" implies, but without the nostalgic aversion to politics?

CHILDREN, COMMUNITY, AND POLITICS: MAKING THE CONNECTION

One puzzle that childhood presents for individualistic Americans is that
children require involuntary attention from a voluntaristically conceived
community. The citizens I met in Amargo knew that taking care of children
is not voluntary, but, in their fear of invisible complexity, they rarely questioned whether purely voluntary solutions could solve all the problems that
children face, rarely asked whether any institutional changes might be necessary. Institutional changes might require more mundane, daily, expensive
attention, might not so cleanly separate private life from the state and politics, and might be more enduring (but less voluntary) than volunteers'
after-hours goodness could offer. In contrast, the people I met in both
Amargo and Snowy Prairie said it is important for children to feel "connected to something" and "a part of things." The everyday ethics of child
raising reveal a hidden morality; while adults like those interviewed in *Habits of the Heart* (or Robert Wuthnow's *Acts of Compassion*) may confidently
speak as if all adults are, or should be, independent and self-interested, the
same adults would probably say that children should be neither. So, the case
of childhood is an especially interesting one in which to observe the interplay between voluntary solidarity and demands for institutional change.

Further, not even the most libertarian adult believes that children can
"do their own thing." Recent authors like Alberto Melucci, Anthony Giddens, and Zygmunt Bauman[17] describe what they consider to be a characteristic of "post-traditional" society: the cultivation of a self that does not
attribute moral decisions to tradition or authority but aims to take full responsibility for its own action and never consider any action inevitable,
never firmly settle into one univocal understanding of reality—a kind of
mandatory existentialism for all. These authors, in various complex and interesting ways, tie this new kind of selfhood to the completion of the project of modernity, which forces an unbearable burden of individuation in a
global society that seems to be lying in ambush, poised to dislocate, speed
up, and vaporize the comfortable anchors of everyday life. The burden
these scholars describe is to retain any sense of purpose in the face of this
global onslaught.

The adults I have heard in Snowy Prairie say very clearly that children
need a kind of love and steadiness that abstract, speedy, bodiless, transitory
relationships cannot sustain. In contrast, Melucci and the other recent authors either romanticize or simply do not imagine child raising in their theorizing. Children cannot be the authors of their own lives, and when intro-

ducing them to that "world" that will fall to ruin if it is not passed down, caregivers are forced to take a stand. Here, there is always a decision to be made, whether conscious or not, about how to represent the world. In this way, child raising is the most basic, mundane, everyday link in the chain of tradition. Yet, Melucci and the rest are right that modernity has given us a new way of being a person, a way we have not fully grasped in our commonsense theories. And whatever that new self is, it offers an especially interesting problem for child raising.

This problem is, in Hannah Arendt's formulation, that in contrast to adults' political education through active citizenship, children's "education" is necessarily authoritarian. It is, Arendt states, unfair to force children to solve the political problems created by adults, and introducing politics too early to children undermines their ability to gain firm footing in a reality they have barely begun to know. If it is impossible to question the ground on which you walk while walking,[18] Arendt says, it is unfair to question the political ground on which children are learning to walk while teaching them to take steps. Instead

> the educators here stand in relation to the young as representative of a world for which they must assume responsibility although they themselves did not make it, and even though they may, secretly or openly, wish it were other than it is. . . . Vis-à-vis the child it is as though [the educator] were a representative of all adult inhabitants, pointing out the details and saying to the child: This is our world.[19]

Arendt's solution is to shelter children from politics completely. What she misses is that children cannot help but notice the shakiness of the political ground;[20] in fact, part of learning to walk on this ground is learning to take its shakiness into account. Children learn to walk whether adults teach them or not, and they assess and question the world's moral steadiness even when adults try to make it seem as if it is not shaking. In other words, children do question the ground they walk on.

If adults take children's ravenous questioning seriously, then conversation about, and with, children can actually force adults to decide where they stand. But in American politicians' rhetoric[21] and in citizens' groups like the volunteers and activists in Amargo, discussion of children and community stops conversation just where it should start; for it should start by asking how we can continue moral education in a way that does not *only* "shelter," "protect," and "insulate" children from the world (to use some of the metaphors I have heard in fieldwork), but also teaches them to analyze and appreciate their inevitable, complex connections to wider institutions. The discussion usually stops, that is, where Durkheim began it, ninety years ago, when he asked how to raise children to recognize and reflect on the bonds that they already inevitably have. Adults' job is to acknowledge and awaken children's awareness of these bonds, as members of families, nations, and humanity. Of these three, as Durkheim puts it, "there is one that enjoys primacy over others—political society, the nation";[22] unlike a family, the nation is not purely personal, and unlike global humanity, it is embodied in real, powerful institutions. Durkheim's question is whether we can teach this sense of connection to children without a seemingly natural, shared, God-given tradition. He turned this problem around and around, saying, first, in *Moral Education,* "We must rediscover the moral forces basic to all moral life . . . even if up to the present that morality has only existed in religious guise. We have to seek out the rational expression of such a morality, that is to say, apprehend such morality in itself, in its genuine nature, stripped of all symbols."[23]

Later, in *The Elementary Forms of the Religious Life,* Durkheim adds that no society can exist without such symbols, that human reality is made of symbols. If this later Durkheim, who took symbols seriously, had looped back to the topic of moral education, perhaps he would have asked, What kinds of deeply shared symbols can societies create, connecting children to the wider world?[24] Is moral education possible in a world in which most adults hold little faith in common political entities? How can adults imagine raising good citizens in bad states?

To consider these questions, I first turn to the volunteer groups that I studied. These groups had the most widely accepted ways of talking about "community," and the most standard understandings of the purpose and place of political speech. They worked hard caring for children, but their quest to cultivate a good society for "the children" was impaired by fear that conducting open-ended political conversation in public would be dangerous. Volunteers *could* talk about their concern for the wider world but only behind the scenes; in meetings and other public situations, they assumed that a good citizen should inspire faith and that this and social critique were mutually exclusive. When the door snapped shut on political conversation, "the children" were the hinge. The paradox is, the more volunteers cared about "community," the more they felt they had to muzzle political conversation in public situations.

VOLUNTEERS: COMMUNITY AND MORAL EDUCATION WITHOUT POLITICS

Volunteer groups tried hard to ignore problems they could not fix readily and without much discussion—not because members were apathetic, but because they were trying to inspire faith and hope among fellow citizens. Volunteers assumed that the purpose of speaking in meetings was to show that regular citizens *can* make a difference on issues that are close to home. This meant publicly claiming to care only about problems that could be solved with hands-on, local, shoulder-to-shoulder work, defining all other problems as unrelated to "the children" and therefore not worth discussing in public. They assumed that cultivating community and community spirit for children meant avoiding politics.

So, volunteers in the Parent League, a group of parents of high school students, devoted their meetings to discussion of "doable" tasks like setting up a Royal Dog Steamer to cook hot dogs at track meets or trucking thousands of cans of soft drinks to the end-of-senior-year festivities. Conducting political discussion in public was considered immoral, because it could undermine the buoyant spirit of community that they sought to create. When newcomers tried to open up discussion in meetings, they were politely ignored. But behind the scenes, volunteers showed that they did care that the roof had caved in on one classroom earlier that year, that the building was unheated, that there was a long-standing flood in another classroom, that there had been several race riots that year at school, and that Nazi skinheads were recruiting on the school grounds. They just did not want to talk about such issues in public; doing so would shatter the nostalgic connection between childhood, apolitical community, hope, and faith in democracy.

In interviews, I heard these refrains used interchangeably: "close to home," "my vested interest," "not political," and "for me and my children" (and, as I have argued elsewhere,[25] these expressions were especially puzzling when used by volunteers to explain their apathy regarding the chemical plants and nuclear battleship station nearby, since the volunteers themselves had told me that the plants were dangerous and often had spills and fires and that the nuclear station "could melt down any minute"). In one group interview, I challenged volunteers, saying that the environmental activists, anti-crime volunteers, and, indeed, members of *all* the groups I was studying also said they were involved "for the children." The volunteers backtracked momentarily, saying "Mmm," and "Yeah," and "That's a real good question. You *could* tie it all to kids." But moments later, they were back to saying, "Just about everything I've ever volunteered for in my adult life has to do with kids," and "I would do things that involve my children."

The "for the children" vocabulary was more troubled than it might seem; it did not just demonstrate a clear desire to protect children from harm. For example, "for the children" did not include talking to them about registering for the draft, one volunteer, Danielle, told me with alarm. When her son turned eighteen, he told her he would have to register for the draft: "And you know, we had never talked about it. Never! Never! Do you still have to register? And I thought about that for days."

Much like public officials, volunteers often said that the family is the cause of all social problems, and should be the cure. For example, at one public forum, the police lieutenant said, "The crime is usually a symptom of a bigger problem which usually goes back to the family structure." The police chief added, "There are ten thousand arrests in Amargo per year. We should focus on the source: the family is the first unit." And at another public meeting, the official introduction began, "It all starts with the family."

But when young people themselves were asked to hold a public forum about an issue of their choice, they discussed AIDS one year, nuclear war another year, and child care another. As Danielle noted, her son "always says" that since the town housed a major nuclear weapons base, "there's a bomb with 'Amargo' written on it." These issues worried the children, but the parents never discussed them in meetings. Perhaps—to go back to Arendt's worry—the children's concerns should hint at the possibility that children inevitably question the world at the same moment that they are becoming acquainted with it. Children's imaginations keep going out the door of the home, even if adults' do not.[26]

The problems, however, were not what volunteers *believed* but what they assumed they could *say in public* and how they could create a forum for public discussion. The most important belief in operation was a belief about the purpose and place of talk itself, about how political conversation fitted into good citizenship; volunteers believed that it did not fit, because it could erode hope and faith. Many scholars of American political culture[27] have noted a nearly universal allegiance to the ideal of a democratic republic, a belief in the principle of responsible, participatory citizenship. In fact, volunteers' public silence was part of an effort at convincing themselves and fellow citizens that they should be active participants in a real "community"—a society that they imagined to be in the great tradition of democratic participation *minus the public sphere*. This mode of citizen participation has a noble lineage; Michael Schudson[28] shows that in the early days of the United States, election days were primarily celebrations of solidarity, trust in leaders, assent to being governed. This was how early Americans interpreted the principles of democracy. Schudson says that these former colonists, now citizens, considered political debate among citizens dangerous because it could undermine solidarity. Like them, the contemporary volunteers I studied clearly cared about the common good, and, although doing projects that did not specifically benefit themselves or their children personally, they were concerned to create a sense of community for the children and thought this had to mean silencing public critique and discussion about the wider world.

Robert Putnam[29] famously mourns the decline of similar sorts of civic associations in America—purely voluntary, face-to-face groups, from bowling leagues to Lions Clubs. This decline, he argues, has led to a decline in democratic participation—but he does not define democracy in a way that necessarily includes public conversation. Like the volunteers, Putnam imagines that civic life will necessarily foster democracy, but he does not worry about the quality of conversation involved. In contrast, theorists of participatory democracy[30] put citizens' open-ended deliberation at the center of democratic politics, arguing that democracy works not just because people "join groups" but because they have thoughtful political conversations in these groups. And local groups are not, for these theorists, necessarily completely detached from larger organizations (nor were they so detached in actual U.S. history).[31]

Such groups and networks may make life more livable in innumerable ways; they may be the yeast that leavens all other kinds of collective action[32] and makes risky acts of altruism possible.[33] But they do not necessarily inspire political debate. In fact, volunteers preempted political debate and counterposed voluntary solutions to institutional ones. In these two ways, the togetherness that Putnam applauds came at the expense of the kinds of discussion that would help people to work with "invisible complexity"—to entertain solutions that did not fit into the nostalgic ideal, to tie the cultivation of hope to the cultivation of critique. Putnam and others say that voluntary associations are the headwaters of democracy; but, unless these associations get beyond the nostalgic image of community, they will likely bottle up political conversation.

In my study, volunteers' and social service workers' understandings of the purpose of public speech resonated perfectly; each assumed that we all know what is to be done and that, if the goals are already set, there is no use talking about them publicly. All we have to worry about is how to get there. As a volunteer in Amargo, I had difficulty finding something to do that required more than simply plugging myself into a predesigned project—delivering meals to housebound elderly people, working alone with needy children. For example, at one meeting of the Just Say No team—a group of volunteers, city officials, and social service workers fighting drug abuse—a volunteer announced that a social service administrator was "looking for volunteers to supervise the playground in the morning before school starts": "A lot of parents have to leave for work at 6 or 6:30 A.M., and there are no before-school programs even in the elementary schools, so the parents have no choice but to just dump their kids—first graders, second graders, even—on the playground, sometimes before it's even light out, and just hope for the best."

Scrounging for volunteers was the *only* possibility discussed. The same pattern occurred over and over; another time, when we learned that at the age of eighteen foster children are turned out on the streets, we quickly decided to start a blanket drive.

A deep desire for faith in voluntary goodness fueled social service workers' idea of a Caring Adult Network, or CAN. The CAN was always introduced with the image of a neighborhood in which any Mom would poke her head out of the kitchen window, ready to help: "If a child is home alone with a problem, that child could go to any of the neighbors in the community, because they'd all be part of the Caring Adult Network." (Snowy Prairie, the city I am now studying, has a similar program.) Though most people in this booming new post-suburb had not lived there very long, and probably would not stay very long, and were almost never there during the day, and did not share a history there, the image of the CAN was compelling; adults could all share in raising the community's children, "so that," as volunteers and social service workers often said, "the community is like an extended family for the children."

A recent illustration of how CAN could function was often told: adults on a city bus had noticed a small, poor, ragged child and began to look after him, greeting him and making sure he got off at the right stop and into the school building (on the days he came to school). When I told one volunteer that I thought the story was touching, she sadly told me that he stopped coming one day and nobody knew why. I had heard the happy part of this story told publicly several times, but no one had ever told the sad ending in public. Thus, overwhelming and potentially political questions appeared but mysteriously vanished from public discussion. Volunteers certainly noticed such problems, but they wanted to believe that people are good inside and can act on that goodness without debating about *how* to be good and without asking for help from institutions. When speaking of supportive, caring community, no one ever asked why Americans had abandoned such community, or why voluntary community participation was declining; volunteers' and social service workers' only explanations blamed the family, which was also considered the only source of hope. Running in a self-contained circuit from child to family to community and around again, speakers' imaginations could not extend to the wider world.

In the 1970s and 1980s, many leftist critics of "the welfare state" said that citizen participation was better than the cold hand of bureaucracy and that the welfare state was good only at controlling people, "policing the family,"[34] and extending tentacles of bureaucracy into the everyday lives of local communities. The Right agreed, adding that welfare was also too expensive, and cut the funds. And social service workers—as anti-bureaucracy as other Americans—thought they were genuinely "creating community" by enlisting volunteers. While this way of creating community certainly might come in handy in an era of social service cutbacks, these workers were not just cynically roping in free labor; like volunteers, they assumed that such direct involvement was the answer to the cold emptiness of suburban life. So, everyone hated bureaucracy, including the bureaucrats themselves.

The irony is, the social service workers' anti-bureaucratic nostalgia resulted in a great hum of activity toward an unquestioned, preset goal that kept good people busy without giving them any space for free, public discussion. Everyone might as well have been working in the stereotypical image of a bureaucracy.[35] According to the nostalgic imagination, we *care* for reasons that are so obvious and so shared that we do not need to talk about them. In hope of restoring this unspoken faith, volunteers had to break the political connections linking childhood, community, and politics. Nostalgic language offered a place where the "buck stops." Hope, generativity, and togetherness thus became detached from critical reflection.

"THIS IS A FAMILY EVENT, NOT A POLITICAL EVENT"—IS THERE ROOM FOR ACTIVISTS?

When they first started speaking out publicly, activists in a local anti-toxics group sounded just like volunteers. Activists told the press and officials that they were involved "for the children" on issues "close to home"; in public speeches, they often physically surrounded themselves with children; and they did not hold public meetings for open discussion. "Backstage," however, in smaller meetings, parties, dinners, poster-making sessions, and other informal get-togethers, activists' sense of what was good "for the children" extended far beyond their own locale and their own children (backstage, they argued that the United States needed new laws regulating, for instance, toxic production). When *not* speaking to the press or public officials, activists trawled American culture for a "hidden language" of global childhood and community. Echoing a concern I heard from many activists, Maryellen said, "If it's not our kids, it'll be someone else's kids. People always ask, 'Well, yeah, but what are you gonna do with all that toxic waste?' That's something we should talk about, since it's not just a local issue. We shouldn't just fight off the thing to have some other community that's less organized get stuck with it!" She could say this in a small group meeting, but this language had no place in the public forum. Off the record, she could speak about "the children" in a way that did not equate the idea of childhood with "local and unpolitical."

Activists tried to call their project a "community" project but were rebuffed, because their agenda, unlike the volunteers', was "political," and "politics" and "community/family" were considered incompatible. For example, a member told me, as she and I marched in front of the group's float, how the activists were able to have this float in the annual town parade. It was a black-sheathed pickup truck with a cardboard smokestack, carrying adults, children, a big lump of ugly-colored cotton sticking out of the smokestack, and the Wizard of Ooze, slimy and smiling in a gown, waving like a prom queen, holding a grayish black artichoke on a stick to look like a malignant Statue of Liberty's torch. Every few minutes, we all broke out in a scary yell.

The activist, Diane, said she had had to "twist the arm of the guy who was in charge of signing people up for the parade even to let us in it *at all*. He was hesitant because, he said, 'This is a *family* event, not a political event.'"

Diane had had to argue, "What's political about a toxic incinerator? It's not political!" I was surprised to hear her say this, but it made sense when she repeated the rest of the conversation. The official had said that not everyone agreed on the subject; Diane had countered with, "Everyone in town agrees! The only people who don't agree are the ones who would make money off it, and they don't even live here, most of them." The official had then said he would have to ask the parade committee when it met, that Monday. "So I said to him," Diane proudly reported (in a wheedling voice, octaves higher than her usual), "'Gee, we'd *really* like to work on the float this weekend,' so he said, 'Oh, heck, go ahead and work on it—what the hell.'"

However, he had made one proviso: *No handing out leaflets.* As we paraded behind the glittering marching band and the handspringing teenage gymnasts, it was clear that without the leaflets, spectators could not possibly understand why we adults were there—except maybe as a preview of Halloween. Another group member, Henry, walked somewhat behind the float, handing out leaflets to the onlookers who lined the sidewalks. Diane commented, a bit angrily, "If it's against the rules, you can be sure Henry's doing it." There was similar debate surrounding participation in other community/family events, such as the annual July 4th celebration. Activists were not sure whether they should challenge the idea that "community/family" must equal "not political," and were not sure whether "everyone in town agrees" meant that theirs was not a political group.

But the "family, not political" definition of community was the only one that was readily available, even though no one gave it much credence and it was impossible to put into practice; into the remainder of the equation, into the gap between what one activist called "kissy-face, huggy-bear" community and the impossibility of its realization, came the total rejection of community—a definition of "radicalism" with a long history in American politics.[36] This radical style involved making statements that were shocking and cynical about the public's stupidity and reciting unbearably depressing facts about the fate of the world. For instance, one activist, a musician, proclaimed at a planning meeting for a concert to publicize the toxic incinerator, "People will go, 'Duh, a free concert—let's go!'" Another entertainer commented he would like to do an audience IQ test and licked a finger and held it in the air—saying, in effect, most audiences' brains were wind tunnels.

The other members did not like this "radical" approach, instead asking, "What can we do, other than music?" and other questions aimed at restoring a sense of earnestness, a sense of a public not totally duped. Activists often seemed to be falling off the edge of despair; in backstage whispers, they worried that the incinerator company's shiny, expensive public relations packages would easily sway local public opinion—even though the same activists sounded upbeat and confident in public. In interviews, they spoke with heartfelt fear for the fate of the planet.

Such deep fear of, and disgust with, the public and the political system may ring true, but it makes the connection between children and politics hard to imagine. For this model of citizenship, Arendt's criticism makes sense; this mode would teach children to revile the world before they learned to revere it. The question is, again, whether adults can teach children to do both at once: to be decent, well-mannered people and to understand that their lives are inseparable from the institutions around them. But institutions presented a riddle for the activists. If warm and fuzzy "community" was unavailable to activists, and total rejection was too rude and dispiriting, should they reject institutions, too? All institutions?—or were any trustworthy? This quandary arose when unions approached the group, offering to unite union concerns for workplace safety and job security at the chemical plants with activists' environmental concerns. For a long time, activists ignored this opportunity. One remembered having to join a union as a teenager, to get a job, and "talking to the guy across an acre of marble [his desk]."

Government and corporate officials addressed activists *as if* the activists cared only about the safety of their own families and their own property, as if activists shared the common aversion to connecting children/community to anything broader. Finally, after about a year of involvement, activists rebelled against the officials' assumption; but when the nostalgic, volunteer-style language of community/children faded from the activists' public speech, it was a struggle to find another public language for talking about children and community. Members began letting their own children come to demonstrations throughout the region and spoke proudly about their children's knowledge of environmental politics, city politics, state politics, and activism. Now and then, activists caught evanescent glimpses of a more open, expansive kind of childhood, but this image never fully materialized. At one meeting, in response to an anti-incinerator article in a high school newsletter, a member urged, "It would be great to have [high school students] come to the Good Neighbor Rally, so it's not just a bunch of old people worried about their property values, but young people worried about—well, basically about their lives!" In reply, another member intoned, parodying a pompous voice, "The Youth of America," as if it was funny to think of something as wholesome and unconflictual as "youth" in the same breath as political activism. And he said he liked the idea but that, even when the activists wanted to invite young people, they too discussed them as if "youth" had no broader vision but were only "worried about their lives."

Activists could not neatly fit their agenda into the children/community model and were wondering how to create a third kind of community that could include politics and institutions. They were not sure whether political involvement came at the expense of family/community; it might spoil the fun of "family" events like the local parade, might involve rejecting "community" and the generative obligation to keep hope alive, through expression of despair.

A typical sociologist might argue that activists were using the rhetoric of "close to home and for the children" strategically, trying to get a foot in the door by whatever means possible. But activists wanted to inspire public debate and broad, global concern. They did not merely want to win this specific battle. This "close to home and for the children" rhetoric undermined activists' very reasons for entering public debate; they did so primarily to encourage grassroots political participation, to inspire fellow citizens to ask important questions and become the genuinely active public that the activists felt American democracy demands.

Bellah would invite us to take the symbolic reality seriously: The activists themselves were puzzling through their own action; like the volunteers, they were trying to figure out how to be good citizens within the symbolic reality available, with the "tools" in their boxes.[37] Meanwhile, for both volunteers and activists, overwhelming cultural pressure created *publicly speakable* metaphors of "the children" and "community" that made private, domestic concerns seem unconnected to global issues—that made it seem as if "the children" could fill us with a shared, unquestioned faith and thus end the debate.

RAISING HOPEFUL YOUTH IN THE "CULTURE OF DEATH"

Does speech about children and community always end the dialogue between security and critical awareness? Who can enact the "mindful"[38] child raising and community that does not try so hard to block out the wider world, that invites discussion rather than end it as quickly as possible? Does speaking about or with children always shorten rather than stretch the threads of solidarity? As Durkheim or Bellah would say, the bonds are already there; the point is to discover them sociologically by examining if, how, and where adults actually try to teach children they are connected to the world.

Highlighting these discussions allows us to notice, on the one hand, the public-spirited deliberation that springs up in private life—when parents and children, separately or together, converse in preschoolers' play groups, for example. On the other hand, focusing on discussions about child raising also helps us to notice the public-spirited deliberation that springs up inside bureaucracies. For the remainder of this essay, I will focus on the latter. If raising children is not just a private activity, we might be able to hear morally and politically charged conversations about it threading through all kinds of institutions, dragging public-spirited questions into a wide range of sites that most social theory would not consider "civic." Maybe noticing these wavering edges of civic life can inspire people to imagine interesting ways of connecting private, civic, bureaucratic, and political life.[39]

BUREAUCRATS WORRYING ABOUT
USURPING VOLUNTARY ASSOCIATIONS' PLACE

Perhaps civil society is not so neatly detached from the bureaucracies that are entrusted to care for the young. Social workers, teachers, school administrators, librarians, community center coordinators, and after-school program organizers often try to draw children and families into activities and discussion aimed at engaging the wider world. Here, we have the fascinating case of state and nonprofit agencies often trying to *create* civil society, with the bureaucrats' goal—paradoxically, for most social theory—to encourage grassroots participatory citizenship by encouraging young citizens or even whole families to gather in ongoing groups to discuss issues that are simultaneously deeply political and deeply personal.[40]

These strange mixtures of volunteers and nonprofit and state agencies have been a growing part of American civic life for decades.[41] The nonprofit agencies are the "mailing list groups" whose growth Putnam disparages;[42] their donors mail checks but never meet and talk in the face-to-face gatherings that are crucial for democracy. What Putnam misses is that these same organizations can use the money garnered from the mailing list to encourage volunteer groups to form, to help volunteer groups coordinate their efforts, or to draw adults into civic life through their children. Whether these efforts work remains to be observed, but there is no reason a priori to assume that these local, underpaid bureaucrats cannot at least sometimes encourage children, or parents, to form civic groups.

In the study I am just beginning in Snowy Prairie, the bureaucrats' goal was not just to do things *for* young people. For example, when teenagers and adults gathered in a dim, windowless room one glorious summer evening for the first of a series of meetings planning the January celebration of Martin Luther King, Jr., Day, the adults consistently refused to tell the young people what to do. The latter understood that this refusal was an important part of the event, that adults wanted to cultivate "youth leadership"; the point that organizers publicly repeated with most pride was that "youth played a big part in planning and organizing" the previous year's celebration at which four hundred young people had gathered for a successful all-day event. The bureaucrats' question this summer evening was whether youth themselves would like to plan the next year's event: What theme did they want this year, if any? What speakers, if any? What workshops, if any?

What community service, if any? Over and over, adults said, "It's up to you to plan what you want to do," and "What I'm saying, I guess, is, 'You have a lot of control.'" The adult facilitator asked, "How would one of you like to sit where I'm sitting, and organize the meeting—facilitate it?"

These public servants very much wanted to avoid usurping voluntary associations' power. Walt, for example, told me he was a "community organizer" for citizens, not a social worker for clients. His agency's main activity was planning ongoing groups and events for youth and families; his primary goal was to have more citizens, and more diverse citizens, involved in the process of planning whatever projects the agency sponsored. Often, these social service agents worked alongside volunteer groups—*aiming*, at least, to take their orders *from* the volunteers. Or, they tried to help volunteer groups do what the groups could not do on their own. Whether and how they succeeded is a crucial question, but it was remarkable how hard the bureaucrats tried to put citizens in the center of the planning process.

In one of the first meetings I attended, Walt's group discussed organizing a "youth calendar," listing local activities for youth on a website and on flyers—especially focusing on community service activities. At first, I worried that the bureaucracies would be doing a job that voluntary associations could do, and I was surprised to hear that this was the bureaucrats' main worry as well. They began the meeting by saying that many events for youth were sponsored by volunteer groups that lacked publicity and that the calendar would link the groups, schools, youth centers, and other organizations and institutions by sending them information about each other's projects. They said that volunteer groups often did not know about events until it was too late for youth groups to plan the private transportation necessary for any activity in a sprawling suburb like Snowy Prairie. They discussed how many hours someone would have to put into the project, whether it could be done instead by two persons, and how steady and long term a commitment it would require. After a long debate, members convinced themselves that hiring someone for the job would not be too bad, even though, as one said, "It doesn't appeal as much to my idealistic idea of 'Let's get the youth involved in doing youth stuff,' but the alternative gets away from lots of headaches." In short, the bureaucrats were like volunteers in many ways, and many worked hours for which they were not paid or worked as volunteers after their paid work ended.

"CREATING A NEW CULTURE" FROM A CULTURALLY NEUTRAL BUREAUCRACY

The state is not just a monolithic "system" that works automatically through the media of money and power; it is as mediated by language as is the rest of life.[43] State workers are cultural beings; the weapons detector at the door of the faceless city-county building does not screen out bureaucrats' cultural selves.[44] "The state" is embodied in smaller groupings, which cohere because people in them talk to each other.[45]

There is good reason to suspect that bureaucrats might be less averse to confronting "invisible complexity" than are volunteers. Bureaucracies *are* the complex institutions that a nostalgic imagination fears. They are the suppressed part of childhood/community, the part Americans do not want to accept. Over and over, these bureaucrats, preschool teachers, and other caregivers say they "aim to change the culture, not just to give kids something to do." They say they seek to "create a new culture" that simultaneously encourages "diversity" and "connection" (two very popular words) and that invites youth to care about the world and to feel responsible for its upkeep—to bear "civic responsibility," as several bureaucrats put it. The bureaucrats' imaginations always go beyond individualism, sometimes go beyond nostalgia, and rarely are technocratic (or, at least, not intentionally).

Among bureaucrats' efforts at "changing culture" are their attempts to create or popularize new American holidays: Earth Day, Juneteenth, Kwanzaa, Cinco de Mayo, Martin Luther King, Jr., Day, and others. At least a hundred U.S. cities have gotten federal grants to make the planning for Martin Luther King, Jr., Day into a youth-oriented civic affair; in Snowy Prairie, this meant dozens of meetings for teenage volunteers to decide what kind of celebration to design. During one, a teenager asked, "Is it a day for doing community service things we're doing anyway, or is it about Martin Luther King, and all these things are happening because of him and his teaching?" The adults said this was a good question. One said, "You could make his life more central—it's up to you." Another agreed, adding, "But there's no money yet, so you have to keep that in mind." Here we have the unprecedented case of bureaucracies creating a new, partly grant-driven holiday in which average young people are partly entrusted with creating a tradition to hand down to themselves, with consciously deciding not only what will happen but also picking the people who will decide what will happen.

In Snowy Prairie, these public celebrations are held usually in dreary, blank-walled places, with folding literature tables from organizations like the Tenant Resources Center, Headstart, prison rights projects, centers for child abuse prevention, domestic violence shelters—not exactly the most festive set of pamphleteers, but institutional and complex. Perhaps new holidays will help make invisible complexity something that one could imagine celebrating—or at least imagine associated with celebration. The events showcase local musicians and local dancers and, unlike "holiday" (Christmas) fairs, offer little to buy. Compared to other holidays, these events have their connection with the wider world less through commercial culture (through corporations) and more through local groups and bureaucracies.

Volunteers and bureaucrats together are creating, through these holidays, a new kind of civic culture, and this culture's moral, political valence cannot be guessed simply by knowing that "bureaucrats" helped to create it. People who are trying to "change the culture" cannot be culturally blank themselves. In the planning of the Youth Calendar, a question that kept arising and would not get solved or disappear was how to define "youth services activities." First, one bureaucrat avoided defining the term, trying to abdicate with the neutrality that could make bureaucracies morally and culturally tone-deaf: "It's not our job—if it's a youth group, fine. If it's a Scout group, fine. It's not our job to *prescribe* what a youth opportunity is . . . whether church, schools groups, we're just giving a heads-up to say it's happening." But, later, this same speaker reflected on the question that several others had persistently raised, and agreed that, indeed, "There's the question of whether to have some review system, like would we include 'Rave' or 'Youth Nazi Service Day,' or 'Lick an Alien Day'?!" In passing a world on to children, adults have to take a stand, even adults who try to hide behind bureaucratic neutrality.

Other examples of conscious efforts at "changing the culture" might include the projects of local children's museums and nature centers, or daycare providers' attitudes toward children's games and conducting of philosophical conversations with children. In just one typical hour of fieldwork at a day-care center, I heard a teacher tell children who invited her to play that she did not "want" to play "prisoner" ("I could pretend to put you in my pocket instead!"), and later, that she did not want to play a shooting game. I heard the children themselves, during this typical hour, debate about what to do with a spider in the sandbox. The day before, the teacher and students had discussed whether bringing guns, slingshots, and karate kicks to the "Oogoslobians"—a topic the five-year-olds had spontaneously brought up—would solve their problems; the teacher had first tried to dismiss the children's concern ("Don't worry, you won't be going to Yugoslavia any time soon"), but, when they persisted, she had told them that more violence, guns, and stones would not solve the problems.

Arendt says, "Education in the modern world . . . by its very nature cannot forget either authority or tradition, and yet must proceed in a world that is neither structured by authority nor held together by tradition."[46] But, in the typical morning on the playground, or in the planning of a youth calendar, we hear a form of authority that does not consciously attribute its power to any specific tradition but could become meaningful and shared and actively debated. The day-care workers and the youth services providers spoke together with reverence and awe when retelling the conversations they had with children. In the fieldwork I have done so far, I have already heard some of these conversations with children last much longer than

most adults would linger over philosophical dialogue. Such playground discussions could become the personally respectful, uncompetitive, unhurried
"ordinary conversations" that the philosopher Nel Noddings[47] describes
(contrasting this form of conversation to Habermas's ideal of impersonal
argumentation) as central to moral education. The institutions that license
and certify day-care centers, such as the National Association for the Education of Young Children, publish elaborate discussions and rules regarding teachers' roles in conversation, instruction, and play; but this does not
mean these conversations are hopelessly rule-bound and rationalized. Even
if the adults would stand for that, the children would not; in these conversations, children often take the lead.

Arendt argues strongly against letting children take the lead and against
making children "learn by doing," as American progressive educators since
Dewey have urged. She calls progressive education an abdication of authority that forces children too early into the harsh, terrifying, unsteady light of
politics. What she misses is that progressive education itself has become a
steady part of the American democratic tradition and that it requires enormous effort and authority to create situations that will actively open up
space for genuine participation, to force children out of the *unfreedom* they
are already in through having entered our commercialized, segregated,
risky world. This is far from abdication.

For example, at one monthly meeting of Youth Services Providers, a
loose network of social service workers and private and nonprofit youth services workers (including the agencies that sponsored the Martin Luther
King Day), an after-school program leader enthusiastically described a series of countywide festivities for youth:

> The goal is to create a community so they can get to know each other. I know
> in our work, we've spent a lot of time trying to get five communities together
> and ended up with five different clumps—kids from each community sticking
> together and not getting to know each other. It's taken time for us to realize
> that we have to structure it *very intentionally* to get them out of their clumps.
> Because people naturally tend to sit with who they know.

Another service worker agreed, but a representative of a 4H Club asked,
"Where *do* we want to go? Why is the goal to have youth get to know people
from different communities?"

A county youth services coordinator later commented, "The *theory* is that
they are all segregated. By community, race, economic group, rural versus
urban, whatever. And we were interested in breaking that down . . . and [his
boss, an elected official] has said that her goal is to increase youth contact
between communities." "And," a social worker noted, "the surprising thing
is that when youth got together to talk about what they had in common,

what they had that was different, what the ideal youth community would look like, what impressed me was that they *didn't* what to just stick with their own community."

These bureaucrats were consciously trying to create civic life and to orchestrate it actively, more actively than do any volunteer groups I have ever encountered. In our segregated society, the seemingly natural mingling that is supposed to happen in voluntary associations usually requires explicit planning. For example, the parents' organization at one Snowy Prairie school held a meeting aimed at encouraging "diversity," and a diverse set of adults did attend, coming from all the far-flung neighborhoods in the school district; but they each sat with their neighbors, in just those segregated "clumps" that the bureaucrats urged the teenagers to abandon. There was no polite way for the parent volunteers to acknowledge the segregation and inequality aloud. But when passing on a world to children, adults may be able to attempt, like the bureaucrats of the youth programs, to notice and correct more of its problems and not abdicate responsibility.

My point is not to extol these bureaucrats' efforts, or to say that all bureaucrats care about civic participation or necessarily succeed in inspiring it, or to deny that many privileged parents, teachers, and bureaucrats in the United States also may eagerly seek to reproduce class inequality. But these bureaucrats are at least trying to evoke a concern for the common good. And, like the volunteers' understanding of commitment to the common good, the bureaucrats' still suffers from forms of individualism that trivialize power or culture or both. For example, when students tried to clean up the local river in a civic education project,[48] the adults foundered on questions of power and politics. In effect, teachers said, "Did the corporation say it *needed* to dump metal into the water? Then we'd best stop testing the water for metal," "Is the water too toxic to touch? Get rubber gloves or find another river." Where the adults could not imagine the next political step, they truncated the students' investigations. Another example illustrates trivialized understanding of culture. In a typical social studies project on "diverse cultures of our state," students built large cardboard displays that dwelled almost entirely on food, music, and holidays. Like many schools around the country, Snowy Prairie's often hold "multicultural potlucks" to which each family is told to bring its "own culture's" dish; about one, several parents made jokes like "Yeah, I'll bring white bread and mayonnaise." This kind of multiculturalism has a long history in the United States; Michael Olneck[49] argues that it makes "culture" into lists of foods, musics, holidays, and clothes—items that are portable, that individuals can don outside of actual lived culture; it thus individualizes while simultaneously invoking nostalgia. Yet not all such efforts are necessarily apolitical and individualistic;[50] to swim against this individualistic and nostalgic current of the prevailing culture, adults who do not already have active political imaginations—most Americans, that is—have to learn alongside their students. If there are still fund-raising bake sales and car washes, canned food drives, mitten drives, scarf drives, hat drives, blanket drives, and toy drives, even with these the point is not that the canned peaches or the polar fleece will solve the problems but that people have gathered, cared, and, above all, reflected. These efforts are often called "service learning" projects. Broadly defined, "service learning" sends students out to get involved in projects that somehow make someone's life better, and then to reflect on that involvement. This kind of education has been going on for decades, but it has recently gained new momentum. This momentum comes from food pantry organizers who like having extra help, current and former political activists who like the participatory, critical edge, crime-prevention officials who like keeping youth off the streets, national programs like Americorps and the Corporation for Public Service that like having new participants, communitarians who like the emphasis on "responsibility," nonprofit and religious institutions of all stripes, and sociologists and other odd bedfellows, whose conversations and relationships will be interesting to observe.

Even for adults with powerful political imaginations, blending care and reflection is a puzzle. Whenever young people were not present, the child-centered bureaucrats self-critically pondered the "reflection" portion of service learning. At one such meeting to plan Martin Luther King Day, one of the adult organizers said, "It's a struggle to do what service learning really is about. It's a process. But what we end up with is a series of random acts of service [everyone chuckles]. . . . So they go pick up trash and that's nice and all, but it doesn't get at the learning component." In another such meeting, one participant, Dan, demanded, "Did [the children] have a sense of connection to something larger?" After some discussion, someone else said, "When they saw how big it was, that made them want to be integrated in the planning process."

Dan persisted, "And the thing that's good about bigger is? Is it *just* that it's bigger or that it's connected to something national?" Later, he added, "It shouldn't just be about planning events, but changing the youth culture." The puzzle for the bureaucrats arises from a difficulty in connecting children to a larger culture of democratic participation; the adults want to tie the children's activities to something larger but are not sure what is on that larger, national, cultural, political end of the connection. There is nothing very solid on that end; the rope dangles.

Heroically, the adults and children keep trying. Local practitioners insist that the core of service learning is "reflection." In a workshop on the topic, the leader stated, "If you work at a food pantry for your service project, the key to it all [becomes] to ask why there is hunger and what our society can do about it."

COMMUNICATING THE "BROKEN COVENANT":
HOPE AND CRITIQUE IN THE GENERATIVE BUREAUCRACY

So, why *is* there hunger, and what can our society do about it? A deeper problem with these civil servants' efforts is that "facing the facts" is impossible, not just for children or bureaucrats, but for everyone. In a conference of environmental educators, several speakers were, themselves, overwhelmed by environmental problems. In a shaking voice, one said,

> We generate 4 pounds of trash a day per person curbside, that's what we *see*, but there's 120 pounds per day that we *don't* see, . . . 27 pounds of stone and cement a day, 19 pounds of coal, 11 pounds of wood. . . . We in the First World consume 80 percent of the world resources, but only 20 percent of the world's population is in the first world. In the U.S., we consume 30 percent of the world resources, but only 4.7 percent of the world's population is in the U.S.

Her conclusion:

> Who's responsible? Corporations? We're looking for something outside of ourselves, but it's a crisis of mind and spirit. We're trying to blame the systems that we have created. . . . We're talking about not only the invisible costs to the environment but real people. It's one of my missions in life to get to people that it's not just about materiality, but sort of the spirituality of that materiality. We consume stuff that has people's *lives* in them.

She then sang a song by the group Sweet Honey in the Rock, a song about imagining who made her shirt and what were the wretched conditions of that distant person's life. But in undoing commodity fetishism, this speaker became overwhelmed; the question thus becomes, how can an adult who feels this frighteningly *connected,* like one exposed nerve that stretches around the world, "protect" children? Note that she did not individualize the problem, did not end with an absurdly cheery message about making a difference by recycling and personally using less cement.

In contrast to volunteers, civil servants who fully recognize the impossibility of their task *still have to keep going.* They can't go home. Bureaucrats might not try as hard as volunteers do to avoid expressing discouraging ideas. In this way, they are more like parents than are volunteers; they cannot quit when they hit such a breathtaking aporia.

Similarly, in a fourth-grade current events class, I heard many disturbing facts, related with little buffer. Current events classes of the past relied on Cold War enemies for a comforting plot line, but current renditions offer little comfort. *My Weekly Reader,* the preeminent midcentury news publication for children, offered ongoing celebration of progress and of America-against-the-Russians and ignored the rest of the world. In contrast, *Newscurrents,* a popular contemporary current events curriculum, is resolutely neutral about American domination of world politics and routinely covers stories outside of Europe and the United States. Observing fourth- and fifth-grade classrooms through a semester, I heard two teachers, two substitute teachers, and several teachers' aides wrestle against feeling overwhelmed. An example is the following interchange that occurred on the day that NATO started bombing Serbia. This event was not in *Newscurrents* yet, because it had just happened.

> *Mr. Mueller* (a typically liberal but not "leftist" fourth-grade teacher): I had a really philosophical discussion with Ben before class. He wanted to know why we should bomb Serbia. We said that we are like a big brother—but when the big brother goes away, the problems are still there. We likened it to capital punishment—getting even.
>
> *A student:* But the Serbians should be taught a lesson for trying to beat up on a little country.
>
> *Mr. Mueller:* Yes, but what are you gonna do? You can't spank them. That's what I'm saying—that's why it was such a philosophical discussion, because it's hard to answer. *I* don't have any clear-cut answers. [He looked over to me at this point—something he almost never did. From a couch in the far corner, I say, "Who does?"]
>
> *Mr. Mueller:* No one does. No one does. There are no easy answers [long pause]. You could try economic sanctions—keep away what they really need. Do you think we got involved in the Middle East because they've got oil or because they don't?
>
> *Several kids:* They do.
>
> *Mr. Mueller:* Think of all the things we use oil for.
>
> *Another student:* Cars, [and] . . .
>
> *Mr. Mueller:* The US has 5 percent of the world's population and consumes more than 30 percent of the world's resources. *Something's not right there.* Now *that's* a philosophical statement on my part.

When we examine this conversation, we note that first this teacher says he has no answers, then he offers a critique of the entire world order, one that implicitly implicates all the persons in the room. The teacher of an old-style current events class could not have easily voiced such radical doubt and guilt. Over the course of just one semester, Mr. Mueller had to explain ozone depletion, the worldwide disappearance of frogs (which many scientists attribute to global environmental disturbances), capital punishment, global warming, the shortage of good day care, school shootings and the safety measures taken to prevent them, and nuclear war, as well as old-fashioned evils like war, poverty, and bigotry. A teacher's aide and I often joked about how little we envied his task, and marveled at his courage.

Similarly, participants in a national e-mail network of teachers and librarians continuously and passionately debate the politics and morality of children's books. They argue, for example, about whether presenting the horrors of the Holocaust, European Americans' treatment of Native Americans, and African American slavery is too frightening and depressing, or whether *not* detailing the horrors of human history trivializes past and current problems. How do librarians, bureaucrats, news producers, social workers, and teachers balance their duty to raise hopeful youth with their duty to raise politically aware youth? How do they communicate what Bellah called America's "broken covenant"[51] without invoking incapacitating despair? And, how does the view from the bottom of the social hierarchy differ from the view from the middle or top? And how, if at all, does it affect the discussion if the people who are asking these questions in public are paid civil servants, not volunteers in freely chosen civil associations?

MEASURABLE OUTCOMES AND IMMEASURABLE GOODNESS

Political and moral discussion unfolds differently in semibureaucratic settings than in voluntary associations. When the people asking the questions are paid social workers and youth, they confront different dilemmas than do volunteers and activists. Let us examine just one of these dilemmas.

The bureaucrats who organize the youth projects have to justify their projects by describing measurable effects on individuals and society. They are especially eager to help poor students and students of color, and need the funds to do so. Thus, more than half of the four hundred youth in this very white city's Martin Luther King Day celebrations have been African American, Asian, or Latino, and have arrived in groups organized by their Urban League after-school programs or by their low-income neighborhood community centers. And many of the grants that paid for the youth activities are "prevention" grants for averting drug use, tobacco use, violence, and alcohol use, the aim being to get youth "off the streets" by engaging them in community service.

Does this matter? Organizers did not *want* it to matter; none of their publicity hinted at it. The idea was that anyone who serves is blessed, "whatever your IQ or socioeconomic status," as one speaker put it at the celebration (making me wonder if any young listeners thought, Good, even though I'm dumb, I can serve). Lines from King were quoted many times and inscribed on placemats, pins, posters, and folders: "Everyone can be great, because anyone can serve. You don't have to have a college degree to serve. . . . You only need a heart full of grace and a soul generated by love."

On the other hand, the social service agencies had to justify their projects to potential funders by marketing them as therapy-like programs with "measurable outcomes" for "at-risk youth." One religiously motivated black social worker, James, said (in a variation of what he and others often repeated),

> This [week of high-profile community service activity for youth] is to show that we're doing all these *things,* that kids are not out on the street causing trouble, that we need more money. That's what we're ultimately doing this

week for. Maybe [a bit tongue-in-cheek now] we could get police records on lower youth crime that week, that's lower because kids are busy doing community service.

And, with funding drying up, social workers complained that they had to spend more time and effort demonstrating "measurable outcomes." One of James's dilemmas was to balance his struggle to counteract measurable injustice with the idea that people should feel immeasurably blessed no matter where they stand in the socioeconomic hierarchy, to balance his desire to produce children who make good grades and go to college with "you don't need a college education to serve."

The suburban white children, along with most of the children of color involved in the King Day community service projects, heard adults say that King's message was about "giving to others." When explaining why they were involved in community service, many children spoke about "making our community better"—usually with a big, self-conscious, self-deprecating giggle. But I was initially puzzled by another interpretation I kept hearing from black children; at one gathering, a social services worker asked about fifty middle-schoolers to write, on hand-shaped construction paper cutouts, "three things you could do to help your community." Although most wrote "shovel snow for old people" or "baby-sit for my neighbors" or "visit a senior center," several said, "I could get a job" or "I could do my homework." At first, I thought these kids simply had not heard the question; however, their responses made complete sense after I heard adults telling young people, in various meetings, that King's idea of nonviolence was "about not beating each other over the head when you disagree"—as if "you," not the violent legal and political system that King resisted, are the perpetrator of the violence. A black police officer gave a long speech at one King Day celebration, saying that King's message was about "choosing to learn to read, choosing not to be a drug dealer, choosing to go to college." Though this was not adults' most common rendition of King's message, those accustomed to being treated as "at-risk" and worthy of attention only if that attention resulted in "measurable outcomes" heard it quite clearly. In justifying their work to funders, caregivers thus sometimes made children feel as if they themselves were both the problem and the solution.

But adults addressed *all* children as potential victims and as potential perpetrators of school shootings, poverty, environmental crisis, even of war in the Balkans. All children were held responsible for using twenty-seven pounds of stone and cement per day, consuming more than their share of the world's resources. The poor or nonwhite students were also held responsible for their own "outcomes." This is the problem to which Arendt pointed when she said that children should not be forced to bear the burden of fixing the world that their parents cannot fix.

One of the dilemmas that these bureaucrats face, which voluntary associations and families rarely encounter, is that they *have* to take sociological categories seriously, even while they believe that "you need a heart full of grace and a soul generated by love." They have to acknowledge that the children's lives are inseparable from the institutions around them and also that the institutions are rotten—and still leave the young people hopeful that they can change these institutions.

Thus, this instrumental language, which measures children and categorizes them by race and class, also sometimes inspires social critique, encouraging participants to ask why our society puts so many youth "at risk." When speaking to each other, out of young people's presence, the social workers treat the poor, black, Asian, or Latino students' problems as social problems and hope that the young people's "outcomes" will outstrip the unjust odds. But it is very difficult for the adults to say this directly to the young people themselves; the adults want to avoid undermining what little authority the adult world offers these children. When George W. Bush was finally named president, one of the young people in the King Day planning group said, "Oh no, he's gonna take away our rights," and the adult in charge could tell her not to worry, that Bush had a lot of people to answer to, but she could not say that she shared the girl's worries—something she could say in other contexts. Similarly, social service agencies held "Recognition Events" to give awards to children who were in "regular school attendance" but who would not normally be expected to be. But the adults at these events never stated why certain (black or Southeast Asian) kids were getting awards for something that was expected of all kids; that would be demoralizing.

Still, many of these adults also wanted children to cultivate a political vision, to put their responsibility in perspective, to see that individual feats of extraordinary personal morality were only one part of the solution, to see that picking up trash was not enough, to see that (as the head of the local NAACP noted at an Urban League breakfast honoring extraordinary young people) "even if these extraordinary kids have managed to break through the system that holds them back, we have to ask why so many of our [African American] youth are in these circumstances to begin with." This is just the kind of political vision that volunteer groups in Amargo tried to avoid cultivating, thinking it would be discouraging. Like the volunteers, the bureaucrats wanted to say that each individual could become extraordinary, that people were not simply products of measurable circumstances (whether of overprivilege or of underprivilege)—that "you make a difference" no matter who you are. The dilemma for public servants was to teach children to confront the world while feeling blessed in the world; to measure and categorize and count in order to reveal social injustice; and also to find gratitude even for blessings they learn they should not have—like those twenty-seven pounds of stone and cement.

All children were invited to feel simultaneously thankful for and guilty about and outraged at and afraid of the system that brought them their unfair advantages or unfair disadvantages. Adults had to balance a social-scientific imagination with another kind of imagination. *Both* are sources of hope. The question is how adults and children weave together immeasurable appreciation and guilt, hope and critical vision, personal and political responsibility, in everyday conversation: can we communicate the broken covenant without communicating despair?

GENERATIVE BUREAUCRACY
AND UNDEBATABLE RESPONSIBILITY

Nurturing children in a society that hinders generativity is potentially a riddle for all adults, including those inside bureaucracies. Bureaucrats can bring an abstract social-scientific imagination to bear on social problems,[52] but their faith in science is less than total. They also share America's anti-bureaucratic culture, and the tensions and agreements between these two symbolic worlds could yield interesting dilemmas and debates. Could such double vision offer a "fruitful interchange," somewhat like the one Bellah describes in "Between Religion and Social Science"? Like the interchange between social science and a transcendent religious vision, perhaps this could "recognize the multiplicity of the human spirit, and the necessity to translate constantly between different scientific and imaginative vocabularies."[53]

Like other Americans, the bureaucrats' political imaginations sometimes float on a stream of generativity. Generativity is not a "transcendent vision" in the sense that Bellah describes, but trying to raise hopeful and generous youth is a death-defying leap of imagination and faith when one lives in what the bureaucrats often called "our culture of death." Like a transcendent religious vision, the grounds for this "generative" faith cannot be measured because they do not exist. Rather, they do not exist in what Bellah calls the "nightmare" of "ordinary reality." But they exist in another, powerful way, as another kind of socially practiced reality.

Instead of simply celebrating or condemning public agencies, we could ask how they might inspire public discussion and how this might differ from the discussion that voluntary associations usually inspire; we could ask how these agencies can or cannot create an understanding of children and community that confronts invisible complexity instead of trying to ignore it. An imagination that equates children, family, and community with hope will, ironically, not allow us to cultivate, or even notice, the life-giving generativity that courses through society. But, since the bureaucrats are not part of the timeless childhood/family/community nexus, they may be in a promising position to open up public discussion of generativity; if respect for public conversation itself is what distinguishes a cloying communitarianism from the searching, never-finished "mindfulness" that Bellah and his co-authors describe, then listening to these bureaucrats' conversations may reveal individuals groping through a dangerous but potentially life-giving generativity, both recognizing and fearing the connection between deep, personal moral education and the vastly complex wider world.

THIRTEEN

On Being a Christian and an American

Stanley Hauerwas

1. ON BEING A SECTARIAN, FIDEISTIC TRIBALIST

I have a well-deserved reputation for being an unapologetic Enlightenment basher. I do not believe something called ethics can be shown to exist or to be justified on Kantian-like grounds of reason alone. I have no use for moral or political liberalism in any of their guises. I do not believe in inalienable rights. I tire of the ongoing futile project to show that freedom of the individual can be reconciled with equality. I do not even believe that a good society can or should be egalitarian if this means all hierarchical considerations bear the burden of proof. Accordingly, many of my colleagues in that strange field called Christian ethics suggest I am a sectarian, fideistic tribalist.

By this, they mean I am trying to convince Christians that we do not have a stake in the "wider world." My often-made claim that the first task of Christians is not to make the world more just but rather is to make the world the world is interpreted as a call for Christians to withdraw from the world or at least from America. That I should be so understood by those working in Christian ethics is quite intelligible if, as I have argued elsewhere, the subject of Christian ethics in America has always been America. Christian ethicists no longer think, as did Walter Rauschenbusch, that their task is to Christianize the social order, but they continue to share Rauschenbusch's presumption that America is the appropriate subject for Christian ethical reflection and action. My refusal to accept this presumption means I cannot help but be interpreted as a traitor to my class or, at least, my discipline.

I confess I have been tempted, and no doubt at times have succumbed to the temptation, to continue to criticize American liberalism in a manner that only confirms such characterizations of my position. Yet I confess I have grown weary of that game. I simply cannot muster energy for yet one more attempt to show the incoherence of liberal political philosophy or practice.

Liberalism, both politically and economically, is doing such a good job of self-destructing it needs no help from me. More important, such a tactic manifests, theologically, a lack of faith. I believe that the American experiment, as some like to put it, is in deep trouble. Yet Christians are obligated to be a people of hope, not wishing for the lives of our non-Christian brothers and sisters to be worse than they need to be.

Some years ago I wrote an article titled "A Tale of Two Stories: On Being a Christian and a Texan."[1] I wrote the article mainly to please myself and to honor my parents, but also in response to criticism that I failed to appreciate that Christians are constituted by stories other than the Christian story—a point a Texan is not likely to overlook. However, I confess my self-description as a Texan was insufficient. I am also an American. As much as I might like—as a Texan or as a Christian—to deny or avoid that I am an American, I know that any such denial would be self-deceptive. Even more important, I have to acknowledge I love the land and the people called American.[2] Of course, the issue is not my love of America but rather how such a love should be shaped and governed by the love of God.

So I should like to take this as an opportunity to explore, in a more constructive way than is my "normal mode," what positive role the church might have in the project called America. Contrary to the critics of my position, I have no wish to have Christians withdraw from service to their neighbors— even their liberal neighbors. The object of my criticism of liberalism has never been liberals, but rather to give Christians renewed confidence in the convictions that make our service intelligible. In short, I have never sought to justify Christian withdrawal from social and political involvement; I have just wanted us to be involved as Christians.

From my perspective, the problem is not liberalism but the assumption on the part of many Christians that they must become liberals to be of service in America. When that happens I believe Christians betray their non-Christian neighbors, because we rob them and ourselves of exemplification of truthful speech forged through the worship of God. What follows is my attempt to suggest what I take to be some mistaken strategies for the negotiation of America by Christians. My criticism of these strategies, however, is meant to make intelligible my claim that Christians have no service more important than to be a people capable of the truthful worship of God.

2. THE PROBLEM WITH THE SEARCH FOR FOUNDATIONS

I noted above that the subject of Christian ethics in America was America.[3] The birth as well as the intelligibility of Christian ethics as a discipline drew on institutions we now call mainstream Protestant Christianity. These mainstream churches assumed a deep compatibility between Christianity and American democracy. For most members of such churches, it was unthinkable that being a Christian might in any way render problematic full participation in American life. Christian ethics accordingly was understood as that mode of reflection that helped churches develop policies to make American ideals of freedom and equality more fully institutionalized in American life.

For both internal and external reasons, Christian thinkers learned, as I suggested above, not to describe their task as Christianizing the social order. The appeals of the Social Gospel to Jesus, as well as the movement's optimism about progress, were subjected to the withering critique of Reinhold Niebuhr. For Niebuhr, the Christian ethical problem became how to achieve relative justice in a world in which love can never be realized. Though Niebuhr understood himself to be a theologian, or at least a social ethicist, his work is almost completely devoid of any account of the church.[4] Yet I think it also true to say that he continued to assume the viability of Protestant Christianity as the background for the stance he developed toward social problems. Such an assumption, of course, has become increasingly problematic.

The problematic nature of this project is not due to the increasing loss of membership, social status, and political power of mainstream Christianity. No doubt such losses are not unimportant for understanding the loss of a distinctive voice of Protestant Christianity in America. Yet I think more important has been the increasing recognition that even if such churches remained socially and politically powerful, they would have nothing distinctive to say as Christians about the challenges facing this society. That such churches have nothing distinctive to contribute is not surprising since their social and political power originally derived from the presumption that there was no essential difference between the church and the principles of the American experiment. That presumption may, of course, also help explain the decline of such churches, because it is by no means clear why you need to go to church when such churches only reinforce what you already know from participation in a democratic society.

The increasing loss of social and political influence of Protestant Christianity has not meant Christian theologians and ethicists have abandoned the attempt to make America correspond to some assumed ideal. Faced, however, with America's increasingly diverse population, such an endeavor has been disciplined by the assumption that when Christians enter the public realm they cannot use Christian language. Rather, some mediating language is required and is assumed justified in the name of a common morality or by natural-law reasoning. For those who remain in the tradition of mainstream Protestantism, this justification often takes the form of trying to show that Rawls, or some Rawls-like, account of justice, is the kind of bridge Christians need to justify our participation in the formulation of public policies necessary to govern a diverse society.[5]

I have no intention to be drawn into debates concerning the adequacy of Rawls's account of justice. Yet I want to make clear why the attempt to use Rawls for developing a way for Christians politically to participate in America distracts us from understanding as Christians the contribution we might make. Nicholas Wolterstorff provides a trenchant analysis of Rawls that makes clear why Rawls is such a distraction. Wolterstorff notes that the reason Rawls thinks a basis for constitutional democracies is necessary is because political issues remain contested in our society. For example, it is not clear how liberty and equality can be expressed among the basic rights and liberties of citizens in a manner that answers both the claims of liberty and those of equality. From Wolterstorff's perspective, Rawls seeks a way to resolve this conflict in the American tradition between Locke and Rousseau—that is, between freedom and equality—by offering his two principles of justice based on common human reason.

Yet Wolterstorff asks, how one can possibly move from

> a tradition with internal unresolved conflicts, to a pair of principles which resolves those conflicts, by doing nothing other than analyzing that tradition and elaborating the principles embedded therein? How can common human reason, exercised reasonably, propel one across the chasm separating unresolved conflicts from proposals for resolution? The essence of Rawls' strategy is to make do with our common human reason working on the public political culture of our constitutional democracies. Nothing more than that. Of course analysis and elaboration can in principle clarify for us the content and contours of our public political culture. But if there's conflict in our public political culture as to the relative weighting of liberty and equality, then the application of "our common human reason" to this culture will *make clear* to us that there is this conflict. It won't yield a proposal as to how they *ought to be* weighted—unless, perchance, our common human reason is a source of moral principles. But that's the Lockian view which Rawls is trying to avoid, by proposing to extract the relevant moral principles from the extant culture rather than from Reason. If the culture is of different minds as to the relative weighting of liberty and equality, then any proposal as to how they *ought* to be weighted will perforce go beyond what can be extracted from that culture itself.[6]

Wolterstorff, I think, rightly concludes that, contrary to Rawls, we must learn to carry on in a politics without a foundation. We shall have to conduct our political deliberations without a shared political basis—that is, without a neutral or coherent set of principles sufficient to adjudicate conflicts. Which means, according to Wolterstorff, our best strategy is to move from one set of deliberations to another, employing whatever set of considerations we think may be persuasive for the persons with whom we are in conversation. A Rawlsian political unity of overlapping consensus is neither possible nor desirable, but all we need, Wolterstorff argues, is the unity that emerges from dialogue among persons each of whom approaches the dialogue with his or her own distinct frame of conviction, and each of whom is willing to live within the confines of a democratic constitution and with the results of fair votes. That's all the unity we have ever had, in these constitutional democracies of ours characterized by religious, moral, and philosophical pluralism. We don't need, and have never had, an ever-present, never-changing foundation on which all of us who are "reasonable" agree and on the basis of which all of us conduct our deliberations. . . . Agreement must be wrought ever anew in ever new ways among ever new parties. For two hundred years now that's been enough for the endurance of pluralistic constitutional democracies. We have no guarantee that it will prove sufficient on into the distant future. Only hope.[7]

I believe one of the great advantages of Wolterstorff's way of understanding our situation is that it does not ask Christians to learn some third language in order socially and politically to participate in America. If this is a "pluralist" society—a description I find far too complimentary—then I see no reason that Christians (any more than Jews or secularists) should be asked to put their convictions in some allegedly neutral language to talk with one another. Of course, "talk with one another" may be a far too innocent way to put the matter in the light of controversies such as those about abortion and assisted suicide. The problem is not that we do not talk with one another but that such talk makes no difference. Yet we will make little progress even in finding our disagreements as long as we search for a "foundation" assumed necessary before the conversation begins.

3. ON TELLING THE AMERICAN STORIES

A more promising way to begin to think about how Christians might contribute to the ongoing American project is that proposed by Martin Marty in his recent book, *The One and the Many: America's Struggle for the Common Good*.[8] That Marty is a historian rather than a philosopher is the reason I find the account he provides promising. Rather than look for foundations, he directs our attention to the stories that constitute the life of that strange entity called America. In this respect he develops a strand of Christian reflection exemplified in H. Richard Niebuhr's *The Kingdom of God in America*, Reinhold Niebuhr's *The Irony of American History*, and the work of Robert N. Bellah. (No matter how Bellah has tried to distance himself from his early work on civil religion of America, I believe it is to his credit that the kind of analysis he and his colleagues provided in *Habits of the Heart*, as well as in *The Good Society*, is in moral continuity with his attempt to name the American civil religion. Bellah's passion has been the attempt to discover the story or stories that can make our common as well as our individual lives as Americans morally good.)

One of the virtues of approaches like Bellah's and Marty's is that they have the potential to take account of aspects of American life that are morally richer than liberal theory can account for. It is often suggested, for example, that liberalism has worked in America exactly because it has been parasitic on forms of life for which liberalism takes no responsibility or that it may even undermine. Marty's focus on narratives about this nation, then, provides an opportunity for thicker accounts of such American characteristics as generosity, a thicker account that can in turn help us better understand America's politics.

That I find these historical and sociological approaches more promising for articulating how Christians might make a contribution in the American context does not mean I agree with what Marty, for instance, takes that contribution to be. To his credit, Marty has discovered Alasdair MacIntyre. Not only does Marty credit MacIntyre for helping us see how important it is that we discover the narratives we inhabit, but he also takes seriously MacIntyre's judgment that "many citizens in their various competitive groups do inhabit incommensurable universes of discourse, universes that lack a basis of comparison and hence an ability to communicate."[9] Yet Marty thinks MacIntyre's pessimism can be countered by drawing on Felix Frankfurter's contention that this society is not held together by law, creed, or ideology, but by sentiment.

Marty quotes Frankfurter that "the ultimate foundation of a free society is the binding tie of cohesive sentiment" and observes that such sentiment remains available for us even in today's multicultural society.[10] Indeed, Marty, the great celebrator of America, has taken to heart the increasing sense that America is not constituted by one story. Accordingly he criticizes Jefferson and the other founders for using the ideology of the Enlightenment to produce sameness and repress difference. In particular, he criticizes the development of the "common school" as well as the texts used in those schools for the repression of difference in the name of creating a common culture. Yet Marty cannot bring himself to abandon the attempt to create a common "sentiment" through what he calls the "commensurable possibilities in storytelling."[11]

He thinks this possible, if we learn to think of the nation less as a community and more in terms of Michael Oakeshott's "civil association."[12] An association does not demand a credal bond or personal intimacy but rather requires us, like porcupines, to stand at a distance from one another learning the delight in the other that only the distance can produce. Drawing on the work of the Calvinist social theorist Althusius, Marty suggests that we best understand a commonwealth not as a community of communities but rather as an association of associations. This formulation would allow people in various groups to live in partly incommensurable universes of discourse and yet find it valuable to interact in ways other than military force and cultural conflict. Rather than reaching for guns, people will learn to "reach for argument, and the telling of stories from different perspectives is a form of argument. One cannot have a republic without argument."[13]

Marty's story remains the optimistic story of America. He expects the conflicts to continue but believes that in the longer future,

> [e]very story well told, well heard, and creatively enacted will contribute to the common good and make possible the deepening of values, virtues, and conversation. At the outset I described this book as an effort to contribute to the restoration of the body politic, or, with the many groups in view, the bodies politic. We have been speaking throughout of the "re-storying" of the republic and its associations. The advice for every citizen who wishes to participate in American life and its necessary arguments: start associating, telling, hearing, and keep talking.[14]

In short, Marty seems to think all this will work out if we just learn to be nice to one another.

Whatever one may think about the strength and/or weakness of Marty's account, what I find striking is the absence of any theological justification. Marty, like Reinhold Niebuhr, assumes his task is to make America work. The story Marty tells is the story of an America in which Christians get to have a role. That such is the case should not be surprising, since Marty represents the discipline of American religious history. Accordingly, it never seems to occur to him that he needs to tell the church's story of America. As a result, he fails to see how the story of America can tempt Christians to lose our own story and in the process to fail to notice the god we worship is no longer the God of Israel.

In this respect it is fascinating to compare Marty's account of the challenges before American life with MacIntyre's reading of America. What Marty finds admirable about American life—our desire to get along by being likable people—MacIntyre finds our greatest defect. MacIntyre observes:

> This wanting to be liked is one of the great American vices that emerges from this refusal of particularity and conflict. Americans tend under the influence of this vice to turn into parodies of themselves—smiling, earnest, very kind, generous, nice people, who do terrible things quite inexplicably. We become people with no depth, no depth of understanding, masters of technique and technology but not of ourselves. Colonel Tuan of the Army of the Republic of Vietnam, which we so generously aided and then so treacherously betrayed, was once asked by Paul Theroux what he thought of the Americans. He called them "well-disciplined" and "generous." "But we also think that they are a people without culture. . . ." He did not mean by this that they lacked high culture. He meant that he could not recognize what it was about them that made them Americans in the way that he was Vietnamese. And that I think is what happens to people with no story to tell of themselves, people who do not con-

front their future as a narrative future. They, or rather we, become superficial people, people with surfaces, public relations people.[15]

From MacIntyre's perspective, Marty's account of the role of stories only reproduces the liberal presumption that the "good thing" about America is how being an American makes you aware, alienates you, from your story.[16] That is why, for MacIntyre, what he calls "the American idea" cannot help but be tragic. It is tragic because the conflict between the basic American principles of every person being able to live, to be free, and to pursue happiness cannot be reconciled with the demand for equality. Slavery is but the most obvious contradiction of the American dilemma. According to MacIntyre, this contradiction represents a conflict so

> deeply embodied in the American character that no care for a surface appearance of consistency or a superficial disguise for hypocrisy could have got rid of it. It is the contradiction between a profound commitment to the principles of equal rights and liberty on the one hand and an equally profound commitment to individualistic practices which generate inequality and unfreedom on the other. American history is the tragic working out of this internalized contradiction.[17]

Marty regrets the general tendency in America for historical amnesia, but he fails to see that a loss of memory is at the heart of the American project. Indeed, as I suggested above, Rawlsian strategies for securing justice require just such a loss of memory. Justice requires the presumption that a genuine break with the past is possible. This is why MacIntyre suggests that America is not just a country but a metaphysical entity, "an intelligible abstraction always imperfectly embodied in natural reality. It is always *not yet,* it is always radically incomplete; and because the values it aspires to incarnate were from the first seen as *the* essential values, anyone and everyone may be summoned to take part in that completion."[18] Thus, America was the attempt to found a historical tradition to connect a particular past to a universal future,

> a tradition that in becoming genuinely universal could find a place within itself for all other particularities so that the Irishman or the Jew or the Japanese in becoming an American did not cease thereby to be something of an Irishman or a Jew or a Japanese. In assuming the burden of this task America took unto itself a genuinely Utopian quality, the quality of an attempt to transcend the limits of secular possibility. America's failures are intimately connected with this grasping after impossibility; but so are its successes.[19]

The tragic character of American history is unavoidable, since rights cannot help but conflict with rights; yet the very moral commitments that shape such a conflict produce a people incapable of recognizing, much less responding, to such conflicts. America is at once the name of an aspiration to liberty and equality of rights and the name of the power that stands in the way of that aspiration. As a result, Americans find themselves at war not only with one another but also with themselves. MacIntyre observes that "citizens of other nations are free to measure what their government and society does by *external* standards of liberty and right and can choose between their loyalty to these absolutes and their loyalty to their own nature; but the American finds that these absolutes *are* his constitution, that he cannot disown his national allegiance without disowning these moral absolutes or vice versa."[20]

Nothing that MacIntyre has said about America requires him to deny Marty's sense that we need a shared history.[21] MacIntyre doubts we can look to academic historians to supply us with such a story just to the extent that such a history, through its elimination of evaluative judgments, of heroes and heroines, seeks to abolish history as a story.[22] Our problem is that such history as well as our political culture has made us quite literally speechless (though of course we go on talking, but such talking represents no more than the clash of opinion). In a striking illustration, MacIntyre offers one exception to our inability to create a common story through public speech—the Vietnam War Memorial. The "Memorial is significant because it both records the names of the dead and also, by style and substance, says that we do not know what to say to or about them. It is a monument to inarticulateness; *both* to our not knowing what to say to and about the dead now, except that they are our dead and dead because of us, *and* to our inarticulateness at the time of the Vietnam war."[23]

MacIntyre acknowledges that it may seem odd to speak of inarticulateness at the time of Vietnam since so much was said at that time. Yet he argues that we spoke at such length because we could not communicate. The war simply revealed, therefore, that we were not able to speak intelligibly to one another on matters that were so deep. And, of course, it is exactly such inability that we have worked hard to forget, by consoling ourselves with rhetorics of consensus and pluralism. Thus, projects such as Marty's mask our loss of shared political speech as well as our lack of communal imagination, "deprivations closely related to our inability to master and to make our own the narrative of ourselves."[24] Shared sentiment cannot help but be sentimental without a more determinative narrative that helps name the truth, the tragic truth, that America is constituted by wrongs so wrong that nothing can be done to make them right.[25]

4. GOD AND AMERICA

If you are schooled in the art of revivals, this should make you attentive to the religious payoff here. For if the analysis I have provided is close to being right, then surely the gospel should have something to say about how to go on as a people who can have a shared past by confessing their sin. Here it seems Christians have something constructive to offer to our politics. We have a story of sin and forgiveness forged in the practices of confession and reconciliation that at least offers the kind of hope Wolterstorff suggested we need. The claim that the first task of the church is to be the church, even in America, could turn out to be good news if the challenge before us as Americans is learning how to be a people who can make our past truthfully ours. That the first task of the church is to be the church is, therefore, anything but a withdrawal strategy.

Yet revival conversions have a well-deserved reputation for not lasting. As tempting as the strategy suggested in the last paragraph may be, I think it would be a mistake to try to make Christianity look good by supplying substance and practice that the liberal narratives of America cannot supply. The ascendancy of liberal ideology and practice in America could be seen as very good news for Christians. In fact, the very emptiness liberalism creates invites someone to fill the space. That Americans lack a strong moral account to justify and/or guide their relations to one another seems to make Christianity, or at least a surrogate, all the more necessary. Indeed, this can look like the best possible of all worlds as Christianity gets to supply the morality without having to govern. Put in terms of the analysis above, Christianity becomes the master story to sustain a republic that officially can have no master story.

A story not unlike this has been tempting for liberal and conservative Christians alike. Liberal Christians assume that something like a religious appeal is necessary, or at least important, to sustain the quest for justice; conservative Christians assume that without Christianity people cannot develop the virtues necessary to sustain a free society. Thus, for both, the importance of intermediate institutions of which the church seems a ready exemplification. Calls for Christians to make the family work are but the out-working of such strategies. The only problem is that the only institution more destructive of the family than capitalism is Christianity.

I am not entirely unsympathetic with some of the suggestions made by those who try to give Christians a role in American society shaped by these strategies. My problem is not that such strategies are wrong; rather, my problem is that this way of conceiving the relation of the church to American society makes the church less than the church. The problem, then, is not as I framed it in the title that I first thought to give this essay, "Why Christianity Will Never Work in America." Even though I believe that the fundamental presuppositions that shaped much of American life and government were meant to destroy or at least marginalize the church, I believe with God's help the church may even survive in America. Rather, the problem is that when Christians in America take as their fundamental task to make America work, then we lose our ability to survive *as church*. We do so because in the interest of serving America, the church unwittingly becomes governed by the story of America that Marty tells. That is a story meant to make our God at home in America.

There is no better indication of the Americanization of the church than the god worshiped by Christians in America. For most American Christians, the crucially important thing about God is that God exist and that God's most important attribute be love. This is not a recent development, but, if Thomas Jenkins is right, it began in the late eighteenth century in such figures as Timothy Dwight and was developed in the nineteenth century by such theologians as Noah Porter. In particular, Porter, drawing on the enlightenment celebration of stoicism and modern science, emphasized the importance of emotional restraint and rationality. According to Jenkins:

> This centered on one trait in particular: benevolence. Benevolence was the key emotion emulated by people and ascribed to God. As the historian James Turner put it: "As the archetype of morality, God expressed the most elevated human ethics. He thus above all had to be—perhaps the favorite adjective of enlightenment divines—benevolent: disinterestedly willing the happiness of all his creatures."[26]

Jenkins traces the career of this god through the development of liberal and conservative theology and literary figures of the nineteenth and twentieth centuries. We should not be surprised that the result was a vague god vaguely worshiped or at least vaguely considered. For example, the influential liberal theologian, minister, and writer Theodore Munger drew on Thomas Arnold's understanding of God as "a power not ourselves working for righteousness."[27] Such a view finds its most sophisticated expression in William James's suggestion, "God is the natural appellation, for us Christians at least, for the supreme reality, so I will call this higher part of the universe by the name of God."[28]

James's god, I believe, is not remarkably different from Reinhold Niebuhr's god. Of course Niebuhr's god was a god of judgment, but such judgment was, as Jenkins suggests, the expression of law, history, and the order of the world.[29] Christ was also the symbol of sacrificial love for Niebuhr, but the very language of symbol was used to protect against any need to make classical Christological claims that require trinitarian displays of who God is. So in spite of Niebuhr's reputation as one who attempted a recovery of orthodoxy, his account of God remained more theist than Christian—that is, a theism combined with a sentimental Christ. Niebuhr may well be the greatest representative of a theology shaped to make America work. But if that is the case, it is a deep judgment on such theology just to the extent Christians lost the reality of God found in cross and resurrection.

I am not suggesting that the American god Jenkins describes was the result of the Christian accommodation to America, but I think it also undeniable that the attenuated god of American Christianity is necessary for a people who believe they are the future of humankind. I believe, therefore, Christians can do nothing more significant in America than to be a people capable of worshiping a God who is to be found in the cross and resurrection of Jesus of Nazareth. The worship of such a God will not be good for any society that desires a god made in the image of the bureaucrat.[30] A people formed by the worship of a crucified God, however, might just be complex enough to engage in the hard work of working out agreements and disagreements with others one small step at a time.

FOURTEEN

Politics as the "Public Use of Reason"
Religious Roots of Political Possibilities

William M. Sullivan

I. THE "PUBLIC USE OF REASON": INTELLECTUALS AND POLITICS

Modern democratic societies aspire to guide their affairs by the "public use of reason." This phrase, which sums up a concept that is one of the most important of the Enlightenment's legacies to the modern world, was put into circulation, if not coined, by Immanuel Kant. Kant defined "the public use of reason" as criticism and debate on questions of public import by educated citizens, independent of the power of potentates and states. The novel idea was that such discussion could significantly influence rulers and governments by generating what came to be known as "public opinion."[1] Enlightenment was to mean progress in self-determination, the opening up to more persons a share in determining those conditions of life affecting everyone. Previously, of course, the determination of these general conditions had been the monopoly of state and church.

Enlightenment, in Kant's understanding, meant a revitalization and vast expansion of the ancient idea of politics as public discussion aiming at justice and the common good. The new "public sphere of opinion" that was developing in European countries such as Britain and France gave concrete form to these hopes for enlightenment, suggesting the possibility of a new era of international peace marked by the "republican constitution of states." This scenario of political and moral progress promised persons of reason, such as Kant, a special importance as educators and counselors to their societies, an aspiration that has during the past two centuries closely linked intellectual talent with the presumed improvement of public affairs.[2]

This ideal of public reason depended upon two premises. One was that humans had the capacity to exercise collective control over social processes. The other was that history could be trusted to allow persuasion rather than force to assume a stronger role in human affairs. This latter hope was articulated in Alexander Hamilton's characterization of the significance of the

American Revolution as having decided in the affirmative "the important question, whether societies of men are really capable or not of establishing good government from reflection and choice." The alternative, the historical ubiquity of which Hamilton fully understood, was that societies would be "forever destined to depend for their political constitutions on accident and force." Should the American republic fail in this endeavor, Hamilton continued, the event would "deserve to be considered as the general misfortune of mankind."[3]

Hamilton enlarged on this Enlightenment confidence in the powers of rational persuasion when he singled out for leadership in republican society those trained in the liberal professions. Because of this education, such a person was most "likely to prove an impartial arbiter" between rival classes and interests in civil society, ready to promote any interest "so far as it shall appear to him conducive to the general interests of society."[4] Embedded in hopes for the public use of reason, then, was the Enlightenment's confidence that reason could reveal natural law, thus upholding universal natural rights and therefore the possibility of a cosmopolitan civilization that would encompass older divisions among groups. Partisans of this "party of reason" shared a tacit faith that it would prove possible to overcome both historical contingency and cultural, especially religious, particularity. These, after all, were the forces that had caused so much misery in Europe during the wars of religion following the upheaval of the Protestant Reformation, forces that the age of Enlightenment determined to subdue.

The twentieth century has not been kind to these hopes. World War I exploded the nineteenth century's expectation that progress in science, technology, and the generation of wealth would propel the advance of liberal political freedoms and humane values. In the following decades, the secular ideologies spawned by the Enlightenment and revolution redoubled the horrors of religious wars with the amplified powers provided by modern technology. Then, in a stunning historical reversal, the Allied victory in World War II rekindled confidence in the possibility of collectively directing the forces of modern civilization toward human betterment, which even the Cold War and the nuclear threat could not wholly overpower. The period after 1945 also saw the astonishing rebirth of liberal democracy in Europe and its emulation around the world. Even the intransigence of the Soviet Union, aggressively asserting the alternative, Marxist variant of Enlightenment hopes for progress, helped indirectly by providing a powerful external stimulus to reform in the direction of greater social justice in the Western countries.

In all the developed Western countries, the arrangements of those decades combined a "mixed economy" of free enterprise managed by governments with a political consensus in favor of social inclusion.[5] The results added up to what one historian has called the "Golden Age," three decades of historically unprecedented improvement in the level of health, longevity, material prosperity, education, and social participation for virtually all classes and groups. Economic growth, combined with stability in social and political life, fostered trust and confidence in the future, producing a rich soil for the growth of democratic culture. By the end of the Cold War period, social analysts were pointing to a historical shift in values from obsession with security to the more adventurous and open quests of "postmaterialism," by which they meant a new concern with the moral and aesthetic quality, as well as the material security, of life.[6]

To a point, the history of this "Golden Age" vindicated the hopes of the Enlightenment's partisans. Especially in the United States and Britain, intellectuals with broad public understanding were important figures in shaping and directing public opinion. However, from the vantage point of the turn of the new century, the fragility of these accomplishments is all too apparent. Political stability and the gains in social justice are at risk everywhere, due to the unrestrained forces of an increasingly global capitalism. In this climate, concern for the future of democratic polities requires that we acknowledge, far more than the inherited doctrines of modernization would suggest, the cultural and institutional sources that supported and made possible such a remarkable efflorescence of humane public purpose.

Close investigation of the British and American cases, however, reveals that the hopes of public reason have in fact been carried, as well as limited and channeled, by deeper social currents. Social events are not only driven by causal forces ranging from demography to ecology; they are also shaped, in ways still imperfectly understood, by symbolic activity and codes of meaning. As social thinkers such as Emile Durkheim and Max Weber have emphasized, the categories of cultural activity—not least the great culturally formative codes of religion—have introduced a realm of relative freedom into human affairs through the possibilities afforded by ritual activity, political deliberation, and scientific inquiry itself. The divergence between such historically linked and culturally akin nations as Britain and the United States can serve as a pointed example of the powerful effects that differing cultural, and particularly religious, histories can have on the institutional and ultimately the intellectual possibilities for politics in modern nations.

II. THE POSTWAR "GOLDEN AGE":
THE KEY ROLE OF INTELLECTUALS

At the core of the achievements of the "Golden Age" was a moral change: all the developed countries greatly expanded those aspects of life that came to be treated as public matters and thus as objects of common responsibility. Health, education, employment, culture, science, insurance against catastrophic events, as well as physical infrastructure and, eventually, the natural environment—and, in some nations, rural and urban heritage—came to be seen as interconnected aspects of advanced civilization. Further, it was agreed that these matters could be at least partially understood and directed by conscious collective action. As this postwar Western order developed, a kind of "middle way" seemed to have been found between the Scylla of prewar economic instability and national aggressiveness and the Charybdis of total absorption of society by the state in Soviet Communism. The mixed economy gave the capitalist market due freedom while subordinating economic rationality to political and cultural values. Tolerance for pluralism and supports for individual autonomy seemed reconcilable with greater social justice and participation in national life.

One indispensable condition of the "Golden Age" was increased linkage of the spheres of knowledge, inquiry, education, and culture with institutions of the economy and the state. More than Kant could have imagined, state and society, experts and other citizens, became linked in mutual influence and collaboration. In all the Western developed countries, such linkages formed a new matrix of public discourse and debate, a genuine if limited institutionalization of the ideal of "public use of reason." Among the most conspicuous causes as well as effects of these developments was the prominence of intellectual talent in the service of practical and public goals.

Closer focus on and comparison of the British and American cases, however, reveals significant differences within the broad similarities—divergences that can illuminate the ways in which cultural and religious history work to shape the horizon of political possibility in modern societies. The common features of Anglo-American thinking during the first half of the twentieth century, but also the distinctly American, as opposed to British, features of these developments, are illustrated in the work of several of the most influential and celebrated public intellectuals of the era. John Maynard Keynes and William Beveridge personified the new importance of the intellectual figure in Britain. In the United States, there was the "Brain Trust" around Franklin Roosevelt's New Deal, calling public attention to the new importance gained by figures of intellectual distinction in public life. The possibilities of this kind of leadership had already been adumbrated by figures of the Progressive era such as Louis Brandeis. The postwar form would be shaped by younger figures such as James Bryant Conant.

III. KEYNES AND BEVERIDGE: CULTURE AND CLERISY

Keynes has become synonymous with the economic regime of those decades of prosperity, especially in the Anglo-American world, while Beveridge's idea of a "welfare state" to provide social cohesion through institutions of civic membership has come virtually to define the political ideals of that era. If Keynes and Beveridge exemplify a kind of leadership that for a period promised to actualize rule by "public use of reason," then it is important to notice the cultural and institutional bases of their role. Culturally, Keynes and Beveridge were the heirs and beneficiaries of a militant tradition in British intellectual life, centered around thinkers, known as "New Liberals," such as T. H. Green, L. T. Hobhouse, and J. Hobson. Similar intellectual developments were taking place in the United States, beginning around the turn of the century, in the broad "Progressive" movement, including figures such as Herbert Croly, John Dewey, and Jane Addams, who were often directly influenced by British thinking of the New Liberal kind. All these developments were part of a larger, transatlantic current of debate and discussion that established a new perspective on long-lamented social ills such as poverty, urban disorder, and disease.[7]

What was new, and shared by these groups, was the belief that social problems were the results of failures in social organization rather than of individual incompetence or vice. As the historian Harold Perkin notes, "Problems thus defined as institutional and societal, rather than moral and individual, cried out for collective, professional solutions rather than moral discipline or exhortation."[8] The effect on politics, and ultimately on the shape of Britain and the United States as the twentieth century unfolded, was vast and dramatic. Despite the similarities in thought, however, the social position, the intellectual style, and, above all, the results of these developments were quite different in Britain and in the United States. Trying to account for these differences brings the important divergence in the institutional history and finally in the cultural, particularly religious, experience of the two polities into sharp relief.

It is striking that Keynes's recent biographer, Robert Skidelsky, characterizes Keynes as consistently speaking "in the name of culture rather than expertise." In claiming a right to direct affairs, Skidelsky notes, Keynes "addressed the world as a priest, not as a technician. And though he rearranged its theology, economics spoke through him, as a church, not as a branch of the differential calculus."[9] What Keynes relied upon were "those larger frameworks of thought which had proportioned knowledge to the purposes of human life," frameworks closely connected to the sense of larger purpose Skidelsky terms "religion."[10]

We misunderstand Keynes, Skidelsky argues, if we see him simply as an academic economist and fail to recognize his self-understanding as "a member of the British 'clerisy'—a secular priesthood setting standards of value and behavior, practicing the arts of leadership and mutual accommodation."[11] The same applies to Beveridge, author of the famous wartime reports on social insurance and full-employment policies that provided the architecture of the postwar welfare state. Beveridge, like Keynes, came from a professional family and was educated at public (that is, private boarding) school and then at Oxford University. Like many idealistic Oxford undergraduates in the late nineteenth and early twentieth century, Beveridge was drawn into social service at Toynbee Hall in the slums of London's East End, putting his philosophical and social-scientific training to work in studying unemployment. While Keynes pursued an academic career in economics at Cambridge University, Beveridge worked in the high civil service, developing a widening system of social insurance that provided the practical basis for the postwar order. Along with many lesser-known figures, Keynes and Beveridge exemplified the combination of intellectual and practical energies in the public service that the ideal of the clerisy was meant to evoke.

The term had been coined in the nineteenth century by Samuel Taylor Coleridge to describe his hopes for a new kind of intellectual to help guide and improve a society reeling from the joint dislocations of industrial capitalism and revolutionary democracy. Coleridge called for the establishment of what he called the "National Church"—not a religious organization but a system of educational and scholarly institutions to be endowed independently of the state. What Coleridge was urging was a further development in the long-term English process of making the national church a public resource by creating a prestigious and independent institutional system to link education and culture with the progress of the nation. Coleridge's clerisy, like August Comte's "savants," and G. W. F. Hegel's "universal class," were to aspire beyond one-sided views, and to exemplify excellence in generalized cultivation and practical wisdom rather than in a narrow specialization. They were to educate the nation's future teachers, civil service, writers, leaders, and intellectuals, infusing them with the "spirit of the state" to counteract the narrowing tendencies that Coleridge saw at work in the all-pervasive "spirit of commerce."

This ideal became powerful in nineteenth-century Britain. Through figures such as Thomas and Matthew Arnold, John Stuart Mill, and T. H. Green, it greatly changed the nation's educational system, shaped its first true civil service, and helped to inspire the social responsibility state of the twentieth century. But it was an ideal that mingled uneasily with the egalitarianism of the democratic ethos. The "public use of reason" was inherently ambiguous. It proclaimed a share in public affairs open to all. Yet deliberation was a complex and difficult skill, involving breadth of experience and judgment rather than routine application of rules that all could learn; it could not be reduced to the simple procedures of majority rule. In this sense, the public use of reason was difficult to reconcile with democratic liberalism.

More clearly than Beveridge, Keynes brought these tensions together, most clearly in his more speculative writings on economics, moral philosophy, and the future of civilization. These were typically essays designed not for specialists or officials but for the general public. Keynes's family descended from Dissenting Protestants, who professed a rigorous regard for liberty of conscience and a strong vocational ethic. This spirit had been broadened by apprenticeship in the leading institutions of the clerisy. Keynes in turn leavened the call of duty with G. E. Moore's ethical philosophy, which postulated personal cultivation and friendship as the core values of a life worth living. This complex background provides some understanding of the reason he insisted that economic growth was never an end in itself and that capitalism could never by itself produce a decent or humane civilization.

The point, Keynes liked to insist, was to maximize not material abundance but "goodness" in that sense of cultivated humanity that Moore advocated. It was the role of the economist, and especially the economist-statesperson, to use governmental economic policy to make possible a swifter advance from obsession with security and accumulation to those values that today are sometimes called "post-materialist." Thus, Keynes consistently looked not to business or the markets—even though he made and lost large sums in the stock market—but to government and cultural institutions as the important agents of social progress. Since wealth was a means rather than an end, Keynes advocated not only state regulation of the national economy, as is well known, but also the involvement of the state in shaping and altering the "preferences" of individuals.

As nations become more affluent, argued Keynes, states should invest and work to lead citizens to expand their preferences beyond material consumption toward the "higher pleasures." To confront the deflationary crisis of the Great Depression of the 1930s, Keynes famously advocated deficit spending and public investment. However, as early as the 1920s he advocated extensive public investments, quite apart from economic emergency, in culture, education, grand civic architecture, and "protecting the countryside"—not to improve economic performance but to enhance the quality of national life. Even higher education, access to which Keynes thought should be expanded and made less class-dependent, ought, he believed, to be seen less as a kind of economic investment in a skilled workforce than as a way to enhance civilization by spreading enjoyment of the higher pleasures.[12] It is not clear that these ideas flow from the discipline of economics. But they are consistent with Keynes's sense of calling as a member of the national clerisy: counseling and persuading his fellow citizens to consider the ethical dimension of the collective life, the question of how they might use their growing national wealth to "live wisely and agreeably and well."

IV. TRANSATLANTIC DIVERGENCE: SCIENCE AND MANAGEMENT

The gap between British and American social policy in the postwar era was graphically apparent in American reactions to both Keynes's economic ideas and the Beveridge Plan. New Dealers, like their British counterparts, had hoped that the experience of national solidarity in World War II would translate into popular support for the consolidation and extension of the so-cial reforms of the 1930s, such as Social Security and governmental respon-sibility for employment. But, while British opinion quickly rallied around Beveridge's proposal that national solidarity required the tangible integu-ment of common public supports, his wartime lecture tour of the United States evoked no lasting resonance among Americans. After initial enthu-siasm, the tone of the response was mostly dismissive, even from ardent Progressives.

To most Americans, even most New Dealers, it seemed obvious that the emphasis for the future should lie not in the "democratization of risks" but in the expansion of opportunities. Material consumption, not public provision, seemed the more authentically American means of social cohe-sion.[13] The same spirit appeared immediately after the war—even as many experts feared a postwar depression—in the rejection of proposals that the federal government should guarantee a job to every citizen.[14] A similar fate awaited efforts to institute universal, federally supported health care, both in the early postwar years and again during the Clinton administration of the 1990s.

Thus, while the United States adopted the concepts of state management of the national economy proposed by Keynes at Bretton Woods, the form in which Keynes's ideas were implemented differed significantly from the Brit-ish case. In the United States, "the policy mix was conservative throughout, emphasizing price stability and the balance of payments as much or more than unemployment." Further, at the core of the great postwar economic boom stood not only Keynesian economic managers, but "high cold war de-fense expenditures [that] gave the government the fiscal leverage it needed on the economy" without trespassing on the freedom of big business and fi-nance to set the nation's economic priorities.[15]

The intellectual currents and figures that dominated these develop-ments also mark an important contrast to the Keynes-Beveridge settlement in Britain. As Alexis de Tocqueville had noted, the law had long been Amer-ica's preeminent public profession. Until well into the twentieth century, if any group could have claimed to function as an American clerisy, it was the elite bar, and the new prominence of national corporations and finance en-hanced the importance and prestige of business lawyers in and out of gov-ernment service. Beginning early in the new century, however, a new form of expertise began to develop: expert management. With the successes of technology and applied science came the application of principles of effi-cient allocation in business corporations and other institutions. As the idea of management developed in both business and government, it seemed to herald a new way in which the old American ideals of individual initiative and voluntary cooperation could be applied to the complicated conditions of the new times without risking radical political conflict.

Over time, a "national class" of college- and university-trained personnel gained prominence. The sympathies and outlook of this new middle class were diverse, yet supportive of progress through economic development and applied scientific method in both technology and social organization. The institutional basis of this class was the consolidated corporate economy that emerged through intense strife in the decades around 1900. The new institutions that ran this vast economic network brought relative stability out of the near-chaos of late-nineteenth-century laissez-faire. They did this by applying new techniques of management and control to all areas of production, personnel, distribution, and innovation.

At the same time, the leaders of the new corporate system endowed and fostered a wave of institutional innovation in higher education. This produced, for the first time in the United States, institutions that combined specialized research with teaching. These universities drew ambitious and talented students from across the nation and fitted them with the skills and social connections useful for the emerging national institutions. These graduates formed the country's first large class whose perspective and loyalties were more national than regional, with moral and cultural standards more cosmopolitan than those of most of their fellow citizens.[16] With important support from the new-style philanthropic institutions devoted to research, which had been established by the great industrialists such as Carnegie and Rockefeller, these institutions also supported a spreading network through which expert knowledge came to join the interests of business and of research as well as the concerns of efficiency and of national power.[17]

The new national class did not share a uniform understanding of itself or its responsibilities, however. It was divided in its loyalties between two rival programs through which the American elites struggled to control the unruly dynamism of the new industrial society. One of these programs supported the private, corporate order established by financiers—above all, by J. P. Morgan. The other produced the regulatory state pioneered during the administration of Theodore Roosevelt and adapted by Woodrow Wilson. There was real divergence between the two; for the first party, private control and voluntarism were sacrosanct, while for the Progressives of the Roosevelt or Wilson sort, the good of the nation required public institutions of a scale and power to regulate private activity so that it did not overwhelm individuals and communities. At the same time, both parties shared the premise that the goal was national progress in both material abundance and individual freedom, although they differed significantly over how each of these terms was to be understood. Both parties also saw deliberate planning and expert management as essential for such progress, differing mostly over what should be the focus of the loyalties as well as the priorities of the experts.

V. EXPERTISE TRUMPS "CULTURE"

Something of the spirit, as well as the ambiguities, of the public aspirations of this American national class becomes apparent in considering the lives of some of its most influential scions during the first half of the century. Louis Brandeis and James Bryant Conant helped to shape the institutional order of those postwar decades when American power reached its zenith, the period that some called the American Century. Between them, they illustrate some differences, as well as the shared consensus, of this American approximation to a clerisy, forming a revealing contrast to their British counterparts. Where the British clerisy centered around the idea of "culture" promoted by Mathew Arnold, these American intellectuals in active life came to exalt technical competence and expertise into preeminence.

Dubbed the "people's lawyer," Brandeis sought through the law to make traditional individual initiative and responsibility compatible with the era of institutionalized science and large-scale organizations. By bringing the methods of the new social sciences and the "scientific management" of Frederick Winslow Taylor into the workings of the law, Brandeis was updating the American tradition of using the bar and the bench as primary means of social adaptation and control. Appointed to the highest bench by Wilson, this Harvard-educated son of immigrant German Jewish parents embraced both the New England spirit of patrician reform and the new enthusiasm for expert planning and economic efficiency. Brandeis pioneered the use of social science as a resource for legal argument, thought of law as a technology for social reform, and sought "social inventions" to reduce the "friction" in the workings of social mechanisms.

Yet, if Brandeis was an innovator, his was innovation in the service of the traditions of the reforming wing of the New England establishment. He remained devoted to the culture and values of that elite provincial culture of which Harvard University was in his time still the emblem. He celebrated the enlarging effects of legal practice on the characters as well as the intellects of attorneys. He held strong moral convictions about the importance of legal principle as opposed to technique. Perhaps the most characteristic of the Progressive opinions Brandeis shared was his advocacy for bringing the moral standards of the traditional learned professions into business practice. Brandeis saw modern society as an interplay of mostly blind forces, which could remain in balance only through the intervention of persons with wide sympathies and broad vision. He sought to use legal regulation as a tool of social engineering to provide solutions to economic and political conflicts. His legacy of trying to combine economic efficiency with social harmony through legal and administrative innovation helped define the New Deal and the postwar developments of the American regulatory state.

Conant anticipated much about the American future by training not in the law but in science. His career of scientific and educational leadership established the lineaments of the American system of education in the second half of the twentieth century. As much as any figure, Conant could rightly be called the parent of the contemporary national class. In this sense, his legacy is as important as any in determining the distinguishing qualities of the American meritocracy. As president of Harvard during the crucial decades linking the depression with postwar prosperity, Conant led that university's transformation into a genuinely national center of learning. At Harvard, Conant supported a highly influential effort to develop a kind of national curriculum that could combine an emphasis on science and practicality with historical understanding and civic values. From his highly visible position, he extended educational testing into a system for selecting a national educated class, through devices such as the Scholastic Aptitude Test and the National Merit Scholarships. Spurred by the nation's wartime success with classifying and channeling the workforce, the postwar Conant system provided a new degree of career mobility for increasing numbers of Americans, especially after the reforms of the 1960s opened possibilities for far more women and minorities than ever before.

Conant sought to legitimate his meritocratic ideal on grounds of social utility. He argued that the new system brought the best talent to where it could most advance the national interest. In the process, the system enhanced the prestige of scientific, technological, and managerial expertise, so that while Americans were famous for their coolness toward European high culture, they were deeply awed by the competence in which the growing meritocracy specialized. Advancement through the increasingly open national educational system required demonstrations of academic merit, while large investments in education—public as well as private—came to be seen as essential features of American democracy. To a considerable extent, Conant's ideals came to define American middle-class aspirations. They stressed keeping education, government, and eventually business open to all. The aim of the system was to advance the cause of democracy and equality.

At the same time, the idea of advancement by merit worked to define life as a competition for success in which achievement came to be taken as a demonstration of individual worthiness. Achievement, in fact, came to overshadow virtually all other virtues. The mostly unnoticed result was, and is, to emphasize invidious distinctions between winners and losers. Over time, acceptance of these distinctions and of the institutions through which they have been generated has increased the prestige of the national class, its causes and tastes. However, it is less clear that it has increased popular esteem for this class. Nor, as has become increasingly evident, have these developments instilled in this remarkably privileged class a sense of solidarity with less successful fellow citizens. Indeed, the institutionalization of the meritocratic system has coincided with the drift of the United States into the rank of the most unequal society in the developed world.

VI. EXPLAINING THE AMERICAN DIFFERENCE

The sense of what was "reasonable" politically was thus quite different in the American context from what was considered possible in Britain. Different polities, it is clear, are differentially hospitable to political ideas, making the welfare state seem a rational development of national identity for Britons while making the expansion of individual opportunity to consume seem equally "natural" as a policy goal for Americans. The numerous possibilities for personal advancement that the American consumer society provided had huge psychological implications, at least for white Americans, making "each individual appear so much more responsible for his or her own fate." By contrast, the class structure of Britain enabled even working-class individuals to

> find satisfaction in collective experience; though his individual fate was frustrating, he did not need to lose self-respect. His counterpart in the United States, even in the relatively rare instance in which he joined a political movement, was confronted with the powerful ethos of his society: he believed in his heart that he had nobody to blame but himself.[18]

These differences are also reflected fairly clearly in the political philosophies dominant in the two nations. The differences correspond to an enduring contrast within the liberal political consensus the two societies share. The contrast is rooted in differing social visions that accent freedom differently in each case. The dominant American approach, identified with the thinking of John Locke, stresses the importance of minimizing reliance upon centralized power and public authority, identifying these as potential threats to individual liberty. For this philosophy, freedom means allowing individuals to work out their own welfare. Identity and purpose are thought to reside in individual labor, private property, and the family, all considered pre-political in nature. Government is said to exist by contract, as an instrument to protect individual rights against the inconveniences of the pre-political situation. It is easy to see why this approach, so familiar to Americans, has shown such elective affinity for reliance upon the capitalist market as the organizing system for social life.

In the land of his birth, Locke had significantly less influence. The British path into modernity has significant affinities with another kind of liberal philosophy, first clearly articulated by Montesquieu, although picked up by later British thinkers such as Coleridge, J. S. Mill, and T. H. Green. This viewpoint has had American adherents and has even played an important role in the United States, but it remains always the minority position, except in moments of exceptional national mobilization. It was given memorable expression in the American context by Hamilton, then revived by Progressive-era thinkers such as Herbert Croly.

This public philosophy disputes the notion that either individuals or societies can define themselves independently of their political constitution. This form of liberalism continues the civic republican concern with developing common purposes through institutions. Here institutions are seen as carriers of identity and meaning that transcend individuals. For this reason, institutions can provide the bases for affiliation and for patterns of shared living that work to transform the purposes of individuals by consciously placing individual activity within a broader drama of development. Democracy in its complete sense is here conceived as developmental—as in the philosophy of John Dewey.

The basic idea is that human development requires a depth of involvement in common projects so as to call out individual capacities that, while expanding the individual's possibilities, also enhance a larger life. The political problem then becomes how to make public authority accountable to and responsible for these common ends. This tradition accepts centralized power as a necessary concomitant of the differentiated complexity of modern societies but seeks to balance central power with organized citizen activity through a variety of intermediate associations. It has therefore emphasized the importance, for liberty, of enabling people leading otherwise private lives to experience the psychological and moral broadening that comes through active citizenship. Seeing liberty as a matter of achieving balance among strong and opposing forces, this tradition has been sympathetic to the idea of a clerisy as a valuable steadying force in liberal polities.

At the core of these differences lies an opposition deeper than concepts alone—something in the nature of a spirit or *habitus*. It shows up in opposing understandings of the very institutions that make up social life. Americans tend to see institutions as instruments, tools that individuals may use to advance purposes of which the origins and ends are conceived as entirely extrinsic to the institutions themselves.[19] By contrast, British life has been built around certain institutions that have seemed to embody key patterns of moral meaning in the society. As Robert Wiebe has emphasized, the struggle for democracy was quite different on the opposite sides of the Atlantic. If Americans, spread across a vast continent, assumed that "they could create a democracy without the state," writes Wiebe, "Europeans, congregating in cities[,] . . . needed the state to create their democracy." For European democracy, "everything hinged on controlling the state, which became invested with all kinds of conflicting hopes for security, order, and justice, [while] American democracy, thriving on suspicion of the state, invested far fewer hopes in it."[20] If social conditions were a large part of the explanation of these important differences, however, there are other sources of the different ways in which Americans and Europeans, even the British, have pursued freedom.

VII. RELIGION AND DIVERGENT ROADS TO MODERNITY

Why, then, these determining differences? Alexis de Tocqueville cautioned that in accounting for traits of national societies, geography counts for less than laws, and laws are less influential than *les moeurs*—the *mores*, or "habits of the heart," that set the tone of both collective and individual life. Here the peculiar religious history of the United States may well have been decisive. "The U.S.," Seymour Martin Lipset has noted, "is the one country in the world dominated by the religious doctrines of Protestant 'dissent'—the Methodists, Baptists, and other sects." Lipset went on to emphasize the massive effects of this "ascetic Protestantism" in a society free of an inherited feudal status order such as prevailed in France and in Great Britain itself during the early modern period. "The teaching of these denominations," Lipset added, "called on people to follow their conscience, to be responsible for their own individual actions, with an unequivocal emphasis not to be found in those denominations which evolved from state churches (Catholics, Lutherans, Anglicans, Orthodox Christians)."[21]

The consequences, according to Lipset, have included a peculiar preoccupation with personal morality in American public life—a morality displayed, above all, through diligence in work and economic achievement, along with family responsibility. But this legacy has also tended to understand morality in a specific way, as a matter of the converted heart. This understanding, ultimately derived from Pietistic Protestantism, typically sharply divides the formation of moral character from intellectual cultivation. Moral formation is thought to take place in family and work, while intellectual training and artistic cultivation can be regarded as sources of moral skepticism and even degeneracy, so that culture has often been seen by Americans as the enemy of moral integrity.

These tendencies are diametrically opposed to the dispositions typical of a nation such as France, descending from a Catholic culture in which humanistic education has been virtually equated with moral formation, or England, in which the Anglican church continued the medieval pattern of general responsibility for education and passed on to the state responsibility for the support of the poor. For Americans, by contrast, poverty has been like character: first a matter of individual accountability and only secondarily an affair of collective responsibility. Indeed, "responsibility," for Americans, has meant primarily responsibility for oneself, made manifest in diligence and achievement. This understanding shares little with the more typical European understanding of responsibility as duty deriving from membership in an interdependent whole. So, for example, two-thirds of the American public consistently subscribe to the idea that poverty, even in significant numbers, is basically the responsibility of the poor. By contrast, among the British, approximately the same percentage regard the existence of widespread poverty as primarily a social, or collective, responsibility.[22]

These oppositions recall Ernst Troeltsch's famous contrast between the *church* and the *sect* as historical forms of social organization in the Christian church. For Troeltsch, the Christian ideal has always contained two poles. One pole receives expression in the sect, as evidenced in the religious forms of the Reformation that gained ascendancy in the early English colonization of North America. Here, "communal forms rest on the principle of a mature, free, conscious decision by the adult individual, on the constant control of faith and morals," so that the religious community is seen as an "association" of free individuals. In this understanding of Christianity, argues Troeltsch, "divine law is more important than sacrament," while individual achievement is decisive rather than grace. Where the church type has "sacraments of penance and forgiveness of sins, the other [sect type] has congregational discipline and the expulsion of the unworthy."[23] The great strength of the "sect type" has been energy and renewal; its negative legacy has been an indifference and cruelty to those considered outside the circle of light. It is the continuation of this pattern in the moral understanding of American society that, as Lipset argues, continues to make the American polity unique among Western nation-states.

The church, for Troeltsch, manifests an organic understanding of the Christian community as a vehicle of divine presence in the world. This conception has never been entirely absent in any Christian movement, but in American history it was the late arrival. The church is an accommodation on the part of Christians with the worlds of nature and history; it places fewer demands on believers but incorporates them all, at whatever state of adherence they may be. As a consequence, the church "corresponds to the Christian conception of grace . . . and the objective holiness of all, even amid personal sinfulness . . . while the idea of subjective perfection recedes into the background." While the sect is simply an association of individuals, the church understands itself to be "an institution of salvation, a work of God and not humans, a miraculous establishment endowed with divine truths and powers of salvation that is not produced and constituted by its members . . . and which bestows on its members an indelible character."[24] This understanding of institutions as wholes greater than the sum of their parts and as embodying trans-individual moral meanings has been one of the most persistent legacies of Christendom to European nations. It is the social condition for an effective clerisy. But it is a decidedly weaker second voice to the strong sectarian bass in America.

To put this contrast another way: the sect attempts to separate itself from the world, enforcing that separation by making high demands on individuals for various kinds of achievement. But it provides little support beyond pervasive discipline. Hence, its penchant for testing and expulsion as a way to maintain purity and organizational morale. By contrast, the church inclines toward including the world, or at least accepting many of its basic features, making fewer demands on individuals. At the same time, it provides strong supports for individuals while emphasizing diverse ways of remaining connected with the community it encompasses. American versus European attitudes toward poverty, state action in the economy, the welfare state—even toward morality—generally resonate with these distinctions.

This contrast appears even in those institutions that are commonly, even uniquely, shared by the two polities, such as the professions. British professionalism has tended to emphasize status, "the ideology of liberal education, and public service"—particularly "in opposition to the growth of industrialism and commercialism"—far more than has American professionalism. In the American case, the polarities have tended to be defined by a focus on social responsibility versus a concentration on the prestige of technical competence. British professionalism has focused on such values as "personal service, a dislike of competition, advertising and profit, a belief in the principle of payment in order to work rather than working for pay, and in the [moral] superiority of the motive of service."[25] These values, however, only make sense when the professional occupation is seen primarily as participation in institutions whose value and prestige derive from what they are and represent as much or more than from their efficiency in the division of labor.

Reform in both Europe and the United States has typically drawn on political visions combining the emphasis of the church tradition on strong common institutions with a sectarian spirit of renewal and change. At the core of these reformist political visions has been faith that strong institutions can create and support aspirations that help to develop individuals, galvanizing their energies by a sense of joint responsibility for improving the larger community. This was the ground from which the British idea of the clerisy sprung.

VIII. THE "PUBLIC USE OF REASON"
AND AMERICAN AMBIVALENCE

Culture shapes and conditions the great Enlightenment ideal of guiding the common life through the public use of reason. It is therefore the complex, historically developing patterns of particular cultures, rather than abstract norms of rationality alone, that determine what practical possibilities will be considered "reasonable" in a particular time and place. Or so this comparison of the differing British and American responses to challenges faced by the two societies through much of the twentieth century has tried to argue. Each nation made important choices at midcentury, choices that shaped their respective futures in indelible ways. In balancing achievement and competition with equity and security, British leadership and popular opinion moved in ways quite different from those of their American counterparts, even though the same intellectual resources circulated on both sides of the Atlantic and even though on each side there was public allegiance to the same political principles of democracy and capitalism.

American culture itself is not univocal. The sectarian Protestant cultural code has never been entirely determinative. Americans continue to show signs of bewilderment and displeasure at where the relentless pursuit of their dominant values of individual freedom and achievement are taking their society. Americans, that is to say, remain ambivalent about the outcomes of their individualist culture. Americans wish very much to be self-reliant; indeed, they feel that they have a duty to be so, to "make something of themselves." They intensely desire to "find themselves" in highly individualized private life. Yet they fear that a life without sustaining commitments to others and the larger society is empty and moribund. They take pride in a kind of scrappy individual resourcefulness that distrusts institutions and commitments unless these show obvious, short-term payoffs—a tendency that shows no signs of stopping as connections among Americans become looser and looser. Yet Americans also long for the order and permanence they sense is lacking in their lives, feeling nostalgia for an imagined past of bucolic communities or dreaming of it appearing magically through some new technological development, against all facts.

This back-and-forth pattern is classic ambivalence, enacted on a mass scale. The problem is both with the institutional heritage and with the bent of the cultural code. It is not the case, however, that there have been no powerful correctives at work that have, at some historical moments, shifted the institutional pattern toward stronger forms of social solidarity. Figures who announced and promoted the broader, more "church"-like conception of American possibility, such as Croly at the turn of the century and a variety of important intellectuals in later decades, have been important to the history of America in the twentieth century. They found support and ultimately shaped new institutional patterns when they enunciated the idea that strong institutions are needed to call out and support the creative capacities of individuals and that persons become individuals most fully through their energetic contribution to the common good. But their position has been a minority voice. And the result of such debates and shifts in the present is really more a stalemated skirmishing than an enduring synthesis.

It is for this reason that the idea of a clerisy, and the public work of those intellectuals who embody its values, is of potential importance for

American society. Such thinkers provide a crucial angle on collective self-understanding by upholding and revealing an insight of enormous value. This insight is the sense of larger possibility and fuller life that flows from understanding how institutions of common life can carry intrinsic value, as bearers of meaning that can save individual lives from futility. Such thinkers bring to awareness a possibility that is always threatened with eclipse in America: that, at their best, public institutions can bring into the lives of all citizens something of the "splendor" the ancient Greeks believed was the gift of "political" life, the life of the city. Even when it is against the odds, and against the grain, to make these things apparent is an activity good for its consequences but also a good in itself.

Meaning and Modernity
America and the World

Robert N. Bellah

METANARRATIVES

From early in my life, I have been concerned with large issues of meaning. In adolescence, I was exposed to a mainline Protestantism from which I absorbed a prophetic Christianity with a strong social-justice component. In college, this prophetic Christianity got transformed into Marxism, which seemed more up-to-date to me at the time, more scientific. In graduate school, disillusionment with Marxism was followed by absorption in the sociological theories of Talcott Parsons and a tentative return to Christianity with the help of the writings of Paul Tillich. I am confessing, in other words, to an obsession with metanarratives and grand theories from an early age, an obsession that I have never lost. From a postmodernist point of view, this might make me a modernist, though neither the postmodernists nor I know clearly enough what modernity is to have any idea what might follow it. To proclaim the end of metanarrative is already to be sufficiently tainted by what is being rejected as to produce only a new metanarrative.

It is a cliché today to speak of history as speeding up (just as it is a cliché to say that we have never been so diverse), and to define modernity as a period of rapidly increasing change. In the broad perspective of geological and biological time, the genus *Homo* has evolved remarkably rapidly for several million years. Since the "cultural explosion" of forty thousand to fifty thousand years ago, human social and cultural change has proceeded with an extraordinary rapidity. The stereotypical contrast of a rapidly changing modernity with a stagnant and unchanging "traditional society"—an idea that,

I am grateful for this extraordinary collection of papers both because of their own value and because they have stimulated me in this epilogue to think new thoughts.

unfortunately, owes more than a little to Max Weber—is surely wrong. But something about modernity makes it different from earlier social conditions, and it has been the task of sociology from the beginning to try to explain what that something is. It would not be an exaggeration to say that sociology began as an effort to explain modernity to itself. In so doing it was necessary for the founders of sociology—certainly for Marx, Weber, and Durkheim—to think systematically about what came before modernity to understand how modern societies are different from all preceding ones. Weber's notion of a development from societies based on kinship and neighborhood, through societies organized by bureaucracy or feudalism, to modern capitalism was a version of a story told in different ways by Marx and Durkheim. These thinkers did not invent this story, which goes back through Hegel, to whom they were all indebted, to Christian salvation history, but it is not my purpose here to trace that genealogy. My own effort to situate modernity in relation to what preceded it, coming out of this sociological tradition, was first expressed in my 1964 article on religious evolution,[1] and it is my hope to complete a fuller version before too long.

In my first version, drawing directly from Weber (and, unconsciously at the time, from Hegel), religion played a very important role in the emergence of modernity. Weber began his study of religion in 1904 with his famous *The Protestant Ethic and the Spirit of Capitalism*. It is clear, however, that if we consider not only that essay but the place of the Protestant ethic argument in Weber's work as a whole, that he believed that ascetic Protestantism was an indispensable catalyst for the emergence of a new form of society, which he called modern capitalism, but which he saw as a new kind of civilization, not just a new kind of economy. Never before the Reformation in the West had the control of a landholding elite in an agrarian society been broken through. Once established, however, capitalism became a worldwide phenomenon, even though taking different forms in different non-Western areas. Thus Protestantism, though occurring in only one tradition, was, indirectly but crucially, an indispensable precondition for the emergence of modernity cross-culturally.

In searching for the root causes of modernity and of why it arose first in the West, Weber embarked on the most ambitious set of comparative studies ever undertaken. In the course of his study of the great traditions he came to believe that religious events in the first millennium B.C. were of critical importance. In each of the world religions that emerged at that time there arose prophets or saviors who radically rationalized previous forms of what he called magical religion. In each case, the emergent figure (Confucius, the Buddha, the Hebrew prophets, Socrates, Jesus) preached a systematic form of ethical conduct quite different from the diffuse ritual and sacramental practices that preceded it. By calling these new symbolic

forms "rationalized," Weber was pointing to the fact that they were more coherent, more cognitively and ethically universalizing, more potentially self-
critical (reflexive), and more disengaged from the existing society than
what had preceded them. Karl Jaspers, a close friend and student of Weber's, called the period of the emergence of these religions the "Axial Age."[2]
S. N. Eisenstadt speaks of the world religions as axial religions, and their related civilizations as axial civilizations.[3] If one follows Weber's argument that
religion is the indispensable catalyst for the emergence of modernity, as
I do, then one can see that the axial religions, even though they emerged
millennia before modernity, were its indispensable precondition.

In my 1964 article, I proposed a simplified way of looking at the shape
of religious evolution. I argued that whereas tribal and archaic religions
were primarily this-worldly in orientation—which is what Weber, perhaps
unwisely, meant by the word "magical"—the axial religions were world-
rejecting (and thus, for Weber, very importantly, magic-rejecting), although
they differed as to whether this rejection was to be worked out within the
world (ethically) or as far as possible outside the world (mystically). It was
the leverage of axial religion in a transcendental reference point, outside
the world, so to speak, that made it possible to criticize and in principle to
revise the fundamental social and political premises of existing societies.
Whereas in tribal and archaic societies self and society were seen as embedded in the natural cosmos, the axial religions and philosophies made it possible in principle for the self to become disembedded from society and society from the given world of nature. It should be remembered, however,
that in its radical consistency axial religion was never more than the religion
of a minority; the majority continued to entertain beliefs and practices continuous with archaic or even tribal religion, which is what Weber meant by
the return to the garden of magic.

With the Protestant Reformation, the belief in a radically transcendent
God had dramatic this-worldly consequences: the consistent demands of an
axial ethic were to be expected from everyone and in every sphere of daily
life. An entirely new degree of disembeddedness of self from society, and
society from nature, became possible. But in the subsequent development
of modernity, although the this-worldly dimension remained dominant, its
transcendental basis became transformed into immanentism, thus returning the modern world in a much different way to the this-worldly immanentism of pre-axial times. This new form of immanentism, however, did
not lead to a reembeddedness of self and society in the cosmos but rather
to ever-increasing degrees of differentiation and disembeddedness. Weber
clearly observed this transition, but viewed it almost entirely negatively. The
modern world of rationalization would run on its own bureaucratic and
economic energies without any transcendental sanction, would become an

iron cage.[4] Charles Taylor has described the same transformation in less somber hues as "the affirmation of ordinary life" and has stressed, following Hegel, growing individuation.[5]

The influence of the Protestant Reformation on the emergence of modern society has been the subject of a vast literature. A significant recent development, however, has been the recognition of the importance of a "disciplinary revolution," particularly associated with the Calvinist wing of the Reformation.[6] The disciplinary revolution operated at a number of levels: a new code of systematic ethical action expected from believers, new institutions capable of enforcing this code, and new solidary organizations strong enough to influence political and economic developments.[7] What was in one sense a new level of control, because largely internal and shared by laity and clergy alike, turned out to have explosive energies in releasing new possibilities, not only in the economic sphere, which so fascinated Weber, but in the spheres of nation-building, democratic politics, science, and technology as well. Philip Gorski's contribution to this volume explores the dynamic but ambiguous contribution of the Protestant disciplinary revolution to the emerging political order of modern societies. The transformation of Protestant codes, under a variety of influences and pressures, into such tendencies as utilitarianism, liberalism, Jacobinism, and socialism—and, more recently, individualism and fundamentalism—has also significantly affected the shape of and the tensions within modern society.

In my 1964 article, I stressed the importance of the self as a focus for understanding the specific nature of modernity: "The historic [axial] religions discovered the self; the early modern religion found a doctrinal basis on which to accept the self in all its empirical ambiguity; modern religion is beginning to understand the laws of the self's own existence and so to help man take responsibility for his own fate." I spoke of the emergence of "a dynamic multidimensional self capable, within limits, of continual self-transformation and capable, again within limits, of remaking the world, including the very symbolic forms with which he deals with it, even the forms that state the unalterable conditions of his own existence." In my thinking at that time, the church was quite marginal, and I spoke of "an increasingly fluid type of organization in which many special purpose subgroups form and disband." I described modern society as "a self-revising social system in the form of a democratic society" and further argued that "it is the chief characteristic of the more recent modern phase that culture and personality themselves have come to be viewed as endlessly revisable."[8] It is almost as if I were, in 1964, a postmodernist before the fact. My later reservations about some of this will become evident below.

THE UNITED STATES AND JAPAN

While my focus in "Religious Evolution" was on the religious dimension of social development, I was also conscious of the political dimension and the variable linkage of religion and politics, as had been my teachers. In an essay published only three years later, "Civil Religion in America,"[9] this linkage came to the fore. Before discussing this, for me, life-changing essay, I want to back up a bit and point out that I began my scholarly life as a Japan specialist—indeed, the first version of what came to be "Civil Religion in America" was delivered as a Fulbright lecture in spring 1961, during my Fulbright year in Japan, soon after the Inaugural Address of John F. Kennedy, which plays a significant role in that essay. That talk was not an effort to speak to an American audience, but to explain to the Japanese, who had been so sternly lectured to by the Occupation on the critical importance of the separation of church and state, why no American president could be inaugurated without mentioning God in his inaugural address.

My doctoral dissertation, published in 1957 as *Tokugawa Religion*,[10] had argued that, although there was nothing like the Protestant Reformation that could have inaugurated modernity in Japan, there were functional equivalents of aspects of Protestantism that made the Japanese more capable than most non-Western societies of responding effectively to the challenge of modernization when it arrived. The book had been received with sharp criticism by Maruyama Masao, Japan's leading social scientist at the time, for eliding too easily the differences between Japan and the West and for being insufficiently aware of the negative aspects of the Japanese tradition. A different series of lectures that I gave at International Christian University in Tokyo, also in spring 1961, under the title "Values and Social Change in Modern Japan,"[11] in which I developed a more critical perspective on aspects of the Japanese tradition, was in part a response to Maruyama. In those lectures, I described a series of Japanese efforts to attain a transcendental perspective, beginning with Shōtoku Taishi in the seventh century, continuing with the major figures of Kamakura Buddhism, especially Shinran and Dōgen, in the thirteenth century, touching on Tokugawa Confucians such as Ogyū Sorai, and concluding with Christians since the Meiji Period, particularly Uchimura Kanzō. I pointed out how in each case the moment of transcendence was quickly submerged. The particularistic "ground bass" of Japanese society that I had described in *Tokugawa Religion* reasserted itself, soon drowning out the transcendental melody that had appeared in the upper register. I did not use the term "non-axial," which S. N. Eisenstadt would use in his book *Japanese Civilization*[12] (as well as in his chapter in this volume), but the germ of that idea was present in my lectures. While I shall return shortly to Eisenstadt's interesting comparison of the United States and Japan, here I shall only note that U.S.–Japan comparisons were very much in my mind from the beginning of the sixties.

Turning now to the 1967 essay "Civil Religion in America," I should note that the response to it was one of the great surprises of my life. I had not particularly wanted to contribute to the *Daedalus* issue on religion in America, because I did not feel I knew enough about America. The germ of what I had to say had already been expressed in my Fulbright lecture of 1961, but I developed the basic idea in the context of national controversy over involvement in the Vietnam War, and I saw the essay as an opportunity to use central elements in the American tradition to criticize our military policy. I did not imagine that my basic insight, derived from the Durkheimian notion that every coherent society will express itself in some kind of religious symbolism, was controversial. I was soon disabused of that idea when I learned that at least two subscribers to *Daedalus* canceled their subscriptions because "Bellah is seeking to undermine the separation of church and state."[13] But more surprising than the opposition was the widespread "aha" response that "Bellah has expressed clearly what we knew vaguely all along" and the civil-religion industry in scholarly publication that ensued.

The many invitations to speak and write on related subjects that the *Daedalus* article stimulated, and my feeling that turning them down in a period of national crisis would not be responsible, led me to an intensive period of self-education in American studies, as I had no serious scholarly preparation for what was to come. I had made significant progress by the time I was asked to give the Weil Lectures at Hebrew Union College/Jewish Institute of Religion in Cincinnati in fall 1971, lectures published in 1975 as *The Broken Covenant*,[14] my most substantial effort to describe what I meant by civil religion in America. As in the original essay, my focus was on the nation. I argued that American civil religion was not a competitor to church religion, which it never challenged, but operated at a different level. My focus, however, was on the nation religiously conceived and marginally, if at all, on the church.

Nonetheless, I did argue that the Protestant Reformation was the single most significant archetype underlying American self-understanding, particularly in the colonial and revolutionary periods. And I argued for a deep analogy between the Protestant idea of conversion as liberation from the bondage of sin, followed by covenant as the institutional expression of the social life of the converted, and revolution as liberation from the bondage of political oppression, followed by constitution as the institutional expression of the social life of the liberated. That is, as conversion was to covenant for the New England colonists, so revolution was to constitution for the new nation. Although I didn't put it that way, I was clearly arguing that the nation, if not replacing the church, was modeled on the (Protestant) church at its deepest level of self-understanding. G. K. Chesterton made this point when he spoke of the United States as "a nation with the soul of a church." The ominous side of this analogy was not overlooked in the book; indeed, it was expressed in its very title, *The Broken Covenant*. Chapter 2, "America as a Chosen People," pointed to the fact that (European) Americans were long able to overlook two primal crimes that haunted our country from the beginning, the genocide of the American Indians and the enslavement of Africans, by assuring themselves that they were a chosen people. I quoted Melville's ironic words:

> Long enough have we been skeptics with regard to ourselves, and doubted whether, indeed, the political Messiah had come. But he has come in *us*, if we would but give utterance to his promptings. And let us always remember that with ourselves, almost for the first time in the history of the earth, national selfishness is unbounded philanthropy; for we cannot do a good to America, but we give alms to the world.[15]

The dangers inherent in the idea of a messiah nation unleavened by the strong consciousness of divine judgment (as expressed, for example, in Lincoln's Second Inaugural Address) was, indeed, the central message of the book. Nonetheless, the question of whether the critique went deep enough is something to which I will return below. Whatever else *The Broken Covenant* was doing, Jeffrey Alexander and Steven Sherwood are quite right, in their chapter in this volume, to point out that its use of myth and symbol in a narrative context moves well beyond the conception of culture I had received from Parsons.

By the late seventies, the definitional debates over the meaning of civil religion were beginning to make me question whether the term was still viable. In 1978 I published an article, "Religion and the Legitimation of the American Republic," in which I wondered whether the problematic nature of American civil religion was not itself an index of the problematic nature of the American nation, caught in the never resolved tension between a civic republicanism and a constitutional liberalism.[16] The hope for renewal of the civil religion that was still expressed in the last chapter of *The Broken Covenant* was, in this essay, replaced by doubt about the coherence of the project and particularly by pessimism about the viability of the republican aspect of our polity. Andrew Delbanco, in a recent book (to which I shall refer below), asks whether, in my 1967 essay, I was describing a vital symbol system or writing its obituary.[17] By 1978 I was almost convinced that I had done the latter.

Although it was not until 1989 that I publicly stated that I would no longer use the term "civil religion,"[18] I had already tacitly abandoned it in

1985 in *Habits of the Heart* (written with the editors of the present volume), where the American tradition was seen as divided into four strands—biblical religion, civic republicanism, utilitarian individualism, and expressive individualism—and in which it was argued that the two forms of individualism had become our first language, with biblical religion and civic republicanism surviving only as second languages.[19] While much that I had previously treated under the rubric of civil religion was now expressed in terms of biblical religion and civic republicanism, these two were no longer fused, and, perhaps most important, there emerged for the first time the beginning of a serious treatment of the church, in chapter 9, "Religion," which I drafted initially. Serious attention to the church as an institution in its own right was deepened in *The Good Society*, written by the same five authors, particularly in chapter 6, "The Public Church," initially drafted by Steven M. Tipton. Still, in both books the focus was on the cultural, political, social, and economic problems of the United States.

In recent essays my appreciation of axial religion and my doubts about the American project have grown ever stronger,[20] but it is only in response to the essays in this volume, particular those of S. N. Eisenstadt and Stanley Hauerwas, that I am ready to undertake a new formulation of my position. I will use the contrast between Japan and the United States to make my point.

Both in *Japanese Civilization* and in his essay in this volume, Eisenstadt speaks of Japan as a non-axial civilization. It is not that Japan has not been exposed to axial religions and civilizations. Since at least the seventh century, Japan has been deeply influenced by Buddhism and Confucianism, as well as by Indian and particularly Chinese civilization. And since the sixteenth century Japan has been influenced by Christianity and Western civilization. But in the face of these religious and civilizational influences, the Japanese have not rejected their pre-axial civilizational premises; instead they have continuously revised them without abandoning them. Outside cultural influences have been appreciated and understood with intelligence and sensitivity but then used to bolster the non-axial premises of Japanese society rather than to challenge them. This is not the place to defend that argument, but it is implicit in much of my work on Japan and explicit in that of Eisenstadt.

Because the Japanese have been aware of axial principles, have understood them thoroughly, and yet have rejected them, preferring instead to adapt them to the reformulation of Japan's own archaic heritage, and because the Japanese have done so with such dynamism and openness to change that Japan has not been "traditional" in the pejorative sense of the term, Eisenstadt argues that Japan should be called non-axial rather than pre-axial. Yet there is one sense in which Japanese civilization can be called pre-axial. The underlying premises of Japanese society, though they can be reformulated with great sophistication, cannot be challenged. They are off the board, so to speak, when it comes to serious discussion of fundamental change.

I would like, for once, to take what Eisenstadt has left at least in part implicit and make it explicit, in this case with respect to America. At the very beginning of his paper, comparing the Japanese and U.S. cases, he argues that, in contrast to the non-axial quality of Japanese civilization, "the United States constitutes probably a crucial—if not *the crucial*—illustration of one of the fullest developments from within Axial civilizations." I want to push just beyond Eisenstadt in arguing that the United States has, from early on, operated with the tacit assumption that it has not just fully developed but actually *transcended* the axial age, that it is a *post-axial* civilization. If America in this understanding is a realized utopia, a version of the Kingdom of God on earth, then its fundamental assumptions cannot be challenged any more than can those of the Japanese. If the Japanese have continuously sought to avoid the introduction of the fundamental tension between ultimate truth and social reality that characterizes axial civilizations, the Americans have collapsed that fundamental tension by believing that it has been resolved in their own society. If the Japanese are in some sense pre-axial, the Americans are in some sense post-axial, or at least in both cases they work very hard at believing they are. This accounts for the American taboo on socialism and for many difficulties our society attempts to avoid facing.

Let us consider what in each case the unassailable premises are. Eisenstadt calls our attention to two fundamental aspects: the construction of collective identity and the basic premises of social and political order. There are remarkable similarities as well as "mirror-image" differences in the two cases. Both Japanese and Americans define *nation* and *people* in sacred terms. In Japan, this sacredness is primordial: Japan is the divine land, created by the gods, and the Japanese people are descended from the gods. While the American identity of "chosen people" and "promised land" uses images that could be seen as primordial, it is future-orientation that is stressed. The chosen people is composed of the people who have chosen to become part of America. The promised land is open to all. America is the land not of the past but of the future: messiah nation or redeemer nation, or in Lincoln's words "the last best hope of earth."

The basic premises of social and political order differ in the two cases relative to the different constructions of collective identity. In the Japanese case, the individual is seen as embedded in a network of social relations, which is in turn embedded in cosmological reality. The Japanese case is remarkable in the degree to which it has been able to maintain dynamism and openness to change within the framework of embeddedness, which is itself unassailable. In America, it is disembeddedness that is sacralized. If America is the new Jerusalem, then there is need for neither church nor state: each individual is free to realize himself or herself as he or she sees fit. If the Japanese have a strong version of social realism, the Americans have an ontological individualism. In both cases, it is not the fundamental premises that are open to question but only the failure to realize them. In both cases, the fundamental premises can be seen as "polluted" by various evil forces, from which they must be defended, but they cannot be attacked.

GOD, NATION, SELF

Andrew Delbanco's recent book, *The Real American Dream*,[21] has greatly helped me clarify the American situation in my own mind, by showing how the fundamental premises have varied over time. Delbanco organizes his small book into three chapters, "God," "Nation," and "Self." These he sees, using Emersonian terminology, as "predominant ideas" that have successively organized our culture and our society, providing a context of meaning that can bring hope and stave off melancholy. In speaking of *God* as the predominant idea that first organized our culture, Delbanco is thinking primarily of the New England Puritans of the seventeenth and eighteenth centuries. *Nation* became the predominant idea from the time of the Revolutionary War until well into the twentieth century. Most recently, *Self* seems to have replaced, or if not replaced, subordinated, God and nation as predominant. Delbanco does not argue for strict chronological epochs, seeing many overlaps, but I will push just a bit beyond him to argue that all three ideas were present at the very beginning and that, although these changed in degree of dominance ever since, some of our deepest problems arise from the form of Protestant Christianity that first put its stamp on colonial culture.

Certainly the Puritans were focused on God; indeed, they were God-obsessed. But from the beginning, both nation and self were significant subtexts. If one takes even so great a document as John Winthrop's 1630 sermon, "A Model of Christian Charity," preached on board the *Arbella* in Salem harbor just before its landing, we find a fusion of church and nation that leads Winthrop to a conscious identification of the Massachusetts Bay Colony with ancient Israel. If Winthrop took Moses' farewell sermon (Deuteronomy 30) as his basic text, he had copious New Testament allusions to strengthen his case, perhaps the most famous (notorious?) of which is the metaphor of a city on a hill: "[W]e shall be as a City upon a Hill [Matthew 5 : 14]; the eyes of all people are upon us." It took Ronald Reagan to embellish this City with the adjective "shining," found neither in Matthew nor in Winthrop but suggestive of the long-lasting tendency to identify America with the City of God.

It has often been pointed out that the Protestant Reformation paved the way for modern nationalism by breaking the hold of the international church and replacing it with state churches. "The glory of God was replaced by the glory of the nation; by a curious dialectic the Reformation paved the way for this development."[22] But the American case was extreme in fusing the glory of God with the glory of the nation in the sense of millennial hopes fulfilled: America as redeemer nation for all the world. A sense of the judgment of God hanging over the nation was evident in the closing lines of Winthrop's sermon, where he warned that we shall "perish out of this good land" if we do not obey God's commandments. A sense of God's judgment was never more evident than in Lincoln's Second Inaugural Address, where he attributed the sufferings of the war to the judgment of God against slavery and quoted Psalm 19:9, "the judgments of the Lord are true and righteous altogether." But, as Roger Williams pointed out in criticism of the views of Winthrop, the basic problem came not from the absence of a sense of judgment (though such a sense often would be absent) but from the basic confusion of the nation with the communion of the saints. For Williams, the error was to confuse "a *people,* naturally considered," with the millennial ark of Christ, a confusion the result of which would be "to pull *God* and *Christ* and *Spirit* out of Heaven, and subject them unto *natural,* sinful, inconstant men."[23] Although Williams had a very problematic view of the church, he knew it could not be identified with a nation. For Lincoln, as far as we know, the church had lost all significance; it was only the nation that had to bear, unworthy though it was, the great mission.

The Protestant temptation to confuse church and nation was linked to the very same conception of the church that would open the door to the confusion of God and self. On the face of it, nothing could be further from the Puritan mind. The conquest of the self so as to make oneself transparent to God was the center of Puritan piety. And yet the very focus on the individual struggle was, as Sacvan Bercovitch points out in his book *The Puritan Origins of the American Self,* finally a form of self-assertion:

> the individual affirming his identity by turning against his power of self-affirmation. But to affirm and to turn against are both aspects of self-involvement. We can see in retrospect how the very intensity of that self-involvement— mobilizing as it did the resources of the ego in what amounted to an internal Armageddon—had to break loose into the world at large.[24]

Just as Lincoln represents a critical step toward a nation that has replaced the church, so Emerson represents a critical step toward a self that has replaced the church, one ratified by William James in his *Varieties of Religious Experience,* which, while Puritan in its fascination with individual religious experience, is not only free from, but inimical to, any "institutional form" that that religious experience might take. James divides religion into two "branches," the personal and the institutional. He chooses to focus entirely on personal religion, leaving institutional religion aside as it lives "at second hand upon tradition."[25] Yet in this case too the Puritans foreshadowed later developments. Delbanco quotes John Cotton in the seventeenth century as saying: "If . . . the Papists aske, where was the Church visible, before *Luther?* The answer is, it was visible, not in open Congregations . . . but in sundry members of the church "—in, that is, individual members who were persecuted by the church in their day. When John Donne said in a sermon that every believer "hath *a Church* in himself,"[26] he was certainly not speaking of the natural self, but of the converted self. Yet the locus of the church in the individual, with the church as an association only coming into existence through the voluntary action of the already converted, was the very notion that opened the door not only to the elevation of the self, but of the nation, to transcendent status. With respect to the fatal notion that the church consists only of the already converted, Roger Williams was, if anything, even more extreme than Winthrop, however right he was to reject the conflation of church and nation. Delbanco sums up his story about America in a paragraph near the end of his book:

> The history of hope I have tried to sketch in this book is one of diminution. At first, the self expanded toward (and was sometimes overwhelmed by) the vastness of God. From the early republic to the Great Society, it remained implicated in a national ideal lesser than God but larger and more enduring than any individual citizen. Today, hope has narrowed to the vanishing point of the self alone.[27]

What I am arguing, moving beyond Delbanco's argument, is that the entire story of declension[28] is present in germ, so to speak, in the very form of Protestant Christianity of the first colonists. An axial critique of the fundamental premises of American society and culture, then, would require not only a critique of ontological individualism and its strange complementarity with the confusion of God and nation, but a critique of the Protestant Reformation itself, at least in its most influential American forms. Such a critique would show that the United States is not the City of God that it claims to be, but only another tired version of the city of man, with all the Augustinian horrors this implies. The great Protestant mistake—into which also some Catholics have at times fallen—was to confuse religion and nation, to imagine that America had become a realized eschatology. Our participation in the great wars of the twentieth century only confirmed our sense of ourselves as beyond history, uniquely chosen in the world to defend the children of light against the children of darkness. The long twilight struggle of the Cold War allowed us to continue in that illusion. But now that we have no mission, no enemy, and no Antichrist to combat, we can see that the Protestant individualism responsible for so much of the best in our society has left us with almost nothing to hold us together.

It is now time to turn to Stanley Hauerwas's chapter, "On Being a Christian and an American," which continues a long-standing, and to me very instructive, dialogue between us. I want to make explicit, perhaps for the first time, how much I am in agreement with him. Needless to say, there are still points of difference, but in the present case, rather than resist the implications of his argument, I wish to go somewhat beyond them. I want to agree with Hauerwas that "the first task of the church is to be the church." For too long we have failed to see that the Kingdom of God on earth is not the nation but the church, and the church only as a foretaste of it, because the church, as an earthly as well as a divine institution, is not without blemish. But for the Protestant church to be the church would require a degree of self-criticism at least as profound as that which the Catholic church undertook in the Second Vatican Council. The formula of letting the church be the church and the culture be the culture will not work in a society like ours where the church is the chrysalis of the culture.

Here I want to assert that most of the current talk about our being more pluralistic than ever is empty wind. Our culture has always been Protestant to the bone and still is. Catholics and Jews have been Protestantized for a long time, and multiculturalism is doing the same thing for the "diverse" groups for which it speaks. I am not saying that there are not differences; in particular, I am not saying that the religious differences, in spite of assimilation to Protestantism, do not count, because they do. But ours is an overwhelmingly monocultural society and the heart of that monoculture is a secularized Protestantism. Thus, a genuine recovery of the church in America would involve not only the disavowal of the confusion of nation and church (Hauerwas says "the church unwittingly becomes governed by the story of America," but I have argued that it became so quite wittingly), and not only the repudiation of the therapeutic domination of both liberal and evangelical churches in which God exists largely to improve self-esteem, but even more a reexamination of the very understanding of the church in the reformed tradition.

A church made up of already converted individuals cannot be the church that could provide any alternative to the culture it has spawned. As far as letting the culture be the culture, this is fine as long as we recognize that the very Enlightenment liberalism that Hauerwas abhors, as well as much else in our culture, both good and bad, is the offspring of the Protestant Reformation and unintelligible in any other context. I am not at all arguing for the repudiation of the Reformation, the Enlightenment, or liberalism (nor, do I think, is Hauerwas) but for the realization of their limits and of, in spite of their great achievements, the degree of responsibility they bear for our present profound cultural predicament. I agree with Hauerwas that theology, ethics, and ecclesiology make up a single package and are unintelligible when separated. My challenge is for him to depict a viable ecclesiology for the American church. He has drawn from the Mennonite, Catholic, and Methodist traditions, but I have yet to see how it all comes together in a church that is genuinely reformed and genuinely catholic.[29]

RELIGION, ECONOMICS, POLITICS

Several essays in this volume treat aspects of religion in America, and each expands the picture I have drawn in significant ways. Albert Raboteau's moving account of the life of Howard Thurman depicts a man for whom personal religious experience was indeed central and who operated very much in the American free church tradition, but with the intent of moving toward a larger community and overcoming the painful differences and exclusions that our privatized spirituality usually manages to overlook. Any effort to rethink Protestantism today must take Thurman seriously.

The essays of Harvey Cox, John Coleman, and Robert Wuthnow all develop aspects of Delbanco's third phase of American religious history. In the prologue to his book, in naming the three ideas whose sequence he will describe, Delbanco writes, "God, nation, and . . . what? the market? the recreational self?"[30] thereby suggesting that the market is, in some degree, a synonym for the term he ultimately uses for his third idea, the self. Harvey Cox's depiction of "The Market as God" suggests that the market, though closely related to the free-floating individual, is a less benign deity than its devotees might think, placing more constraints on free-floating selves than self-lovers might wish. The institutional constraints of the market is a theme to which I will return. John Coleman's essay, "Selling God in America," treats the degree to which religion has actually become marketized in America, both in theory and in practice—the logical outcome of the third stage in Delbanco's scheme. But Coleman notes that not far below the surface of our burgeoning marketized religious life is a "spiritual hunger and identity-seeking," together with a "massive spiritual illiteracy," that marketized religion seems unable to alleviate.

Wuthnow gives a somewhat (but only somewhat) more upbeat picture of our present religious condition, as indicated by the title of his essay, "Reassembling the Civic Church," which develops arguments put forth in his recent book, *Loose Connections.*[31] He argues that the porous institutions in our society are the natural result of a decline of the pressure of external threats that tend to hold people in tightly bounded groups, which may well be the case; however, Wuthnow seems to overlook the coercive nature of some of what he calls "brokering mechanisms." In the typical case of Bill

Hartwig, with which he begins the chapter, he cites the university that allowed Bill to move away from home and begin a new life as such a brokering mechanism. But brokering mechanisms may be a term for institutional rules that are as coercive in their own way as any traditional *Gemeinschaft*. John Meyer and his collaborators have pointed out that the educational and occupational systems have a determinative effect on the lives of the citizens of modern societies.[32] One's last educational degree, for example, has an enormous influence on one's life chances in such societies. If, in one sense, going to a university is an option that offers new degrees of freedom, in another perspective, not going to a university closes off a wide range of possibilities essentially forever. And if one does go to a university, one must accept a rigid set of rules as to what counts as adequate performance, rules that will only be further elaborated when one enters the occupational world. Freedom and coercion may be more closely linked than appears. One need not resort to Foucault, but only to John Meyer, to understand how modern society constitutes freedom as a mechanism of coercion. Still, Wuthnow is helpful in showing us how people cope with a society in which older institutions such as family, neighborhood, and church have indeed become porous even while the market, education, and occupation have grown increasingly coercive. The capacity of short-term, limited-purpose groups to meet significant needs in our society, particularly within the context of the church, is convincingly shown both in his chapter and in other recent work.

Ann Swidler, in "Saving the Self: Endowment versus Depletion in American Institutions," paints a darker picture of loose connections and porous institutions than does Wuthnow. She points out how marketization undercuts all noneconomic functions of institutions, even economic institutions, with the result that pressures on individuals increase exponentially. Much of the focus on the self in our culture is an effort to shore up persons who have little institutional support and must make up their lives as they go along, juggling conflicting obligations along the way. Nina Eliasoph shows how depleted selves in "post-suburban" communities turn to family and "the children" to find a secure anchoring for dealing with social problems. The result is, on the whole, an eviscerated public language and a diminished capacity even to imagine politics as a shared quest for the good. She does nonetheless find a remnant among what she calls "cultural bureaucrats," who can relate the deeply shared American preoccupation with children to larger issues that would open the way to civic participation.

Both Steven M. Tipton's and Richard Madsen's essays deal with the linkage between institutions and moral languages and so may be considered together. They both exemplify the distinctive position of the *Habits* group, that moral languages are rooted in institutional contexts and are unintelligible without them but draw from religious and philosophical sources and are not mere reflexes of their institutional contexts. Traditions of moral discourse shape as well as are shaped by such contexts. Tipton's "Social Differentiation and Moral Pluralism" is a careful specification of the links between social settings and styles of moral evaluation in the major institutional spheres of American life. In so doing, it gives substantial reality to moral quandaries that otherwise hang in midair. It would be interesting to link this essay with Swidler's discussion, to see how some institutional contexts may be impinging on others with depletion as a result.

Madsen's essay, "Comparative Cosmopolis: Discovering Different Paths to Moral Integration in the Modern Ecumene," takes the relation of moral language to social setting that Tipton described and puts it in cross-cultural comparison. In so doing, Madsen points out a major limitation of *Habits of the Heart* and *The Good Society* as bases for comparative work: their focus on middle-class life. Madsen sees the point of this focus in the middle class having been, above all, the carrier of modernity and the purveyor of its cultural dynamic to everyone else. But, for comparative purposes, the approach of these books will be much more applicable in the advanced industrial societies of Europe and Asia than in most of the third world. And, even among the developed nations, Madsen points out, there are significant axes of variation. His use of Mary Douglas's grid/group scheme is most suggestive. By arguing that the United States is a society with strong grid and weak group, he sheds light on my response to Wuthnow's chapter. Wuthnow's "porous institutions" are really examples of Douglas's weak group category, for the institutional rules (strong grid) can be quite coercive, even though group membership is indeed porous. I would want to qualify Madsen's analysis of Japan as a strong grid/strong group society. Japan is, for a developed society, indeed characterized by an unusually strong group orientation, but I would argue that for such a society grid orientation (institutional rules) is relatively weak, and much that is handled by formal rules in other such societies is managed through informal personal contact in Japan. Indeed, to continue the "mirror-image" metaphor, among industrial nations the United States is the most extreme in the strong grid, weak group category and Japan the most extreme in the strong group, weak grid category.

The last two essays on which I want to comment move (as does Madsen) beyond the United States. Charles Taylor, as a Canadian, knows us well, yet views us from the middle distance and so can tell us important things. William Sullivan uses the contrast between the United States and Britain as a useful point of entry. What is especially interesting to me is that—maybe because both are philosophers—Taylor and Sullivan begin to help me see how to move beyond the post-axial claims of American culture to begin to envision a world in which, indeed, the church is the church and the culture is the culture. In particular, they can help us think about what politics in a chastened—that is, axial—American society might look like.

Taylor, in his essay "Democracy, Inclusive and Exclusive," shows why a degree of common identity is necessary in any society that claims to be self-governing. Citizens must share enough to understand each other when they deliberate about matters of common concern. Because of our millennial claims, this issue may have been more salient in the United States than in some other modern societies—Canada, for example—but in none is it missing. In each, there has been a tendency to exclude those who seem culturally incomprehensible, or to forcibly assimilate them. When awareness of differences reaches a sufficient degree of sophistication, however, the possibility emerges of respecting the real differences that are present and including those who are different in a common enterprise that transcends those differences. I would suggest that this is the actual problem in Canada, but largely a rhetorical problem in the United States, because our cultural differences are in fact not nearly as profound as we like to think. For the United States, the problem is to nurture differences that are only incipient, so that Taylor's solution of inclusive pluralism might be a reality rather than a disguised form of assimilation.

Sullivan's chapter, "Politics as the 'Public Use of Reason,'" by comparing the United States and Britain, suggests the difference between a politics based on the assumption that all fundamental problems are solved in a realized utopia (United States) and the more normal axial politics of a society where at least some know that its fundamental premises are in question (Britain). In a realized utopia, not only is the church not in any strong sense necessary (a 1988–89 survey found that one-third of Americans believe "people have God within them, so churches aren't really necessary"),[33] but so is politics. All problems will be solved if we only get the family together (Eliasoph's chapter) or if we can only "take control of our lives" (Swidler's chapter). What used to be politics is now a matter of technical expertise. It was John F. Kennedy who said, speaking of the chief task of contemporary government, the management of the economy, that we need "technical answers, not political answers."[34] Whereas some British cultural leaders—what Sullivan, following Coleridge, calls the clerisy—saw the problems of modern society in terms of culture and institutions, that is, the fundamental formative influences on the way people live, the newly emerging national class in America thought in terms of expertise and management. In a realized utopia, people should be free to do whatever they want, whether it be to make money or to undertake a "spiritual journey," with the state reduced to a technical mechanism. The notion that some forms of life are better than others and that it is the job of the intellectual class—the clerisy, in Coleridge's terms—to help the public decide which is better already sounds fatally "elitist" to American ears. In the vacuum that follows, rational-choice theory makes eminent sense, especially when it is expanded beyond the sphere of economics to include marriage and even religious choices. The fit between a free church tradition, in which the priesthood of all believ-

ers comes close to the godhood of all believers, and an apolitical technical management of society with the sole aim of increasing GDP, is remarkably tight.

What the British comparison suggests is not that the British have it right
and we have it wrong—British society, like all modern societies, has plenty
of unresolved problems—but that the British have both a more temperate
view of the nature of their own society and more ample resources for addressing its basic problems. Among these resources is a church, however
pushed to the margins, with a tangible understanding of its own reality as a
separate institution (ironically, in spite of the survival of an attenuated establishment) and, not unrelated, the notion that fundamental issues of culture and the quality of institutions belong in the sphere of public debate. I
think there is much to be said for the idea that America needs something
like the British clerisy, although I suspect the term cannot cross the Atlantic. If this be denounced as elitist arrogance, I am not afraid of the charge.

As long as American society continues to experience an apparent (but by
no means universally shared) prosperity, it is unlikely to abandon the notion that it is a collection of independent individuals with a minimal church
and a minimal state and no need to ask any fundamental questions. Should
we run into severe difficulties—and the experience of history suggests that
we will—then we may look to whatever marginal resources we have to rethink the course on which we have been embarked virtually since the first
colonists landed on these shores. If I am right, there is certainly no ideal
past to which we can look, for our deepest problems were there in germ
from the beginning. Nor are there any perfect heroes to point the way. In
Habits, we showed a certain lack of enthusiasm for Benjamin Franklin and
Walt Whitman, while our admiration for John Winthrop and Thomas Jefferson was relatively unrestrained. But, as I have suggested in this chapter,
Winthrop bears a heavy burden for beginning us on a wrong path, much as
we still have to learn from him. My enthusiasm for Jefferson is also severely
tempered today, not because of supposed sexual peccadilloes or even because of his ugly views about race, reprehensible though they are, but because he contributed so much to the suspicion of institutions and government in our tradition. His hatred of cities, which led to the creation of
Washington, D.C., as a miserable village in a swamp, is only emblematic of a
regressive individualism barely tempered by a residual republicanism. Even
Lincoln, who remains for me the greatest American, combined a substantive politics of moral judgment about slavery, which lost him the senatorial
election against Stephen Douglas, with a conception that the universal
spread of small property would solve all our problems.[35] And, as I have
noted above, since Lincoln ignored the church, he left us with only his
example of moral leadership in the political sphere, an example seldom if
ever imitated.

If, then, we have few models, and they ambiguous ones, perhaps we can turn to the rest of the world in a way Americans, with their belief in their own immaculate exceptionalism, have seldom done. Perhaps we are just one more tired example of Augustine's city of man, and we can learn from other nations that have known this all along. Hauerwas asks why Christianity won't work in America, but he knows, as I do, that only the recovery of a tangible, visible church not submerged in a redeemer nation or dissipated into a collection of individual seekers could make Christianity possible here.

CONCLUSION

If, as I have argued, the American project has been in major respects self-deluding, what does that imply about the metanarrative with which I began this epilogue? Such a metanarrative must say something about a scheme in which a historic or axial age is followed by an early modern and a modern one. In my original essay on religious evolution, I made the point that the "stages" were not discrete, that nothing is ever lost. I argued that even aspects of tribal and archaic religion survive among us. What I did not recognize clearly enough is that the axial age remains as determinative for us as ever, that we have not left it behind, that what I called the early modern and the modern were only phases of working out its implications. The texts of the Bible and of classical Greek philosophy remain central. The task of understanding, interpretation, and application is a demanding one, as it has always been, and carrying it out in our historical circumstances is particularly daunting, but nothing that has followed those texts means that they can be left behind.

The Reformation and the great waves of change that have followed it were radical fulfillments of many of the promises of axial religion at the same time that they were subversions of it. For the Reformation, the text of the New Testament and the events recounted therein were central. Not only was the New Testament in almost every line a response to the Hebrew Bible and unintelligible without it, its reception in the West occurred in a culture saturated with Platonic/Aristotelian philosophy (and successor movements) that indelibly shaped its meaning. Some Protestants wanted to reappropriate the Bible without regard to the intervening history, but they did not succeed. Neither the Enlightenment nor any of the great ideological movements of the twentieth century have supplanted the axial heritage; often they have acted it out in parody even as they imagined themselves rejecting it.

The great project of modernity, beginning with the Reformation, was the leap into freedom. One tendency in the Reformation imagined that we could as individuals relate directly to God without the mediation of any living tradition or the community that carries it. To the extent that the Reformation led to the enfranchisement of the laity, the priesthood of all believers, it was a fulfillment of axial teachings. And the idea of the priesthood of all believers did help subjects to become citizens when changes in church polity stimulated changes in national polity. But this important leap of freedom was also a first step in the sacralization of disembeddedness. And we have seen the consequences of these moves in the American case, the strengthening of the state going hand-in-hand with an in good part illusory freeing of the individual.

The Enlightenment leapt further into freedom, imagining that we could live by disembodied reason alone. But the next turn in the process of disembeddedness was the disembedding of the economy from traditional constraints, and the consequent depletion of all those institutions that formerly protected the lifeworld.[36] In the capitalist world, the individual was left more alone than ever, vulnerable to the great ideological movements that swept the world in the twentieth century, movements that falsely promised security in an increasingly insecure world.

Today the collapse of "real existing socialism," unveiling it as the illusion it always was, has not only tarnished the image of successful democratic socialist achievements such as universal health care, but has been taken as a signal of the triumph of global capitalism. Globalization is the new watchword, again promising unexampled increases in freedom, yet providing us with, in Thomas Friedman's words, a "golden straitjacket" (Friedman seems to be unconscious of the consequences in mythology for those who turn everything into gold).[37] Those who claim there are no limits to economic growth seem to be in command, if anyone is, in the process of globalization.

But if socialism fell so recently, can capitalism, based on the same economically reductionist illusions, be far behind? Viable institutions cannot be replaced by monetary transactions and electronic technology. The idea that there are no limits to economic growth is surely a lie, and acting as if it were true is suicidal. We can say that there are no limits to growth, or, more modestly, that if there are we don't yet know them, *if* we are speaking of psychocultural growth. But the kind of growth that requires the destruction and consumption of the biosphere cannot but stop psychocultural growth, because its biological consequences are terminal.

Part of our reassessment of ourselves as still historic cultures, however much we have been transformed, for good and for ill, by the successive waves of modernity, is the realization that the organic metaphor still applies to us. I am pointing not to the old organic metaphor of rigidly hierarchical societies (though hierarchy in some form is a necessary characteristic of both biological and social systems) but to something like Habermas's notion of a *lifeworld* in contrast to administrative and market systems, which, when not adequately anchored in the lifeworld, can destroy normative community. Our growing understanding that biological and cultural evolution are deeply interconnected helps us to see that culture is the living membrane that connects us to the natural world and that institutions are the biosocial organs that allow us to live in this new environment.[38] The Japanese sacralization of embeddedness, of trying to avoid the leaps of freedom as far as possible—without, of course, giving up the spoils of capitalism—is not open to us. But our own hypertrophied disembeddedness is endangering the very basis of life on this planet.

We are rational, but, as Alasdair MacIntyre has reminded us, this is not the whole truth about us for we are dependent rational animals: "Acknowledgment of dependence is the key to independence."[39] What I have called disembeddedness can only be relative to continuing, though changing, forms of embeddedness, which leads us to consider once again whether there is such a thing as human nature. As Aristotle would say, in one sense there is, in another sense there is not. If we think that there is a definite human nature that we can specify in detail, we are surely wrong. But if we say there is nothing generally true of humans, we are also wrong.

Our nature begins with the fact that we are a single biological species, but it does not end there. Justice, for example, as an actual practice is found in all human societies and in some primate ones as well.[40] Perhaps only the axial civilizations have discovered the philosophical concept of justice, and they in slightly different though not incompatible forms.[41] If there is a human nature, even though we may know it only tentatively and in part, then it makes sense to speak of a human telos, a human purpose, something "for the sake of which" we live our lives. I am not speaking in any determinist sense. We can see all too clearly that humans often fail to realize their telos. But if we have a nature, then a good form of life that fulfills the potentialities of our nature *is* our telos. And how do we know what is a good form of life? The organic metaphor helps us, here, to see that our lives are always part of a larger whole, a longer story, that points to something higher than human life, and from which ultimately the standards for a good form of life come. This is what all the axial religions and philosophies have called, in one way or another, God. Those who believe that the telos of human life is most fully expressed in the worship of God have the special responsibility of modeling for us a good form of human life. None of this implies we will get there. We can use our freedom to destroy the possibility of any telos at all—to make an end of all ends, so to speak.

One way of putting our present situation would be to say that reality—God—is asking us to embark on a transformation of our way of life, a transformation that would restore our organic relationship to each other and to the biosphere, asking us to struggle to see whether we can reconcile the conflicts between freedom and equality that are inherent in our kind of society with the requirements of that organic relationship. This is the task that the greatest (and most Christian) modern philosopher, Hegel, set for us. We rightly aspire to rational independence, but we can only attain it when we recognize that we are mortal creatures who need air to breathe and are dependent from birth to burial on the hands of others.[42] Freedom must be embodied; the truth lies in reconciliation. If the modern efforts to leap into freedom, noble though many have been, have led to a form of life that is not sustainable, the axial vision is still alive to help us find a new way.

NOTES

INTRODUCTION

1. Michel Foucault, *The Order of Things: An Archaeology of the Human Sciences*.
2. Pierre Bourdieu, *Distinction: A Social Critique of the Judgement of Taste*.
3. E. P. Thompson, *The Making of the English Working Class*.
4. Robert N. Bellah, *Beyond Belief: Essays on Religion in a Post-Traditional World*.
5. Paul Ricoeur, *The Conflict of Interpretations: Essays in Hermeneutics*.
6. Mary Douglas, *How Institutions Think*.
7. Robert N. Bellah, *Tokugawa Religion*.

1. "MYTHIC GESTURES"

1. The intellectual-cum-personal relationship between Bellah and Geertz deserves sustained attention. Particularly as graduate students and young social scientists, they were close, as indicated by Geertz's effort in the early 1970s to bring Bellah to the Princeton Institute for Advanced Study as its second permanent social science member (Geertz was the first). Because they shared a more culturalist perspective than Parsons and because both became major figures in launching cultural sociology, it is difficult to separate, at least for the purpose of this essay, discussion of the two.

2. Alvin Gouldner, *The Coming Crisis of Western Sociology*, 212.

3. Robert N. Bellah, *Beyond Belief: Essays on Religion in a Post-Traditional World*, 260.

4. Ibid., 21.

5. Ibid., 44.

6. Ibid. An implicit corollary to this evolutionary perspective is the adoption of Parsons's conception of "structured strain," in which crises and pathologies confronting society are mere impediments to an overall evolutionary trend, impediments resulting from the ever-growing complexity and autonomy of the differentiation arising from adaptive upgrading:

It remains to be seen whether the freedom modern society implies at the cultural and personality as well as at the social level can be stably institutionalized in large-scale societies. Yet the very situation that has been characterized as one of the collapse of meaning and the failure of moral standards can also, and I would argue more fruitfully, be viewed as one offering unprecedented opportunities for creative innovation in every sphere of human action.

7. Ibid., 171.
8. Ibid., 172.
9. Ibid., 181.
10. Ibid., 175.
11. Ibid., 176.
12. Ibid., 44.
13. Ibid., 186.
14. Hayden White, *The Content of the Form.*
15. Bellah, *Beyond Belief,* 186.
16. Ibid., xvii.
17. Ibid.
18. Ibid., 260.
19. Sacvan Bercovitch, *The Puritan Origins of the American Self.*
20. Robert N. Bellah, *The Broken Covenant: American Civil Religion in a Time of Trial.*
21. Ibid., 157.
22. Ibid., xi.
23. Ibid., xii.
24. Ibid., xiii.
25. Ibid., 142.
26. Ibid., 1.
27. Ibid., 63.
28. Ibid., 3.
29. Hayden White, *Metahistory, Tropics of Discourse,* and *The Content of the Form.*
30. Emile Durkheim, *The Elementary Forms of the Religious Life,* 13.

2. SOCIAL DIFFERENTIATION AND MORAL PLURALISM

1. This essay draws widely on the work of Robert N. Bellah, and is deeply indebted to it, including his "New Religious Consciousness and the Crisis in Modernity" in *The New Religious Consciousness,* ed. Charles Glock and Robert N. Bellah; and chapter 2 of *Habits of the Heart,* by Robert N. Bellah, Richard Madsen, William M. Sullivan, Ann Swidler, and Steven M. Tipton. To my four coauthors, collegial critics and friends, I am most grateful.

2. Cf. Alasdair MacIntyre, *After Virtue;* Jeffrey Stout, *Ethics after Babel;* Ann Swidler, "Culture in Action: Symbols and Strategies," 137–166; and Roger Friedland and Robert R. Alford, "Bringing Society Back In," in *The New Institutionalism in Organizational Analysis,* 232–266.

3. For elaboration of this view of ethical styles and moral traditions, see my *Get-*

ting Saved from the Sixties, chapters 1 and 5. For elaboration of the taxonomy of styles of ethical evaluation, see Ralph B. Potter, "The Structure of Certain Christian Responses to the Nuclear Dilemma, 1959–1963," 363–398.

4. From the Revised Standard Version of the *Bible* (New Oxford Annotated Edition).

5. William K. Frankena, *Ethics,* 13–16.

6. On the Bible's many ethical styles and their centrally anti-authoritarian nature, see Walter Breuggemann, *Theology of the Old Testament: Testimony, Dispute, Advocacy.* This paper aims to clarify, not close, the gap between modernist definition of the authoritative and the regular ethical styles and the premodern matrix of the biblical and the republican cultural traditions, by sketching these traditions in terms related yet irreducible to the categories of the authoritative and regular styles of ethical evaluation in their conventional usage in modern ethics. I am indebted to Robert N. Bellah on this point.

7. Mary Douglas, "Cultural Bias"; Bellah, "Religious Evolution."

8. Cf. Max Weber, "The Social Psychology of the World Religions."

9. Emile Durkheim, *The Elementary Forms of the Religious Life,* 207–225.

10. Erik Erikson, "Life Cycle."

11. Douglas, "Cultural Bias" and "Grid and Group"; also, Douglas (ed.), *Essays in the Sociology of Perception,* 3–7, 15, 78.

12. Emile Durkheim, *The Division of Labor in Society,* 31–67, 101–148.

13. Michael Walzer, *Spheres of Justice,* 190–196.

14. A. W. H. Adkins, *Moral Values and Political Behavior in Ancient Greece,* especially chs. 2, 5; also his *Merit and Responsibility,* chs. 11–16, especially pp. 230–240.

15. Pierre Bourdieu, *An Outline of a Theory of Practice,* 164–171, 200n20; and Douglas, "Cultural Bias," 10.

16. On natural law, reason, and rights, cf. Plato, *Laws;* Ernst Bloch, *Natural Law and Human Dignity,* 7–65; Hobbes, *Leviathan,* part I, chs. 5, 12–15; Locke's *Two Treatises of Government* and *An Essay Concerning Human Understanding;* Thomas L. Pangle, *The Spirit of Modern Republicanism,* chs. 16–21. On the religious roots of modern citizenship, see Louis Dumont, "A Modified View of Our Origins: The Christian Beginnings of Modern Individualism."

17. Alvin Gouldner, *The Coming Crisis of Western Sociology,* 69.

18. Frankena, *Ethics,* 30–35; John Rawls, "Two Concepts of Rules."

19. Cf. Karl Marx, "The Grundrisse," 222–244.

20. Durkheim, *The Division of Labor,* 316–322. See, for example, the hedonic utilitarian reinterpretation of Jeremy Bentham, *Principles of Morals and Legislation,* ch. 2.

21. Cf. John Rawls, *Theory of Justice,* 11–22; Michael Sandel, *Liberalism and the Limits of Justice,* 165–183.

22. Douglas, "Cultural Bias," 21, 26; also Adam Smith, *The Theory of Moral Sentiments,* part 3, chs. 5–6.

23. Peter L. Berger, Brigitte Berger, Hansfried Kellner, *The Homeless Mind,* 41–62; Douglas, "Cultural Bias," 20–21; Weber, "Bureaucracy."

24. Immanuel Wallerstein, *The Modern World-System,* vol. I, pp. 16–38, 133–136, 158–162, 347–357. Also Karl Polanyi, *The Great Transformation,* 68–76; Charles E.

Lindblom, *Politics and Markets*, 43–44; and John W. Meyer, John Boli, George Thomas, Francisco Ramirez, "World Society and the Nation State."

25. Bellah et al., *Habits of the Heart*, 71–75.

26. On emotivism and intuitionism, see MacIntyre, *After Virtue*, 14–18; H. D. Ross, *The Right and the Good*, 18–23.

27. Douglas, "Cultural Bias," 19–20, 26.

28. Smith, *Moral Sentiments*, part 1, sec. 1, ch. 3; part 3, ch. 2.

29. Ibid., part 1, sec. 3, ch. 2; ibid., part 6, sec. 1.

30. Ibid., part 1, sec. 1, chs. 1–3; ibid., part 3, chs. 3–5; ibid., part 6, ch. 3.

31. See Berger et al., *The Homeless Mind*, 190–196; Philippe Aries, *Centuries of Childhood;* Lawrence Stone, *The Family, Sex, and Marriage: England 1500–1800* on the rise of "affective individualism".

32. Alexis de Tocqueville, *Democracy in America*, 506–508, 530–534, 584–592.

33. Robert E. Lane, *Political Ideology*, 57–81; Charles Tilly, *Durable Inequality;* William Julius Wilson, *When Work Disappears* and *The Bridge over the Racial Divide;* and Claude S. Fischer, Michael Hout, Martin Sanchez Jankowski, Samuel R. Lucas, Ann Swidler, and Kim Voss, *Inequality by Design.*

34. Melvin L. Kohn, *Class and Conformity*, xxvi–xxvii, xxxiv–xxvi, 189–193, 200–203.

35. Carol Gilligan, *In a Different Voice*, chs. 1, 6.

36. Lawrence Kohlberg, "Moral Development," 489–490. Cf. Gilligan, *In a Different Voice*, chs. 1, 6; Seyla Benhabib, *Situating the Self*, 148–202; Susan Moller Okin, *Justice, Gender, and the Family.*

37. C. Wright Mills, *White Collar*, xvii. See Tipton, *Getting Saved from the Sixties*, 209–218; Arlie Hochschild, *The Managed Heart.*

38. Note, for example, the sweeping economistic conclusions of Pierre Bourdieu, *Outline of a Theory of Practice*, 171–197, and the ubiquity of judgments of taste in class struggles over cultural classification and the underlying relations of power in such classification, according to Bourdieu, *Distinction*, 479–484.

39. James Hampton, "Giving the Grid/Group Dimensions an Operational Definition," 78.

40. See, for example, how William H. Sewell, "A Theory of Structure: Duality, Agency, and Transformation," qualifies Bourdieu, *Outline of a Theory of Practice*, ch. 2; also how Friedland and Alford, "Bringing Society Back In," qualifies Meyer et al., "Ontology and Rationalization in the Western Cultural Account"; and how Stout, *Ethics after Babel*, qualifies MacIntyre, *After Virtue.*

41. Tipton, "Republic and Liberal State: The Place of Religion in an Ambiguous Polity"; Bellah, "Religion and the Legitimation of the American Republic"; Michael Sandel, *Democracy's Discontent*, 4–54.

42. Kristin Luker, *Abortion and the Politics of Motherhood*, chs. 7–8.

43. Ibid., 3–8.

44. Paul DiMaggio, John Evans, and Bethany Bryson, "Have Americans' Social Attitudes Become More Polarized?" 710, 715, 715n23, 716. On the predominance of "rights talk" in U.S. abortion debates, see Mary Ann Glendon, *Abortion and Divorce in Western Law.* On the sovereignty of individual conscience in U.S. culture, see Bellah, "Is There a Common American Culture?"

45. MacIntyre, *A Short History of Ethics*, 90.

46. Potter, "The Logic of Moral Argument."
47. Tipton, *Getting Saved from the Sixties,* 281.
48. Taylor, *Hegel and Modern Society,* 160.
49. Clifford Geertz, "Thick Description," and "Ethos, World View, and the Analysis of Sacred Symbols," 3–30, 126–141.

3. SAVING THE SELF

The ideas for this essay originated as a talk at Congregation Netivot Shalom in Berkeley. A fuller version was given as the Elsie Lipset Memorial Lecture at Stanford University. I also want to thank audiences at St. Mary's College, the California Sociological Association, Notre Dame University, and the Jewish Communal Affairs Committee of San Francisco for their valuable comments. I am grateful to the Sloan Center for Working Families at the University of California, Berkeley. I am indebted, as ever, to my coauthors and friends Robert N. Bellah, Richard Madsen, William M. Sullivan, and Steven M. Tipton, and to my husband, Claude Fischer.

1. Robert Wuthnow, *The Restructuring of American Religion.*
2. Bellah, Madsen, Sullivan, Swidler, and Tipton, *Habits of the Heart.*
3. See Michele Dillon, *Catholic Identity.* Of course, affirmation of the religious value of the oppressed and excluded is firmly founded in the Christian Gospels and can hardly be regarded as radical innovation. But contemporary claims for religious inclusion do not focus on sin and forgiveness, or even on the need for a cleansing rebirth, but on the assertion of the value of the individual and on the validation of marginalized social identities.
4. Both quotations in this paragraph are from Bellah et al., *Habits of the Heart,* 229. Note the remarkable similarity in views of hell reported by James Davison Hunter in *Evangelicalism* (p. 39) among a very different population—Evangelical college students and seminarians. He quotes several as saying that the idea of eternal damnation is incompatible with their understanding of God's mercy. One says, "I hope that hell would be like soul sleep—a kind of nothingness—but the Bible doesn't say that. I can't imagine a loving God being so cruel forever and ever." Another says, "At Judgment we are judged by our deeds and by the light we have to live by. People who[m] God considers wicked will be cast into the lake of fire right along with the Beast—at which point they go 'piff' and they are gone. I don't believe in eternal torment—it may be but it seems to be inconsistent with God's nature."
5. Andrew Greeley and Michael Hout, "Americans' Increasing Belief in Life after Death," find that, overall, the proportion of Americans who believe in life after death increased from the 1970s to the 1990s. The authors attribute this change to the aggressive efforts made, particularly by the Catholic Church, to indoctrinate immigrants in more orthodox theology and practice, as the churches entered a newly competitive religious environment. Nonetheless, as shown by the recent *U.S. News and World Report* survey noted in Jeffrey Sheler, "Hell Hath No Fury," belief in hell is compatible with a very mild sense of sin and damnation. While *U.S. News* finds the proportion of Americans who believe in hell growing, those who believe in hell are more likely to see it as "an anguished state of being" than as an actual place of physical torment.

6. Indeed, Michael Hout, Andrew Greeley, and Melissa Wilde, in "The Demographic Imperative in Religious Change" and a series of related papers, question the notion of a decline in mainline religion and of any shift to fundamentalism. Analyzing General Social Survey data by cohorts, they find that the growth of fundamentalist denominations has come entirely from members' greater fertility, due to earlier age at first marriage and higher birthrates.

7. Ibid., 18.

8. I am indebted to a stimulating paper by Kay Eskenazi, "Salvation and Religious Goals in New Religions," for insight into the kinds of "salvation" offered by the new religions. She notes "the transformation from a flawed ethical self [in the traditional salvation religions] to a worthy psychological self [in the new religions]" (p. 57). She also points out that "[w]ithout exception, each new religion promises that practicing the techniques associated with its system will enhance believers' capacities to accomplish personal inner-worldly goals. Each grounds this promise in a description of some metaphysical reality–symbolized differently in different religions–that can serve as a source of infinite power" (p. 58).

9. See Harriet Whitehead, *Renunciation and Reformulation.*

10. See Joseph Gusfield, "Nature's Body and the Metaphors of Food."

11. Among hundreds of recent titles are Barrie R. Cassileth, *The Alternative Medicine Handbook;* Michael H. Cohen, *Complementary and Alternative Medicine;* William Collinge, *The American Holistic Health Association Complete Guide to Alternative Medicine.* For a study of holistic health practices, see J. A. English-Lueck, *Health in the New Age.*

12. See the *University of California, Berkeley, Wellness Letter* and the *Harvard Health Letter,* as well as Andrew Weil's many books, including *Health and Healing; Natural Health, Natural Medicine;* and *Spontaneous Healing.*

13. Sigmund Freud, *Civilization and Its Discontents.* See Mary Douglas and Aaron Wildavsky, *Risk and Culture,* for a related analysis of how concerns about social boundaries are related to perceptions of technological and environmental risk.

14. In Bellah, Madsen, Sullivan, Swidler, and Tipton, *The Good Society,* we define an "institution" as "a pattern of expected action of individuals or groups enforced by social sanctions, both positive and negative" (p. 10). We emphasize the distinction between institutions ("normative patterns imbedded in and enforced by laws and mores") and particular organizations. We use the examples of the corporation, of the family, and of baseball.

> There are certainly better families and worse, happier and more caring families and ones that are less so. But the very way Americans institutionalize family life, the very pressures and temptations that American society presents to all families, are themselves the source of serious problems. (p. 11)

> [B]aseball, with its purposes, codes, and standards, is a collective moral enterprise, an institution in the full sense, and Americans care deeply about it. As an institution, baseball is more than the actual players and organizations who play the game during any given season. That is why we can see the sport as sometimes succeeding, sometimes failing, in becoming what baseball ought to be. (p. 39)

W. Richard Scott, in *Institutions and Organizations,* 33, develops a complementary definition emphasizing the cognitive and regulative as well as the normative aspects of institutions. Ronald L. Jepperson, "Institutions, Institutional Effects, and Institutionalism," offers the clearest analysis available of institutionalization as a variable dimension of human enterprises.

15. See Paul Hirsch, *Pack Your Own Parachute.*

16. Peter Schrag in *Paradise Lost* details the devastating effects on California of the weakening of the state's political institutions. The weakness of California's political parties, traced as early as James Q. Wilson's study *The Amateur Democrat,* have been compounded in recent years by the frequent reliance on statewide initiatives instead of the legislative process and by the effects of term limits.

17. See Norman Nie, Sidney Verba, and John Petrocik, *The Changing American Voter;* Michael Schudson, *The Good Citizen,* ch. 6.

18. In *Voice and Equality,* Sidney Verba, Kay Lehman Schlozman, and Henry Brady note the decline in voting, but point out that other forms of political participation held steady, while the number who report having contacted a public official or contributed money to a party or candidate has increased. (But see Steven J. Rosenstone and John Mark Hansen, *Mobilization, Participation, and Democracy in America.*) Verba et al. note that "[w]hat we see at the level of the individual may reflect, in part, the widely discussed decline of political parties and invigoration of interest groups. However, it probably reflects as well a parallel transformation of both sets of institutions, whereby nationalization and professionalization have redefined the citizen activist as, increasingly, a writer of checks and letters" (p. 73).

19. What are now called neoconservatives originally developed the view that America's problem was not that government was too powerful but that it was too weak to govern effectively (see, e.g., Edward C. Banfield, *Political Influence;* Samuel P. Huntington, *American Politics*). But increasingly critics on the Left, wishing wider social protections and a more vibrant democracy, also see weak political institutions as a limitation on democratic politics (see Theda Skocpol, *Protecting Soldiers and Mothers* and *Social Policy in the United States*). The disintegration of the former Soviet Union and turmoil in Eastern Europe also have served as a chastening reminder that the overthrow of undemocratic political institutions does not guarantee democracy unless effective new political institutions can be established.

20. For an interesting treatment of this issue, see Lauren B. Edelman, Christopher Uggen, and Howard S. Erlanger, "The Endogeneity of Legal Regulation."

21. See John E. Chubb and Paul E. Peterson (eds.), *Can the Government Govern?*

22. Bellah et al., *The Good Society,* 130–138.

23. Schrag, *Paradise Lost.*

24. Claude S. Fischer, Michael Hout, Martín Sanchez Jankowski, Samuel Lucas, Ann Swidler, and Kim Voss, *Inequality by Design.*

25. Schrag, *Paradise Lost.*

26. See Juliet Schor, *The Overworked American.*

27. Andrew Cherlin, *Marriage, Divorce, Remarriage,* 126–129. Noting that both men and women show "substantial attachment to marriage." Cherlin puts the difficulty this way:

> The paradox is that when Americans finally enter a marriage, they judge it increasingly by a single standard–personal fulfillment–that is difficult to maintain. . . . Indeed, with personal fulfillment accepted as such a predominant indicator of marital health, it is difficult for unhappy individuals to remain married. Fifty years ago, even thirty, unhappy couples hesitated to divorce; now they are almost compelled to. (p. 130)

28. Norman M. Bradburn, *The Structure of Psychological Well-Being;* Cherlin, *Marriage, Divorce, Remarriage.*

29. Lenore Weitzman, *The Divorce Revolution.*

30. Terry Arendell, *Divorce;* Barbara Defoe Whitehead, *The Divorce Culture.*

31. Lenore Weitzman, *The Divorce Revolution. See* the insightful analysis of the ways changes in divorce law affect marriage in Susan Westerberg Prager, "Shifting Perspectives on Marital Property Law."

32. Fischer et al., *Inequality by Design.*

33. Arlie Russell Hochschild, *The Time Bind.*

34. Jodi Wilgoren, "More Than Ever, First-Year Students Feeling the Stress of College."

35. See Michel Foucault, "Afterword."

36. Robert Wuthnow, *Sharing the Journey;* Mariana Valverde, *Diseases of the Will.*

37. Tipton, *Getting Saved from the Sixties.*

38. Hochschild, "The Commercial Spirit of Intimate Life and the Abduction of Feminism."

39. Alan Wolfe, in his recent analysis of American moral life, *One Nation, After All,* and Anthony Giddens, in his reflections on contemporary intimacy, *The Transformation of Intimacy,* note similar phenomena, although they give these a different spin. Wolfe notes that contemporary Americans have stressful lives but have developed selves, styles, and modes of living that allow them to cope with these stresses. On the whole, I would agree, but I would point out the very high level of psychic functioning that such a life presumes. Giddens sees enhanced possibilities for intimacy in the liberation from traditional domestic obligations. Here I am more skeptical.

40. Hochschild, *The Time Bind,* 222–229.

41. Wuthnow, *Sharing the Journey.*

42. Found in Jules Harlow (ed.), *Mahzor for Rosh Hashanah and Yom Kippur,* 499–501.

4. MIRROR-IMAGE MODERNITIES

1. Robert N. Bellah, *The Broken Covenant;* "Civil Religion in America"; *Tokugawa Religion; Beyond Belief.*

2. S. N. Eisenstadt, *Japanese Civilization.*

3. For an analysis of these theories, see, for instance, Eisenstadt, *Tradition, Change, and Modernity;* for a principled view on multiple modernities, see Eisenstadt, "Multiple Modernities in an Age of Globalization." See also Eisenstadt, *Die Vielfalt der Moderne: Heidelberger Max-Weber-Vorlesungen.*

4. Eric Voegelin, *From Enlightenment to Revolution;* Eisenstadt, *Revolution and the Transformation of Societies.*

5. H. Blumenberg, *Die Legitimat der Neuzeit;* Eisenstadt (ed.), *Post-Traditional Societies;* John W. Meyer, John Boli, and George Thomas, "Ontology and Rationalization in the Western Cultural Account."

6. Edward Shils, *Center and Periphery;* Eisenstadt, L. Roniger, and A. Seligman, *Centre Formation, Protest Movements, and Class Structure in Europe and the United States.*

7. Bellah, "Civil Religion in America."

8. Frank Dobbin, *Forging Industrial Policy;* Dobbin, John Sutton, John Meyer, and W. Richard Scott, "Formal Promotion Schemes and Equal Employment Opportunity Law."

9. Dorothy Ross, "Socialism and American Liberalism."

10. W. Sombart, *Why Is There No Socialism in the United States?* Kim Voss, *The Making of American Exceptionalism;* Dobbin, *Forging Industrial Policy.*

11. Nathan Glazer, *The Limits of Social Policy.*

12. Paul Boyer, *Urban Masses and Moral Order in America, 1820–1920;* Voss, *Making of American Exceptionalism.*

13. Eisenstadt, Roniger, and Seligman, *Centre Formation, Protest Movement and Class Structure.*

14. See Yehoshua Arieli, *Individualism and Nationalism in American Ideology.*

15. G. Mosca, *The Ruling Class.*

16. Michael Kazin, *The Populist Persuasion.*

17. Sacvan Bercovitch, "Afterword."

18. Leo Marx, "Pastoralism in America"; *The Machine in the Garden.*

19. S. Vlastos, "Opposition Movements in Early Meiji, 1869–1885"; Y. Sugimoto, "Structural Sources of Popular Revolts and the Tobaku Movement at the Time of the Meiji Restoration."

20. Robert Scalapino, *The Early Japanese Labor Movement.*

21. J. Livingston, J. Moore, and F. Oldfather (eds.), *Postwar Japan, 1945 to the Present.*

22. To some extent this was made possible by the differences between the electoral systems of the two societies. The Socialist and Communist Parties did not become, except for a very short period, part of the ruling coalition.

23. Scalapino, *Early Japanese Labor Movement.*

24. See G. Bernstein (ed.), *Recreating Japanese Women, 1600–1945,* especially articles by L. Dasplica Rodd; B. Molony, and M. Silverberg. See also O. Kasza, "The State and the Organization of Women in Pre-War Japan"; V. Buckholter-Traschel, *Different Modes of Articulation of Social Protest.*

25. E. Krauss, *Japanese Radicals Revisited;* E. Kraus, K. Steiner, and S. Flanagan (eds.), *Political Opposition and Local Politics in Japan.*

26. T. Ishida, "Conflict and Its Accommodation."

27. See Yoshikaru Sakamoto, "The Emperor System as a Japanese Problem."

28. J. V. Koschmann (ed.), *Authority and the Individual in Japan: Citizen Protest in Historical Perspective.*

29. Matthews M. Hamabata, "Ethnographic Boundaries"; R. Smith, "Gender Inequality in Contemporary Japan."

30. S. H. Neill McFarland, *The Rush Hour of the Gods;* Shiseyoshi Murakami, *Japanese Religion in the Modern Century;* C. Blacker, "Millenarian Aspects of the New Religions in Japan."

31. H. Harootunian, "Late Tokugawa Culture and Thought."

32. T. Rimer (ed.), *Culture and Identity.*

33. S. Nolte, *Liberalism in Modern Japan.*

34. Gary D. Allinson, "Citizenship, Fragmentation, and the Negotiated Polity"; Michio Muramatsu, "Patterned Pluralism under Challenge: The Policies of the 1980s"; Margaret A. McKean, "State Strength and the Public Interest."

35. Allinson, "Citizenship, Fragmentation, and the Negotiated Polity"; Muramatsu, "Patterned Pluralism under Challenge." See also Frank Schwartz, "Of Fairy Cloaks and Familiar Talks"; T. Ishida, "Emerging or Eclipsing Citizenship?"

36. Allinson, "Citizenship, Fragmentation, and the Negotiated Polity."

37. M. Waida, "Buddhism and the National Community." See also C. Blacker, "Two Shinto Myths: The Golden Age and the Chosen People," and J. R. Werblowski, *Beyond Tradition and Modernity*.

38. Peter Nosco, *Confucianism and Tokugawa Culture*.

39. K. Wildman Nakai, "The Naturalization of Confucianism in Tokugawa Japan."; Peter Nosco, Introduction to *Confucianism and Tokugawa Culture*.

40. An interesting illustration of the persistence of such conceptions of the Japanese collectivity can be found in the attitude of some distinguished twentieth-century Japanese leftist intellectuals to Marxism. Intellectuals such as Kotuku or Kawakawi Hajime attempted to deemphasize the "materialistic" dimensions of Marxism and infuse them with "spiritual" values. While most such Chinese intellectuals emphasized the transcendental and universalistic themes of "classical" Confucianism, the Japanese emphasized the "kokutai," the Japanese national community or essence. Cf. G. A. Hoston, "A 'Theology' of Liberation? Socialist Revolution and Spiritual Regeneration in Chinese and Japanese Marxism."

41. See also Gilbert Rozman (ed.), *The East Asian Region*.

42. Peter Nosco notes that some Confucian-inspired Tokugawa intellectuals viewed the Tokugawa as recipients of the mandate of heaven, but they avoided the converse implication that "heaven might withdraw its mandate from any specific regime" until the last years of Tokugawa rule. See Nosco's introduction to *Confucianism and Tokugawa Culture*. See also Francis Hsu, "Filial Piety in Japan and China"; Herschel Webb, *The Japanese Imperial Institution in the Tokugawa Period*.

43. H. Watanabe makes a similar observation concerning the striking difference between the relationship of a samurai to his lord and the relationship of the Chinese scholar-official to the emperor. See Watanabe, "The Transformation of Neo-Confucianism in Early Tokugawa Japan."

44. Seymor Martin Lipset, *The First New Nation; American Exceptionalism*.

45. Terence Ball and J. G. A. Pocock (eds.), *Conceptual Change and the Constitution;* Bernard Bailyn, *The Ideological Origins of the American Revolution*.

46. Rogers M. Smith, "Beyond Tocqueville, Myrdal, and Hartz."

47. Judith Shklar, *American Citizenship*.

48. Gordon S. Wood, *The Radicalism of the American Revolution*.

49. Shklar, *American Citizenship*.

50. Wendy F. Naylor, "Some Thoughts upon Reading Tocqueville's *Democracy in America*."

51. Shklar, *American Citizenship*.

52. Robert H. Wiebe, *Self-Rule; The Search for Order 1877–1920*.

53. Elina H. Gould has lately shown that the British confrontation with American independence and with the premises of the American Revolution generated a related strong "conservative" counterrevolution in British political discourse. See her "American Independence and Britain's Counter-Revolution."

54. George Kateb, "Democratic Individuality and the Meaning of Rights"; Olaf Hansen, *Aesthetic Individualism and Practical Intellect*.

55. Daniel Bell, "'American Exceptionalism' Revisited."
56. Massimo L. Salvadori, *Europa America Marxismo.*
57. Ann Swidler, "Inequality and American Culture."
58. Adam Seligman, "The Failure of Socialism in the United States: A Reconsideration."
59. R. W. B. Lewis, *The American Adam;* Terence Ball, *Reappraising Political Theory.*
60. Bellah, "Civil Religion in America"; *Broken Covenant.*
61. Lewis, *American Adam.*
62. Sacvan Bercovitch, "New England's Errand Reappraised."
63. Joyce Appleby, "New Cultural Heroes in the Early National Period."
64. Bellah, "Civil Religion in America"; *Broken Covenant.*
65. Appleby, "New Cultural Heroes" and *Liberalism and Republicanism in the Historical Imagination;* P. Johnson, "God and the Americans."
66. See Eisenstadt, *Power, Trust and Meaning,* especially chs. 1 and 8.

5. CALVINISM AND REVOLUTION

1. Max Weber, *Gesammelte Aufsätze zur Religionssoziologie.*
2. Michael Walzer, *The Revolution of the Saints: A Study in the Origins of Radical Politics.*
3. Robert M. Kingdon, *Geneva and the Coming of the Wars of Religion in France, 1555–1563; Geneva and the Consolidation of the French Protestant Movement.*
4. Walzer, *Revolution of the Saints,* 115.
5. Ibid., 114.
6. Phyllis Mack Crew, *Calvinist Preaching and Iconoclasm in the Netherlands, 1544–1569,* 59.
7. G. Groenhuis, *De Predikanten,* 163.
8. Ibid., 165 ff.
9. The theological debates are copiously recounted in Douglas Nobbs, *Theocracy and Toleration: A Study of the Disputes in Dutch Calvinism.* A fuller treatment, giving greater attention to the social and political context, may be found in A. Th. Van Deursen, *Bavianen en Slijkgeuzen.* A less sympathetic portrait is contained in Jan Den Tex, *Oldenbarnevelt,* vol. 3.
10. Kingdon, *Geneva and the Coming.*
11. Ibid., appendix 2.
12. F. P. Van Stam, *The Controversy over the Theology of Saumur, 1635–1650.*
13. Perez Zagorin, *Rebels and Rulers, 1500–1660.*
14. Martin Van Gelderen, *The Political Thought of the Dutch Revolt,* 270–276.
15. Charles Tilly, *European Revolutions, 1492–1992.*
16. This is the strategy followed in Theda Skocpol's *States and Social Revolutions,* far and away the most influential book on the subject, and one that has had an enormous impact on sociology. The approach recommended here is more in line with that developed in Tilly's *European Revolutions.*
17. This section draws primarily on Wim P. Blockmans, "A Typology of Representative Institutions in Late Medieval Europe"; Brian Downing, *The Military Revolution and Political Change;* Karol Gorski, *Communitas princeps corona regni: Studia selecta;*

Gouvernés et gouvernants; Otto Hintze, "Typologie der ständischen Verfassungen des Abendlandes"; Helmut G. Koenigsberger, *Estates and Revolutions;* A. R. Myers, *Parliaments and Estates in Europe to 1789;* Kazimierz Orzechowski, "Les systèmes des assemblées d'états: Origines, évolution, typologie"; Gianfranco Poggi, *The Development of the Modern State.*

18. The phenomenon of peasant representation was limited mainly to Scandinavia and the Southern German territories.

19. Here again, there were important exceptions, such as Scandinavia, which had a quattro-curial system, and Hungary, where there were four separate chambers.

20. See Downing, *Military Revolution;* David Eltis, *The Military Revolution in Sixteenth-Century Europe;* Thomas Ertman, *Birth of the Leviathan;* J. R. Hale, *War and Society in Renaissance Europe;* Geoffrey Parker, *The Military Revolution.*

21. This is not to deny, of course, that differences over fine points of theology, e.g., the "real presence" of Christ in the Eucharist, could give rise to bitter disputes in the sixteenth century, and not only within the clergy. Nevertheless, Calvin's social and political views were still quite moderate when compared to those expounded by millenarian sects such as the Anabaptists.

22. Luther's stance against popular resistance during the Peasants' War (1525) is notorious. Less well known are his later pronouncements, which allowed resistance by the "lower magistrates." This constitutionalist theory of resistance was further elaborated by jurists in Hessia and probably formed the basis of Calvin's views (on this, see especially Quentin Skinner, *Foundations of Modern Political Thought*).

23. Julian H. Franklin, *Constitutionalism and Resistance in the Sixteenth Century;* Robert M. Kingdon, "John Calvin's Contribution to Representative Government"; Skinner, *Foundations.*

24. The narrative is based on the following standard accounts of the Dutch Revolt: Pieter Geyl, *The Dutch Revolt;* S. Groenveld et al., *De tachtigjarige oorlog;* Geoffrey Parker, *The Dutch Revolt,* I. Schöffer, *De Lage Landen,* 132–268. Notes in the text refer to more specialized works.

25. James Tracy, *Holland under Habsburg Rule, 1515–1565.*

26. Michiel Dierickx, *L'érection des nouveaux diocèses aux Pays-Bas, 1559–1570.*

27. Crew, *Iconoclasm.*

28. E. H. Kossman and A. F. Mellink, *Texts Concerning the Revolt of the Netherlands,* document 4, 62–66.

29. Solange Deyon, *Les "casseurs" de l'été 1566: L'iconoclasme dans le nord.*

30. A. L. E. Verheyden, *Le conseil des troubles.*

31. A. A. Van Schelven, *De Nederduitsche Vluchtelingskerken der XVIe eeuw in Engeland en Duitschland.*

32. H. M. Grapperhaus, *Alva en de Tiende Pennig.*

33. J. C. A. De Meij, *De Watergeuzen in de Nederlanden, 1568–1572.*

34. H. A. E. Van Gelder, *Revolutionnaire Reformatie.*

35. J. W. Koopmans, *De Staten van Holland en de Opstand.*

36. Kossmann and Mellink, *Texts Concerning the Revolt of the Netherlands,* document 23, 126–132.

37. André Despretz, "De Instauratie der Gentse Calvinistische Republiek (1577–79)"; J. Decavele (ed.), *Het Eind van Een Rebelse Droom; Brugge in de Geuzentijd.*

38. H. Q. Janssen, *De Kerkhervorming in Vlaanderen.*

39. Kossmann and Mellink, document 37, 165–172.

40. Ibid., document 49, 216–228.

41. Geoffrey Parker, *The Army of Flanders and the Spanish Road, 1567–1659: The Logistics of Spanish Victory and Defeat in the Low Countries' Wars.*

42. F. G. Oosterhoff, *Leicester and the Netherlands, 1586–1587.*

43. Jan Den Tex, *Oldenbarnevelt,* vol. 1.

44. Werner Hahlweg, *Die Heeresreform der Oranier und die Antike;* Jan Willem Wijn, *Het Krijgswezen in den Tijd van Prins Maurits.*

45. S. J. Fockema-Andreae, *De NederlandseStaat onder de Republiek;* Robert Fruin, *Geschiedenis der Staatsinstellingen in Nederland;* Marjolein C. 't Hart, *The Making of a Bourgeois State: War, Politics, and Finance during the Dutch Revolt.*

46. W. P. C. Knuttel, *De Toestand der Nederlandsche Katholieken ten Tijde der Republiek;* A. Th. Van Deursen, *Bavianen en Slijkgeuzen: Kerk en Kerkvolk ten Tijde van Maurits en Oldebarnevelt.*

47. I am aware that fiscal crises have come to be seen as a key cause of revolutions since the pioneering work of Theda Skocpol on this subject, and I do not wish to downplay their significance in the outcome of the Dutch Revolt. But I think it is important to point out that fiscal crises and "state breakdown" were a chronic condition in the "absolutist" monarchies of the early modern period, and that their association with revolution was far from perfect. I should also hasten to add that the second key precondition for revolution that Skocpol adduces, peasant revolt, was conspicuously absent from the Dutch case and, indeed, from all the cases examined in this chapter. It may be objected that the Revolt and other events examined here were not "real" revolutions. But this is not the place to engage in definitional debates about what does or does not constitute a revolution. I can only hope that the material I present is sufficient to convince the reader of the revolutionary character of the conflicts in question and note that the logic of early modern revolutions was somewhat different from the modern revolutions treated in Skocpol's work.

48. Rients Reitsma, *Centrifugal and Centripetal Forces in the Early Dutch Republic: The States of Overijssel, 1566–1600.*

49. James D. Tracy, *A Financial Revolution in the Habsburg Netherlands: Renten and Renteniers in the County of Holland, 1515–1565.*

50. This narrative draws on standard accounts of the Wars of Religion, such as Robert J. Knecht, *The French Wars of Religion, 1559–1598;* J. H. Mariéjol, *La Réforme et la Ligue;* Pierre Miquel, *Les guerres de religion;* Holt Mack, *The French Wars of Religion, 1562–1629;* Michel Pernot, *Les guerres de religion en France, 1559–1598;* J. H. M. Salmon, *Society in Crisis: France in the Sixteenth Century;* and Nicola M. Sutherland, *The Huguenot Struggle for Recognition.* It also draws on several regional studies: Philip Benedict, *Rouen during the Wars of Religion;* Barbara B. Diefendorf, *Beneath the Cross: Catholics and Huguenots in Sixteenth-Century Paris;* Mark Greengrass, "The *Sainte Union* in the Provinces: The Case of Toulouse." And for military issues, it draws primarily on James B. Wood, *The King's Army: Warfare, Soldiers, and Society during the Wars of Religion in France, 1562–1576.*

51. Lucien Romier, *Les origines politiques des guerres de religion;* Romier, *Le royaume de Cathérine de Medici.*

52. J. Russell Major, *Representative Government in Renaissance France*.

53. Robert Harding, *Anatomy of a Power Elite: The Provincial Governors of Early Modern France*.

54. Jean Delumeau, *Naissance et affirmation de la Réforme;* Janine Garrisson, *Les protestants du Midi;* Mark Greengrass, *The French Reformation*.

55. Kingdon, *Geneva and the Coming*, 54–88.

56. Major, *Representative Government*, 58–96.

57. Henri Hauser, *La naissance du protestantisme;* Samuel Mours, *Le protestantisme en France*, vol. 1; Garrisson, *Protestants*, 231–244.

58. Benedict, *Rouen;* Denis Crouzet, *Les guerriers de Dieu: La violence au temps des troubles de religion, vers 1525–vers 1610;* Natalie Z. Davis, *Society and Culture in Early Modern France*, ch. 6; Diefendorf, *Beneath the Cross;* Mark Greengrass, "The Anatomy of a Religious Riot in Toulouse in May 1562"; Penny Roberts, *A City in Conflict: Troyes during the French Wars of Religion*.

59. Major, *Representative Government*.

60. Garrisson, *Protestants*, 167–200; G. Griffiths, *Representative Government in Europe in the Sixteenth Century*, 254–297.

61. David Parker, *La Rochelle and the French Monarchy*.

62. Frederic J. Baumgartner, *Radical Reactionaries: The Political Thought of the French Catholic League*, 101 ff.

63. On the ways in which consensus building was affected by the internal organization of representative assemblies, see especially Thomas Ertman, *Birth of the Leviathan*.

64. Mours, *Protestantisme*, especially 248–249.

65. Léonce Anquez, *Histoire des assemblées protestantes;* Garrisson, *Protestants*, 161–222; Griffiths, *Representative Government*, 255–260.

66. This section draws heavily on the following works: Juliusz Bardach, "Gouvernants et gouvernés en Pologne au Moyen-Âge et aux temps modernes"; Bardach, "L'élections des députés à l'ancienne diète polonaise, fin XVe–XVIIIe siècles"; Norman Davies, *God's Playground: A History of Poland*, vol. 1: *The Origins to 1795*, ch. 7; K. Gorski, *Communitas Princeps Corona Regni*, ch. 5; Antoni Maczak, "The Structure of Power in the Commonwealth of the Sixteenth and Seventeenth Centuries"; Hans Roos, "Ständewesen und parlamentarische Verfassung in Polen"; Henryk Samsonowicz, "Polish Politics and Society under the Jagiellonian Monarchy"; Zygmunt Wojciechowski, *L'état polonais au Moyen Âge;* and Andrzey Wyczanski, "The Problem of Authority in Sixteenth-Century Poland."

67. Stanislaw Russocki, "La naissance du parlementarisme polonais vue dans une perspective comparative."

68. György Bonis, "The Hungarian Feudal Diet (13th–18th Centuries)"; R. J. W. Evans, "Calvinism in East Central Europe: Hungary and Her Neighbours"; Gorski, *Communitas Princeps*, chs. 1, 6, 10; Vaclav Vanacek, "Les assemblées d'états en Bohème à l'époque de la révolte d'états."

69. Zygmunt Wojciechowski, "Les débuts du programme de l' 'Exécution des lois' en Pologne au début du XVIe siècle."

70. James Miller, "The Polish Nobility and the Renaissance Monarchy: The 'Execution of the Laws' Movement."

71. Davies, *God's Playground*, 160–190; Paul Fox, *The Reformation in Poland;* Ambroise Jobert, *De Luther à Mohila: La Pologne dans la crise de la chrétienté, 1517–1648;* Valerian Krasinski, *Historical Sketch of the Rise, Progress, and Decline of the Reformation in Poland;* Reddaway et al., *The Cambridge History of Poland, vol. 1: From the Origins to Sobieski,* ch. 16; G. Schramm, *Der polnische Adel und die Reformation;* Karl Völker, *Kirchengeschichte Polens;* Stanislas Lubieniecki, *History of the Polish Reformation, and Nine Related Documents.*

72. Victor Lucien Tapie, *Une église tcheque au XVIe siècle: L'Unité des Frères;* Rudolf Rican, *The History of the Unity of Brethren: A Protestant Hussite Church in Bohemia and Moravia.*

73. Earl Mose Wilbur, *A History of Unitarianism: Socialism and Its Antecedents;* Stanislaw Kot, *Socinianism in Poland: The Social and Political Ideas of the Polish Antitrinitarians in the Sixteenth and Seventeenth Centuries.*

74. Quoted in Krasinski, *Reformation in Poland,* vol. 1, 295–300.

75. A. F. Pollard, *The Jesuits in Poland,* 26.

76. Ibid., 27.

77. Reddaway et al., *Cambridge History of Poland,* 344.

78. Jobert, *De Luther à Mohila,* 209; Bardach, "L'élections des députés," 51–52.

79. Wilbur, *Unitarianism,* 343.

80. Krasinski, *Reformation in Poland,* vol. 2, 54–60; Lubieniecki, *History of the Polish Reformation.*

81. Cited in Davies, *God's Playground,* 342.

82. I should perhaps point out that this state of affairs flies in the face of the Marxist axiom that states that popular violence invariably leads the "ruling classes" to close ranks. While this does indeed happen in some cases, it would probably be more accurate to say that popular violence has revolutionary (as opposed to reactionary) consequences only when there are preexisting breaks within the ranks of the ruling classes. On this point, see Michael Mann, *The Sources of Social Power,* vol. 2: *The Rise of Classes and Nation-States, 1760–1914.*

6. COMPARATIVE COSMOPOLIS

1. Robert N. Bellah (ed.), *Emile Durkheim on Morality and Society,* xviii.

2. Talcott Parsons, *The Structure of Social Action.*

3. Talcott Parsons, *The Social System.*

4. Robert N. Bellah, Richard Madsen, William M. Sullivan, Ann Swidler, and Steven M. Tipton, *Habits of the Heart: Individualism and Commitment in American Life.*

5. Robert N. Bellah, Richard Madsen, William M. Sullivan, Ann Swidler, and Steven M. Tipton, *The Good Society.*

6. Robert N. Bellah, "Religious Evolution," 20–50.

7. As one of these coauthors, I would attest that we contributed through our empirical work to that sense of the complexity of American life and helped to enrich the theoretical apparatus for representing that complexity. Nonetheless, we were able to work together so well because we all accepted the basic parameters of Bellah's vision. It is these parameters that I am now trying to explicate and extend to comparative sociology.

8. *Habits of the Heart* has been translated into German, Spanish, Italian, Japanese, Chinese, Russian, Vietnamese, and Bulgarian; *The Good Society* has been translated into Chinese and Japanese.

9. Bellah, *Emile Durkheim*, ix–lv.

10. Ibid., ix–x.

11. Ibid., xxv.

12. Bellah et al., *Habits of the Heart*, 3–8.

13. Ibid., 297–307.

14. Pierre Bourdieu, *Distinction: A Social Critique of Judgment and Taste.*

15. Alexis de Tocqueville, *Democracy in America*, 508.

16. Ibid., 508.

17. Seymour Martin Lipset, *Political Man: The Social Bases of Politics.*

18. Bellah et al., *Habits of the Heart*, 148.

19. Mary Douglas, *Natural Symbols: Explorations in Cosmology.*

20. Ibid., 77–92.

21. Alasdair MacIntyre, *After Virtue*, especially 22–33.

22. Douglas, *Natural Symbols*, 89–91.

23. Ibid., 171.

24. Ibid., 186.

25. Ibid., 19–58.

26. See Ezra F. Vogel, *Japan's New Middle Class.*

27. Tocqueville, *Democracy in America*, 448–449.

28. Ibid., 446–447.

29. Ibid., 447.

30. Bellah et al., *Habits of the Heart*, 221.

31. Jürgen Habermas, *The Theory of Communicative Action*, vol. 2, 77.

32. Robert N. Bellah, "Beyond Economic Competitiveness: Education for Citizenship and Democracy," 5.

33. Douglas, *Natural Symbols*, 72–73.

34. Bellah, "Beyond Economic Competitiveness," 14.

35. Max Weber, "Science as a Vocation," 148.

36. Robert N. Bellah, "Max Weber and World-Denying Love: A Look at the Historical Sociology of Religion."

37. Ibid; also, Max Weber, "Politics as a Vocation," 128.

38. Ibid.

7. MAMMON AND THE CULTURE OF THE MARKET

It was under the imaginative eye of Robert N. Bellah that, as a doctoral student at Harvard in the late 1950s, I was first exposed to Max Weber and Emile Durkheim. The influence of all three is evident in this chapter and is gratefully acknowledged. A shortened version of this piece appeared in *The Atlantic*, March 1999.

1. Emile Durkheim, *The Elementary Forms of Religious Life.*

2. There are important exceptions to this obliviousness. See, for example, Mi-

chael Taussig, *The Devil and Commodity Fetishism in South America;* Mary Douglas and Baron Isherwood, *The World of Goods.*

3. On ritual, see Edmund Leach, "Ritualization in Man in Relation to Conceptual and Social Development"; Victor Turner, *From Ritual to Theater: The Human Seriousness of Play;* Sally Falk Moore and Barbara Myerhoff (eds.), *Secular Ritual.*

4. Francis Fukuyama, *The End of History and the Last Man.*

5. Karl Polanyi, *The Great Transformation.*

6. E. R. Dodds, *The Greeks and the Irrational.*

7. For a historical overview of this phenomenon, see Piero Camporesi, *Bread of Dreams: Food and Fantasy in Early Modern Europe.*

8. See Jackson Lears, *Fables of Abundance.*

9. For a fascinating account of how Christians in the first five centuries of Christianity both used and were used by the prevailing cultural and religious symbolism of the day, see Thomas F. Matthews, *The Clash of the Gods.*

10. Kathryn Tanner, *The Politics of God.*

8. SELLING GOD IN AMERICA

1. Alexis de Tocqueville, *Democracy in America.* See vol. 1, chapter 11, on the free press; vol. 2, bk.2, ch.20, on manufacturing; vol. 2, bk. 3, ch. 21, on reasons for the rarity of revolutions. Tocqueville uses the phrase "a commercial nation" in vol. 1, p. 219.

2. For the metaphor of a market imperialism, see Michael Walzer, *Spheres of Justice,* 120–121. Robert Rogat Loeb, *Soul of a Citizen: Living with Conviction in a Cynical Time,* speaks of an American "addiction" to greed and consumerism. Note that I am, in places, ironic in my "celebration" of commercial culture and its promotion of a kind of religion in the United States.

3. On free associations, see Tocqueville, *Democracy in America,* vol. 1, ch. 12.

4. Robert Wuthnow, *Acts of Compassion,* 325.

5. Robert Putnam, *Making Democracy Work.* I treat of religion and social capital in my essay "Under the Cross and the Flag" and in my forthcoming book, *Public Discipleship: Paradenominational Groups and Citizenship.*

6. Robert N. Bellah, Richard Madsen, William M. Sullivan, Ann Swidler, and Steven M. Tipton, *Habits of the Heart.*

7. Jon Butler, *Awash in a Sea of Faith.*

8. R. Lawrence Moore, *Selling God: American Religion and the Marketplace of Culture,* 4.

9. Seymour M. Lipset, "Comments on Luckmann," 187.

10. This point is documented in Butler, *Awash in a Sea of Faith.* For a subtle parsing of what is true and not true about the secularization hypothesis, see Jose Casanova, *Public Religions in the Modern World.*

11. Andrew Greeley, *Religious Change in America.*

12. Wade Clark Roof and William McKinney, *American Mainline Religion.*

13. Sidney Verba, Kay Schlozman, and Henry Brady, *Voice and Equality.*

14. R. Stephen Warner, "Work in Progress: Toward a New Paradigm for the Sociological Study of Religion"; Colleen McDannell, *Material Christianity.*

15. Moore, *Selling God,* 11.

16. Ibid.

17. See Lewis Leary, *The Book Peddling Parson: An Account of the Life and Works of Mason Locke Weems, Patriot, Pitchman, Author, and Purveyor of Morality.*

18. Moore, *Selling God,* 111.

19. Cited in ibid., 121.

20. Ibid., 105.

21. Cited in ibid., 211.

22. Dianne Winston, *Red, Hot, and Righteous: Urban Religion and the Salvation Army.*

23. Robert Orsi, *Thank You, St. Jude,* 16.

24. Moore, *Selling God,* 237.

25. McDannell, *Material Christianity,* 222.

26. Butler, *Awash in a Sea of Faith,* 275.

27. Donald Miller, *Reinventing American Protestantism: Christianity in the New Millennium.*

28. Butler, *Awash in a Sea of Faith,* 273.

29. Moore, *Selling God,* 9.

30. Ibid., 144.

31. Warner, "Work in Progress," 1058.

32. R. Stephen Warner, "Religion, Boundaries, and Bridges."

33. Ibid., 219.

34. Moore, *Selling God,* 272.

35. Warner, "Work in Progess," 1062.

36. Ibid., 1067.

37. Ibid., 1069.

38. Ibid., 1077.

39. George Gallup, *The Unchurched American—Ten Years Later,* 3.

40. Warner, "Work in Progress," 1079.

41. Ibid., 1079.

42. Christian Smith, *American Evangelicalism: Embattled and Thriving,* cf. table 2.8, 49.

43. Barbara Wheeler, "You Who Are Far Off: Religious Division and the Role of Religious Research." For the decline of the liberal Protestant churches, see Thomas Reeves, *The Empty Church.*

44. See John A. Coleman, S.J., "Exploding Spiritualities: Their Social Causes, Social Location, and Social Divide."

45. Moore, *Selling God,* 276.

46. Randall Balmer, *Mine Eyes Have Seen The Glory: A Journey Into the Evangelical Subculture in America,* 212.

47. Warner is not wedded to a rational-choice model of the human actor. Rodney Stark, however, insists that an appeal to a rational-choice model of the human actor is part and parcel of his use of the market analogy. Stark, *The Rise of Christianity,* 169–184.

48. Robert N. Bellah, *Beyond Belief,* 237–259.

9. IN SEARCH OF COMMON GROUND

1. Louis Armstrong, "(What Did I Do to Be So) Black and Blue."

2. Howard Thurman's search for common ground seemed an apt subject for a festschrift in honor of Robert N. Bellah, for several reasons. Bellah's interest in the cultural and institutional expressions of religious experience, his scholarly study and personal advocacy of the symbols of civic and national community, and his appreciation of critical opposition to dehumanizing trends within modernity all resonate profoundly with central elements of Thurman's thought. For much of Bellah's career, he and Thurman lived in close proximity—the one in Boston separated from the other in Cambridge only by the Charles River and, at a later period, the one in San Francisco separated from the other in Berkeley only by the Bay. I do not know whether the two ever met personally.

3. Several important analyses of Thurman's life and thought have been written. In my view, the most helpful include Walter E. Fluker, *They Looked For a City: A Comparative Analysis of the Ideal of Community in the Thought of Howard Thurman and Martin Luther King, Jr.;* Alonzo Johnson, *Good News for the Disinherited: Howard Thurman on Jesus of Nazareth and Human Liberation;* Mozella G. Mitchell (ed.), *The Human Search: Howard Thurman and the Quest for Freedom, Proceedings of the Second Annual Thurman Convocation;* Alton B. Pollard III, *Mysticism and Social Change: The Social Witness of Howard Thurman;* Luther E. Smith, Jr., *Howard Thurman: The Mystic as Prophet;* Walter Earl Fluker and Catherine Tumber (eds.), *A Strange Freedom: The Best of Howard Thurman on Religious Experience and Public Life.* The publication of Thurman's papers is in process.

4. Howard Thurman, *With Head and Heart: The Autobiography of Howard Thurman,* 20–21.

5. Ibid., 5–6.

6. Howard Thurman (ed.), *A Track to the Water's Edge: The Olive Schreiner Reader,* xxvii–xxviii.

7. Thurman, *With Head and Heart,* 73.

8. Ibid., 112–114.

9. Howard Thurman, *Why I Believe There Is a God: Sixteen Essays by Negro Clergymen with an Introduction by Howard Thurman,* xi.

10. Thurman, *With Head and Heart,* 134.

11. Howard Thurman, *Footprints of a Dream: The Story of the Church for the Fellowship of All Peoples,* 24.

12. Ibid., 32.

13. Lerone Bennett, Jr., "Howard Thurman: Twentieth-Century Holy Man," 76, 84.

14. Thurman, *Common Ground,* 28.

15. Ibid., 44.

16. Ibid., 76.

17. Ibid., 80.

18. Ibid., 82–83.

19. Ibid., 57–58.

20. Ibid., 67–68.

21. Ibid., 80.

22. Ibid., 88.

23. Ibid., 92–93.

24. Thurman, *With Head and Heart,* 245–247.

25. For an enlightening discussion of the painful cost of becoming white, see Thandeka, *Learning to Be White: Money, Race, and God in America.*

10. REASSEMBLING THE CIVIC CHURCH

1. William J. Bennett, "Moral Corruption in America"; E. J. Dionne, *They Only Look Dead: Why Progressives Will Dominate the Next Political Era.*

2. George Rodrigue, "Gingrich Aims for Kinder Image"; Wayne Woodlief, "Practicing What They Preach."

3. Robert D. Putnam, "Bowling Alone: America's Declining Social Capital"; Putnam, "Tuning In, Tuning Out: The Strange Disappearance of Social Capital in America"; *P.S.: Political Science and Politics;* Robert N. Bellah, Richard Madsen, William M. Sullivan, Ann Swidler, and Steven M. Tipton, "Individualism and the Crisis of Civic Membership."

4. Henry G. Cisneros, *Higher Ground: Faith Communities and Community Building.*

5. For a valuable overview of the changing civic or "public" role of congregations, see Martin E. Marty, "Public and Private: Congregation as Meeting Place."

6. George H. Gallup, Jr., *Religion in America: 1996 Report;* Andrew Greeley, "The Other Civic America."

7. Robert N. Bellah, Richard Madsen, William M. Sullivan, Ann Swidler, and Steven M. Tipton, *Habits of the Heart: Individualism and Commitment in American Life.*

8. James Davison Hunter, *Culture Wars;* John A. Hall (ed.), *Civil Society: Theory, History, Comparison.*

9. Robert N. Bellah, Richard Madsen, William M. Sullivan, Ann Swidler, and Steven M. Tipton, *The Good Society.*

10. Lester C. Thurow, *The Future of Capitalism: How Today's Economic Forces Shape Tomorrow's World.*

11. David Popenoe, *Life without Father: Compelling New Evidence That Fatherhood and Marriage Are Indispensable for the Good of Children and Society;* Sara McLanahan and Gary Sandefur, *Growing Up With a Single Parent: What Hurts, What Helps.*

12. Theda Skocpol, *Boomerang: Clinton's Health Security Effort and the Turn against Government in U.S. Politics.*

13. Robert Wuthnow, *The Crisis in the Churches: Spiritual Malaise, Fiscal Woe.*

14. The larger argument about porous institutions and evidence supporting it are presented in Robert Wuthnow, *Loose Connections: Civic Involvement in America's Fragmented Communities.*

15. Useful treatments of *reassembling* in the history of American religion include Donald G. Mathews, "The Second Great Awakening as an Organizing Process, 1780–1830"; and Nathan O. Hatch, *The Democratization of American Christianity.*

16. Although space does not permit a broader conceptual discussion of civil society, my usage is similar to that of Ernest Gellner, *Conditions of Liberty: Civil Society and Its Rivals,* and Adam Seligman, *The Idea of Civil Society;* and see Robert Wuthnow, *Christianity and Civil Society: The Contemporary Debate.*

17. Frank F. Furstenberg, "The Future of Marriage."

18. Joe Zeff and Pat Lyons, *The Downsizing of America*.

19. Among many other discussions of the changes in neighborhoods, see Alan Ehrenhalt, *The Lost City: Discovering the Forgotten Virtues of Community in Chicago of the 1950s*; Claude S. Fischer, "Ambivalent Communities: How Americans Understand Their Localities."

20. Alejandro Portes and Ruben G. Rumbaut, *Immigrant America: A Portrait*; Thomas J. Espenshade (ed.), *Keys to Successful Immigration: Implications of the New Jersey Experience*.

21. On "leaving home," *see* Bellah et al., *Habits of the Heart*, 56–62.

22. On the characteristics of markets that are conducive to porous institutions, see especially Charles E. Lindblom, *Politics and Markets: The World's Political-Economic Systems*; Robert E. Lane, *The Market Experience*; Oliver E. Williamson, *Markets and Hierarchies*.

23. These results are from my Civic Involvement Survey, conducted through in-person interviews with 1,528 nationally representative respondents in January and February 1997; see Wuthnow, *Loose Connections*, for further details. The figures in the text are odds-ratios computed from logit regression models; the figure for divorce is significant at the .08 level, all others are significant at or beyond the .05 level of probability.

24. Wade Clark Roof, *A Generation of Seekers: The Spiritual Journeys of the Baby Boom Generation*; Dean R. Hoge, Benton Johnson, and Donald A. Luidens, *Vanishing Boundaries: The Religion of Mainline Protestant Baby Boomers*.

25. Princeton Religion Research Center, *The Unchurched American—Ten Years Later*, 44–45; common reasons given for ceasing to attend church in this national survey included moving to a new community, finding other activities, feeling out of place, work schedule, and becoming divorced or separated.

26. R. Stephen Warner, "The Place of the Congregation in the Contemporary American Religious Configuration" and *New Wine in Old Wineskins*.

27. These results are based on an analysis of the 462 Protestants in the Civic Involvement Survey who said they belonged to a specific congregation. The percentages of those who attended churches with one thousand or more members, compared with the percentages among those who attended churches with fewer than two hundred members, were, respectively, as follows: raised in a suburb or city, 59, 43; work contacts mostly outside one's own community, 61, 49; knowing fewer than half the people in one's neighborhood, 73, 58; having lived at six or more addresses in one's life, 70, 44; residing at present address for one year or less, 16, 10; attending a congregation outside one's own neighborhood, 63, 43; attending a congregation located in a city or suburb, 84, 50; having attended college, 75, 49; defining "community" as the region in which one lives, 20, 6; defining "community" as one's own neighborhood, 32, 40; having no children, 29, 18; having worked at present job less than one year, 17, 12; having ever been divorced, 34, 25; age 30 to 49, 48, 32; having at least one parent who graduated from college, 38, 22; making long-distance telephone calls at least once per week, 55, 37; using the Internet or e-mail, 27, 17. (Members of medium-sized congregations fell in between on all of these comparisons.)

28. Although most discussions of large Protestant congregations have focused on the exceptionally large and rapidly growing "megachurch," the studies emphasize many social factors mentioned here as characteristic of the members (or "seekers") attending these churches. See Bill Hybels and Lynne Hybels, *Rediscovering Church: The Story and Vision of Willow Creek Community Church;* Richard Olson, *The Largest Congregations in the United States: An Empirical Study of Church Growth and Decline;* Scott L. Thumma, "Sketching a Mega-Trend: The Phenomenal Proliferation of Very Large Churches in the United States"; Nancy L. Eiesland, "Contending with a Giant: The Impact of a Megachurch on Exurban Religious Institutions."

29. The respective percentages of members of large and small congregations who said they attended worship services about every week were 45 and 47; who regularly attended a Sunday school class, 39 and 37; who participated in a Bible study or prayer group, 46 and 47; who had six or more close friends in the congregation, 73 and 54.

30. The percentages of self-identified religious conservatives in large and small congregations, respectively, were 42 and 50; of moderates, 46 and 40; and of liberals, 13 and 10. When asked to describe the theological orientation of their congregation, the respective percentages who said "moderate" were 38 and 25.

31. Several examples of large mainline Protestant churches that have become places both of reassembling and of promoting civic involvement are profiled in Randall Balmer, *Grant Us Courage: Travels along the Mainline of American Protestantism;* see also Marilee Munger Scroggs, "Making a Difference: Fourth Presbyterian Church of Chicago." Public roles, apart from civic involvement, of congregations are emphasized in my book *Producing the Sacred: An Essay on Public Religion.*

32. Among members of large churches, 71 percent had done some volunteering while 62 percent in medium-sized and in small congregations had.

33. Thirty-two percent of those in large churches said they had done volunteer work in a poor inner-city area at some time in their life; 23 percent in small churches had done so, and 16 percent in medium churches. The proportions of members saying they had attended meetings during the past year concerning community issues were 43 percent in large churches, 30 percent in medium churches, and 31 percent in small churches.

34. Putnam, "Tuning In, Tuning Out."

35. The mean number of voluntary organizations to which respondents said they belonged was 2.2 among those in large churches, 1.8 among those in medium churches, and 1.3 among those in small churches.

36. The number of volunteer activities in which respondents have engaged in the past year is not significantly related to size of congregation but when examined in a multiple regression analysis, is significantly related to respondent's education and income and to whether the congregation is located in a suburb. Number of hours spent volunteering per week is significantly associated only with income; number of memberships in civic and other voluntary organizations, however, is significantly related to size of congregation, when one controls for these other factors (it is also positively associated with higher levels of education and income).

37. In a multiple regression analysis of the Civic Involvement Survey data, the relationship (beta) between the number from a list of twelve service activities that

members reported their church helping to sponsor and the size of the congregation was .327, controlling for location of the congregation (city, suburb, or small town) and for the education and income levels of the respondent.

38. Controlling for location of congregation, size, and education and income of respondent, the number of volunteer activities in which respondents have engaged in the past year is positively associated with the number of service programs sponsored by their congregation (beta = .324, significant beyond the .001 level of probability).

39. The social service activities of congregations are examined in Virginia A. Hodgkinson and Murray S. Weitzman, *From Belief to Commitment: The Community Service Activities and Finances of Religious Congregations in the United States,* 23–24; for each of the more than thirty specific activities included in the study, large congregations were more likely to be engaged than small or medium-sized congregations (the study did not distinguish between Protestant churches and Catholic parishes). In my survey, respondents were asked about activities their congregations "help to sponsor" in order to heighten the chances that members of small congregations acting in cooperation with other churches might respond affirmatively; still, the differences were considerable; for instance, the respective percentages in large, medium, and small congregations that responded affirmatively to each of the following were day care activities, 61, 45, 29; tutoring programs, 43, 31, 24; helping low-income families, 45, 20, 12; AIDS-related activities, 41, 41, 27; food distribution to the needy, 93, 87, 80; recovery programs for alcoholics, 55, 29, 24; job-seekers' programs, 45, 20, 13; counseling, 79, 71, 59; ministries to prisoners, 52, 32, 20.

40. The respective percentages for participating in a coalition with other churches were large, 66; medium, 52; small, 40; and for engaging in service activities with other nonprofit organizations, 55, 51, and 32.

41. In another paper, I have examined the differences in civic involvement among evangelical churches that are organized around a congregational model of polity and mainline Protestant churches that are organized around a federated model of polity, showing that the former are more likely to promote activities within the congregation, while the latter are more likely to encourage involvement in other community organizations; see Wuthnow, "Mobilizing Civic Engagement: The Changing Impact of Religious Involvement."

42. Examples of how these financial commitments may limit social ministries are presented in Wuthnow, *The Crisis in the Churches.*

43. In my 1991 survey of the U.S. labor force (described in *God and Mammon in America*), I asked about congregation size and financial contributions of members. In congregations with one thousand or more members, average giving was $2,429, compared with $1,204 in congregations of from two hundred to less than one thousand members and $1,044 in congregations with less than two hundred members; as a proportion of reported family income, the respective figures (based on 558 cases) were 4.6 percent, 2.0 percent, and 2.9 percent. A possible reason for these differences: in large congregations, 50 percent of members said they had heard a sermon about personal finances in the past year, compared to 40 percent in medium-sized congregations and only 36 percent in small congregations.

44. Wuthnow, *Crisis in the Churches;* John D. McCarthy and Jim Castelli, *Religion-sponsored Social Service Providers: The Not-So-Independent Sector.*

45. Some suggestive observations on the role of size in Jewish congregations are given in Robert C. Liebman, "Finding a Place: The Vision of *Havurah.*"

46. In the Civic Involvement Survey, the mean number of volunteer activities in which individuals had been engaged in the past year in large, medium-sized, and small parishes, respectively, were 2.7, 2.1, and 1.2; the mean number of programs that the parishes helped to sponsor were 5.6, 4.8, and 4.5.

47. For comparisons of congregations in different kinds of communities, see Nancy Tatom Ammerman, *Congregation and Community.*

48. I am grateful to Susan Eckstein of Boston University for sharing her preliminary findings from a study of volunteering in an Italian American working-class community in Boston; the generalizations in the text are also drawn from qualitative interviews conducted as part of my research on civic involvement.

49. See especially Eiesland, "Contending with a Giant."

50. On mistrust, see Tim Nelson, "The Church and the Street: Race, Class, and Congregation."

51. For an example, see Wuthnow, *The Crisis in the Churches,* ch. 3.

52. On the role of inner-city churches, see Wuthnow, *Loose Connections,* especially ch. 5.

53. I have written about support groups as agencies that both facilitate and ease the dislocations of social fluidity in *Sharing the Journey: Support Groups and America's New Quest for Community.*

54. From personal conversations with Loren Mead, Carl H. George, and several other church planners.

55. Ongoing research on new immigrant congregations by R. Stephen Warner and Helen Rose Ebaugh is particularly relevant; see also Kelly H. Chong, "Religion, Ethnicity, Authority: Evangelical Protestantism and the Construction of Ethnic Identity and Boundaries among Second-Generation Korean-Americans"; Won Moo Huhr and Kwang Chung Kim, "Religious Participation of Korean Immigrants in the United States."

56. This point is well argued by McCarthy and Castelli, *Religion-sponsored Social Service Providers.*

57. Using logit regression analysis, I examined five social characteristics that are associated with low levels of volunteering, comparing how these characteristics functioned among people who belonged to no congregation and among people who were members of any Protestant congregation (controlling for education and gender). Belonging to a congregation appears to function best as a substitute for being integrated into one's neighborhood; thus, among nonmembers, the odds of having done volunteer work during the past year were only .422 as great among those who knew few of their neighbors as among those who knew more of their neighbors, whereas among Protestant members, this figure was .664 (both coefficients are significant at the .05 level). Substantively, these figures suggest that knowing one's neighbors makes less difference to volunteering if one is a church member than if one is not. Being a church member also seemed to reduce the negative effect on volunteering of being unemployed and of being African American. But it did not change the negative effect of having a low income. A somewhat more consistently positive picture of the effect of church membership on learning civic skills is pre-

sented in Sidney Verba, Kay Lehman Schlozman, and Henry E. Brady, *Voice and Equality: Civic Voluntarism in American Politics,* although their findings also suggest exceptions.

11. DEMOCRACY, INCLUSIVE AND EXCLUSIVE

1. Michael Sandel, *Democracy's Discontent.*
2. Gérard Noiriel, *Le creuset français.*

12. RAISING GOOD CITIZENS IN A BAD SOCIETY

1. Erik Erikson, *Insight and Responsibility,* 152–153.
2. Hannah Arendt, "The Crisis in Education," 132.
3. Ibid., 196.
4. Robert N. Bellah, Richard Madsen, William M. Sullivan, Ann Swidler, and Steven M. Tipton, *The Good Society,* 274.
5. Robert N. Bellah, *The Broken Covenant: American Civil Religion in Time of Trial.*
6. G. W. F. Hegel, "Philosophy of Right and Law," 269; emphasis in the original translation.
7. M. Gottdeiner and George Kephart, "The Multinucleated Metropolitan Region: A Comparative Analysis."
8. I have changed names of people and places, and some distinctive features of the setting and individuals, to protect the anonymity of those portrayed in both studies. The studies of "Amargo" come from Nina Eliasoph, *Avoiding Politics: How Americans Produce Apathy in Everyday Life.*
9. Robert Putnam, "Bowling Alone: America's Declining Social Capital"; *Making Democracy Work.*
10. Derek Phillips, *Looking Backward: A Critical Appraisal of Communitarian Thought.*
11. Paul Lichterman, *The Search for Political Community: American Activists Reinventing Commitment,* calls this the "see-saw model."
12. Robert N. Bellah, Richard Madsen, William M. Sullivan, Ann Swidler, and Steven M. Tipton, *Habits of the Heart,* 183.
13. See also Christopher Lasch's "The Communitarian Critique of Liberalism" and *The True and Only Heaven.*
14. J. L. Austin, *How to Do Things with Words.*
15. Erving Goffman, *The Presentation of Self in Everyday Life.*
16. In Nina Eliasoph, "Making a Fragile Public: A Talk-Centered Study of Citizenship and Power," I gather together more direct evidence for these dramatic shifts between backstage and front stage speech.
17. Alberto Melucci, *The Playing Self;* Anthony Giddens, *Modernity and Self-Identity;* Zygmunt Bauman, *Postmodern Ethics.*
18. See Charles Taylor's discussion of this dilemma in *Sources of the Self: The Making of Modern Identity,* 491.
19. Arendt, "The Crisis in Education," 189.
20. Both Jean Elshtain, "Political Children," and J. Peter Euben, *Corrupting Youth:*

Political Education, Democratic Culture, and Political Theory, make this point in very sensitive ways.

21. Henry Jenkins, "Introduction: Childhood Innocence and Other Modern Myths."

22. Emile Durkheim, *Moral Education,* 79.

23. Ibid., 20. (This collection was originally written as lectures in 1902–3 and published posthumously in 1922.)

24. This is not the place to review this vast body of work. If anything is a constant in American secular moral education, it is worry—from the writings of the nineteenth-century educator Horace Mann down to former Secretary of Education William Bennett. As David Purpel and Kevin Ryan say in an often-quoted essay, moral education "comes with the territory" (in Durkheim, Moral Education, 9). It is impossible to avoid; it happens in gym class, on the playground, at lunch; the puzzle is how to go about it in a country with no state religion.

25. In "Close to Home: The Work of Avoiding Politics" and in Avoiding Politics.

26. In *No Reason to Talk about It: Families Confront the Nuclear Taboo,* David Greenwald and Steven Zeitlin's family interviews show especially poignantly the deep, jarring psychological conflict between children's drive to learn and adults' drive to protect children.

27. For instance, Robert Lane, *Political Ideology;* Bellah et al., *Habits of the Heart;* David Halle, *America's Working Man;* Jennifer Hochschild, *What's Fair?*

28. Michael Schudson, *The Good Citizen: A History of American Civic Life.*

29. Putnam, "Bowling Alone"; *Making Democracy Work.*

30. Bellah and coauthors; Alexis de Tocqueville, *Democracy in America;* John Stuart Mill, *On Liberty;* John Dewey, *The Public and Its Problems;* Hannah Arendt, *The Human Condition;* Jürgen Habermas, *Theory of Communicative Action,* vols. 1 and 2; and others.

31. Theda Skocpol, "Civic America Today."

32. Michael Walzer, "The Civil Society Argument."

33. Samuel Oliner and Pearl Oliner, *The Altruistic Personality.*

34. Jacques Donzelot, *Policing the Family.*

35. Brian O'Connell, "What Voluntary Activity Can and Cannot Do for America."

36. Christopher Lasch, *The New Radicalism in America, 1889–1963: The Intellectual as a Social Type;* and Paul Lichterman, "Elusive Togetherness: Religion in the Quest for Civic Renewal."

37. Ann Swidler, "Culture in Action."

38. Bellah et al., *The Good Society.*

39. An absolutely crucial question I am leaving out is how these settings might help people weld themselves into a powerful political force; this potential is a defining feature of the classic public sphere. Perhaps the question is whether what James Scott, in *Domination and the Arts of Resistance: Hidden Transcripts,* calls a "hidden transcript" can overtake the "public transcript." Some of the settings I am describing have little access to wide publicity.

40. Exploring these actually existing connections between public and private, which people implicitly make in everyday life, is one way of addressing the questions raised by various theorists; while thinking through this project, I especially have the works of Nancy Fraser, Jeff Weintraub, and Bonnie Honig in mind.

41. Steven Rathgeb Smith, "Civic Infrastructure in America: The Interrelationship between Government and the Voluntary Sector." Similarly, in *The Necessity of Politics*, Christopher Beem recaptures Tocqueville from the Right's anti-political agenda; Beem correctly argues that Tocqueville's (as well as Hegel's) concept of civil society had politics and the state at its center.

42. Sidney Verba, Kay Schlozman, and Henry Brady, *Voice and Equality*, also documents the growth of "check writing" and the decline of face-to-face participation.

43. I am referring, of course, to Habermas's "system/lifeworld" distinction (*Theory of Communicative Action*). My point is that this boundary is not an object in the world, but one that people continually create and question and make real and question again. (Craig Calhoun, *Critical Social Theory: Culture, History and the Challenge of Difference*, makes this point well.)

44. Elihu Katz and S. N. Eisenstadt, "Some Sociological Observations on the Response of Israeli Organizations to New Immigrants"; and Elihu Katz and Brenda Danet, "Bureaucracy as a Problem for Sociology and Society."

45. Charles Fox and Hugh Miller, *Postmodern Public Administration: Toward Discourse;* John Forester, *The Deliberative Practitioner: Encouraging Participatory Planning Processes.*

46. Arendt, "Crisis in Education," 195.

47. Nel Noddings, "Conversation as Moral Education."

48. Maria Powell, "Truth and Consequences in 'Testing the Waters.'"

49. Michael Olneck, "Terms of Inclusion: Has Multiculturalism Redefined Equality in American Education?"

50. See Grant Reeher and Joseph Cammarano (eds.), *Education for Citizenship: Ideas and Innovations in Political Learning,* and Jacques Benninga (ed.), *Moral, Character, and Civic Education in the Elementary School,* for some thoughtful service-learning efforts.

51. Bellah, *The Broken Covenant.*

52. Alvin Gouldner, *The Future of Intellectuals and the Rise of the New Class.*

53. Bellah, "Between Religion and Social Science," 246.

13. ON BEING A CHRISTIAN AND AN AMERICAN

1. Stanley Hauerwas, "A Tale of Two Stories: On Being a Christian and a Texan," 25–45.

2. I recently received a letter from a friend that nicely expresses my own ambivalent reactions to the current United States of America. My friend is not a Christian but a committed Aristotelian. In his letter, he said:

> I flew to L.A. with my father for my brother's wedding. The ceremony in my brother's back yard was one of the weirdest I ever attended, performed by an "ordained minister" in a strange California New Age group that my new sister-in-law is involved in called "The Movement for Spiritual Inner Awareness." I had to bite my lip to keep myself from laughing. On reflection, however, there's something seriously wrong with a culture that can abide this sort of crap. It was an object lesson in how right Harold Bloom was in marking gnosticism as "the American religion." It also reinforced my commitment to philosophy as an important hedge against gnosticism, since even the most die-hard Plo-

tinian anti-materialist will be constrained to arguing his or her point rather than assuming it is pneumatically self-evident. Bah.

You can probably garner from the above that I am not in a particularly jovial mood. Certain circumstances surrounding the wedding have depressed and soured me, and a great number of the guests at the wedding had characters that bothered me no end. America is a civilization that makes it very difficult indeed to take one's life seriously, and while I hate being haughty (or crabby), I find most of my fellow countrymen and women rather hard to take of late. I am far too much of a tight-ass (and proud of it, too) to feel terribly comfortable here. I admire the reticence and lack of ostentatious self-display you find in most Europeans and Asians as much as I disdain the shallowness and "fun-loving" mindset of many of my compatriots. (I always thought "fun-loving" to be a disguised insult.) The plane ride home was a bit of an epiphany, because the weather was clear from L.A. to N.Y. and I spent most of my time just scanning the amazingly diverse and astonishingly beautiful landscape: the aspens were turning gold in the Rockies, the maples and oaks were bright red in the Alleghenies, and I had bird's-eye views of both L.A. and N.Y.C., the latter being especially beautiful at 20,000 feet. What you have in America is almost unbearably intense scenic beauty, virtually everywhere, combined with an almost equally intense social, political, cultural and moral ugliness. (Well, maybe not "ugliness" but emptiness.) My wife is always quick to point out the perils of this "grass is always greener" attitude I am apt to fall into, and she's surely right about it. Nevertheless I don't think I'm entirely wrong either.

3. For a more developed account of this theme, see my "Why Christian Ethics Is Such a Bad Idea" and "Christian Ethics in America (and the JRE): A Report on a Book I Will Not Write."

4. It is not just that Niebuhr had no or little role for the church in his thought; but it is by no means clear what status his theological claims have. In an extraordinary paragraph (p. xxvi) in the preface to the 1964 edition of *The Nature and Destiny of Man,* Niebuhr observes about his book:

> I placed a special emphasis on the eschatology of the New Testament with its special symbols of the Christ and anti-Christ, taking them as symbols of the fact that both good and evil grow in history, and that evil has no separate history, but that a greater evil is always a corruption of a greater good. I believe that the perils of a nuclear age substantiate this interpretation much more vividly than I expected when I presented the thesis. But I am now not so sure that the historic symbols will contribute much to the understanding by modern man of his tragic and ironic history with its refutation of the messianic and utopian hopes of the Renaissance and Enlightenment.

That Christ only stands on the edge of history was always clear in Niebuhr's work, but that one may not need even the "symbol" is something else again. Interpreted as charitably as possible, one can only assume that this observation is not about Christ, but rather the "understanding by modern man."

5. See, for example, Edmund Santurri, "Rawlsian Liberalism, Moral Truth, and Augustinian Politics." Santurri argues that Christians have a stake in a Rawlsian political strategy to the extent the latter can be saved from Rorty-like skepticism by providing an Augustinian justification. Yet the truth Santurri thinks Augustine supplies is that "order is better than disorder." I find it hard to understand why Augustine is thought necessary to sustain that "truth." Santurri's article is followed by commentaries by David Dawson, Jean Elshtain, Timothy Jackson, Gilbert Meilaender, and Michael White.

6. Nicholas Wolterstorff, *From Presence to Practice: Mind, World, and Entitlement to Believe.* I am indebted to Wolterstorff for making his manuscript available to me. The quote appears on p. 353 of the manuscript.

7. Ibid., 358.

8. Martin Marty, *The One and the Many: America's Struggle for the Common Good.*

9. Ibid., 71–72.

10. Ibid., 22.

11. Ibid., 74–76.

12. Ibid., 120–129.

13. Ibid., 154.

14. Ibid., 225.

15. Alasdair MacIntyre, "How to Be a North American," 16.

16. I originally thought I might use this essay to explore the difference between the hyphens—that is, the difference between what it means to be, for example, a German-American and a Christian-German and/or Christian-American. That America alienates us from our story of origin is not unique, because so does Christianity. Indeed, I suspect one of the problems for Christians in America is the temptation to confuse those two quite different alienations.

17. Alasdair MacIntyre, "The American Idea." This article as well as "How To Be a North American" need to be more widely known as they would make easy dismissals of MacIntyre's philosophical arguments much more difficult.

18. Ibid., 61. I should note that MacIntyre makes clear that what he calls "the American idea" is not a single or unitary reality but presents very different aspects from different points of view and at different times.

19. Ibid., 66. MacIntyre cites as "successes" the increase in the number of Americans who graduate from high school, the number of African Americans who graduate from college, and the availability of health care to the poor. MacIntyre is, also, particularly critical of those forms of anti-Americanism, characteristic of Europeans, that seek to make America the scapegoat for the sins of Western modernity. Such anti-Americanism is a sign of failure to recognize that in the "democracies of the West you cannot reject America because in the end, if you are honest, America is you. Every American has two nationalities, his own and that from which his or her ancestors originally sprang, whether in Europe, Asia, Africa, or in North America itself. But the counterpart to this is that free persons anywhere also have two nations, whether they like it or not—their own and the United States" (ibid., 68). MacIntyre is not suggesting, I think, that this is a "good thing" but rather that this is the way things are. As I suggested above, the way America alienates us from our origin is quite interesting to compare to how becoming a Christian alienates us from our past. I think the difference is quite simple—the church is not a utopian possibility but a concrete community across time.

20. Ibid., 61.

21. The "we," of course, needs to be specified. MacIntyre maintains that the boundaries of a culture cannot be identified with political boundaries. This is particularly important for Americans since we must realize that "there is no adequate way of telling our common story unless we understand how to relate to Mexican understandings of Mexican history and to Canadian understandings of Canadian his-

tory, whether of Québecois or of English-speaking Canadians." MacIntyre, "How to Be a North American," 14.

22. For a fascinating argument to reclaim history as a moral enterprise, see David Harlan, *The Degradation of American History*. There Harlan notes:

> American culture cannot be thought of as a single conversation carried on by a limited number of distinct and autonomous voices. It is not, as the champions of multiculturalism contend, that American culture has become too pluralistic and diversified to carry on such a conversation—as if we had become a collection of isolated, marginalized, and exotically distinct subcultures, each one speaking its own private language. In fact, it is pretty much the opposite, for all those putatively distinct subcultures have actually been commingling in the night, combining and coalescing with an unrelenting ferocity. . . . This is the point at which Eliot and even Oakeshott fail us. If we are to have the predecessors we need, we must find them ourselves—find them and arrange them such that we can see ourselves as the latest in a long sequence or tradition of such thinkers. (pp. 206–207)

That is the task of history according to Harlan. He is quite pessimistic that history as a social science is capable of such a role.

23. MacIntyre, "How to Be a North American," 18. MacIntyre is surely right to praise the Vietnam War Memorial, but I think much more can be said about the monument's significance. That the monument pulls us into itself while we see ourselves reflected in the black marble is surely a representation of how we were drawn into the war. Most of us were spectators to the deaths of those whose names are now on the wall. It is right therefore to see ourselves reflected in their deaths. Moreover, the long, slow path out of Vietnam mimics the long, slow path into the war. That the monument is, moreover, a slash into the earth is not accidental. The blood spilled in Vietnam by American and Vietnamese surely cries out from the ground itself. It is the voice of Abel. Of course, such a reading of the memorial is made possible by the Bible. MacIntyre has no reason to resist such a reading, though others might.

24. Ibid., 18.

25. Some no doubt would assume that the war in Vietnam constitutes such a wrong, but I do not. The way the United States exited that war may well constitute such a wrong. Slavery and the genocide against the native Americans are certainly points that make us begin to think about such wrongs.

26. Thomas E. Jenkins, *The Character of God: Recovering the Lost Literary Power of American Protestantism*, 21.

27. Ibid., 137–138.

28. William James, *The Varieties of Religious Experience*, 425.

29. Jenkins, *The Character of God*, 169.

30. James (in his quite wonderfully obtuse restraint) observes when considering the character of what "over-beliefs" one might hold: "It would never do for us to place ourselves offhand at the position of a particular theology, the Christian theology, for example, and proceed immediately to define the 'more' as Jehovah, and the 'union' as his imputation to us of the righteousness of Christ. That would be unfair to other religions, and, for our present standpoint at least, would be an over-belief." *Varieties of Religious Understanding*, 431.

14. POLITICS AS THE "PUBLIC USE OF REASON"

1. Immanuel Kant, "What Is Enlightenment?"

2. Jürgen Habermas has described this process in *The Structural Transformation of the Public Sphere: An Inquiry into a Category of Bourgeois Society.*

3. Alexander Hamilton, John Jay, and James Madison, *The Federalist Papers*, no. 1.

4. Alexander Hamilton, *Federalist Papers*, no. 35.

5. Eric Hobsbawm, *The Age of Extremes: A History of the World, 1914–1991*, 257–336.

6. Ronald Inglehart, *The Silent Revolution: Changing Values and Skills in Advanced Industrial Society.*

7. Daniel T. Rogers, *Atlantic Crossings: Social Politics in a Progressive Age.*

8. Harold Perkin, *The Rise of Professional Society: England since 1880*, 357.

9. Robert Skidelsky, *John Maynard Keynes: The Economist as Saviour, 1920–1937*, 407.

10. Ibid., 408.

11. Ibid., 8.

12. The quotations are from "Economic Possibilities for Our Grandchildren," cited by Robert Skidelsky in "Two Cheers for Consumerism."

13. Rodgers, *Atlantic Crossings*, 498. See also Olivier Zunz, *Why the American Century?* 88–92.

14. Louis Galambos and Joseph Pratt, *The Rise of the Corporate Commonwealth: United States Business and Public Policy in the Twentieth Century*, 133–137.

15. Ibid., 180.

16. Robert Wiebe, *Self-Rule: A Cultural History of American Democracy*, esp. 141–149.

17. Zunz, *American Century*, 4–23.

18. Ibid., 91.

19. This is one of the key concepts put forward in the analysis of contemporary American life in *The Good Society* by Robert N. Bellah, Richard Madsen, William M. Sullivan, Ann Swidler, and Steven M. Tipton.

20. Wiebe, *Self-Rule*, 182–183.

21. Seymour Martin Lipset, *The First New Nation: The United States in Historical and Comparative Perspective*, xxxvi. See also Lipset, *American Exceptionalism: A Two-Edged Sword.*

22. Lipset, *American Exceptionalism.*

23. Ernst Troeltsch, *Religion in History*, 221.

24. Ibid., 220.

25. This point has been emphasized in criticism of these features of British society as essentially anti-modern by Martin J. Wiener, *English Culture and the Decline of the Industrial Spirit, 1850–1980*, 22–23.

EPILOGUE: MEANING AND MODERNITY

1. Robert N. Bellah, "Religious Evolution."

2. Karl Jaspers, *The Origin and Goal of History.*

3. One might mention, among many relevant works, especially S. N. Eisenstadt (ed.), *The Origins and Diversity of Axial Age Civilizations.*

4. Max Weber, *The Protestant Ethic and the Spirit of Capitalism,* 181.

5. Charles Taylor, *Sources of the Self,* 209.

6. Philip Gorski, "The Protestant Ethic Revisited: Disciplinary Revolution and State Formation in Holland and Prussia."

7. S. N. Eisenstadt, "Origins of the West: The Origin of the West in Recent Macrosociological Theory: The Protestant Ethic Reconsidered."

8. Bellah, "Religious Evolution," 42–44.

9. Robert N. Bellah, "Civil Religion in America." Reprinted as ch. 9 of Bellah, *Beyond Belief: Essays on Religion in a Post-Traditional World.*

10. Robert N. Bellah, *Tokugawa Religion.*

11. Robert N. Bellah, "Values and Social Change in Modern Japan." The second and third lectures were published under the same title as ch. 7 in Bellah, *Beyond Belief.*

12. S. N. Eisenstadt, *Japanese Civilization.*

13. That the article remained controversial was brought home to me by the fact that those who opposed my appointment to the School of Social Science at the Institute for Advanced Study at Princeton in 1973 used this article as evidence of my obvious incompetence.

14. Robert N. Bellah, *The Broken Covenant: American Civil Religion in Time of Trial.*

15. Ibid., 39.

16. Robert N. Bellah, "Religion and the Legitimation of the American Republic." Reprinted as the Afterword to the University of Chicago Press 1992 edition of *The Broken Covenant.*

17. Andrew Delbanco, *The Real American Dream: A Meditation on Hope,* 95.

18. Robert N. Bellah, "Comment on James A. Mathisen, 'Twenty Years after Bellah: Whatever Happened to American Civil Religion.'"

19. Robert N. Bellah, Richard Madsen, William M. Sullivan, Ann Swidler, and Steven M. Tipton, *Habits of the Heart: Individualism and Commitment in American Life,* 1985 (paperback edition with a new introduction, 1996).

20. I think of two papers published in the *Journal of the American Academy of Religion:* Robert N. Bellah, "Is There a Common American Culture?" and Robert N. Bellah, "Max Weber and World-Denying Love: A Look at the Historical Sociology of Religion."

21. Delbanco, *The Real American Dream.*

22. Francisco O. Ramirez and John Boli, "On the Union of States and Schools," 194.

23. Sacvan Bercovitch, *The Puritan Origins of the American Self,* 110.

24. Ibid., 20.

25. William James, *The Varieties of Religious Experience,* 34–35. Charles Taylor offers a useful brief commentary on *Varieties* in his "Transformations in Religious Experience: The William James Lecture," 18–20. Taylor here stresses the contemporaneity of James's views just in the degree to which the personal is favored over the institutional.

26. Bercovitch, *Puritan Origins,* 11.

27. Delbanco, *The Real American Dream*, 103.

28. Delbanco, who started his scholarly career as a student of New England Puritanism, uses this very Puritan term to characterize the historical course he is describing: *The Real American Dream*, 41–42. His story is not pessimistic, however, as he believes that the hunger for meaning, unappeased by exclusive concentration on the self, will eventually lead Americans to larger concerns.

29. Stanley Hauerwas has given us hints concerning his ecclesiology in two recent books: *In Good Company: The Church as Polis*, especially ch. 1; and *Sanctify Them in the Truth: Holiness Exemplified*, especially chs. 4, 9, and 11, and in the sermons in part 4. It is clear from these references that Hauerwas is not happy with the idea of the church as a voluntary association, nor does he accept the distinction between the visible and the invisible church. He writes mainly about the local church, but it is hard to think that his ideal church polity would be strictly congregational.

30. Delbanco, *The Real American Dream*, 11.

31. Robert Wuthnow, *Loose Connections: Civic Involvement in America's Fragmented Communities*.

32. See, for example, John Meyer, "Self and Life Course: Institutionalization and Its Effects."

33. Wade Clark Roof, *Spiritual Marketplace: Baby Boomers and the Remaking of American Religion*, 85.

34. Robert Reich, *The Next American Frontier*, 81.

35. Delbanco, *The Real American Dream*, 74, and elsewhere. Delbanco's measured treatment of Lincoln is exemplary.

36. Karl Polanyi, *The Great Transformation*.

37. Thomas L. Friedman, *The Lexus and the Olive Tree*.

38. In *Habits of the Heart* we tried to assess our cultural resources, and in *The Good Society* we argued that good institutions are the basis of any viable society.

39. Alasdair MacIntyre, *Dependent Rational Animals*, 85.

40. Frans de Waal, *Good Natured: The Origins of Right and Wrong in Humans and Other Animals*.

41. Xiao Yang, "Trying to Do Justice to the Concept of Justice in Confucian Ethics."

42. See James Stockinger's critique of Locke, as cited in *The Good Society*, 104.

BIBLIOGRAPHY

Adkins, Arthur W. H. *Merit and Responsibility*. Oxford: Oxford University Press, 1960.
———. *Moral Values and Political Behavior in Ancient Greece*. New York: W. W. Norton, 1972.
Allinson, Gary D. "Citizenship, Fragmentation, and the Negotiated Polity." In *Political Dynamics in Contemporary Japan*. Edited by Gary D. Allinson and Yasunori Sone. Ithaca and London: Cornell University Press, 1993.
Ammerman, Nancy Tatom. *Congregation and Community*. New Brunswick: Rutgers University Press, 1997.
Anquez, Léonce. *Histoire des assemblées protestantes*. Geneva: Slatkine Reprints, 1970 [1859].
Appleby, Joyce. *Liberalism and Republicanism in the Historical Imagination*. Cambridge, Mass.: Harvard University Press, 1992.
———. "New Cultural Heroes in the Early National Period." In *The Culture of the Market: Historical Essays*. Edited by Thomas L. Haskell and Richard F. Teichgraeber III, 163–188. Cambridge: Cambridge University Press, 1995.
Arendell, Terry. *Divorce: Women and Children Last*. Berkeley and Los Angeles: University of California Press, 1986.
Arendt, Hannah. "The Crisis in Education." In *Between Past and Future*. New York: Penguin, 1977.
———. *The Human Condition*. Chicago: University of Chicago Press, 1958.
Arieli, Yehoshua. *Individualism and Nationalism in American Ideology*. Cambridge, Mass.: Harvard University Press, 1964.
Aries, Philippe. *Centuries of Childhood*. New York: Knopf, 1962.
Armstrong, Louis. "(What Did I Do to Be So) Black and Blue." In *Giants of Jazz: Louis Armstrong*, by *Time-Life*, STL-Jo1 P3 14674, 1978.
Austin, J. L. *How to Do Things with Words*. Oxford: Oxford University Press, 1965.
Bailyn, Bernard. *The Ideological Origins of the American Revolution*. Cambridge, Mass.: Harvard University Press, 1992.

Ball, Terence. *Reappraising Political Theory: Revisionist Studies in the History of Political Thought.* Oxford: Oxford University Press, 1995.

Ball, Terence, and J. G. A. Pocock, eds. *Conceptual Change and the Constitution.* Lawrence: University of Kansas Press, 1988.

Balmer, Randall. *Grant Us Courage: Travels along the Mainline of American Protestantism.* New York: Oxford University Press, 1996.

———. *Mine Eyes Have Seen the Glory: A Journey into the Evangelical Subculture in America.* New York: Oxford University Press, 1989.

Banfield, Edward C. *Political Influence: A New Theory of Urban Politics.* New York: Free Press, 1961.

Bardach, Juliusz. "L'élections des députés à l'ancienne diète polonaise, fin XVe–XVIIIe Siècles." *Parliaments, Estates and Representation,* 5, 1 (June 1985): 45–59.

———. "Gouvernants et gouvernés en Pologne au Moyen-Âge et aux temps modernes." In *Gouvernés et gouvernants: Recueils de la société Jean Bodin pour l'histoire comparée,* vol. 4, 255–285. Brussels: De Boeck University, 1965.

Bauman, Zygmunt. *Postmodern Ethics.* Cambridge, Mass.: Blackwell, 1993.

Baumgartner, Frederic J. *Radical Reactionaries: The Political Thought of the French Catholic League.* Geneva: Librairie Droz, 1975.

Beem, Christopher. *The Necessity of Politics: Reclaiming American Public Life.* Chicago: University of Chicago Press, 1999.

Bell, Daniel. "'American Exceptionalism' Revisited: The Role of Civil Society." *The Public Interest* 95 (1989): 38–56.

Bellah, Robert N. *Beyond Belief: Essays on Religion in a Post-Traditional World.* New York: Harper and Row, 1970.

———. *The Broken Covenant: American Civil Religion in Time of Trial.* New York: Seabury Press, 1975.

———. *Tokugawa Religion: The Culture of Modern Japan.* New York: Free Press, 1985.

———. *Tokugawa Religion: The Values of Pre-Industrial Japan.* Glencoe, Ill.: Free Press, 1957.

———. "Beyond Economic Competitiveness: Education for Citizenship and Democracy." Speech given at the National Catholic Education Association/Department of Chief Administrators of Catholic Education Annual Meeting, Pittsburgh, October 20, 1992.

———. "Civil Religion in America." *Daedalus* 96:1 (1967): 1–21.

———. Comment on James A. Mathisen, "Twenty Years after Bellah: Whatever Happened to American Civil Religion." *Sociological Analysis* 50:2 (1989): 147.

———. "Is There a Common American Culture?" *Journal of the American Academy of Religion* 66:3 (Fall 1998): 613–625.

———. "Max Weber and World-Denying Love: A Look at the Historical Sociology of Religion." *Journal of the American Academy of Religion* 67:2 (1999): 277–304.

———. "New Religious Consciousness and the Crisis in Modernity." In *The New Religious Consciousness.* Edited by Charles Y. Glock and Robert N. Bellah. Berkeley and Los Angeles: University of California Press, 1976.

———. "Religion and the Legitimation of the American Republic." In *Varieties of Civil Religion,* by Robert N. Bellah and Philip E. Hammond. New York: Harper and Row, 1980.

————. "Religion and the Legitimation of the American Republic." *Society* 15:4 (1978): 16–23.

————. "Religious Evolution." *American Sociological Review* 29:3 (1964): 358–374.

————. "Values and Social Change in Modern Japan." *Asian Cultural Studies* [International Christian University, Tokyo] 3 (1963):13–56.

————, ed. *Emile Durkheim on Morality and Society.* Chicago: University of Chicago Press, 1973.

Bellah, Robert N., Richard Madsen, William M. Sullivan, Ann Swidler, and Steven M. Tipton. *The Good Society.* New York: Alfred A. Knopf, 1991.

————. *Habits of the Heart: Individualism and Commitment in American Life.* New York: Harper and Row, 1986 [1985].

————. *Habits of the Heart: Individualism and Commitment in American Life.* Berkeley: University of California Press, 1996 [1985].

————. "Individualism and the Crisis of Civic Membership." *Christian Century,* May 8, 1996, 514–515.

Benedict, Philip. *Rouen during the Wars of Religion.* Cambridge: Cambridge University Press, 1981.

Benhabib, Seyla. *Situating the Self.* New York: Routledge, 1992.

Bennett, Lerone, Jr. "Howard Thurman: Twentieth-Century Holy Man." *Ebony* 33:4 (February 1978): 76, 84.

Bennett, William J. "Moral Corruption in America." *Commentary,* November 1995, 29.

Benninga, Jacques, ed. *Moral, Character, and Civic Education in the Elementary School.* New York: Columbia University Teachers College Press, 1991.

Bentham, Jeremy. *An Introduction to the Principles of Morals and Legislation.* Edited by Wilfrid Harrison. Oxford: Basil Blackwell, 1948.

Bercovitch, Sacvan. "Afterword." In *Ideology and Classic American Literature.* Edited by Sacvan Bercovitch and M. Jehy. Cambridge: Cambridge University Press, 1996.

————. "New England's Errand Reappraised." In *New Directions in American Intellectual History.* Edited by John Higham and Paul K. Conkin, 85–104. Baltimore: Johns Hopkins University Press, 1979.

————. *The Puritan Origins of the American Self.* New Haven and London: Yale University Press, 1980 [1975].

Berger, Peter L., Brigitte Berger, and Hansfried Kellner. *The Homeless Mind.* New York: Vintage Books, 1974.

Bernstein, G., ed. *Recreating Japanese Women, 1600–1945.* Berkeley and Los Angeles: University of California Press, 1990.

Blacker, C. "Millenarian Aspects of the New Religions in Japan." In *Tradition and Modernization in Japanese Culture.* Edited by D. Shively. Princeton: Princeton University Press, 1971.

————. "Two Shinto Myths: The Golden Age and the Chosen People." In *Themes and Theories in Modern Japanese History: Essays in Memory of Richard Storry.* Edited by Sue Henny and Jean-Pierre Lehmann, 64–78. Atlantic Highlands, N.J.: Athlone Press, 1988.

Bloch, Ernst. *Natural Law and Human Dignity.* Cambridge, Mass.: MIT Press, 1986.

Blockmans, Wim P. "A Typology of Representative Institutions in Late Medieval Europe." *Journal of Medieval History* 4 (1978): 189–215.

Blumenberg, H. *Die Legitimat der Neuzeit.* Frankfurt: Suhrkamp, 1987.

Bonis, György. "The Hungarian Feudal Diet (Thirteenth–Eighteenth Centuries)." In *Gouvernés et gouvernants, recueils de la société Jean Bodin pour l'histoire comparée,* vol. 4, 287–307. Brussels: De Boeck University, 1965.

Bourdieu, Pierre. *Distinction: A Social Critique of the Judgement of Taste.* Translated by Richard Nice. Cambridge, Mass.: Harvard University Press, 1984.

————. *Outline of a Theory of Practice.* Cambridge: Cambridge University Press, 1977.

Boyer, Paul S. *Urban Masses and Moral Order in America, 1820–1920.* Cambridge, Mass.: Harvard University Press, 1978.

Bradburn, Norman. *The Structure of Psychological Well-Being.* Chicago: Aldine, 1969.

Breuggemann, Walter. *Theology of the Old Testament: Testimony, Dispute, Advocacy.* Minneapolis: Fortress Press, 1997.

Briggs, B. Robin. *Early Modern France.* New York and London: Oxford University Press, 1977.

Brugge in den geuzentijd. Bruges: Werkgroep Herdenkingsbundel, 1982.

Buckholter-Traschel, V. *Different Modes of Articulation of Social Protest: Social Movements in Japan.* Kyoto: Kyoto International Student House, 1984.

Butler, Jon. *Awash in a Sea of Faith.* Cambridge, Mass.: Harvard University Press, 1990.

Calhoun, Craig. *Critical Social Theory: Culture, History, and the Challenge of Difference.* Oxford: Blackwell, 1995.

Camporesi, Piero. *Bread of Dreams: Food and Fantasy in Early Modern Europe.* Chicago: University of Chicago Press, 1989.

Casanova, José. *Public Religions in the Modern World.* Chicago: University of Chicago Press, 1994.

Cassileth, Barrie R. *The Alternative Medicine Handbook: The Complete Reference Guide to Alternative and Complementary Therapies.* New York: W. W. Norton, 1998.

Cherlin, Andrew J. *Marriage, Divorce, Remarriage.* Rev. ed. Cambridge, Mass.: Harvard University Press, 1992.

Chong, Kelly H. "Religion, Ethnicity, Authority: Evangelical Protestantism and the Construction of Ethnic Identity and Boundaries among Second Generation Korean Americans." Paper presented at the Annual Meeting of the American Sociological Association, New York, 1996.

Chubb, John E., and Paul E. Peterson, eds. *Can the Government Govern?* Washington, D.C.: Brookings Institution, 1989.

Cisneros, Henry G. *Higher Ground: Faith Communities and Community Building.* Washington, D.C.: Department of Housing and Urban Development, 1996.

Cohen, Michael H. *Complementary and Alternative Medicine: Legal Boundaries and Regulatory Perspectives.* Baltimore: Johns Hopkins University Press, 1998.

Coleman, John A., S.J. "Exploding Spiritualities: Their Social Causes, Social Location, and Social Divide." *Christian Spirituality Bulletin* 5:1 (Spring 1997): 9–15.

————. *Public Discipleship: Paradenominational Groups and Citizenship.* N.p., n.d.

————. "Under the Cross and the Flag." *America,* May 11, 1996, 6–14.

Collinge, William. *The American Holistic Health Association Complete Guide to Alternative Medicine.* New York: Warner Books, 1996.

Conradt, Nancy M. "John Calvin, Theodore Beza, and the Reformation in Poland." Madison: University of Wisconsin Press, 1974.

Crew, Phyllis Mack. *Calvinist Preaching and Iconoclasm in the Netherlands, 1544–1569.* Cambridge: Cambridge University Press, 1978.

Crouzet, Denis. *Les guerriers de Dieu: La violence au temps des troubles de religion, vers 1525–vers 1610.* Seyssel: Champ Vallon, 1990.

Davies, Norman. *God's Playground: A History of Poland.* Vol. 1: *The Origins to 1795.* Oxford: Clarendon, 1981.

Davis, Natalie Z. *Society and Culture in Early Modern France.* Stanford: Stanford University Press, 1975.

De Meij, J. C. A. *De Watergeuzen en de Nederlanden, 1568–1572.* Amsterdam: Noord-Hollandsche Uitgevers Mij., 1972.

de Tocqueville, Alexis. *Democracy in America.* 2 vols. Edited by J. P. Mayer. Garden City, N.Y.: Doubleday, 1969; New York: Anchor Books, 1974; New York: Vintage Books, 1990 [1831].

Decavele, J., ed. *Het Eind van Een Rebelse Droom.* Gent: Stadsbestuur, 1984.

Delbanco, Andrew. *The Real American Dream: A Meditation on Hope.* Cambridge, Mass.: Harvard University Press, 1999.

Delumeau, Jean. *Naissance et affirmation de la Réforme.* Vol. 4. Paris: Presses Universitaires de France, 1983.

Den Tex, Jan. *Oldenbarnevelt.* Haarlem: H. D. Tjeenk Willink and Zoon, 1960–66.

Despretz, André. "De instauratie der gentse calvinistische republiek (1577–79)." *Handelingen der Maatschappij voor Geschiedenis en Oudheidskonde te Gent* 17 (1963): 119–229.

Dewey, John. *The Public and Its Problems.* Denver: Alan Swallow, 1926.

Deyon, Solange. *Les "casseurs" de l'été 1566: L'iconoclasme dans le nord.* Paris: Hachette, 1981.

Diefendorf, Barbara B. *Beneath the Cross: Catholics and Huguenots in Sixteenth-Century Paris.* New York and Oxford: Oxford University Press, 1991.

Dierickx, Michiel. *L'érection des nouveaux diocèses aux Pays-Bas, 1559–1570.* Brussels: La Renaissance du Livre, 1967.

DiMaggio, Paul, John Evans, and Bethany Bryson. "Have Americans' Social Attitudes Become More Polarized?" *American Journal of Sociology* 102:3 (November 1996): 690–755.

Dionne, E. J. *They Only Look Dead: Why Progressives Will Dominate the Next Political Era.* Rev. ed. New York: Touchstone Books, 1997.

Dobbin, Frank, John Sutton, John Meyer, and W. Richard Scott. "Formal Promotion Schemes and Equal Employment Opportunity Law: The Institutional Construction of Internal Labor Markets." *American Journal of Sociology* 99 (1993): 396–427.

Dobbin, Frank. *Forging Industrial Policy: The United States, France, and Britain in the Railway Age.* New York: Cambridge University Press, 1994.

Dodds, E. R. *The Greeks and the Irrational.* Boston: Beacon Press, 1957.

Donzelot, Jacques. *Policing the Family.* New York: Pantheon, 1979.

Douglas, Mary. "Cultural Bias." Occasional Paper no. 35. London: Royal Anthropological Institute, 1978.

———. *Essays in the Sociology of Perception.* London: Routledge and Kegan Paul, 1982.

————. *How Institutions Think.* Syracuse: Syracuse University Press, 1986.

————. *Natural Symbols.* New York: Vintage, 1973.

Douglas, Mary, and Baron Isherwood. *The World of Goods.* New York: Basic Books, 1979.

Douglas, Mary, and Aaron Wildavsky. *Risk and Culture: An Essay on the Selection of Technological and Environmental Dangers.* Berkeley and Los Angeles: University of California Press, 1982.

Douglas, Richard M. "Genus and Vocatio: Ideas of Work and Vocation in Humanist and Protestant Usage." *MIT Publications in the Humanities,* no. 71. Cambridge, Mass.: MIT Press, 1965.

Downing, Brian. *The Military Revolution and Political Change.* Princeton: Princeton University Press, 1992.

Drouot, Henri. *Mayenne et la Ligue: Étude sur la Ligue, 1587–1596.* Paris and Dijon, 1937.

Dumont, Louis. "A Modified View of Our Origins: The Christian Beginnings of Modern Individualism." *Religion* 12 (1982): 1–27.

Durkheim, Emile. *The Division of Labor in Society.* Translated by W. D. Halls. New York: Free Press, 1984.

————. *The Elementary Forms of Religious Life.* Translated by Joseph W. Swaim. New York: Free Press, 1965.

————. *The Elementary Forms of the Religious Life.* Translated by Karen E. Fields. New York: Free Press, 1995 [1912].

————. *Moral Education.* New York: Macmillan, 1961 [1922].

————. *Moral Education: A Study in the Theory and Application of the Sociology of Education.* New York: Free Press, 1973.

Edelman, Lauren B., Christopher Uggen, and Howard S. Erlanger. "The Endogeneity of Legal Regulation: Grievance Procedures as Rational Myth." *American Journal of Sociology* 105 (September 1999): 406–454.

Ehrenhalt, Alan. *The Lost City: Discovering the Forgotten Virtues of Community in Chicago of the 1950s.* New York: Basic Books, 1995.

Eiesland, Nancy L. "Contending with a Giant: The Impact of a Megachurch on Exurban Religious Institutions." In *Contemporary American Religion: An Ethnographic Reader.* Edited by Penny Edgell Becker and Nancy L. Eiesland. San Francisco: Altamira Press, 1997.

Eisenstadt, S. N. *Japanese Civilization: A Comparative View.* Chicago: University of Chicago Press, 1996.

————. "Multiple Modernities in an Age of Globalization." In *Grenzlose Gesellschaft?* Edited by Claudia Honegger, Stefan Hradil, and Franz Traxler, 37–50. Opladen: Leshe and Burdrich, 1999.

————. "Origins of the West: The Origin of the West in Recent Macrosociological Theory: The Protestant Ethic Reconsidered." *Cultural Dynamics* 2:3 (1990): 119–153.

————. *Power, Trust, and Meaning.* Chicago: University of Chicago Press, 1995.

————. *Revolution and the Transformation of Societies: A Comparative Study of Civilizations.* New York: Free Press, 1978.

————. *Tradition, Change, and Modernity.* New York: John Wiley, 1977 [1973].

———. *Die Vielfalt der Moderne: Heidelberger Max-Weber-Vorlesungen, 1997*. Berlin: Velbruck Wissenschaft, 2000.

———, ed. *The Origins and Diversity of Axial Age Civilizations*. Albany: State University of New York Press, 1986.

———. *Post-Traditional Societies*. New York: W. W. Norton, 1972.

Eisenstadt, S. N., Luis Roniger, and Adam Seligman, eds. *Centre Formation, Protest Movements, and Class Structure in Europe and the United States*. London: Frances Printer, 1987.

Eliasoph, Nina. *Avoiding Politics: How Americans Produce Apathy in Everyday Life*. New York: Cambridge University Press, 1998.

———. "Making a Fragile Public: A Talk-Centered Study of Citizenship and Power." *Sociological Theory* 14:3 (1996): 262–289.

Elshtain, Jean Bethke. "Political Children." In *Feminist Interpretations of Hannah Arendt*. Edited by Bonnie Honig, 263–284. University Park: Pennsylvania State University, 1995.

Eltis, David. *The Military Revolution in Sixteenth-Century Europe*. London and New York: I. B. Tauris, 1995.

English-Lueck, J. A. *Health in the New Age: A Study of California Holistic Practices*. Albuquerque: University of New Mexico Press, 1990.

Erikson, Erik. *Insight and Responsibility*. New York: W. W. Norton, 1964.

———. "Life Cycle." In *International Encyclopedia of the Social Sciences*. Edited by David L. Sills. New York: Macmillan/Free Press, 1968.

Ertman, Thomas. *Birth of the Leviathan: Building States and Regimes in Medieval and Early Modern Europe*. Cambridge: Cambridge University Press, 1997.

Eskenazi, Kay. *Salvation and Religious Goals in New Religions*. Berkeley: California Institute of Integral Studies, 1997.

Espenshade, Thomas J., ed. *Keys to Successful Immigration: Implications of the New Jersey Experience*. Washington, D.C.: University Press of America, 1997.

Euben, J. Peter. *Corrupting Youth: Political Education, Democratic Culture, and Political Theory*. Princeton: Princeton University Press, 1997.

Evans, R. J. W. "Calvinism in East Central Europe: Hungary and Her Neighbours." In *International Calvinism*. Edited by Menna Prestwich, 167–196. Oxford: Clarendon Press, 1985.

———. *The Making of the Habsburg Monarchy, 1550–1700*. New York: Oxford University Press, 1979.

Fischer, Claude S. "Ambivalent Communities: How Americans Understand Their Localities." In *America at Century's End*. Edited by Alan Wolfe, 79–90. Berkeley and Los Angeles: University of California Press, 1991.

Fischer, Claude S., Michael Hout, Martin Sanchez Jankowski, Samuel R. Lucas, Ann Swidler, and Kim Voss. *Inequality by Design*. Princeton: Princeton University Press, 1996.

Fluker, Walter Earl. *They Looked for a City: A Comparative Analysis of the Ideal of Community in the Thought of Howard Thurman and Martin Luther King, Jr.* New York: University Press of America, 1989.

Fluker, Walter Earl, and Catherine Tumber, eds. *A Strange Freedom: The Best of Howard Thurman on Religious Experience and Public Life*. Boston: Beacon Press, 1998.

Fockema-Andreae, S.J. *De Nederlandse Staat onder de Republiek.* Amsterdam: Noord-Hollandse Uitgevers, 1961.

Forester, John. *The Deliberative Practitioner: Encouraging Participatory Planning Processes.* Cambridge, Mass.: MIT Press, 1999.

Foucault, Michel. "Afterword: The Subject and Power." In *Michel Foucault: Beyond Structuralism and Hermeneutics.* 2d ed. Edited by Hubert Dreyfus and Paul Rabinow, 208–226. Chicago: University of Chicago Press, 1983.

————. *The Order of Things: An Archaeology of the Human Sciences.* Translated by A. Sheridan-Smith. New York: Random House, 1970.

Fox, Charles, and Hugh Miller. *Postmodern Public Administration: Toward Discourse.* Thousand Oaks, Calif.: Sage, 1995.

Fox, Paul. *The Reformation in Poland.* Baltimore: Johns Hopkins University Press, 1924.

Frankena, William K. *Ethics.* Englewood Cliffs, N.J.: Prentice-Hall, 1963.

Franklin, Julian H., ed.and trans. *Constitutionalism and Resistance in the Sixteenth Century.* New York: Pegasus, 1969.

Fraser, Nancy. "What's Critical About Critical Theory? The Case of Habermas and Gender." In *Feminism as Critique.* Edited by Seyla Benhabib and Drucilla Cornell, 31–55. Minneapolis: University of Minnesota Press, 1987.

Freud, Sigmund. *Civilization and Its Discontents.* Translated by James Strachey. New York: W. W. Norton, 1961.

Friedland, Roger, and Robert R. Alford. "Bringing Society Back In: Symbols, Practices, and Institutional Contradictions." In *The New Institutionalism in Organizational Analysis,* edited by Walter W. Powell and Paul J. DiMaggio. Chicago: University of Chicago Press, 1991.

Friedman, Thomas L. *The Lexus and the Olive Tree.* New York: Farrar, Straus and Giroux, 1999.

Fruin, Robert. *Geschiedenis der Staatsinstellingen in Nederland.* 2d rev. ed. Edited by H. T. Colenbrander. The Hague: Martinus Nijhoff, 1922.

Fukuyama, Francis. *The End of History and the Last Man.* New York: Free Press, 1992.

Furstenberg, Frank F. "The Future of Marriage." *American Demographics* (June 1996): 34–40.

Galambos, Louis, and Joseph Pratt. *The Rise of the Corporate Commonwealth: United States Business and Public Policy in the Twentieth Century.* New York: Basic Books, 1988.

Gallup, George. *The Unchurched American—Ten Years Later.* Princeton: Princeton Religious Research Center, 1988.

Gallup, George H., Jr. *Religion in America: 1996 Report.* Princeton: Princeton Religion Research Center, 1996.

Garrisson, Janine. *Les protestants du Midi.* Toulouse: Privat, 1988.

Geertz, Clifford. *The Interpretation of Cultures.* New York: Basic Books, 1973.

Gellner, Ernest. *Conditions of Liberty: Civil Society and Its Rivals.* London: Penguin, 1994.

Geyl, Pieter. *The Revolt of the Netherlands, 1555–1609.* London: Cassel 1988 [1932].

Giddens, Anthony. "Living in a Post-Traditional Society." In *Reflexive Modernization:*

Politics, Tradition, and Aesthetics in the Modern Social Order, by Ulrich Beck, Anthony Giddens, and Scott Lash, 56–109. Stanford: Stanford University Press, 1994.

———. *Modernity and Self-Identity.* Cambridge: Polity, 1991.

Gilligan, Carol. *In a Different Voice.* Cambridge, Mass.: Harvard University Press, 1982.

Glazer, Nathan. *The Limits of Social Policy.* Cambridge, Mass.: Harvard University Press, 1988.

Glendon, Mary. *Abortion and Divorce in Western Law.* Cambridge, Mass.: Harvard University Press, 1987.

Glock, Charles Y., and Robert N. Bellah, eds. *The New Religious Consciousness.* Berkeley and Los Angeles: University of California Press, 1976.

Goffman, Erving. *The Presentation of Self in Everyday Life.* Garden City, N.Y.: Doubleday, 1959.

Gorski, Karol. *Communitas Princeps Corona Regni. Studia Selecta.* Warsaw: Panstwowe Wydawnictwo Naukowe, 1976.

Gorski, Philip, "The Protestant Ethic Revisited: Disciplinary Revolution and State Formation in Holland and Prussia." *American Journal of Sociology* 99:2 (1993): 265–316.

Gottdeiner, M., and George Kephart. "The Multinucleated Metropolitan Region: A Comparative Analysis." In *Postsuburban California: The Transformation of Orange County since World War II,* by Rob Kling, Spencer Olin, and Mark Poster, 31–54. Berkeley and Los Angeles: University of California Press, 1991.

Gould, Elina H. "American Independence and Britain's Counter-Revolution." *Past and Present* 154 (1997): 107–141.

Gouldner, Alvin. *The Coming Crisis of Western Sociology.* New York: Basic Books, 1970; Avon Books, 1971.

———. *The Future of Intellectuals and the Rise of the New Class.* New York: Oxford University Press, 1979.

Gouvernés et gouvernants, recueils de la société Jean Bodin, vols. 4–5. Brussels: De Boeck Université, 1965.

Grapperhaus, H. M. *Alva en die Tiende Penning.* Deventer: Kluwer, 1982.

Greeley, Andrew. "The Other Civic America." *American Prospect* (May–June 1997): 36–39.

———. *Religious Change in America.* Cambridge, Mass.: Harvard University Press, 1989.

Greengrass, Mark. "The Anatomy of a Religious Riot in Toulouse in May 1562." *Journal of Ecclesiastical History* 34 (1983).

———. *The French Reformation.* Oxford: Basil Blackwell, 1987.

———. "The Sainte Union in the Provinces: The Case of Toulouse." *Sixteenth Century Journal* 34 (1983): 469–496.

Greenwald, David, and Steven Zeitlin. *No Reason to Talk about It: Families Confront the Nuclear Taboo.* New York: W. W. Norton, 1987.

Griffiths, G. *Representative Government in Europe in the Sixteenth Century.* Oxford: Clarendon, 1968.

Groenhuis, G. *De predikanten.* Groningen: Wolters-Noordhof, 1977.

Groenveld, S., et al. *De Tachtigjarige Oorlog.* Zutphen: De Walberg Pers, 1993.

Gunst, Péter. "Agrarian Systems of Central and Eastern Europe." In *The Origins of*

Backwardness in Eastern Europe. Edited by Daniel Chirot, 53–91. Berkeley and Los Angeles: University of California Press, 1989.

Gusfield, Joseph. "Nature's Body and the Metaphors of Food." In *Cultivating Differences.* Edited by Michele Lamont and Marcel Fournier, 75–103. Chicago: University of Chicago Press, 1992.

Habermas, Jürgen. *The Structural Transformation of the Public Sphere: An Inquiry into a Category of Bourgeois Society.* Cambridge, Mass.: MIT Press, 1989.

————. *Theory of Communicative Action.* Vols. 1 and 2. Boston: Beacon Press, 1985.

Hahlweg, Werner. *Die Heeresreform der Oranier und die Antike.* Berlin: Junker and Dünnhaupt, 1941.

Hale, J. R. *War and Society in Renaissance Europe, 1450–1620.* Baltimore: Johns Hopkins University Press, 1985.

Hall, John A., ed. *Civil Society: Theory, History, Comparison.* London: Polity Press, 1995.

Halle, David. *America's Working Man.* Chicago: University of Chicago, 1984.

Hamabata, Matthews M. "Ethnographic Boundaries: Culture, Class, and Sexuality in Tokyo." *Qualitative Sociology* 9:4 (1986): 354–371.

Hamilton, Alexander, John Jay, and James Madison. *The Federalist Papers, no. 1.* Cutchogue, N.Y.: Buccaneer Books, 1992.

Hampton, James. "Giving the Grid/Group Dimensions an Operational Definition." In *Essays in the Sociology of Perception.* Edited by Mary Douglas. London: Routledge and Kegan Paul, 1982.

Hansen, Olaf. *Aesthetic Individualism and Practical Intellect: American Allegory in Emerson, Thoreau, Adams, and James.* Princeton: Princeton University Press, 1990.

Harding, Robert R. *Anatomy of a Power Elite: The Provincial Governors of Early Modern France.* New Haven: Yale University Press, 1978.

Harlan, David. *The Degradation of American History.* Chicago: University of Chicago Press, 1997.

Harlow, Jules, ed. *Mahzor for Rosh Hashanah and Yom Kippur: A Prayer Book for the Days of Awe.* New York: Rabbinical Assembly, 1971.

Harootunian, H. 1989. "Late Tokugawa Culture and Thought." In *Cambridge History of Japan,* vol. 5: *The Nineteenth Century.* Edited by M. B. Jansen, 168–259. Cambridge: Cambridge University Press, 1989.

't Hart, Marjolein C. *The Making of a Bourgeois State: War, Politics, and Finance during the Dutch Revolt.* Manchester and New York: Manchester University Press, 1993.

't Hart, Marjolein C., Joost Jonker, and Jan Luiten Van Zanden, eds. *A Financial History of the Netherlands.* Cambridge: Cambridge University Press, 1997.

Hatch, Nathan O. *The Democratization of American Christianity.* New Haven: Yale University Press, 1991.

Hauerwas, Stanley. "Christian Ethics in America (and the JRE): A Report on a Book I Will Not Write." *Journal of Religious Ethics* (Twenty-fifth Anniversary Supplement) 25:3 (1998): 57–76.

————. *In Good Company: The Church as Polis.* South Bend, Ind.: University of Notre Dame Press, 1995.

————. *Sanctify Them in the Truth: Holiness Exemplified.* Nashville: Abingdon Press, 1998.

————. "A Tale of Two Stories: On Being a Christian and a Texan." In *Christian Ex-*

istence Today: Essays on Church, World, and Living in Between, 25–45. Durham: Labyrinth, 1988.

———. "Why Christian Ethics Is Such a Bad Idea." In *Beyond Mere Health: Theology and Health Care in a Secular Society.* Edited by Hilary Regan, Rodney Horsfield, and Gabrielle MacMullen, 64–79. Melbourne: Australian Theological Forum, 1996.

Hauser, Henri. *La naissance du Protestantisme.* 2d ed. Paris: Presses Universitaires de France, 1963.

Hegel, G. W. F. "Philosophy of Right and Law." In *The Philosophy of Hegel.* Translated by J. M. Sterrett and Carl J. Friedrich, 221–332. New York: Random House, 1954 [1821].

Hintze, Otto. "Typologie der ständischen Verfassungen des Abendlandes." *Historische Zeitschrift* 141 (1930): 229–48.

Hirsch, Paul M. *Pack Your Own Parachute: How to Survive Mergers, Takeovers, and Other Corporate Disasters.* Reading, Mass.: Addison-Wesley, 1987.

Hobbes, Thomas. *Leviathan.* Edited by C. B. Macpherson. Harmondsworth: Penguin Books, 1968 [1651].

Hobsbawm, Eric. *The Age of Extremes: A History of the World, 1914–1991.* New York: Random House, 1995.

Hochschild, Arlie Russell. "The Commercial Spirit of Intimate Life and the Abduction of Feminism: Signs from Women's Advice Books." *Theory, Culture, and Society* 11 (1994): 1–24.

———. *The Managed Heart.* Berkeley and Los Angeles: University of California Press, 1983.

———. *The Time Bind: When Work Becomes Home and Home Becomes Work.* New York: Metropolitan Books, 1997.

Hochschild, Arlie Russell, with Anne Machung. *The Second Shift: Working Parents and the Revolution at Home.* New York: Viking Penguin, 1989.

Hochschild, Jennifer. *What's Fair?* Cambridge, Mass.: Harvard University Press, 1981.

Hodgkinson, Virginia A., and Murray S. Weitzman. *From Belief to Commitment: The Community Service Activities and Finances of Religious Congregations in the United States.* Washington, D.C.: Independent Sector, 1993.

Hoge, Dean R., Benton Johnson, and Donald A. Luidens. *Vanishing Boundaries: The Religion of Mainline Protestant Baby Boomers.* Louisville: Westminster/John Knox, 1994.

Honig, Bonnie. "Difference, Dilemmas, and the Politics of Home." In *Democracy and Difference.* Edited by Seyla Benhabib, 257–277. Princeton: Princeton University Press, 1996.

Hoston, G. A. "A 'Theology' of Liberation? Socialist Revolution and Spiritual Regeneration in Chinese and Japanese Marxism." In *Ideas Across Cultures: Essays on Chinese Thought in Honor of Benjamin I. Schwartz.* Edited by Paul A. Cohen and Merle Goldman, 165–194. Cambridge, Mass.: Harvard University Press, 1990.

Hsu, Francis L. K. "Filial Piety in Japan and China: Borrowing Variations and Significance." *Journal of Comparative Family Studies* (Spring 1971): 57–74.

Huhr, Won Moo, and Kwang Chung Kim, "Religious Participation of Korean Immigrants in the United States." *Journal for the Scientific Study of Religion* 29 (1990): 19–34.

Humboldt, Wilhelm, Freiherr von. *The Limits of State Action.* London: Cambridge University Press, 1969 [1852].

Hunter, James Davison. *Culture Wars.* New York: Basic Books, 1993.

———. *Evangelicalism: The Coming Generation.* Chicago: University of Chicago Press, 1987.

Huntington, Samuel P. *American Politics: The Promise of Disharmony.* Cambridge, Mass.: Harvard University Press, 1981.

Hybels, Bill, and Lynne Hybels. *Rediscovering Church: The Story and Vision of Willow Creek Community Church.* Grand Rapids, Mich.: Zondervan, 1995.

Inglehart, Ronald. *The Silent Revolution: Changing Values and Skills in Advanced Industrial Society.* Princeton: Princeton University Press, 1977.

Ishida, T. "Conflict and Its Accommodation: Omote-Ura and Uchi-Soto Relations." In *Conflict in Japan.* Edited by E. Krauss, T. Rohlen, and P. Steinhoff, 16–38. Honolulu: University of Hawaii Press, 1984.

———. "Emerging or Eclipsing Citizenship? A Study of Changes in Political Attitudes in Postwar Japan." In *Japan Developing Economies.* Edited by Miyohei Shinohara. Tokyo: Institute of Asian Economic Affairs, 1967.

James, William. *The Varieties of Religious Experience.* In *Writings 1902–1910.* New York: The Library of America, 1987; New York: Mentor Books, 1958. [1902].

Janssen, H. Q. *De Kerkhervorming in Vlaanderen.* Arnhem: J. W. and C. F. Swaan, 1866–68.

Jaspers, Karl. *The Origin and Goal of History.* London: Routledge and Kegan Paul, 1953 [1948].

Jenkins, Henry. "Introduction: Childhood Innocence and Other Modern Myths." In *The Children's Culture Reader.* Edited by Henry Jenkins, 1–40. New York: New York University Press, 1998.

Jenkins, Thomas E. *The Character of God: Recovering the Lost Literary Power of American Protestantism.* New York: Oxford University Press, 1997.

Jepperson, Ronald L. "Institutions, Institutional Effects, and Institutionalism." In *The New Institutionalism in Organizational Analysis.* Edited by Walter W. Powell and Paul J. DiMaggio, 208–226. Chicago: University of Chicago Press, 1991.

Jobert, Ambroise. *De Luther à Mohila: La Pologne dans la crise de la Chrétienté, 1517–1648.* Paris: Institut d'Etudes Slaves, 1974.

Johnson, Alonzo. *Good News for the Disinherited: Howard Thurman on Jesus of Nazareth and Human Liberation.* New York: University Press of America, 1997.

Johnson, P. "God and the Americans." *Commentary* 99:1 (1995): 25–45.

Kant, Immanuel. "What Is Enlightenment?" In *Perpetual Peace and Other Essays.* Translated by Ted Humphrey, 41–46. Indianapolis: Hackett, 1983.

Kasza, O. "The State and the Organization of Women in Pre-War Japan." *Japan Foundation Newsletter* 18:2 (1990): 9–13.

Kateb, George. "Democratic Individuality and the Meaning of Rights." In *Liberalism and the Moral Life.* Edited by Nancy L. Rosenblum, 183–206. Cambridge, Mass.: Harvard University Press, 1989.

Katz, Elihu, and Brenda Danet. "Introduction: Bureaucracy as a Problem for Sociology and Society." In *Bureaucracy and the Public: A Reader in Official-Client Relations.* Edited by Elihu Katz and Brenda Danet, 3–30. New York: Basic Books, 1973.

Katz, Elihu, and S. N. Eisenstadt. "Some Sociological Observations on the Response of Israeli Organizations to New Immigrants." *Administration Science Quarterly* 5 (1960): 113–133.

Kazin, Michael. *The Populist Persuasion: An American History.* New York: Basic Books, 1995.

Kingdon, Robert M. *Geneva and the Coming of the Wars of Religion in France, 1555–1563.* Geneva: Librairie Droz, 1956.

——. *Geneva and the Consolidation of the French Protestant Movement, 1564–1572.* Madison: University of Wisconsin Press, 1967.

——. "John Calvin's Contribution to Representative Government." In *Politics and Culture in Early Modern Europe: Essays in Honor of H. G. Koenigsberger.* Edited by Phyllis Mack and Margaret C. Jacob, 183–198. Cambridge: Cambridge University Press, 1987.

Knecht, Robert J. *The French Wars of Religion, 1559–1598.* New York: Longman, 1996.

Knuttel, Willem Pieter Cornelis, 1854–1921. *De Toestand der Nederlandsche Katholieken ten Tijde der Republiek.* The Hague: Martinus Nijhoff, 1892–94.

Koenigsberger, Helmut. *Estates and Revolutions.* Ithaca: Cornell University Press, 1971.

Kohlberg, Lawrence. "Moral Development." In *International Encyclopedia of the Social Sciences,* vol. 10. Edited by David L. Sills. New York: Macmillan/Free Press, 1968.

Kohn, Melvin L. *Class and Conformity.* 2d ed. Chicago: University of Chicago Press, 1977.

Koopmans, J. W. *De Staten van Holland en de Opstand.* The Hague: Stichting Hollandse Historische Reeks, 1990.

Koschmann, J. V., ed. *Authority and the Individual in Japan: Citizen Protest in Historical Perspective.* Tokyo: University of Tokyo Press, 1978.

Kossman, E. H., and A. F. Mellink, eds. *Texts Concerning the Revolt of the Netherlands.* Cambridge: Cambridge University Press, 1974.

Kot, Stanislaw. *Socinianism in Poland: The Social and Political Ideas of the Polish Antitrinitarians in the Sixteenth and Seventeenth Centuries.* Translated by Earl Morse Wilbur. Boston: John Tanner, 1957.

Krasinski, Valerian. *Historical Sketch of the Rise, Progress, and Decline of the Reformation in Poland.* London: Murray, 1838.

Krauss, E. *Japanese Radicals Revisited: Student Protest in Post-War Japan.* Berkeley and Los Angeles: University of California Press, 1974.

Krauss, E., K. Steiner, and S. Flanagan, eds. *Political Opposition and Local Politics in Japan.* Princeton: Princeton University Press, 1980.

Lane, Robert E. *The Market Experience.* Cambridge: Cambridge University Press, 1991.

——. *Political Ideology.* New York: Free Press, 1964.

Lasch, Christopher. "The Communitarian Critique of Liberalism." In *Community in America.* Edited by Charles Reynolds and Ralph Norman, 173–184. Berkeley: University of California Press, 1988.

——. *The New Radicalism in America, 1889–1963: The Intellectual as a Social Type.* New York: Knopf, 1966.

————. *The True and Only Heaven: Progress and Its Critics*. New York: W. W. Norton, 1991.

Le creuset français. Paris: Le Seuil, 1989.

Leach, Edmund. "Ritualization in Man in Relation to Conceptual and Social Development." In *The Philosophical Transactions of the Royal Society of London*, 29th series, 251: 403–408.

Lears, Jackson. *Fables of Abundance*. New York: HarperCollins, 1994.

Leary, Lewis. *The Book Peddling Parson: An Account of the Life and Works of Mason Locke Weems, Patriot, Pitchman, Author, and Purveyor of Morality*. Chapel Hill: University of North Carolina Press, 1984.

Lewis, R. W. B. *The American Adam: Innocence, Tragedy, and Tradition in the Nineteenth Century*. Chicago: University of Chicago Press, 1955.

Lichterman, Paul. "Elusive Togetherness: Religion in the Quest for Civic Renewal." Unpublished manuscript.

————. *The Search for Political Community: American Activists Reinventing Commitment*. Cambridge: Cambridge University Press, 1996.

Liebman, Robert C. "Finding a Place: The Vision of Havurah." In *"I Come Away Stronger": How Small Groups Are Shaping American Religion*. Edited by Robert Wuthnow, 300–321. Grand Rapids, Mich.: Eerdmans, 1994.

Lindblom, Charles E. *Politics and Markets: The World's Political-Economic Systems*. New York: Basic Books, 1977.

Lipset, Seymour Martin. *American Exceptionalism: A Double-Edged Sword*. New York: W. W. Norton, 1996.

————. "Comments on Luckmann." In *Social Theory for a Changing Society*. Edited by Pierre Bourdieu and James Coleman. Boulder: Westview, 1991.

————. *The First New Nation: The United States in Historical and Comparative Perspective*. New York: W. W. Norton, 1979; New York: Basic Books, 1963.

————. *Political Man: The Social Bases of Politics*. Garden City, N.Y.: Anchor Books, 1963.

Livingston, J., J. Moore, and F. Oldfather, eds. *Postwar Japan, 1945 to the Present*. New York: Random House, 1973.

Locke, John. *An Essay Concerning Human Understanding*. Edited by P. H. Nidditch. Oxford: Clarendon Press, 1979.

————. *Two Treatises of Government*. Edited by Peter Laslett. New York: New American Library, 1965.

Loeb, Robert Rogat. *Soul of a Citizen: Living with Conviction in a Cynical Time*. New York: St. Martin's Griffin, 1999.

Lubieniecki, Stanislas. *History of the Polish Reformation, and Nine Related Documents*. Translated by George Hunston Williams. Minneapolis: Fortress Press, 1995 [1685].

Luker, Kristin. *Abortion and the Politics of Motherhood*. Berkeley and Los Angeles: University of California Press, 1984.

MacIntyre, Alasdair. *After Virtue*. South Bend, Ind.: University of Notre Dame Press, 1984 [1981].

————. "The American Idea." In *America and Ireland, 1976-1996: The American Identity and the Irish Connection*. Edited by David Noel Doyle and Owen Dudley Edwards, 57–68. Westport, Conn.: Greenwood Press, 1980.

————. *Dependent Rational Animals*. Chicago: Open Court, 1999.

————. "How to Be a North American." Federation of State Humanities Councils. Humanities Series, no. 2–88, 1987.

————. *A Short History of Ethics*. New York: Macmillan, 1966.

Mack, Holt. *The French Wars of Religion, 1562–1629*. Cambridge: Cambridge University Press, 1995.

Maczak, Antoni. "The Structure of Power in the Commonwealth of the Sixteenth and Seventeenth Centuries." In *A Republic of Nobles*. Edited by J. Federowicz, Maria Bogucka, and Henryk Samsonowicz, 109–134. Cambridge: Cambridge University Press, 1982.

Major, J. Russel. *Representative Government in Renaissance France*. New Haven: Yale University Press, 1980.

Mann, Michael. *The Sources of Social Power*. Vol. 2: *The Rise of Classes and Nation-States, 1760–1914*. Cambridge: Cambridge University Press, 1992.

Marièjol, J. H. *Lavisse histoire de la France*. Vol. 6: *La Réforme et la Ligue*. Paris: Lavisse, 1911.

Marty, Martin E. *The One and the Many: America's Struggle for the Common Good*. Cambridge: Harvard University Press, 1997.

————. "Public and Private: Congregation as Meeting Place." In *American Congregations*. Vol. 2: *New Perspectives in the Study of Congregations*. Edited by James P. Wind and James W. Lewis, 133–166. Chicago: University of Chicago Press, 1994.

Marx, Karl. "The Grundrisse." In *The Marx Engels Reader*. Edited by Robert C. Tucker. New York: W. W. Norton, 1972.

Marx, Leo. *The Machine in the Garden: Technology and the Pastoral Idea in America*. New York: Oxford University Press, 1964.

————. "Pastoralism in America." In *Ideology and Classic American Literature*. Edited by Sacvan Bercovitch and M. Jehlen, 36–39. Cambridge: Cambridge University Press, 1996.

Mathews, Donald G. "The Second Great Awakening as an Organizing Process, 1780–1830." In *Religion in American History: Interpretive Essays*. Edited by John M. Mulder and John F. Wilson, 199–217. Englewood Cliffs, N.J.: Prentice-Hall, 1978.

Matthews, Thomas F. *The Clash of the Gods*. Princeton: Princeton University Press, 1993.

McCarthy, John D., and Jim Castelli. *Religion-sponsored Social Service Providers: The Not-So-Independent Sector*. Washington, D.C.: Aspen Institute, 1996.

McDannell, Colleen. *Material Christianity*. New Haven: Yale University Press, 1995.

McFarland, S. H. Neill. *The Rush Hour of the Gods: A Study of New Religious Movements in Japan*. New York: Macmillan, 1967.

McKean, Margaret A. "State Strength and the Public Interest." In *Political Dynamics in Contemporary Japan*. Edited by Gary D. Allinson and Yasunori Sone. Ithaca and London: Cornell University Press, 1993.

McLanahan, Sara, and Gary Sandefur. *Growing Up With a Single Parent: What Hurts, What Helps*. Cambridge, Mass.: Harvard University Press, 1994.

Melucci, Alberto. *The Playing Self*. New York: Cambridge University Press, 1996.

Meyer, John. "Self and Life Course: Institutionalization and Its Effects." In *Institutional Structure: Constituting State, Society, and the Individual*, by George M. Thomas et al., 242–260. Newbury Park, Calif.: Sage, 1987.

Meyer, John W., John Boli, and George Thomas. "Ontology and Rationalization in the Western Cultural Account." In *Constituting State, Society, and the Individual,* by George M. Thomas, John W. Meyer, Francisco O. Ramirez, and John Boli, 12–37. Beverly Hills, Calif.: Sage, 1987.

Meyer, John W., John Boli, George Thomas, and Francisco Ramirez. "World Society and the Nation State." *American Journal of Sociology* 103:1 (July 1997): 144–181.

Mill, John Stuart. *On Liberty.* New York: Penguin, 1979 [1859].

Miller, Donald. *Reinventing American Protestantism: Christianity in the New Millennium.* Berkeley and Los Angeles: University of California Press, 1997.

Miller, James. "The Polish Nobility and the Renaissance Monarchy: The 'Execution of the Laws' Movement." *Parliaments, Estates, and Representation,* 3 (1983): 1–23; 4 (1984): 1–24.

Mills, C. Wright. *The Power Elite.* New York: Oxford University Press, 1957.

———. *White Collar.* New York: Oxford University Press, 1951.

Miquel, Pierre. *Les guerres de religion.* Paris: Fayard, 1980.

Mitchell, Mozella G., ed. *The Human Search: Howard Thurman and the Quest for Freedom. Proceedings of the Second Annual Thurman Convocation.* New York: Peter Lang, 1992.

Moore, R. Lawrence. *Selling God: American Religion and the Marketplace of Culture.* New York: Oxford University Press, 1994.

Moore, Sally Falk, and Barbara Myerhoff, eds. *Secular Ritual.* Amsterdam: Van Gorcum, 1977.

Mosca, G. *The Ruling Class.* New York: McGraw Hill, 1939.

Mours, Samuel. *Le protestantisme en France.* Paris: Librairie Protestante, 1959.

Murakami, Shiseyoshi. *Japanese Religion in the Modern Century.* Translated by H. Byron Earhart. Tokyo: University of Tokyo Press, 1983.

Muramatsu, Michio. "Patterned Pluralism under Challenge: The Policies of the 1980s." In *Political Dynamics in Contemporary Japan.* Edited by Gary D. Allinson and Yasunori Sone. Ithaca and London: Cornell University Press, 1993.

Myers, A. R. *Parliaments and Estates in Europe to 1789.* London: Harcourt Brace Jovanovich, 1975.

Nakai, K. Wildman. "The Naturalization of Confucianism in Tokugawa Japan: The Problem of Sinocentrism." *Harvard Journal of Asian Studies* 40 (1980): 157–199.

Naylor, Wendy F. "Some Thoughts upon Reading Tocqueville's *Democracy in America.*" Paper written for seminar of Professor Edward Shils, "Ideas on Social Solidarity," University of Chicago, May 1995.

Nelson, Tim. "The Church and the Street: Race, Class, and Congregation." In *Contemporary American Religion: An Ethnographic Reader.* Edited by Penny Edgell Becker and Nancy L. Eiesland. San Francisco: Altamira Press, 1997.

New Oxford Annotated Bible. Edited by Herbert G. May and Bruce M. Metzger. New York: Oxford University Press, 1973.

Nie, Norman H., Sidney Verba, and John R. Petrocik. *The Changing American Voter.* Cambridge, Mass.: Harvard University Press, 1976.

Niebuhr, Reinhold. Preface to *The Nature and Destiny of Man.* 1964 ed. Louisville: Westminster/John Knox, 1996.

Nobbs, Douglas. *Theocracy and Toleration: A Study of the Disputes in Dutch Calvinism from 1600 to 1650.* Cambridge: Cambridge University Press, 1938.

Noddings, Nel. "Conversation as Moral Education." *Journal of Moral Education* 23:2 (1994): 107–118.

Nolte, S. *Liberalism in Modern Japan.* Berkeley and Los Angeles: University of California Press, 1987.

Nosco, Peter. *Confucianism and Tokugawa Culture.* Princeton: Princeton University Press, 1984.

O'Connell, Brian. "What Voluntary Activity Can and Cannot Do for America." *Public Administration Review* 4–5 (September–October 1989): 486–491.

Okin, Susan Moller. *Justice, Gender, and the Family.* New York: Basic Books, 1989.

Oliner, Samuel, and Pearl Oliner. *The Altruistic Personality.* Glencoe, Ill.: Free Press, 1988.

Olneck, Michael. "Terms of Inclusion: Has Multiculturalism Redefined Equality in American Education?" *American Journal of Education* 101 (1993): 234–260.

Olson, Richard. *The Largest Congregations in the United States: An Empirical Study of Church Growth and Decline.* Ann Arbor: University Microfilms, 1988.

Oosterhoff, F. G. *Leicester and the Netherlands, 1586–1587.* Utrecht: Hes, 1988.

Orsi, Robert. *Thank You, St. Jude.* New Haven: Yale University Press, 1996.

Orzechowski, Kazimierz. "Les systèmes des assemblées d'états: Origines, évolution, typologie." *Parliaments, Estates, and Representations* 6:2 (1986): 105–111.

Pangle, Thomas L. *The Spirit of Modern Republicanism.* Chicago: University of Chicago Press, 1988.

Parker, David. *La Rochelle and the French Monarchy.* London: Royal Historical Society, 1980.

Parker, Geoffrey. *The Army of Flanders and the Spanish Road, 1567–1659: The Logistics of Spanish Victory and Defeat in the Low Countries' Wars.* Cambridge: Cambridge University Press, 1972.

———. *The Military Revolution: Military Innovation and the Rise of the West, 1500–1800.* Cambridge: Cambridge University Press, 1988.

Parsons, Talcott. *The Social System.* New York: Free Press, 1951.

———. *The Structure of Social Action: A Study in Social Theory, and Special Reference to a Group of Recent European Writers.* New York: McGraw-Hill, 1937.

———. *The Structure of Social Action: A Study in Social Theory, and Special Reference to a Group of Recent European Writers.* 2d ed. New York: Free Press, 1968.

Perkin, Harold. *The Rise of Professional Society: England since 1880.* London and New York: Routledge, 1989.

Pernot, Michel. *Les guerres de religion en France, 1559–1598.* Paris: SEDES, 1987.

Phillips, Derek. *Looking Backward: A Critical Appraisal of Communitarian Thought.* Princeton: Princeton University Press, 1993.

Picot, Georges. *Histoire des États généraux.* Paris: Hachette, 1888.

Plato. *The Laws of Plato.* Translated by Thomas L. Pangle. New York: Basic Books, 1988.

Poggi, Gianfranco. *The Development of the Modern State: A Sociological Introduction.* Stanford: Stanford University Press, 1978.

Polanyi, Karl. *The Great Transformation.* New York: Octagon Books, 1975; Boston: Beacon Press, 1957; New York: Rinehart and Company, 1944.

Pollard, A. F. *The Jesuits in Poland.* New York: Haskell House, 1971.

Pollard, Alton B., III. *Mysticism and Social Change: The Social Witness of Howard Thurman.* New York: Peter Lang, 1992.

Popenoe, David. *Life without Father: Compelling New Evidence That Fatherhood and Marriage Are Indispensable for the Good of Children and Society.* New York: Free Press, 1996.

Portes, Alejandro, and Ruben G. Rumbaut. *Immigrant America: A Portrait.* Berkeley and Los Angeles: University of California Press, 1990.

Potter, Ralph B. "The Logic of Moral Argument." In *Toward a Discipline of Social Ethics.* Edited by Paul Deats. Boston: Boston University Press, 1972.

———. "The Structure of Certain Christian Responses to the Nuclear Dilemma, 1959–1963." Th.D. thesis, Harvard Divinity School, 1965.

Powell, Maria. "Truth and Consequences in 'Testing the Waters': Teaching Activism in Environmental Education." Unpublished paper, University of Wisconsin–Milwaukee, 1995.

Prager, Susan Westerberg. "Shifting Perspectives on Marital Property Law." In *Rethinking the Family: Some Feminist Questions.* Edited by Barrie Thorne with Marilyn Yalom, 111–130. New York: Longman, 1982.

Purpel, David, and Kevin Ryan. *Moral Education.* Berkeley: McCutchan, 1976.

Putnam, Robert D. "Bowling Alone: America's Declining Social Capital." *Journal of Democracy* (January 1995): 65–78.

———. *Making Democracy Work.* Princeton: Princeton University Press, 1993.

———. "Tuning In, Tuning Out: The Strange Disappearance of Social Capital in America." Ithiel de Sola Pool Lecture, American Political Science Association, 1995. *P.S.: Political Science and Politics* 27 (1995): 664–683.

Ramirez, Francisco O., and John Boli. "On the Union of States and Schools." In *Institutional Structure: Constituting State, Society, and the Individual,* by George M. Thomas, John W. Meyer, Francisco O. Ramirez, and John Boli, 173–197. Newbury Park, Calif.: Sage Publications, 1987.

Rawls, John. "Two Concepts of Rules." *Philosophical Review* 64 (1955): 3–32.

Rawls, John. *A Theory of Justice.* Cambridge, Mass.: Harvard University Press, 1971.

Reddaway, W. F., J. H. Penson, O. Halecki, and R. Dyboski, eds. *From the Origins to Sobieski (to 1696).* Vol. 1 of *The Cambridge History of Poland.* Cambridge: Cambridge University Press, 1950.

Reeher, Grant, and Joseph Cammarano, eds. *Education for Citizenship: Ideas and Innovations in Political Learning.* New York: Rowman and Littlefield, 1997.

Reeves, Thomas. *The Empty Church.* New York: Free Press, 1996.

Reich, Robert. *The Next American Frontier.* New York: Times Books, 1985.

Reitsma, Rients. *Centifugal and Centripetal Forces in the Early Dutch Republic: The States of Overijssel, 1566–1600.* Amsterdam: Rodopi, 1982.

Rican, Rudolf. *The History of the Unity of Brethren: A Protestant Hussite Church in Bohemia and Moravia.* Translated by C. Daniel Crews. Bethlehem, Penn.: Moravian Church in America, 1992.

Richet, Denis. "Aspects socio-culturels des conflits religieux à Paris dans la seconde moitié du XVIe siècle." *Annales: Economies, Sociétés, Civilisations* 32 (1977): 764–789.

Ricoeur, Paul. *The Conflict of Interpretations: Essays in Hermeneutics.* Evanston: Northwestern University Press, 1974.

Riesman, David. *The Lonely Crowd: A Study of the Changing American Character.* New Haven: Yale University Press, 1965.

Rimer, T., ed. *Culture and Identity.* Princeton: Princeton University Press, 1990.

Roberts, Penny. *A City in Conflict: Troyes during the French Wars of Religion.* Manchester: Manchester University Press, 1996.

Rodrigue, George. "Gingrich Aims for Kinder Image." *Dallas Morning News,* 14 August 1996, 20A.

Rogers, Daniel T. *Atlantic Crossings: Social Politics in a Progressive Age.* Cambridge, Mass.: Belknap Press of Harvard University Press, 1998.

Romier, Lucien. *Les origines politiques des guerres de religion.* Paris: Perrin, 1913.

———. *Le royaume de Cathérine de Medici.* Geneva: Slatkine Reprints, 1978 [1925].

Roof, Wade Clark. *A Generation of Seekers: The Spiritual Journeys of the Baby Boom Generation.* San Francisco: Harper San Francisco, 1993.

———. *Spiritual Marketplace: Baby Boomers and the Remaking of American Religion.* Princeton: Princeton University Press, 1999.

Roof, Wade Clark, and William McKinney. *American Mainline Religion.* New Brunswick: Rutgers University Press, 1987.

Roos, Hans. "Ständewesen und parlamentarische Verfassung in Polen." In *Ständische Vertretungen in Europa im 17. und 18. Jahrhundert.* Edited by Dietrich Gerhard, 310–367. Göttingen: Vandenhoeck and Ruprecht, 1969.

Rosenstone, Steven J., and John Mark Hansen. *Mobilization, Participation, and Democracy in America.* New York: Macmillan, 1993.

Ross, Dorothy. "Socialism and American Liberalism: Academic Social Thought in the 1880s." *Perspectives in American History* 11 (1978): 7–79.

Ross, H. D. *The Right and the Good.* London: Oxford University Press, 1930.

Rozman, Gilbert, ed. *The East Asian Region: Confucian Heritage and Its Modern Adaptation.* Princeton: Princeton University Press, 1991.

Russocki, Stanislaw. "La naissance du parlementarisme polonais vue dans une perspective comparative." *Acta Poloniae Historica* 72 (1995): 33–47.

Sakamoto, Yoshikaru. "The Emperor System as a Japanese Problem: The Case of Meiji Gakuin University." *Prime Occasional Papers,* no. 5. Yokohama, Japan, 1989.

Salmon, J. H. M. "The Paris Sixteen, 1584–94." *Journal of Modern History* 44 (1972): 540–576.

———. *Society in Crisis: France in the Sixteenth Century.* London: Methuen, 1975.

Salvadori, Massimo L. *Europa America Marxismo.* Torino: Piccola Biblioteca Einaudi, 1990.

Samsonowicz, Henryk. "Polish Politics and Society under the Jagiellonian Monarchy." In *A Republic of Nobles.* Edited by J. K. Federowicz, Maria Bogucka, and Henryk Samsonowicz, 49–69. Cambridge: Cambridge University Press, 1982.

Sandel, Michael. *Democracy's Discontent: America in Search of a Public Philosophy.* Cambridge, Mass.: Belknap Press of Harvard University Press, 1996.

————. *Liberalism and the Limits of Justice.* Cambridge: Cambridge University Press, 1982.

Santurri, Edmund. "Rawlsian Liberalism, Moral Truth, and Augustinian Politics." *Journal for Peace and Justice Studies* 8:2 (1997): 1–36.

Scalapino, Robert. *The Early Japanese Labor Movement.* Berkeley: Institute of East Asian Studies, University of California, 1983.

Scheerder, J. *De beeldenstorm.* Bussum: De Haan, 1974.

Schor, Juliet B. *The Overworked American: The Unexpected Decline of Leisure.* New York: Basic Books, 1991.

Schrag, Peter. *Paradise Lost: California's Experience, America's Future.* New York: New Press, 1998.

Schramm, G. *Der Polnische Adel und die Reformation.* Wiesbaden: Franz Steiner, 1965.

Schudson, Michael. *The Good Citizen: A History of American Civic Life.* Cambridge, Mass.: Harvard University Press, 1998.

Schwartz, Frank. "Of Fairy Cloaks and Familiar Talks: The Politics of Consultation." In *Political Dynamics in Contemporary Japan.* Edited by Gary D. Allinson and Yasunori Sone, 217–242. Ithaca and London: Cornell University Press, 1993.

Scott, James. *Domination and the Arts of Resistance: Hidden Transcripts.* New Haven: Yale University Press, 1990.

Scott, W. Richard. *Institutions and Organizations.* Thousand Oaks, Calif.: Sage, 1995.

Scroggs, Marilee Munger. "Making a Difference: Fourth Presbyterian Church of Chicago." In *American Congregations,* vol. 1: *Portraits of Twelve Religious Communities,* 464–519. Chicago: University of Chicago Press, 1994.

Seligman, Adam. *The Idea of Civil Society.* New York: Free Press, 1992.

Sewell, William H. "A Theory of Structure: Duality, Agency, and Transformation." *American Journal of Sociology* 98:1 (July 1992): 1–29.

Shennan, J. H. *The Parlement of Paris.* London: Eyre and Spottiswood, 1968.

Shils, Edward. *Center and Periphery: Essays in Macro-Sociology.* Chicago: University of Chicago Press, 1975.

Shklar, Judith. *American Citizenship: The Quest for Inclusion.* Cambridge, Mass.: Harvard University Press, 1991.

Sikkink, David. "'I Just Say I'm a Christian': Symbolic Boundaries and Identity Formation among Church-Going Protestants." In *Re-Forming the Center: American Protestantism, 1900 to the Present.* Edited by Douglas Jacobsen and Vance Trollinger, Jr., 49–69. Grand Rapids, Mich.: Eerdmans, 1998.

Skidelsky, Robert. *John Maynard Keynes: The Economist As Saviour, 1920–1937.* London: Macmillan, 1992.

————. "Two Cheers For Consumerism." *New York Times,* Op-Ed, August 14, 1998.

Skinner, Quentin. *The Foundations of Modern Political Thought.* Cambridge: Cambridge University Press, 1978.

Skocpol, Theda. *Boomerang: Clinton's Health Security Effort and the Turn against Government in U.S. Politics.* New York: W. W. Norton, 1996.

————. "Civic America Today." Paper presented at American Political Development Seminar, Department of Political Science, University of Wisconsin–Madison, 1998.

————. *Protecting Soldiers and Mothers: The Political Origins of Social Policy in the United States.* Cambridge, Mass.: Harvard University Press, 1992.

————. *Social Policy in the United States: Future Possibilities in Historical Perspective.* Princeton: Princeton University Press, 1995.

————. *States and Social Revolutions.* Cambridge: Cambridge University Press, 1979.

Smith, Adam. *The Theory of Moral Sentiments.* New York: Oxford University Press, 1976.

Smith, Christian. *American Evangelicalism: Embattled and Thriving.* Chicago: University of Chicago Press, 1998.

Smith, Luther E., Jr. *Howard Thurman: The Mystic as Prophet.* Richmond, Ind.: Friends United Press, 1991.

Smith, R. "Gender Inequality in Contemporary Japan." *Journal of Japanese Studies* 13:1 (1987): 1–26.

Smith, Rogers M. "Beyond Tocqueville, Myrdal, and Hartz: The Multiple Traditions In America." *American Political Science Review* 87:3 (1993): 549–566.

Smith, Steven Rathgeb. "Civic Infrastructure in America: The Interrelationship between Government and the Voluntary Sector." In *Civil Society, Democracy, and Civic Renewal.* Edited by Robert K. Fullinwider, 127–150. Lanham, Md.: Rowman and Littlefield, 1999.

Sombart, W. *Why Is There No Socialism in the United States?* White Plains, N.Y.: M. E. Sharpe, 1976.

Stark, Rodney. *The Rise of Christianity.* San Francisco: HarperCollins, 1997.

Stone, Lawrence. *The Family, Sex, and Marriage: England 1500–1800.* New York: Harper and Row, 1977.

Stout, Jeffrey. *Ethics after Babel.* Boston: Beacon Press, 1988.

Sugimoto, Y. "Structural Sources of Popular Revolts and the Tobaku Movement at the Time of the Meiji Restoration." *Journal of Asian Studies* 34:4 (1975): 875–890.

Sutherland, Nicola M. *The Huguenot Struggle for Recognition.* New Haven: Yale University Press, 1979.

Swidler, Ann. "Culture in Action." *American Sociological Review* 51 (1986): 273–286.

————. "Culture in Action: Symbols and Strategies." *American Journal of Sociology* 51:1 (April 1986): 137–166.

————. "Inequality and American Culture: The Persistence of Voluntarism." In *Reexamining Democracy.* Edited by Gary Marks and Larry Diamond, 294–314. London: Sage, 1992.

Tanner, Kathryn. *The Politics of God.* Minneapolis: Fortress Press, 1992.

Tapie, Victor Lucien. *Une église tcheque au XVIe siècle: L'unité des frères.* Paris: E. Leroux, 1934.

Taussig, Michael. *The Devil and Commodity Fetishism in South America.* Chapel Hill: University of North Carolina Press, 1980.

Taylor, Charles. *Hegel and Modern Society.* Cambridge: Cambridge University Press, 1979.

————. *Sources of the Self: The Making of Modern Identity.* Cambridge, Mass.: Harvard University Press, 1988.

————. "'Transformations in Religious Experience': The William James Lecture." *Harvard Divinity School Bulletin* 28:4 (1999): 18–20.

Thandeka. *Learning to Be White: Money, Race, and God in America.* New York: Continuum, 1999.

Thomas, George M., John W. Meyer, Francisco O. Ramirez, and John Boli. *Institu-*

tional Structure: Constituting State, Society, and the Individual. Newbury Park, Calif.: Sage, 1987.

Thompson, E. P. *The Making of the English Working Class.* New York: Random House, 1963.

Thumma, Scott L. "Sketching a Mega-Trend: The Phenomenal Proliferation of Very Large Churches in the United States." Paper presented at the Annual Meeting of the Association for the Sociology of Religion, Miami, 1993.

Thurman, Howard. *Footprints of a Dream: The Story of the Church for the Fellowship of All Peoples.* New York: Harper and Brothers, 1959.

————. *Why I Believe There Is a God: Sixteen Essays by Negro Clergymen with an Introduction by Howard Thurman.* Chicago: Johnson Publishing Company, 1965.

————. *With Head and Heart: The Autobiography of Howard Thurman.* New York: Harcourt Brace Jovanovich, 1979.

————, ed. Introduction to *A Track to the Water's Edge: The Olive Schreiner Reader,* by Olive Schreiner. New York: Harper and Row, 1973.

Thurow, Lester C. *The Future of Capitalism: How Today's Economic Forces Shape Tomorrow's World.* New York: William Morrow, 1996.

Tilly, Charles S. *Durable Inequality.* Berkeley and Los Angeles: University of California Press, 1998.

————. *European Revolutions, 1492–1992.* Oxford: Basil Blackwell, 1992.

Tipton, Steven M. *Getting Saved from the Sixties: Moral Meaning in Conversion and Cultural Change.* Berkeley and Los Angeles: University of California Press, 1982.

————. "Republic and Liberal State: The Place of Religion in an Ambiguous Polity." *Emory Law Journal* 39:1 (1990): 191–202.

Tracy, James D. *Holland under Habsburg Rule, 1506–1566: The Formation of a Body Politic.* Berkeley and Los Angeles: University of California Press, 1990.

Troeltsch, Ernst. *Religion in History.* Edited by James Luther Adams. Minneapolis: Fortress Press, 1991.

Turner, Victor. *From Ritual to Theater: The Human Seriousness of Play.* New York: Performing Arts Journal Publications, 1982.

Valverde, Mariana. *Diseases of the Will: Alcohol and the Dilemmas of Freedom.* Cambridge: Cambridge University Press. 1998.

Van Deursen, A. Th. *Bavianen en Slijkgeuzen. Kerk en Kerkvolk ten Tijde van Maurits en Oldebarnevelt.* Franeker: Van Wijnen, 1991.

Van Gelder, H. A. E. *Revolutionnaire Reformatie.* Amsterdam: P. N. van Kampen and Zoon, 1943.

Van Gelderen, Martin. *The Poltical Thought of the Dutch Revolt, 1555–1590.* Cambridge: Cambridge University Press, 1992.

Van Schelven, A. A. *De Nederduitsche Vluchtelingskerken der XVIe Eeuw in Engeland en Duitschland.* The Hague: Martinus Nijhoff, 1909.

Van Stam, F. P. *The Controversy over the Theology of Saumur, 1635–1650.* Amsterdam and Maarssen: APA–Holland University Press, 1988.

Vanacek, Vaclav. "Les assemblées d'états en Bohème à l'époque de la révolte d'états." In *Gouvernés et gouvernants, recueils de la société Jean Bodin pour l'histoire comparée,* vol. 4, 239–254. Brussels: De Boeck University, 1965.

Verba, Sidney, Kay Lehman Schlozman, and Henry E. Brady. *Voice and Equality: Civic Voluntarism in American Politics.* Cambridge, Mass.: Harvard University Press, 1995.

Verheyden, A. L. E. *Le conseil des troubles.* Flavion–Florennes: Editions Le Phare, 1981.

Vlastos, S. "Opposition Movements in Early Meiji, 1869–1885." In *Cambridge History of Japan,* vol. 5: *The Nineteenth Century.* Edited by M. B. Jansen, 368–431. Cambridge: Cambridge University Press, 1989.

Voegelin, Eric. *From Enlightenment to Revolution.* Durham: Duke University Press, 1975.

Vogel, Ezra F. *Japan's New Middle Class.* Berkeley and Los Angeles: University of California Press, 1963.

Völker, Karl. *Kirchengeschichte Polens.* Berlin and Leipzig: Walter de Gruyter, 1930.

Voss, Kim. *The Making of American Exceptionalism: The Knights of Labor and Class Formation in the Nineteenth Century.* Ithaca: Cornell University Press, 1993.

Waal, Frans de. *Good Natured: The Origins of Right and Wrong in Humans and Other Animals.* Cambridge, Mass.: Harvard University Press, 1996.

Waida, M. "Buddhism and the National Community." In *Transactions and Transformations in the History of Religions,* edited by F. E. Reynolds and T. M. Ludwig. London: E. J. Bailly, 1980.

Wallerstein, Immanuel. *The Modern World-System.* Vol. 1: *Capitalist Agriculture and the Origins of the European World-Economy in the Sixteenth Century.* New York: Academic Press, 1974.

Walzer, Michael. "The Civil Society Argument." In *Dimensions of Radical Democracy.* Edited by Chantal Mouffe, 89–107. New York: Verso, 1992.

———. *The Revolution of the Saints: A Study in the Origins of Radical Politics.* New York: Atheneum, 1970.

———. *Spheres of Justice.* New York: Basic Books, 1983.

Warner, R. Stephen. *New Wine in Old Wineskins.* Berkeley and Los Angeles: University of California Press, 1988.

———. "The Place of the Congregation in the Contemporary American Religious Configuration." In *American Congregations,* vol. 2: *New Perspectives in the Study of Congregations.* Edited by James P. Wind and James W. Lewis, 56–99. Chicago: University of Chicago Press, 1994.

———. "Religion, Boundaries, and Bridges." *Sociology of Religion* 58:3 (Fall 1997): 217–235.

———. "Work in Progress: Toward a New Paradigm for the Sociological Study of Religion." *American Journal of Sociology* 98:5 (March 1993): 1044–1093.

Watanabe, H. "The Transformation of Neo-Confucianism in Early Tokugawa Japan." Paper presented at the Conference on Confucianism of the American Academy of Arts and Sciences, Cambridge, Mass., 1992.

Webb, Herschel. *The Japanese Imperial Institution in the Tokugawa Period.* New York: Columbia University Press, 1968.

Weber, Max. "Bureaucracy," "Politics as a Vocation," "Science as a Vocation," "The Social Psychology of the World Religions." In *From Max Weber: Essays in Sociology.* Translated and edited by Hans Gerth and C. Wright Mills. New York: Oxford University Press, 1958 [1921–22].

———. *Gesammelte Aufsätze zur Religionssoziologie.* Taschenbuchausg Tübingen: J. C. B. Mohr (Paul Siebeck), 1988 [1920].

Weil, Andrew. *Health and Healing.* Rev. ed. Boston: Houghton Mifflin, 1995.

————. *Natural Health, Natural Medicine: A Comprehensive Manual for Wellness and Self-Care.* Rev. ed. Boston: Houghton Mifflin, 1995.

————. *Spontaneous Healing: How to Discover and Enhance Your Body's Natural Ability to Maintain and Heal Itself.* New York: Fawcett Columbine, 1996.

Weintraub, Jeffrey. "The Theory and Politics of the Public/Private Distinction." In *Public and Private in Thought and Practice: Perspectives on a Grand Dichotomy.* Edited by Jeffrey Weintraub and Krishan Kumar, 1–42. Chicago: University of Chicago Press, 1996.

Weitzman, Lenore. *The Divorce Revolution: The Unexpected Social and Economic Consequences for Women and Children in America.* New York: Free Press, 1985.

Werblowski, J. R. *Beyond Tradition and Modernity.* Atlantic Highlands, N.J.: Athlone Press, 1976.

Wheeler, Barbara. "You Who Are Far Off: Religious Division and the Role of Religious Research." *Review of Religious Research* 37 (1996): 266–301.

White, Hayden. *The Content of the Form.* Baltimore: Johns Hopkins University Press, 1987.

————. *Metahistory.* Baltimore: Johns Hopkins University Press, 1973.

————. *Tropics of Discourse.* Baltimore: Johns Hopkins University Press, 1978.

Whitehead, Barbara Defoe. *The Divorce Culture: Rethinking Our Commitments to Marriage and Family.* New York: Vintage, 1996.

Wiebe, Robert H. *The Search for Order, 1877–1920.* New York: Hill and Wang, 1992.

————. *Self-Rule: A Cultural History of American Democracy.* Chicago: University of Chicago Press, 1995.

Wiener, Martin J. *English Culture and the Decline of the Industrial Spirit, 1850–1980.* Cambridge: Cambridge University Press, 1981.

Wijn, Jan Willem. *Het Krijgswezen in den Tijd van Prins Maurits.* Utrecht: Hoeijenbos, 1934.

Wilbur, Earl Morse. *A History of Unitarianism: Socianism and Its Antecedents.* Cambridge, Mass.: Harvard University Press, 1945.

Williamson, Oliver E. *Markets and Hierarchies.* New York: Free Press, 1975.

Wilson, James Q. *The Amateur Democrat: Club Politics in Three Cities.* Chicago: University of Chicago Press, 1962.

Wilson, William Julius. *The Bridge over the Racial Divide.* Berkeley and Los Angeles: University of California Press, 1999.

————. *When Work Disappears.* New York: Knopf, 1996.

Winston, Dianne. *Red, Hot, and Righteous: Urban Religion and the Salvation Army.* Cambridge, Mass.: Harvard University Press, 1999.

Wojciechowski, Zygmunt. "Les débuts du programme de l' 'Exécution des lois' en Pologne au début du XVIe siècle." *Revue historique de droit français et etranger* 29:2 (1951): 173–192.

————. *L'état polonais au Moyen Âge.* Paris: Recueil Sirey, 1949.

Wolfe, Martin. *The Fiscal System of Renaissance France.* New Haven: Yale University Press, 1972.

Wolterstorff, Nicholas. *From Presence to Practice: Mind, World, and Entitlement to Believe.* Gifford Lectures for 1994–95 at the University of St. Andrews, Fife, Scotland.

Wood, Gordon S. *The Radicalism of the American Revolution.* New York: Vintage Books, 1993.

Wood, James B. *The King's Army: Warfare, Soldiers, and Society during the Wars of Religion in France, 1562–1576*. Cambridge and New York: Cambridge University Press, 1996.

Woodlief, Wayne. "Practicing What They Preach." *Boston Herald,* February 16, 1997, 29.

Wuthnow, Robert. *Acts of Compassion: Caring for Others and Helping Ourselves*. Princeton: Princeton University Press, 1991.

———. *Christianity and Civil Society: The Contemporary Debate*. Philadelphia: Trinity International Press, 1996.

———. *The Crisis in the Churches: Spiritual Malaise, Fiscal Woe*. New York: Oxford University Press, 1997.

———. *God and Mammon in America*. New York: Free Press, 1994.

———. *Loose Connections: Civic Involvement in America's Fragmented Communities*. Cambridge, Mass.: Harvard University Press, 1998.

———. "Mobilizing Civic Engagement: The Changing Impact of Religious Involvement." Paper presented at a conference on civic engagement organized by Theda Skocpol, Harvard University, October 1997.

———. *Producing the Sacred: An Essay on Public Religion*. Urbana: University of Illinois Press, 1994.

———. *The Restructuring of American Religion*. Princeton: Princeton University Press, 1988.

———. *Sharing the Journey: Support Groups and America's New Quest for Community*. New York: Free Press, 1994.

Wyczanski, Andrzej. "The Problem of Authority in Sixteenth-Century Poland." In *A Republic of Nobles*. Edited by J. K. Federowicz, Maria Bocucka, and Henryk Samsonowicz, 91–108. Cambridge: Cambridge University Press, 1982.

Xiao Yang. "Trying to Do Justice to the Concept of Justice in Confucian Ethics." *Journal of Chinese Philosophy* 24 (1997): 521–551.

Zagorin, Perez. *Rebels and Rulers, 1500–1660*. Cambridge: Cambridge University Press, 1982.

Zeff, Joe, and Pat Lyons. *The Downsizing of America*. New York: Times Books, 1996.

Zunz, Olivier. *Why the American Century?* Chicago: University of Chicago Press, 1998.

CONTRIBUTORS

Jeffrey Alexander is Professor of Sociology at the University of California, Los Angeles. His most recent books are *Fin-de-Siècle Social Theory: Relativism, Reduction, and the Problem of Reason* (1995), *Neofunctionalism and After* (1998), and *Cultural Trauma* (forthcoming).

Robert N. Bellah is Elliott Professor of Sociology, Emeritus, at the University of California, Berkeley. Among many awards and honors, he is a recipient of the National Humanities Medal.

John A. Coleman, S.J., is Charles Casassa Professor of Social Values at Loyola Marymount University, where he teaches in the Law School and the Department of Sociology. Among his books are *The Evolution of Dutch Catholicism, An American Strategic Theology,* and *One Hundred Years of Catholic Social Teaching.* He is currently doing research on Catholic Charities USA, as part of a study of religion and welfare.

Harvey Cox is Victor S. Thomas Professor of Divinity at Harvard University, where he teaches both at the Divinity School and in the Program on the Study of Religion in the Faculty of Arts and Sciences. His book *The Secular City* (1965) was recently selected by the Faculty of Marburg University as one of the two most decisive books in Protestant theology in the twentieth century.

S. N. Eisenstadt is Professor Emeritus at the Hebrew University of Jerusalem. He has also been a visiting professor at numerous universities, a member of many scientific academies, a recipient of honorary doctoral degrees of the Universities of Tel Aviv and Helsinki and Harvard University, a recipient of the International Balzan Prize, the McIver Award of the American Sociological Association, the Israel Prize and Rothschild Prize in Social Sciences, and the Max Planck Research Award.

Nina Eliasoph is Assistant Professor in the Department of Sociology at the University of Wisconsin–Madison and author of *Avoiding Politics: How Americans Produce Apathy in Everyday Life*. She is currently working on an ethnographic study exploring political conversation and moral education between children and adults.

Philip S. Gorski is Assistant Professor of Sociology at the University of Wisconsin–Madison. His current research focuses on the relationship between religion and politics in early modern Europe. He is completing a book titled *The Disciplinary Revolution: Calvinism, Confessionalism and the Growth of State Power*, to be published by the University of Chicago Press.

Stanley Hauerwas is Gilbert T. Rowe Professor of Theological Ethics at the Divinity School of Duke University. His most recent book is *Sanctify Them in the Truth: Holiness Exemplified*.

Richard Madsen is Professor of Sociology at the University of California, San Diego. Besides being the coauthor of *Habits of the Heart* and *The Good Society*, he is the author of five books on various aspects of morality, religion, and society in Chinese societies.

Albert Jordy Raboteau teaches in the Religion Department at Princeton University. He is the Henry W. Putnam Professor of Religion and has served as chair of his department and as Dean of the Princeton University Graduate School. He taught at the University of California, Berkeley, and served there with Robert Bellah on an interdepartmental committee for the Program in Religious Studies. His field is religions of the Americas, with a specialization in the religious history of African Americans. His books include *Slave Religion, A Fire in the Bones*, and *African-American Religion* (a high school text). He is the coeditor with David Wills of *African-American Religion: A Documentary History*.

Steve Sherwood is a graduate student in the Department of Sociology at the University of California, Los Angeles. His areas of interest include narrative theory, religious and cultural sociology, and the sociology of artists. Publications include "Narrating the Social: Postmodernism and the Drama of Democracy" (1994) and "Theorizing the Enigma: The Problem of the Soul in Durkheim's 'Elementary Forms of the Religious Life'" (1998).

William M. Sullivan is Professor of Philosophy at La Salle University and Senior Scholar at the Carnegie Foundation for the Advancement of Teaching. He is the author of *Work and Integrity* and a coauthor of *Habits of the Heart* and *The Good Society*.

Ann Swidler is Professor of Sociology at the University of California, Berkeley. She is a coauthor of *Habits of the Heart* and *The Good Society,* as well as of *Inequality by Design* (Princeton University Press, 1996). Her most recent book is *Talk of Love: How Middle Americans Use Their Culture* (University of Chicago Press, 2001).

Charles Taylor is Professor of Political Science and Philosophy, Emeritus, at McGill University, Montreal, Canada.

Steven M. Tipton is Director of the Graduate Division of Religion and Professor of Sociology at Emory University and its Candler School of Theology. He is currently working on *Public Pulpits,* a study of religious advocacy in Washington.

Robert Wuthnow is the Gerhard R. Andlinger '52 Professor of Sociology and Director of the Center for the Study of Religion at Princeton University. He is the author of numerous books, including *After Heaven: Spirituality in America since the 1950s* (University of California Press, 1998) and *Loose Connections: Joining Together in America's Fragmented Communities* (Harvard University Press, 1998).

INDEX

abortion debate, 36–38

activists: community/family rhetoric and, 206–9

AGIL system, 4–5

America. See United States

Anjou, Duke of, 97–98

Arendt, Hannah, 195, 200, 213, 214

aristocracy: French Wars of Religion and, 79; in Poland-Lithuania, 99–101

Arminian controversy, 80

Armstrong, Louis, 150

Arnold, Thomas, 234

associations, 229

Balmer, Randall, 148

Barton, Bruce, 141

Bathory, Stephen, 98

Bellah, Robert: concern with religion of, 1; contrasted with Parsons, 2, 4–5, 6–7, 10, 12, 105; on Durkheim, 105, 107; Durkheim and, 13–14; finding of critical voice by, 9–11; on middle class, 111; move from theory to history by, 106; on self, 258; on self-interest, 10–11; symbolic realism, xi, 12; on symbols and myth, 11–12; on Weber, 121

Bellah, Robert (publications): *Beyond Belief,* 4, 9; *The Broken Covenant,* 9–11, 13, 260–61; "Civil Religion in America," 5–7, 11, 13, 228, 259, 260; *The Good Society,* 106, 112, 195, 198, 262, 282n14; *Habits of the Heart,* 42, 106, 108, 109, 110, 111, 112, 118, 137, 196, 198, 262; "Introduction" to *Emil Durkheim on Morality and Society,* 107; "Religion and the Legitimation of the American Republic," 261; "Religious Evolution," 5, 105–6, 108, 256, 257, 258; "The Systematic Study of Religion," 4–5; *Tokugawa Religion,* xiv, 259; "Values and Social Change in Modern Japan," 259

Bercovitch, Sacvan, 265

Beveridge, William, 239–41

Blake, William, xvii

Bourdieu, Pierre, x

Brandeis, Louis, 245

brokering mechanisms, 168–69, 269

Buddhism, 69

bureaucracies, 205; ethical style of, 26–27, 28; generative, 222–23; volunteer groups and, 210–15; youth projects and, 219–22

Butler, Jon, 142

California, depletion of institutions in, 46, 48

Calvinism: in France, 88–94, 102; in Netherlands, 85–88, 102; in Poland-Lithuania, 94–103; revolution and, 78–79, 103–4; sources of radicalism in, 83–84

Canada, 271

capitalism: corporate, 10; Weber and, 256

Caring Adult Network (CAN), 204–5

Compositor:	G&S Typesetters, Inc.
Text:	10/12 Baskerville
Display:	Baskerville
Printer and Binder:	Sheridan Books, Inc.